THE

AND

THE BEST FORGOTTEN

*To Mark and Gloria
with best wishes and
a smile for a while*

RONALD FRAZER

Ronald Frazer

2 Oct 2004

Pen Press Publishers Ltd

First published in Great Britain by
Pen Press Publishers Ltd
39-41, North Road
Islington
London N7 9DP

ISBN 1-904754-39-2

Printed and bound in the UK

A catalogue record of this book is available from the British
Library

Cover drawing by unknown artist.
Efforts were made unsuccessfully to acquire copyright.

About the Author

My Father, a businessman in Belfast where I was born, ensured that I received a good education at a renowned school, with the expectation that it would give me a good start in life. He might as well have saved his hard earned money.

It had always been my ambition to become a professional Opera Singer. Although I was thwarted in this, mainly through my own intransigence, though I had some vocal talent, and to some extent my failure to grab opportunities presented, singing has remained a major influence in my life. It is worse than being in love; though unrequited, it is inescapable.

In pursuit of my somewhat ambitious expectations, I worked intermittently in diverse jobs before reluctantly realising my limitations and, at the age of thirty, taking a job in banking, which unexpectedly led to a successful career of twenty eight years.

It was through my various travails that I met rare and interesting characters and had some very good and bad experiences, which furnished enough material to make me think of writing a book in the hope of entertaining the reader with anecdotes of a haphazard life. It was only after retiring from the Bank and with the constant urging and support of my good friend and former colleague, Isabel Gouveia-Lima, that I finally took up the pen, to relate these experiences.

Equally important, was the enthusiastic support and patience of my wife, whose skills and energy at the keyboard, finally transcribed my illegible scrawl onto computer disk, enabling me to offer it to a Publisher. This book is the result.

Acknowledgements

Back cover caricature by Geoff Kidman, friend and former colleague.

Vedette Records Co., Cologno Monzese (Milano), 1969, whose record sleeve, given to me by Piccaluga, afforded me details of the extensive itinerary of the cities where he performed.

I also acknowledge the good work of all at Pen Press Publishers Ltd for the design and production of this book.

CHAPTER 1

The Coronation of King George VI took place in May 1937, following his succession to the throne after the abdication of his brother Edward VIII in 1936. It was a scene of celebration in Belfast, followed by a royal visit to the city by the new King and Queen Elizabeth on 27th July 1937. That was an eventful year in Belfast, a city already renowned for its industry and the great shipyard of Harland & Wolff, the biggest in the world, creator of the Titanic and her sister ship the Olympic in 1910/11, the largest ships afloat at that time. Another great ship, the Capetown Castle, was launched in September 1937 and Harry Ferguson first introduced his famous tractor at the Royal Ulster Society's Agricultural Show at the King's Hall, Balmoral, in May 1937. He had produced it in spite of his bank's refusal to back him and it went on to world fame and great economic success. The last great ocean liner, one of many to be built at Harland & Wolff, was the Canberra, made in 1960. The linen industry and the great rope works were still viable.

There was much talk of impending war in Europe, but this did not overshadow the celebrations in Belfast, where I was born on 5th July 1937. I already had a brother, Frederick, who had been born in Enniskillen, Co Fermanagh, in August 1935, where my parents had gone to live, my father having taken up employment there. My father, Robert Andrew Frazer, from the small village of Red Rock, in Co Armagh, and my mother, Winifred Agnes Patton, of Belfast, had met during the time they had worked together for D H Wilson, Wholesale Grocer and Butter Merchant, on the Old Lodge Road in Belfast. Mother had been working there as Mr Wilson's Personal Assistant and Secretary, when my father joined the company, following his return from South Africa, whereto he had emigrated as a young man and had worked in Johannesburg for Thrupp's, a large general business, as a manager.

Mother's first job after school, and having attended Miss Dunn's Business School, was with a private detective agency, where she had been sent as a typist and office assistant. It was a rather dingy office and the boss addressed her as 'little missy', instructing her first off, to clean the windows. This did not accord with her own grander ideas of the excitement of sleuthing, and she told him so, tendering her notice to leave immediately. He was conciliatory and prevailed upon her to calm down and settle in for a while. Reluctantly agreeing, she asked for a window cloth and some cleaning liquid and was told to use newspaper. She left to seek other employment.

My mother joined Wilson's and was quickly given responsibility for running the office and organising the staff. Mr Wilson was a martinet, with waxed moustaches and a formidable manner, and Mother often regaled us with stories of his idiosyncrasies. He was a stickler for discipline. On a whim he would dismiss a member of staff, such as on the occasion when, noticing a young store-worker was looking pale and tired, he discovered the lad had been out dancing the previous evening. Mother was instructed to give him his cards, on the grounds that no one could be fit for work after such pursuits. The same applied when Wilson discovered that another staff member had been playing tennis. My mother always had to do the firing. Little did Wilson know that my mother and father both enjoyed that sport; my dad was a good player and Mother often complained that he would never let her win a point.

I met Mr Wilson on several occasions when I was a child. With his waxed moustaches elongated to a fine point, military bearing and beady eye glaring from a monocle, he was a daunting figure to one so young. He was, however, kindly enough to me, showing me the large 56-pound cheeses and boxes of butter imported from New Zealand and Australia. He would show me how to use the butter and cheese tester, plunging it into a block of butter, withdrawing a sample and eating it like a stick of seaside rock. He would call for Mother to close his office door on other occasions, whilst he enjoyed a swig from a bottle of olive oil.

2

Mother had to attend to all his correspondence, including that of a personal nature. He would hand her letters from an aunt in America and other relatives without reading them himself, and she had to read them and reply as she saw fit. He didn't bother to look at her replies either. He was a City Councillor of great probity and full of good works but was ruthless with staff and his own family.

Wilson's only son worked in the business for a short time, for a pittance. He was by all accounts a pleasant, very mannerly young man. He married a lovely lady from Co Donegal, without his father's approval, but died of a sudden illness within a year. Wilson cut his son's widow off without a penny and she had to return home to live with her mother for the rest of her life, in Co. Donegal near Ballybofey. Her husband hadn't got round to signing the life insurance policy he had been arranging. Mother used to visit her every year for a summer holiday around the 12th of July, and they were always great friends. She used to visit us in Belfast; she was lovely and pleasant, but never remarried. Her own mother had been a governess to the Swedish royals and lived into her eighties, a lively character.

On another occasion, Wilson called my mother to take dictation of a letter, which turned out to be to herself, telling her of her own dismissal. She took it down with *sang froid*, typed it up and left it on his desk along with other correspondence for signature. She never did receive it and carried on working the next day, right up until her marriage.

Mother and Father were both musical. She had been organist at Agnes Street Presbyterian Church, while Father became organist and choirmaster at York Street Church on his return from Enniskillen, where he had been the organist in the Presbyterian Church. He was also a tenor with a fine voice who had been encouraged by the organist at Belfast Cathedral, Captain Brennan, to take up a singing career with the words: 'Put your shirt on your voice, young man'. However, a growing family and business responsibilities took precedence. In his youth he had sung with the Armagh Pro Cathedral Choir, where he had been nominated for the musical school. But his father considered that impractical and told him to get out into the world and

3

make something of himself in a 'proper job'.

However, music always played a big part throughout my father's life. He had organised the ship's concert, in which he also featured as a soloist, on the voyage back from Capetown. The programme, with a fine picture of the steamship Themosticles, was on display in the Ulster Museum. He wrote an interesting journal of his time in South Africa, telling of visits to Kimberley Gold Mines, Victoria Falls and the Zambezi, of horseriding on the Veldt, tennis parties and dining at great hotels. He also had a motorbike, which he rode recklessly. On one occasion, during a long journey, he fell asleep and tumbled off it, but thankfully without serious injury. I found his driving licence amongst his papers, dated 30.12.1931, issued by the Province of Transvaal, costing five shillings. I also have a cutting from the Belfast Telegraph, reporting on a concert my father had organised in 1939 at York Street Church, in aid of the district fund for the poor, with an array of artistes and the accompanist, Mr George Lilley, who was a very accomplished organist at a city Presbyterian Church. Father was a long-serving member of the Belfast Philharmonic Chorus, with which he performed in frequent broadcasts of great works from the Ulster Hall. The conductor in the 1950s was Maurice Miles, who had a distinguished career and was very demanding, conducting what was then the City of Belfast Orchestra, which later became the Ulster Orchestra and achieved worldwide fame.

My parents were invited to dinner on one occasion by the great pianist Solomon, a noted interpreter of the works of Mozart, Schubert, Beethoven and Liszt, whose career was tragically cut short by a stroke, although he had a long life. He showed taste and refinement both at the keyboard and socially, and Mother always recalled the occasion of their meeting with great joy.

My brother Fred was born in Enniskillen, where the family lived in a large rented property called Killivilly House, which was outside the town. My parents played their part in the local social scene with their involvement in the church. Mother was often called upon to provide the accompaniment for visiting soloists for she was the better pianist, although she had no singing voice herself. Mrs Whaley, wife of a prominent business-man, particularly requested her playing because she said Mr Frazer made her nervous! Mother accompanied many singers throughout the province, often travelling long distances to do so, and was lucky to get her supper, never mind payment. Some-what different today!

She had many anecdotes to tell. At one concert the baritone was having difficulty. He asked her to stop for a moment, removed his teeth to his pocket and continued his recital. On another occasion a lady was singing the well known song 'I know where I'm going', when a voice from the audience called out in disgust, 'Can you go now?'

A good accompanist is a rare find and Mother was very versatile in her early days. A friend of mine who travelled about singing in concerts related how he always worried about the quality of accompaniment he might expect in country places, for they can make or break you. Once, when singing in a small town in the Republic, he was introduced to his accompanist. Noticing that the pianist had a finger missing from his right hand, the singer feared the worst. Then, on reflection, he thought, 'Perhaps having overcome this affliction, he might be quite good.' (He wasn't!)

The minister of Enniskillen church was a Welshman, small of stature, but with a large tenor voice, who was very enthusias-tic about music and always encouraged it, singing heartily from the pulpit. When asked to perform a wedding at which it was requested there should be no music, he refused, saying it was impossible and ridiculous to contemplate a wedding without music. In the end, the persons concerned were prevailed upon and Mother did the necessary - she and Mrs Whaley giving of their services freely.

The Reverend was a man of character who had a double thumb, which one could not help but notice. Far from causing him any abashment, he displayed it prominently over the edge of the pulpit while he preached the sermon.

Father was the manager of a general goods business in Enniskillen, working for a wealthy man called Plunket. Mother encouraged him to ask for a rise in salary, instead of which the proprietor sent him home with a couple of chickens! That was it, he resigned and the family returned to Belfast where Father started his own wholesale confectionery business on the Old Lodge Road, opposite his previous employer.

When I was born, the family were living with my maternal grandparents in a large double-fronted but semi-detached Edwardian house, at 58 Cliftonpark Avenue. The house had a small front garden with fine wrought iron gate and railings and several steps up to the fine, double outside door and lobby leading to a beautiful inside door with brass bell and knocker and an interesting decorative frosted glass panel. This led to a large hallway, with drawing room to the left and dining room to the right, where there was a piano installed. Behind the drawing room and to the left was a large sun parlour, containing a two-manual pedal organ, a large oaken sideboard bookcase and my grandfather's old office desk. It had a high stool, the desk with sloping surface, surmounted by three frosted glass panels. It looked like something out of Dickens. That was a lovely room in which we loved playing as children. To the back of the hallway was a broad and impressive stairway, to the right of which were the kitchen, with stone floor and open fireplace, scullery and pantry and a washroom with a large 'Belfast' sink.

There was a manageable but walled back garden with two apple trees, a shed and coal hole and a yard, covered with a glass panelled roof. I remember watching as a young child, when painters came to decorate the back of the house, wondering how they would manage to stand on the roof to reach the upper storey without falling through and gashing a leg or two and bleeding to death. Steps at the end of the garden led to a back entry door, where the bins were put out for collection, with rows of houses and streets behind us.

We had several bedrooms and a maid's room at the head and to the side of the first landing and two attics at the top of the house, filled with interesting items and mustiness. When we were young we were somewhat scared of going up there alone.

My maternal grandparents were Frederick Patton and Hannah (nee Wright) who had lived in the house for many years. Grandfather died in 1940, when I was three years of age, so I hardly remember him. He was 63 and Mother often told us of his agonising death from prostate cancer with only aspirin to assuage his suffering. He was short of stature, a businessman who had owned two outfitters shops on the Shankill Road, still a thriving business area, although ravaged by time and the troubles. He was a member of the Loyal Orange Lodge and several items of regalia, medals and sashes and a pair of ceremonial swords, were found in the house after his demise. He was a fine singer, who would have liked to have been a professional. I inherited much of his music. He always wrote his songs on manuscript paper, both words and music, as an aid to memorising them, a device used by Caruso.

Grandma was a tall austere lady, with hair tied back in a bun. She couldn't sing a note, but would drone to us in a tuneless monotone, till my father despaired, for he said that she would ruin our ear for music for ever. She had been brought up in a strict Presbyterian family with much emphasis on church going, and she used to terrify us with tales of having to walk miles to and from church each Sunday and relate the sermon before receiving lunch. This made me very cynical of religion at an early age, for she put the fear of God into us. Indeed, so much was God's all-seeing presence implanted in our minds, I remember at the age of four or five being highly embarrassed when going to the lavatory. I imagined a large eye up in the corner and I used to stand with my trousers down, looking through my legs and asking aloud, 'Can you see me now God?' Receiving no reply, I began to think there wasn't much to it after all and became less concerned.

We shared the house with Aunt Edith, unmarried at that time. She was my mother's sister, younger by two years. She went off and joined the WAAFS (Women's Army Auxiliary Force) at the outbreak of the 1939/45 war and went to England for training, where she met her husband-to-be, Sam Rowan, a Wireless Operator with the RAF who had returned from service in India and Burma. She was a Telegraphist, decoding and relaying Morse Code. They met in the 'Silent Cabin', which was a laugh, for she was and is still, in her 90s, the biggest non-stop talker of all time. He was a taciturn, pipe-smoking chap, who simply read his papers, did his crosswords and raised his eyebrows despairingly now and then. He was a great golfer and a good tennis player. They got married in 1943 and Fred and I went to the wedding with my parents. Valerie, my sister, was born on 15th June 1940 and was too young to go. Winifred, my younger sister, was born later in November 1943.

Members of the household included Grandma, of course, who continued to tell us stories of her childhood but would lighten the gloom by reading *Pinocchio* to us when she could be persuaded to. Then there was Margaret Murphy, our resident maid from Co Monaghan. She was a devout Roman Catholic girl who would often have us in her room, teaching us how to tell our beads with her rosary and making us say our prayers. Margaret and Grandma, looked after us a good deal of the time for Mother worked with Father in the business he had started. Margaret used to take Fred for Easter holidays to the family farm in Co Monaghan, which made me envious for I was too young to go

We went regularly with our parents to Cliftonville Presbyterian Church, where Aunt Edith and Sam were married. Margaret attended the wedding but due to her strict Catholic upbringing, she was unable to enter the church, so she watched from the porch. Years later, Cliftonville Church was taken over by the Rev Ian Paisley's Free Presbyterian Church and was finally burned down during the troubles.

Fred and I joined the Boys Brigade and Lifeboys respectively, similar to the Boy Scouts and Cubs, which gave us something to do in the way of games and exercise, as well as friendships. Margaret continued to pursue her own religion at the local Chapel. We were always very close to her for she looked after us during the week, except on Thursday afternoons, when she had the half day off and Mother was at home instead. Margaret had suffered a tragedy early in her life. Her young sister, who worked for another household, had been cleaning an over mantel with methylated spirits when she caught fire and was severely burned. She lingered during the night but died in the early hours. We were all very upset. Margaret stayed with us till 1947, when we moved house. She eventually married a butcher and did well, her sons going to university, one becoming a doctor. She visited Mother from time to time thereafter, until Mother's death. Margaret still lives in Belfast, I think.

There was no garage at the house so Father rented a lock-up nearby. He always had a car, even on his return from Johannesburg. His first one was an Alfa Romeo and when we were born, he had a fine two-tone black and grey Morris. New cars were impossible to buy, due to wartime restrictions, but we thought the Morris, classical in design, was a beauty. The business premises were filled with shelves, stacked with boxes and jars of sweets and chocolate of every sort. The pervading smell was entrancing. In the early days Father and Mother were often out long hours together, with Fred as a baby lying in the back of the van, travelling round the country drumming up business. Eventually they took on a couple of helpers, a store man and a driver, and the business grew. Father then took over the business and premises of his former boss, the redoubtable D H Wilson, who sold out and retired. This meant that the business was now styled, R A Frazer, Wholesale Grocer, Confectioner and Butter Merchant, with a new heading for the stationery and calendar which was issued annually and distributed to customers.

The premises were much larger, with a general office and Father's private office on the ground floor and a van-yard with a lorry, a large Austin van and a small Ford van and a large store-room. There were two upper store-rooms on the next floor. The building stood on a corner, giving a useful wide main entrance in the side street. Butter and cheese were imported in bulk from New Zealand and Australia, cheese in 56 lb rounds wrapped in muslin, two cheeses to a crate, and butter in 56 lb boxes. Sugar, collected from the docks from Tate & Lyle in Liverpool, was piled high in one hundredweight sacks. Extra butter was kept in the Belfast cold-storage warehouses until required and was re-packaged in 1lb and half-pound rolls by the Cregagh Dairies under the R A Frazer brand name. Cheese was still sold 'loose', either as a full cheese to larger retailers or cut with a cheese wire into smaller lots for sale to smaller shops, where it was then sliced off according to customers' needs. Likewise, dried peas, split green peas, lentils, barley and rice were stacked up in one-hundred weight sacks to be re-packaged into one or half stone paper bags. Sugar was similarly dispensed, according to requirements, before the advent of one and two pound packaging by the suppliers, delivered in 28 lb parcels. Since then, wasteful packaging of all commodities has overwhelmed the consumer. Soup mixture comprising barley, lentils and green-split peas were packaged in cellophane bags under the RAF brand name and sold in dozens to the shops. Tea, arriving in large plywood chests from India and Ceylon, was blended and two qualities in red and green packs were produced by the packers, bearing the RAF brand. Years after my father's death, people were still looking for RAF tea.

Sultanas, raisins and other dried fruit were also received in bulk cardboard cartons and were re-packaged as well. Tinned fruit from South Africa and corned beef from Uruguay and Argentina were also popular, arriving in 6lb tins for slicing or half-pound tins for retail individually. Confectionery of every available description and biscuits were sold, as well as candles, matches, boot and furniture polish, and a certain number of proprietary chemists' lines were stocked, such as Aspro, Aspirin, Mrs Cullen's powders, Beechams pills and powders and cough medicine. Soap powders and bars of Sunlight and Lifebuoy soap were also stocked, as well as breakfast cereals, custard, semolina and tapioca, jams, syrup and treacle, indeed all general groceries.

Father had a number of office and store-room staff and from an early age, I accompanied one of the confectionery salesmen on his journeys in the van, to towns such as Armagh city with its two cathedrals facing each other on adjacent hills, Lisburn, Lurgan, Portadown, Markethill, Larne, Carrickfergus, Ballyclare, Ballymena, Ballynure, Bangor, Ballywalter, Millisle, Donaghadee, Newtownards and further afield to Newcastle, Rathfriland and many others in more distant counties such as North Antrim, Londonderry, Tyrone and Fermanagh. The salesman was called John Craig and he liked to sing hymns in a wavering tenor as we drove - more religion! One day we had lunch at Portadown in a restaurant. We had steak and the bill came to four shillings each. This was much greater than John's usual allowance, so he remonstrated with the proprietress. She explained that she had to buy the meat on the Black Market, for wartime rationing restrictions still prevailed. He argued that that wasn't his fault, without success. Anyway, he recouped his expenses later.

One day D Wilson came to the store and called Miss Patton (my mother) into his 'private office', now in use by Father, of course. Seeing him on the premises, Wilson asked, 'What is that young man doing here?' Mother explained that he was Bob Frazer, her husband and now proprietor, whereupon Wilson ordered her to sack him and to give him his cards. Sensing his state of mind, my mother followed orders, took Father aside and ushered him off the premises. She was able to ring Mrs Wilson who, realising the situation, sent for the authorities, who quietly removed Mr Wilson. He wasn't seen again. It is fair to say that Mother always acknowledged his honesty and refusal to be bribed, or to engage in any chicanery. In ways he was a pillar of society and a leading light in the temperance movement who supported the work of the Salvation Army. He had advanced business ideas for his time and held team-building and think-tank meetings for the staff (those he hadn't fired) at his fine house on the North Circular Road in Belfast.

CHAPTER 2

In 1939, war broke out with Germany and Aunt Edith returned from England. She was posted to Ballyhalbert in Co Down with the WAAFS and worked alongside Sam in the Signals. Father was member of the Home Guard and joined the ARP (Air Raid Protection) squad. In April and May of 1941 Belfast was raided by German bombers. The large shipyard of Harland and Wolff, the aircraft factory of Short Brothers and the Rope Works, the biggest in the world, and the docks, were all prime targets. Earlier in the war, precautions had been taken in the houses and streets, with gas masks and stirrup-pumps being issued. These were great fun and useful for purposes other than fighting fires. Blackouts were imposed and householders taped up all their windows to prevent inward blasts of broken glass. Air Raid shelters were constructed in the streets, sturdy, one-storey buildings of brick and concrete, with flat roofs easily accessible for climbing which provided great play areas for the children.

On April 15th and 16th 1941, Belfast received a severe bombing and about 900 people were killed. We sat in the kitchen, our wooden chairs chattering on the trembling floor, as the bombs exploded around us. Something fell down the kitchen chimney and tumbled out of the burning fire onto the floor. It did not explode. In the dark we were quickly ushered into the candle-lit dining room, where Father played the piano and sang operatic arias, one, appropriately, *Salut Demeure Chaste et Pure*, from Faust. After that raid we had an indoor bomb shelter installed. It consisted of stout supporting steel pillars and a steel roof, with heavy wire grids hanging down round the sides. We could only crouch in there, but at least it would have taken a great weight of debris, should the worst have happened. As it was, our house survived, but a row was flattened behind us and all around the area, bomb craters appeared. Aunt Edith, who had been assisting Father with the fire fighting, received a bad burn on her hand. A warden went to assist a lady standing upright, leaning against the remains of her door post. Though she appeared to be surveying the scenes of devastation around her, she was, in fact, dead.

Mother and we children were quickly evacuated to Killycopple, a remote town-land in Co Armagh, to a small property which Father had acquired. It consisted of a small single-storey cottage, with a corrugated iron roof and a field, with a stream running through at the bottom. Father and Aunt Edith remained in Belfast. I think grandma stayed too. She certainly wasn't with us. We were driven there with a bed on top of the car.

So there we were, with a stream to play in, making mud pies and visiting the flax dams where the retting of the fibres took place, creating a terrible stench and visiting the nearby farm, to purchase whatever produce was available. For Mother it was a less agreeable experience. Her natural affinity was with the city and there she was with the three of us and nothing but isolation. During a thunderstorm, the house rattled and it sounded like a steamroller was being driven across the corrugated roof. Fred was about six years of age and was able to go to the local infants' school, which gave Mother a little respite, but being a 'townie', his presence was somewhat resented and he wasn't happy.

I suffered sunstroke and got the head-staggers and Valerie got a tubercular infection in her neck from infected milk. Fred more or less escaped illness but one day threw me into a bunch of stinging nettles to add to my misery.

Not far away, at Redrock, my father's birthplace, was Black's trading establishment, a customer of the business. General trading in farm foodstuffs, groceries, confectionery and paraffin oil, was carried out here. There was also a large barn across the road from the house, with two petrol pumps outside. Stacks of bags of animal meal were stored there. The house was attached to the shop, which had a low ceiling and a counter from which was dispensed the usual assortment of grocery lines. Sides of bacon were hung from the rafters and it was a satisfying noise and sight of the rashers being cut with the bacon slicer, peeling off into greaseproof paper and being deftly wrapped, to be concealed in shopping baskets. The Blacks were very good to us and we loved to sit in the low-ceilinged living room, well warmed by a welcoming fire, being fed a tasty fry of eggs, bacon and dipped bread. That was luxury living in those days.

Mr Black was a kindly man, who occasionally brought out his huge charabanc of a car, a real bone-rattler. You climbed up two steps to get into it and he thundered along in a quite dangerous manner. There wasn't much traffic about, which was just as well, for he paid no heed to the rules of the road, nor to driving strictly on the left. We always ooked forward to a ride, Mother less so.

A second air-raid took place on 7th May 1941, causing major damage and further bomb craters appeared throughout the city. During all this time, Father stayed in Belfast, looking after whatever business was possible and spending his evenings with neighbours, the Hortons. Mr Horton played the cello and another friend, Mr Symmons, an agent for Mackintosh's confectionery and Sharp's toffee ('Sharp's the word for toffee' was their motto), visited for musical evenings. He was a fine baritone singer, who had won the Dublin Feis Ceoil, the major annual singing contest, still run there and once won by Count John McCormack, the great Irish tenor. Mr and Mrs Symmons were life-long friends of the family and for many years after father's death, Mrs Symmons remained a close friend of my mother. She was from Manchester and reminded you of Gracie Fields, good-looking and jolly, with a handsome fur coat and an engaging personality. She was particularly patient with us. Mr Symmons was a tall, slim gentleman, with a moustache who could make us laugh with his impressions and mimicry. He was not unlike Groucho Marx, especially with his quick asides, often poking fun at his own wife. She was not slow in riposte.

After the bombing, we returned to Belfast, but continued to use Killycopple for holidays and at weekends, until Winifred was born in 1943. We were then evacuated to Millisle in Co Down. Father had rented a house just by the road running along the sea-shore, with clear sea views . American troops, the

14

first in Europe, arrived in Belfast in 1942 and were pursued by children in the streets, seeking gifts of chewing gum and sweets. We later encountered them at Millisle, for we were near Ballyhalbert, with its military installations, further along the coast. We enjoyed a ride on a caterpillar driven armoured amphibian truck. It was nice by the seaside. Other friends had been evacuated there as well, including the Smyths, who used to own a large record shop in Belfast. Mr Smyth looked like Prince Rainier and his father, who was an impresario, had brought the great Caruso to perform at the Ulster Hall, in 1909. The second generation Smyths were friends of the family and he was one of the few people in Belfast to own a Rolls Royce, in the early 1950s. He was a terrible driver and told Mother he had only got it to sit in at the door for the benefit of the neighbours.

As a child, I had terrible trouble with my teeth and with asthma. I remember a cold wet day, when I had to go by bus to Donaghadee to have a tooth pulled. I was miserable after having gas, which caused me horrifying nightmares which recurred for many years. I was in space, flying round the world in darkness approaching a blinding light, horrified at the speed and impetus, into oblivion, with a recurring high-pitched bleep, reminiscent of a sputnik circling the earth in space. I awoke screaming for years afterwards. Coming home in the bus I was bleeding profusely and crying, and I had to stand at the open back of the bus in case I wet myself. An old lady asked my mother if I had been knocked down by a car. I suffered agonies of toothache for years. In this respect I took after my father, who had very deep strong roots to his teeth. He once went to have one extracted and the dentist was the worse for drink. It all finished up with Father lying on his back on the floor, with the dentist's knee on his chest, vainly trying to wrench the offending molar from my father's screaming head.

We had great fun amongst the sand dunes. At weekends, prayer meetings were held outdoors. A small melodeon was erected on the sands and after several evangelical tirades and exhortations from the bible, by the preacher, singing of hymns would commence. There was a small cinema in Millisle also, but I can't remember any particular shows. We loved playing on the sands and rocks. We occupied a fine semi-detached house with a terraced lawn in front and a sizeable vegetable garden at the back. We were paid a penny for plucking dandelions off the front lawn.

A load of horse manure had been delivered for use on the vegetables and had to be soaked before being spread, after it had rotted for some time. To do this, we used a wheelbarrow and a large barrel of rain water beside the house drained off the roof. On emptying the barrel a large dead rat was found at the bottom, which caused some excitement, if not revulsion. Luckily, we had only ever used the water on the garden, although it was greatly recommended for washing, due to its softness and the good lather it could achieve.

We enjoyed the house and father's two cousins, Tom and Harry Frazer, came down for holidays. Tom was a lovely fellow, charming and friendly, who liked singing Negro spirituals, particularly 'Swing Low Sweet Chariot' and 'Standing in the Need of Prayer'. He looked like Al Jolson (without the black face), had a good voice and loved the singing of Paul Robeson. His favourite aria was 'The Song of the Flea', by Mussorgsky. He was an accountant and audited the books for our business. Harry was a well known and wealthy estate agent and a JP in Belfast, whom we saw infrequently, whereas Tom came often as a visitor both to Millisle and Belfast, throughout father's life. One day, Harry broke a toe while cavorting in the sea. To me this seemed most unusual and he didn't receive a lot of sympathy. It did curtail his visits.

Mother was unsettled. The war continued, but when the RAF planes began target practice on the off-shore rocks, flying low overhead with much noise, it was as bad as the air-raids. She preferred the real thing so we returned to Belfast and that ended our evacuation, although we experienced no more raids. Still, we all regret that Father hadn't bought the house in Millisle for what would have been a nominal sum, even in those days. Eventually he did buy a double wooden bungalow on the Donaghadee Road, the other side of Millisle, which we used for holidays for some years. He paid £600 for it and received a written receipt of a jotter page, acknowledging that he was the new owner of the property. The place was finally rented out, care of a local agent, who got more of the rent than we did. The tenants sub-let in Summer and made a fortune. We could never find the receipt after Father's death, so Mother sold the place to the sitting tenants very cheaply and without fuss. It is still there.

So it was back to Belfast. Life continued as did the war, until 1945, when peace was declared. Fred and I were sent to the 'BAP' school, officially the Baptist Junior School, affectionately known as the 'Wee BAP', which was on the Antrim Road. Another school, the Jaffe, at the end of Cliftonville Road, where the boys were antagonistic, was a problem and we had to run the gauntlet of their wrath, sometimes being attacked.

I didn't like school at all. Miss Boggs was our mistress, who shamed me in front of the class one day by bringing Fred in to demonstrate how stupid I had been over some trifle. On another occasion I arrived late in the morning, when school had started. She vented her wrath by giving me three stinging whacks on the palm of the hand with a springy cane. Later on, the Headmaster, having seen me creeping into the class, brought me forward and administered three more blows to the same place with a ruler. I was so taken aback with the injustice of it all that I couldn't even mutter a protest. I have remembered the name of Boggs ever since for it was a figure of fun anyway, due to its geographical and more basic connotations.

As for Figgins, the Headmaster, he was as miserable as he looked, so I guess he got his just desserts. They said at school that he could see out of the back of his head. As far as I'm concerned, he talked out of his backside as well. I don't think I learned a damn thing there, certainly I don't remember anything, but it sowed the seeds of my contempt for bungling authority and pompous nobodies. I was naturally left-handed, but was made to write with my right-hand, which is why my hand-writing today is still atrocious and it probably affected my brain as well.

About this time, I was probably eight years old and I was beginning to take an interest in a couple of girls at the school. One was called Sylvia and the other Ann. Sylvia was blonde and Ann was dark, with glasses, but both were pretty, so much so that I could only admire them from a distance and nothing came of it, though we were friendly enough in a remote sort of way. However, as mentioned earlier, the air-raid shelters in the streets provided ample playing areas and gave opportunities for meeting mixed groups of local children. Naturally, Mother was askance at the thought of our playing in the streets at all. Nevertheless, as a young girl living, as she had, in the same house, she herself had surreptitiously taken advantage of the pleasures that street life provided. She often told of the fun she'd had, swinging on a rope, looped round the lamp-posts, which provided a sling seat on which she and others could swing round the post two or three times, before unwinding in a different direction. Also, spinning of tops with a whip and the running of hoops with a stick were pastimes that I and my brother and sisters all enjoyed. In the shelters on dark nights, we would meet and sometimes, with the light of a torch, show made-up paper reels of 'films' wound through a cut-out opening in a large cornflakes packet and, if lucky, steal a kiss from one or other of the more readily available 'big' girls who were present - very daring and pleasurable!

I had a good friend at school called Ronnie Findlay and we went back and forth together, both for company and moral support. He lived in a street nearby and I was intrigued on occasion when he would carry out a battery which had glass sides, taking it somewhere or other to be charged. Apparently this was used to run a radio in his house, which I couldn't understand, as we had a large electric HMV radiogram at home, on which we could not only hear the radio, but play 78 rpm records from my father's collection of opera singers and other classical music. Caruso in 'La Donna e Mobile' and 'O Sole Mio' on the other side, was my favourite record. Records of Gigli, Chaliapin, Tetrazzini, Galli-Curci, Peter Dawson, Isobel Bailie, Clara Butt and Ursula Van Diemen were available, along with such as Heifitz, Campoli, the great violinists or the overture from Weber's 'Oberon', 'Finlandia' by Sibelius with Toscannini and so on. To hear Galli-Curci, one of the foremost coloratura sopranos ever, singing a simple song like 'Home

Sweet Home', with slightly accented English, was a joy of feeling, expression and a display of great phrasing and breath control. It haunts me still and I have retained it, as well as on LP and CD. Her coloratura in 'Ombra Leggiera'from 'Dinorah', or 'Lo Hear the Gentle Lark', or 'Una Voce Poco Fa' are most memorable. Likewise Tetrazzini, the 'Plump and Jolly Song Thrush', said to have made over £10m in her time and spent the lot, with a bigger voice but equal agility. She was a good friend of Caruso, who was my favourite singer but Gigli was also wonderful in 'Salut Demeure' and 'Che Gelida Manina' with two of the best and most beautiful high Cs ever recorded. I played the Caruso record to destruction, for the pick-up with its sharp steel needle was very heavy and eventually the record was worn thin.

Ronnie Findlay and I remained friends for a long time. One day, coming home from school, he had to collect some sausages from the butcher at the corner of Manor Street. We decided to carry them on our heads, in turns, for the packet was soft and easily balanced. But they fell off several times and the package burst, so we decided to sample them and ate them raw. They were quite pleasant and I've had a fondness for sausages every since, but of the cooked variety - sometimes very nice with marmalade or strawberry jam. When we got to his house, there were only a couple of sausages left and some mush. I beat a hasty retreat and when I told Mother of our escapade, she was horrified, saying I would get 'worms'or suchlike. Nothing happened, although Ronnie did incur his mother's displeasure and he had very little supper that night.

We were encouraged to go to church and Sunday school and to join the Boys Brigade, some of which could be fun. I invited Ronnie along one Sunday afternoon to some such function in the hope of him finding some amusement. It turned out to be an extension of Sunday school, during which we were to sit and make up prayers. Someone would start and then nudge his or her neighbour to continue. When it got to us, we were embarrassed and tongue-tied. I nudged him and he nudged me repeatedly, until it became acrimonious. No prayers were uttered, only a few oaths as the nudges increased in violence and

19

the meeting (and our friendship) broke up. His total distaste for religion preceded my own by some years. My wife mentioned a similar occasion in which she was involved at one time, when a friend whose turn it was to pray was so overwhelmed with nerves that she blurted out, 'Oh God, bless all absent friends here with us to-night'.

During my childhood things were pretty basic. Although we had a car, a radiogram and a piano, we really had little in luxuries and I had to make do with Fred's cast-offs. Of course, wartime precluded the acquisition of many items, both of essentials and treats. Many items and indeed cars, were few and far between. Fred had a tricycle and a pedal car, bought earlier by his grandfather, which I would have loved. I had a set of wooden building blocks and a plank of wood and a hammer and nails to make a boat. I always wanted a pedal car but never got one. From an early age I had an interest in making things. From a set of old pram wheels and a plank of wood I fashioned a 'guider', which consisted of a fixed set of wheels at the back and a front set attached to a cross bar on a swivel, which could be steered by the feet with the aid of a rope. This was a type of vehicle popular at the time and afforded great fun trundling down hills or pushing each other around. A simpler device was a roller skate with a small plank of wood set on top, on which we careered down Fountain Street pavement. An unfortunate accident in striking a lady's leg one day put paid to that, use of the guiding cart being more manageable. Years later I made a couple of such carts for my sisters, though pram wheels had become scarcer. The biggest of these was made with two bicycle wheels at the front, the body made from two large wooden packing cases nailed together and mounted on the complete, sprung, under-carriage of an old pram. Even as late as the 1980s, I made one for my young nephews who had great fun with it.

One day at a fun-fair in Warrenpoint where we had a day out, I found a pound note. This was a lot of money, for we were used to pennies and halfpennies. Even in my time we had used the farthing (one nine-hundred and sixtieth of a pound), before it was phased out. Not knowing what to do, I confided in Fred, who immediately seized it, saying that he would buy us all presents when we got home. The result was that we got Snakes and Ladders and Ludo boards and other simple gifts. The appearance of these items naturally aroused mother's curiosity. Grandma was consulted; she knew nothing about it, except to say that she had seen Fred with a half note i.e. ten shillings, so the secret was out. I never played the Ludo, but the Snakes and Ladders afforded us some fun. I presume Fred benefited by ten shillings after the purchases.

Many items were delivered by tradesmen regularly, often from horse-drawn wagons. Milk, coal, bread and mineral waters were delivered to the house. Milk was dispensed with a long-handled ladle from a churn into household utensils. Bread vans or carts had long drawers which were pulled out to gain access to the goodies at the front end. A long-hooked pole was used to unearth Paris buns, pancakes and pastries. Veda bread, a malted loaf and very tasty toasted, was popular. White 'pan' loaf, cheese or 'beal' end white loaf, wheaten, soda and potato bread were all served. Belfast was renowned for its mineral springs, resulting in many producers of varieties of brown and white lemonade, cream soda, raspberryade, kali water (very good for delicate stomachs), orangeade and sarsaparilla. These were all sold in large bottles, returnable for a 2d deposit, with syphons of soda water sold with a half-crown deposit on the bottle, returnable or exchangeable for a fresh one. The names Ross, Cantrell and Cochrane, and Maclennan were famous, but with many other producers throughout the city. Ross's soft drinks were served on board the great ocean liners visiting the Americas. Another famous name in this production was Lyle & Kinahan, and in my retirement I am living on Lylehill Road in the Village of Templepatrick by the main gateway of Castle Upton, the former home and estate of the late Sir Robin Kinahan, whose fortune was made in this trade. He was also a previous Lord Mayor of the City of Belfast.

Coal merchants sold their wares from the back of a lorry or cart drawn by a horse, dispensed in one cwt bags, the coalman in his long black leather apron, neck scarf and cap, with black leather flap down his back carrying them to be dumped in the coal-hole or cellar. The bags were shaken out and piled, folded double, to be counted as evidence of the number delivered. Many horse-drawn vehicles were used and fresh horse droppings in the shape of well-formed oblong balls were hurled by children at each other like snowballs. People in houses were not ashamed to rush out with a bucket and shovel to collect fresh deposits, for allotments were popular where no gardens existed and the manure was a valuable commodity in those austere days. Cliftonpark Avenue had a smooth concrete surface, excellent for whipping tops and roller skating. It was quite broad with fine houses on each side usually occupied by professional or business people. However, several large houses had been converted into flats, turning them into tenements. Most of the houses are now gone, either destroyed in the blitz or completely ravaged by the subsequent troubles throughout the 70s and 80s and lasting some 30 years. The whole area is still a trouble spot in North Belfast and much disfigured.

Trams were running in the streets of Belfast and could be used over long distances. Trolley buses appeared in the 50s, but were superseded by petrol and diesel vehicles that lacked the charm of the trams. Your could run after the trams and hop on and off at convenient stops. Some were open-topped and some were a fine blue streamlined type, with closed doors with pleasing contours. One big event in my young life was the occasion when a tram took off without its crew from the Cliftonville Depot and careered down the steep road. Aunt Edith and Uncle Sam were aboard, but were able to leap off as it slowed at the top of the Cliftonville Road. It regained momentum and emerged about a mile or so later at the bottom of the road, careered through the traffic lights across the main Antrim Road and demolished a shoe-maker's shop on the other side, finishing up in the side of the Phoenix pub. There were no serious injuries but this became a spectacle which excited us, until the debris was removed.

The last tram in Belfast ran on the 28th of February 1954, a sad occasion. The tram-lines and square-set cobbles were lifted and smooth surfaces put down by degrees. This certainly made for better motoring.

CHAPTER 3

Before and during the war there was much austerity, rationing of food, sweets, petrol, clothing and most commodities was common, everything being in short supply. This rationing persisted for quite some time after the war into the mid-50s.

Men with oxyacetylene torches removed our nice iron gate and railings, along with all others in the streets, and carried them off to make armaments. This completely spoiled the look of the gardens. It is not known how many of these vandalised items actually finished up helping the war effort and rumours abound, but no doubt a few scrap dealers benefited. After the war in 1945, things began to improve. Cinemas and theatres opened up and rebuilding began. The air-raid shelters remained for some years and became derelict and vandalised. Many blitzed sites remained as open spaces for many years, known as waste ground, where traders' stalls were sometimes set up or street entertainers performed. On one occasion, a tent had been erected and some boys were able to get onto the roof and slide down its slopes. This seemed like fun as I enviously watched them, till one fellow became impaled on the metal spike on the top of a pole. He lay there yelling in agony till he was removed and taken off for treatment. Families returned to the city and life began again.

Mother and Father always went to the variety shows which took place each week at the Grand Opera House. Later I would accompany them. The shows were great, with dancing girls, comedians, a singer, a juggler or hypnotist, a contortionist or tap-dancer, maybe a ventriloquist or a troupe of harmonica players, (the Morton Fraser Harmonica Gang, were notable), or a whistler, but always with a well-known star to top the bill. A great show, unlike the present day theatres, dominated by over-amplified pop singers. I was fortunate enough to see such stars as Bob Hope, actually rather boring himself, for he mumbled his quips into the microphone, but he had Gloria De Haven with him. She was gorgeous and he lost no opportunity in embracing and kissing her. She sang and fooled around and was divine in my young imagination. I heard Norman Hockridge, a noted singer, saw Harry Secombe before he became famous in The Goons, but he sang beautifully, and performed his various comedy routines. Laurel and Hardy also visited us and we saw many more stars of variety and stage, the most impressive being Micheal Macliammoir in his one-man show, 'The Importance of being Oscar'. Brilliant!

Next door was the Hippodrome, where the circus was sometimes staged, much preferable to the uncomfortable big top. Particularly impressive was the tight-rope walker, who ascended a rope stretched from the stage to the balcony, with a girl on his shoulders, sliding back down with increasing momentum, to the stage and great applause. There was an armless man who painted with his feet, lit and smoked a cigarette, scratched his head, fired a rifle and did other tricks. Belfast had dozens of cinemas, the greatest being the Ritz, which gave a fine show including a cartoon, Movietone News, a B feature and organ recital, before the main film. Great value for half a crown. If required, you could have a meal in the cinema restaurant before the show. The nearest cinema to us was the Capitol on the Antrim Road, also very good and superior to the Lyceum further down the road. There was another one on the Old Park Road, all of these within walking distance of home. But the great thrill was to go to the famous down-town cinemas, the Ritz, the Hippodrome, the Gaumont or the Regal. The Grand Central Hotel took pride of place in Royal Avenue and was a great venue to eat, meet or be seen.

Aunt Edith and Uncle Sam lived with us for a time after their marriage. Meantime, Grandma was getting older and used to sit reciting tales from her childhood over and over. Many times we heard of her spartan upbringing and austere religious instruction, but some of her stories were interesting too, about Belfast and the early troubles, when an uncle had been shot at the front door. She often mentioned Lord Carson. Grandma

24

was useful at looking after us too and we constantly requested her to read Pinocchio to us until she was demented.

Outside of work, Mother and Father had quite a social life. They played tennis, particularly my father, with Uncle Sam, at the courts by the Waterworks at the corner of the nearby Antrim Road. This area also provided a playground where we could go with impunity, without fear of mugging or interference. The Waterworks had two large reservoirs, with swans and ducks and where people sailed toy yachts. The playground provided much fun, having swings, roundabouts, swing boats, see-saw and climbing apparatus. There were large machines which could fling you off, big swings and other items to amuse us, but we never suffered any injuries of note. There was also an abandoned steam-roller, over which we used to clamber and we enjoyed pretending to drive it. A tram could take you to Bellevue further up the Antrim Road for 1d, where there was the zoo and the Floral Hall, famous for dances. There was a miniature steam railway which took you along the skirt of the Cave Hill, looking down from above and with views across the Belfast Lough and Co Down on the far side. It also afforded good views of the city and the ship yard. Sometimes we would climb Cave Hill and walk across it with Father, then return home exhausted. There was also a general fun fair including dodgems, roll-a-penny, ghost train and rifle range. Father and Mother continued to enjoy the shows, plays on occasion, and Father rehearsed with the Philharmonic regularly. We always went each year to hear him in 'The Messiah'.

Around 1946, it was decided that our schooling should move on. Fred and I were sent for tests at Belfast Academical Institution, one of Belfast's foremost schools. We made little impression, confirming the inadequacy of our learning at the 'BAP'. So much for Boggs and Figgins! In the end we were sent to Portora Royal School in Enniskillen, where Fred had been born.

It was at this time that Father bought a farm at Ballyrobert outside Belfast in the townland of Ballyclare. It comprised 75 acres of land with a small stream running behind it at the bottom of the back field, which flowed under the railway arch that carried the line to Londonderry. Doagh station was not far away. We were unaware that Father was buying this place and Mother thought that he was intending it as a weekend retreat. When we were finally taken to see it and she realised that we were to live there, she was annoyed for she was a townswoman and never liked the country.

The house was called Fairacre and had a nice appearance, but was at the end of a long lane off the Doagh Road, now called the Longshot. That had been part of the famous Ballyclare circuit, where the annual Grand Prix Races took place, before the Dundrod Circuit came into use. The pit-stops had been on that road which made it of interest. There was another back entry to the property from the main Belfast Road, wending through the fields. It was more of a cinder road, but could accommodate vehicles and in one of the fields was a single-storey, double dwelling, which housed the farm labourer and his family and parents. The farm was well-stocked with cattle, pigs, hens, geese and ducks, two goats and four working horses and various hay-making and ploughing machinery.

Meantime, Aunt Edith and Uncle Sam were planning to move to a neat little detached house in Whitehouse Park, down by Belfast Lough. It had a small front garden and a pleasant rear one, backing on to the Belfast/Larne railway line. Grandmother went to live with them. It was lovely to sit on a good day and see and hear the trains passing. Sam worked in the Civil Service and his office moved near to Bangor, which meant he had to get there each day by train.

CHAPTER 4

So it had been decided that we would be sent to Portora Royal School and that we would be returning to a new house. Portora was known as the Eton of Ireland and had been founded by King James VI of Scotland and First of England, in the seventeenth century. It had had many famous pupils, including Oscar Wilde and Samuel Beckett. It was still famous for its rugby and becoming famous for rowing, taking advantage of the beautiful Lough Erne on whose shores it resided. The curriculum was Classics-based, emphasizing Greek and Latin, as well as all the general subjects. It was a boarding school with a large number of day pupils, and attracted students from the Republic of Ireland as well as England and the Colonies. Mother always talked about the boys going down town to attend the local churches in Summer, when they were attired in blazers and boaters, which they often threw skimming away into the waters of the Erne as they crossed the bridge into the town. She enjoyed that.

So it was all hands to the pumps to prepare for us to go there. New clothes, all labelled with Cash's woven name-tapes, were required. Two sets of this and six sets of that, underwear, pyjamas, socks etc. Two pairs of black shoes, sports clothes, shirts and trousers of regulation style were required. Poor Mother was exhausted! Fred and I expressed little interest or excitement in the forthcoming venture and only on the day of departure did trepidation begin to emerge. For one reason or another, Father was unable to drive us to school which was some 80 miles away. So we went with him by train from Belfast's Gt. Victoria Street Station on the afternoon steam train to Enniskillen. It was a nice journey with a meal on board and it was fairly comfortable in the cosy corridor compartment. Many other boys, established pupils, were on board, their experience evident by their swaggering, affected indifference. We arrived in the late evening and took a taxi up to the school.

Portora Royal School stands on a hill overlooking 'The Narrows', where the upper and lower Loughs meet, just outside the town of Enniskillen which in fact is on an island in the river. The site gives a full view of the entire town. It is a most magnificent setting, with a boathouse on the lake shore at the bottom of Portora Hill at The Narrows. There are cricket and rugby pitches on the upper ground and three rugby pitches at lakeside on the other side of the hill, by the Derrygonnelly Road. A new swimming pool was built near the school gates during my time there, which also served the needs of the local youth movements. The new gates had been donated in memory of the Reay brothers, former pupils who had perished in the war. They were officially opened by Lord Granville, then Governor of Northern Ireland. There was a general sports day for the occasion and his Lordship disported himself in the gymnasium, fencing with epée with some of the senior boys. He was a stout gentleman, appearing in his shirt sleeves and braces, sweating profusely but fencing vigorously with much shouting.

In the Autumn of 1947, on my first evening, I was delivered to the Matron of the Prep School, Gloucester House, which is within the grounds at the bottom of the hill, accessed by the main gates, from which a steep drive wends its way to the upper school terrace, where my brother Fred was sent. I didn't see much of him after that except at church on Sundays. I was ten years old. As we had arrived rather late, most of the boys were already in the dormitories in Gloucester House. I was escorted by the Matron, without ceremony, to a dormitory and told to prepare for bed. She then offered me a hot drink of cocoa, which was full of lumps and quite unappealing. I was unable to stomach it and the Matron was quite brusque in ordering me to bed. Father had left to stay in a local hotel overnight and would be returning to Belfast next day without seeing us. I felt isolated.

Next day was even worse. On rising, we were left to get washed and dressed and then directed to the dining room. More horrors! Shredded Wheat to start breakfast, which I could never touch for it seemed to me like straw with candle-grease coating and then boiled eggs, the smell of which quite repulsed me, particular with a room full of 40 cracked open simultaneously. There were one or two new boys with whom I struck up some accord, strengthened by our mutual misery.

Notices were posted on boards with Frazer junior (that was me) assigned to particular classes and day-time duties. I don't remember the procedures in detail but after a short while, the Headmaster, the Rev. Douglas L Graham, appeared and called out mine and several other names, telling us to get to the wall. Without further ado, he told us there was to be no more Latin for us and that we were to fill in those periods with gardening duties. So much for my academic career! (More of the Head later, when I eventually reached the upper school.)

Our Head of Gloucester House was a chap called Taplin, a large, rather ungainly but not unkind man. He had a wide, spade-like chin and an air of tired resignation. He was nick-named 'Hunya', because of the way his lower jaw jutted out and his speech delivery. David Lloyd-Simon, a Welshman, was the music master, with a manic manner. He was very stern. However, it was the only class I actually liked and, detecting that I could sing in tune, he singled me out to perform in front of the class. This resulted in jibes and face-pulling from my fellows, rendering me helpless and earning me a boxing of the ears by the master. The experiment was not repeated. Still, I enjoyed the class well enough and the master entertained us by playing mixed up tunes on the piano, asking us to try and name the different ones disguised therein. Serious teaching of music was for piano, conducted by Lloyd-Simon as extra lessons, for which payment was required. He also taught elocution as an extra, which I took to modify my Belfast accent, but no extra music lessons, which would have been of more interest to me.

Other lessons were conducted in English, Maths, History, French and Geography. We played rugby, athletics and cricket in the lower school and boxing was encouraged in the gym. I was a fighter and was therefore encouraged in that direction and took naturally to rugby, which I liked. I was never any good at athletics, particularly cross-country running and made my asthma an excuse to avoid that futile pastime. I was reasonable at cricket as a slow left-hand bowler and fielding, but not batting. In the first term I was selected for the school play and was assigned three parts. I was awarded the prize for best actor. The awards were decided and presented by Dame Millicent Trimble. I was successful at rugby and was made a Prefect.

The school was predominantly Protestant, and each pupil had to attend the church of his upbringing on Sunday mornings in the town. Being Presbyterian, I (with others) had to attend that church, which was at the far end of town, whereas the Methodist and Church of Ireland were in the centre of town, where the Church of Ireland and Roman Catholic Churches stood opposite each other. In addition, our forced devotions included Sunday School, Bible Classes for the upper school, followed by a full service with a long sermon to boot, whereas the Church of Ireland chaps had a special short service and were back to school long before us, with time for ad hoc sports before lunch. The Rev. Jenkins had by this time retired and been replaced by a serious, rather dull individual. His name escapes me, but he hated the Portorans, whose only source of relief during the service was either playing cards below the pew, or writing in names of up-to-date, upper school rugby teams, with their record of results against other schools, or else reading those more historical lists previously written.

I gradually came to terms with Gloucester House life. In the first term, Mother had arranged for the Rev. Jenkins to take Fred and myself to lunch one weekend. Prior to that we had been met by a former neighbour who had lived beside them in Whaley Terrace. That was near the Redoubt, an annexe to the school, serving as an extra dormitory, where I slept for a couple of years. He took us to lunch, which gave us some respite from school meals. Our day with the Rev Jenkins was much more successful. His son was a magician who entertained us with his tricks and the Reverend was a pleasant and amusing host.

The only relief during the terms was the odd visit by some friend's pater or mater, who would invite you to lunch or a day out to Florencecourt or Bundoran. Occasionally, we would make the odd journey to play away at some other school in a game of rugby. Once we were invited to Ballyshannon by a boy's father, Chief Engineer with the Cementation Construction Co. He arranged for a trawler to take us around the coast. The day was fine and it was a thrill to be borne along on the gentle swell of the Atlantic and to view the splendour of the cliffs from below. A trawl was cast and we enjoyed seeing the net hauled aloft, swinging perilously as the boat bobbed on the waves, till its contents disgorged into the hold in a stream of wriggling silver fish. We were able to land on one of the small rocky islands off shore, a mere dot in the ocean, its steep sides surmounted by a green glassy slope. It was pure joy to sit on the grass, gulls wheeling overhead, as we tucked into a simple lunch of hard-boiled eggs with salt and pepper and buttered wheaten bread.

My first year or so made me very homesick indeed and I used to sit on the grass slope by Derrygonnelly Road, waiting for buses to pass, imagining that they were on their way to Belfast and hoping some day to catch one. Eventually the Head of Gloucester House was replaced by a chap called P L Rice, who was particularly interested in cricket and whose wife set up a horse-riding school . Fred took riding lessons for a time but soon stopped when a horse sat on him. I don't think it did him a lot of good, for many years later he was found to have had an enlarged spleen. We were encouraged in gardening at Prep School and were each allocated a small plot to try to produce useable vegetables. Several sons of the sod were very good, producing lots of edible items. I managed to produce one small vegetable marrow (inedible) and a lot of weeds, so I soon lost interest.

We played table tennis and other indoor games on rainy days in the 'Rec' (we called it 'the wreck'), a wooden recreation hut. We had a crazy PE master who arranged these. He also taught Maths and English, but was active with sports generally. One day, during one of his table tennis tournaments, others of us were running round the hut enjoying a bit of rough and tumble. Suddenly he exploded, chased us round the room and, as a big fellow from Dublin called Perkins, was passing, he felled him

31

with a rabbit punch. I shouted out, 'You've killed him!', whereupon the master started after me, followed by a few others, as we escaped out of the hut and into the main corridor of the school to be cornered in the toilets at the far end. He descended upon us, caught some unfortunate by the throat and started to hammer his head against the door. Others were cowering in the locked lavatories. Eventually, his sanity restored, he calmed down. There was a bit of a scandal and the master was quickly moved to the upper school, where it was thought he might be less of a menace. The consequences would have been greater today but we all recovered. In retrospect, I found the incident very amusing and still today, I laugh uproariously when recounting this episode. In fact, I took extra maths lessons in the upper school with that gentleman, in an effort to improve my general certificate exam results. I recently learned of his death. He wasn't a bad old stick - the victim of a bad temper rather than a bad nature.

This particular master did have another go at me in the gymnasium at the upper school, when I landed on my head following a forward dive over the vaulting horse. I was meant to land on my hands and finish with a forward somersault. My head seemed to disappear into my shoulders and I was lying stunned and gasping, whereupon he kicked me roughly to the side of the hall, muttering, 'You stupid dolt', and other disparagements. I took some minutes to recover and have suffered a creaking neck and pains ever since. He also supervised the Redoubt , where his wife was the resident matron. When I slept there some time later, a new young and attractive matron was installed. She was very friendly and we tried to persuade her to take off her clothes. She wouldn't, but took our fun and games in good spirit.

Both my brother and myself benefited from tuition in maths by the said gentleman and we remained on friendly terms. But there were many genuine injustices at the school, some perpetrated vindictively by the staff. One which particularly hurt me when I was young occurred in Gloucester House. Each fortnight a film was played on the upper school's equipment in the Steele Hall, which we were allowed to attend. That night, the film was 'Way out West', with Laurel and Hardy, and it was so successful that it was rearranged for another showing. I and a few of the other boys had caught a slight cold previously, but we were well on the way to recovery. The whole of Gloucester House greatly looked forward to the re-showing of the film. The matron, however, had other ideas and we were prevented from going on account of our 'illness'. This was an example of unsurpassed spite in my view, and most hurtful.

The Rev. Graham's son was at Gloucester House in my first or second year. He was a real Denis the Menace and would beat everyone up in the dorm at night, with a heavy pillow. He would also climb down the drainpipe in the night and disappear down town. He was eventually removed by his father, much to our relief and amusement, and was sent to a school in England after that.

As we approached the time to be transferred to the senior school, rumours of horrors to come began to circulate, of the viciousness of certain masters. One, who was deadly accurate with the chalk, would hurl it suddenly at a pupil at the slightest provocation, sometimes followed by the wooden backed duster; another would give you the Chinese burn, viciously rubbing his thumb up the side of your temple, almost tearing out the short hairs, or else taking a clump between his fingers and twisting them to excruciation, whilst raising you from your seat. Another, it was said, could wither you with a glance, causing you even more disquiet, such was the venom of his look. There were tales of the beatings one might expect from the Prefects, or the fagging duties one might have to carry out, such as bed-making, shoe-cleaning and other duties. Failure to perform well or to keep the bastards' studies tidy would result in punishment or derision. It turned out that most of these 'monsters' weren't too bad; most of the masters were reasonably fair, though each had his own eccentricities. However, there were some proper sadists among the Prefects: one gave me and a friend a violent beating with a long Scout staff for using one of the rugby balls to play touch rugby on the school's parade ground. He administered six fearful blows to the backside, causing weakness at the knees and bruising of the buttocks, but we suffered no permanent injury and our pride ensured that we displayed no discomfort to him. He was an ugly big oaf and I never had any trouble with him again, but I'm sure we got the better of him somehow.

Having got through the first year at Gloucester House, my time there settled into the routine lessons, sports and permitted extra curricular activities. The daily diet was supplemented with the odd parcel from home. I had a great addiction to sweets, which were still rationed since the war. We were encouraged to have bicycles at school and I acquired an old second-hand rattler. Several of us used to cycle across the Fermanagh border to Blacklion, in the Republic of Ireland, where sweets of limited variety and quality were readily available. This was a round trip of about 12 miles - a lot of effort to acquire a few bars of tough toffee, which was all we could afford. Indeed, our teeth suffered, though no doubt the exercise did us good. My addiction, particularly to chocolate, became so great that I used to purchase others' sweet ration coupons so that I could indulge further without the effort of riding 12 miles. The cost of the coupons, added to the cost of the available confectionery, effected their own limitations. Throughout my life I have remained addicted to chocolate and crave it every day.

CHAPTER 5

Finally, with others of my year, I moved to the upper school, which meant more togging out, for long trousers were now *de rigueur*. We needed school caps and blazers, though boaters were no longer worn, so that expenditure wasn't necessary. The Headmaster, the Rev. Douglas L Graham, was from a Dublin family and of a good social and educational background. He himself had been a pupil at the school before going on to take his degrees. He was a large man of impressive stature, a Classics scholar as well as a clergyman, and he was young for a Headmaster. He had a cauliflower ear, for he had been the Royal Navy heavyweight champion boxer and also a good rugby player in his time. He had a charming and ladylike wife, who kept herself aloof, and my housemaster, A T M Murfet, a Cambridge scholar, declared in his somewhat condescending and comical tones that she had 'enjoyed bad health' for a number of years. This terminology made us howl, as we did on another occasion, when we were talking about a fellow pupil whose father had shops on the north Antrim coast in Portrush, saying that he had done very well. Murfet's disparaging response was, 'Yes, but he did it with his hands'. He said this with a sly twinkle, fully aware that Fred and I came from a business background ourselves. We had many a laugh at that one. I will refer to Mr Murfet later, for he had a considerable influence over me.

The Rev. Graham did not particularly like us and Fred in particular often fell foul of his wrath. I, despite my growing distaste for religion, took the compulsory Synod exams and achieved first place in all Ireland amongst the Presbyterian faction. I was awarded a prize. As if to show his disdain, not only for Presbyterians but for the sons of business, Graham allowed all the other prize-winners to visit his study first to choose their awards. Finally calling me in, he said there wasn't much left but to pick what I liked. I didn't like it, but received some wretched book which, to this day, I have never opened. I hid my own dislike and disappointment and went about my business. Fred and I simply did not meet what Graham considered to be the classical Greek and Latin background and scholastic and social standards of the school. Yet he was to review his opinion in later years.

The school was divided into four 'Houses': Ulster, Munster, Leinster and Connaught, after the four Provinces of Ireland. We were assigned to Connaught, where Fred was already established. Fred more or less ignored me throughout our school days, being my senior by two years. Connaught was considered to be the best House, particularly for rugby, and it was a strange choice, for the Housemaster was A T M Murfet. We never found out his Christian names but he was nick-named Mickey. He was a gentleman and a Cambridge Classics scholar. I had already been ejected from (compulsory) Latin classes by the Headmaster whilst in Gloucester House (it was apparently beyond me), and had never taken up Greek at all. I think Fred continued with his Latin.

'Mickey' had come to the school in about 1920 by a set of strange circumstances. He had been skiing in Switzerland and fell out of the back of a train, sustaining injuries. Returning home, his doctors advised that he should go to Galloway in Scotland to recuperate. Owing to some misunderstanding in the travel arrangements, he finished up in Galway and decided to stay. He found his way to Enniskillen and employment at the school, remaining there till his retirement in about 1960, a confirmed bachelor, living in rooms in the school. He continued to teach Latin and Greek to pupils, amongst whom had been the said Samuel Beckett, whom Mickey described as a strange boy who, even then, wrote incomprehensibly. Beckett, of course, went on to win the Nobel Prize for literature.

Mickey inspired respect and affection amongst the pupils and enjoyed particular allegiance from his House, as well as being Deputy Headmaster. He always wore a bow tie. He maintained an easy discipline, never resorted to physical punishment and made allowance for people's inadequacies. For some reason he encouraged me, probably because I began to emerge as a rugby player and general sportsman who just managed to keep up with the curriculum. He probably liked the fact that he didn't have to teach me Classics. He often drove to school rugby matches in other towns and would take me and a couple of others with him as spectators, to see the school First XV playing in Belfast or Dublin. On one such occasion we were also able to attend an International game at Landsdowne Road where we saw Jack Kyle, Ireland's greatest out-half, whom I met later at our local church in Glengormley.

Often, Mickey regaled us with stories of similar visits to the Republic in the old days, during the troubles in the 1920s. They travelled by train then and he recounted an incident when the train was stopped at Dundalk on the border and several armed men boarded it. They went amongst the carriages, selecting a number of passengers and ordering them off, where they were shot on the platform. The train then proceeded, leaving the platform strewn with corpses. This reminded me of similar stories related by Mother of the times in Belfast when on trams the driver would shout 'Everybody down!', and the passengers dropped to the floor as a hail of bullets sprayed the body-work.

The House rooms were situated beside each other, underneath the Steele Hall, which was used for assemblies, concerts and school plays. Our room was between Leinster and Munster, Ulster being at the top of the corridor. The school prefects had their own study in the main body of the school, next to the library and day-boys had their own quarters and dining room. Friendly rivalry persisted amongst the Houses and each had its own particular characteristics. We were rumbustious. The rooms accommodated 30 or so desks. The walls were half-panelled with tongue and groove wood, painted a dull brown, and the walls above being an even duller green (our House colours) and the desks and other furniture were Spartan. Large round iron pipes along the wall under the windows, provided a modicum of heat and you could sit on them in your leisure time to thaw out. The room was used throughout the school day for Classics lessons, with the master sitting at a sloping desk on a dais at the front. School lessons were conducted in each of these rooms according to the subject of the House-master. Naturally, ours was used by Mickey for Latin and Greek, Munster for Maths, Ulster for French and Leinster for English and French. Other rooms in the main body of the building accommodated History, Geography, Art and English Litera-ture, while Physics and Chemistry were taught in their own labo-ratories. There were music rooms behind the House rooms and above in the Assembly Hall.

A covered corridor gave access to each room, coming in from the quadrangle, with the gymnasium and the point-22 shooting range behind. Steps at each end led up to the cloisters giving access to the dining rooms, Stone Hall and front entrance with stairs to the dormitories. This led to the Old Library, now a history classroom, up three or four stairs past the Prefects' study and into the school Library, which in turn led to an ante-room, before entering the Head's house.

The school enjoyed magnificent views across the lake from the front side and back. One was able to see down almost to Devenish Island, from the playing fields behind with a full pano-rama of the town of Enniskillen from the terrace, which stretched right across the front of the school. Cole's Monu-ment was easily visible, standing in the distance on a hill. The town was off-limits to us, except for church and other official excursions, such as a play or opera by a visiting troupe. The first opera I ever saw was there in the Town Hall: Rossini's 'The Barber of Seville' with piano accompaniment. I was enthralled.

School rules were strict. No alcoholic drink or smoking, no unauthorised visits to town, lights out at 10 p.m., meal times and morning assembly rigidly adhered to with no excuses for lateness, church of your parents' religious persuasion to be at-tended each Sunday, no climbing on roofs, no fraternising with the kitchen maids and so on. People found sneaking out down town to go to the cinema or hoping to meet girls were invari-ably caught, for the town was full of 'spies' reporting back. This did not stop such activities. I decided that I would change religion and go instead to the Church of Ireland, to benefit from the shorter walk and service. This lasted for two weeks, before I was reprimanded by Mickey and ordered to get back to the Presbyterians, where the service was much longer. We were being prepared for Confirmation to take First Communion. We were exhorted to feel the will of God and to be moved by the solemnity. Special tuition was given to learn the Catechism. I was unconcerned by the whole rigmarole, except for depression. On the eve of the ceremony I asked my friend, Paddy Holmes, if he felt any way different. He didn't and we had to go ahead anyway, but to this day I do not take Communion in church, as I feel it would be hypocritical to do so.

In addition to the school curriculum, I took carpentry lessons as an extra, which I enjoyed. I once made a bookcase for Mother, which she greatly looked forward to receiving. However, it was used in the school play before the end of term and then disappeared, so she never did get it. Later I made a smaller bedside cabinet, which she used till her last days. I quite liked Art classes too, and I was two or three times commended by the new Art master for my design of a Chinese plate and my realistic depiction of an apple tree. I was pleased about the apple tree for I was able to visualise it correctly, being familiar with them at home and depicted it accordingly with all its irregularities. I once drew a profile of my sister Valerie on the wall, which impressed my parents and ever after, Art was the only pursuit my parents encouraged me in. Father even went so far as to buy me a book on Augustus John to inspire me.

I struggled with Maths, liked French, History and Geography, couldn't make head nor tail of Chemistry and Physics and enjoyed the English Literature classes with F E Rowlette, the master (I learnt years later that his Christian name was Frazer). He was the one with the notorious reputation for hair torture, which was not as bad as forecast. He was a mild-mannered, likeable man who refereed the rugby games. He used to read us the Sean O'Casey plays: 'Shadow of a Gunman', 'Juno and the Paycock' and so on, effecting the Dublin 'guttie' accent, which excited our interest. We also read plays by Richard Brindsley Sheridan, Shaw and Shakespeare. On occasions, Rowlette would take two or three of us on outings in his car to Boho Caves or Marble Arch. One of my friends, Fred Storey, was from Argentina. He played the mouth organ and had excellent teeth, never going to the dentist, and he could bite the top off a lemonade bottle as easily as with an opener. One day he surprised us when we came upon some horses, by leaping on the back of one and taking off at a gallop across the field. His training on the Pampas was obvious. He was also a nice singer.

We received Religious Instruction classes in a Nissen hut in the school grounds, out amongst the chickens which the Headmaster kept. It had a wooden floor under which the chickens would lay eggs and was beside a field where a donkey grazed. The master hadn't a hope. He could not control the class and made us take copious notes. I adopted a form of indecipherable shorthand, which was in the end meaningless. The classes would descend into chaos, with much desk top rattling, but the master refused to stop, except to remonstrate with us once, saying he would continue the lesson whether we liked it or not. He went on talking in his calm, quiet voice, putting notes on the board and ignoring the clamour. Someone had gathered some eggs from beneath the hut. These were pelted at him and the blackboard was streaming. That finally brought proceedings to a halt. On another day, the master arrived to find the donkey, which by this time had disgraced itself in the middle of the room. That was the end.

The school boasted a Combined Cadet Corps to which one had to belong. At one time there had been an RAF wing but that had been abandoned, leaving the Army and Navy factions. Most were dragooned into the Army, although Fred and a few others managed to join the smaller Naval unit. They were fortunate in being able to spend their time on the lake, in two old whaling boats, pretending to be sailors. We, less fortunate, were subjected to rigid Army uniform code, square-bashing on the parade-ground, signals and weapon training. There was also a field gun which was kept in good order and used on certain parades. There was a pipes and drums band, with kilts as the regulation dress. I enjoyed the weapons training and we had a 202 rifle range, where the shooting team practised for Bisley. I was a good shot, but lacked the patience to be selected. Sten and Bren gun training were also given and we were issued with 303 rifles and occasionally with live ammunition, when we had

40

the opportunity to go to Ballykinler or Colchester Army camps. Each year we were issued with the 303 rifles and blanks and thunder-flashes and sent on night operations against the real RAF at Killadeas. We were warned to protect our rifles at all costs, as the IRA was active even in those days, stealing weapons. To lose your rifle in any circumstances was a grave offence.

Camp at Ballykinler was a real pain to me - hideously boring and uncomfortable in Nissen huts, with poor food. We spent much of the time at the NAAFI, ssupplementing our diet with junk food, or lying in the huts or in the sun (if it ever shone), drinking nut-brown ale. I and others took up pipe smoking, which made me feel dreadful. The next year we were sent to Colchester camp. This was worse. We were under canvas in incessant rain and on putting a foot out you skidded on slimy yellow clay, falling and getting plastered with the stinking mess. The journey to get there meant a train from Enniskillen to Belfast. During the journey some fellows got on the outside and made their way along the sides of the carriages to the end of the train, where they hurled the tail lamps onto the track. This meant a delay on arrival at Belfast, whilst we were berated and the culprits singled out. I forget what their punishment was but the matter was taken most seriously. Finally, a steamboat to Stranraer and a night train journey got us to Colchester. We had to stop at March in the middle of the night; a more desolate place I can't imagine.

The camp was quite large and we were assigned to bell tents - eight or ten to a tent. Next, we had to queue in the pouring rain for issue of straw mattresses and blankets and then for issue of tin plate, mug and cutlery. Back in the tent and spread out, we lay exhausted on the bedding. The flaps were closed and several people smoked, causing a dreadful fug of smoke and steaming clothes. Then we had to queue for food. This was served onto the tin plates where it immediately congealed, so we didn't eat much. To clean up we were provided with dustbins of boiling water. There was so much debris floating on the top that it was hardly worth trying to wash the utensils. However, a quick dip into the boiling water and a rinse in a slightly less contaminated bin did have some effect, especially on your hands if you weren't careful. After that, you rubbed the utensils with sand to remove remnants of grease. The tin soon developed patches of rust.

We were able to do some shooting after further queuing to receive issue of a rifle and five live rounds of 303 ammunition. We then had a long bumpy truck journey to the butts. We were assigned our order for action. Half were despatched up to the targets about 200 yards away, where they had to signal the hits achieved by means of a black and white board on a long pole. With different movements either up or down, backwards and forwards across the face of the target, or rotation of the pole, you were able to signal whether a hit, inner or outer, or a miss had been achieved. This was quite tedious as round after round was fired while you awaited your own turn at the shooting. The impact and whine of the bullets was deafening. Occasionally, whilst you were signalling with the pole in full view, someone would take a pot shot at it. If they were successful in hitting the board or pole it would be painfully wrenched from your hands which could break a wrist. After the first salvo, targets were changed on a pulley and the used target was patched up for future use. Then it was a trudge back and standing in line, await-ing your own turn to lie down on the wet ground to fire off your five shots, followed by a long hike and drive back to queue again to hand in your weapons and account for your shots by producing the spent cartridge cases.

On other occasions we would be marched out in the rain, over the moors, with ground sheets strung around our necks and the water running down the sheet into the backs of our legs. We were to watch demonstrations of anti-tank weapons. Somewhere in the distance was an old hulk of a tank or ar-moured vehicle. Elsewhere in the distance you would hear a report and see a puff of smoke, as a bazooka was fired off. This happened three times, after which you marched across to the distant target, to witness the holes that had been blown in it. Nearly everything about the camp was of interest, but the te-dium of waiting around and the awful weather, dampened the enthusiasm. I was even glad to get back to school.

On the parade ground at school we had to march up and down, bellowed at by the Sergeant Major, left-wheeling, right left turning, presenting arms, forming ranks, shuffling to get our distance and all the usual parade ground manoeuvres. On one occasion I giggled at something. It was quite innocuous but the Colonel, who was also our geography teacher, lost his temper and berated me roundly in front of the whole troop, calling me every nasty name he could think of to demean me. I was so taken aback that I couldn't speak and would probably have been struck if I had. I wondered if he had lost his reason, for he had a large scar down his head and jaw, probably a war wound, which could well have affected his brain. He eventually calmed down. We got on fine in class and generally he was a very likeable man and was most helpful to my brother, Fred, some years later.

Charlie Phipps was a rebel who would not succumb to the discipline. He had had ambitions to join the Fleet Air Arm as a career, but due to early detection of colour blindness, had been told that would be impossible. He was a big fellow but had strained his heart at an early age by rowing too much too soon. Since then, rigid control of oarsmen was imposed to ensure that no one repeated the error of over-training. Training for rowing was very strenuous. The disappointment over his lack of career prospects changed Phipps's outlook and he would not conform. He effected a mode of marching by swinging his left arm with his left foot and his right arm at the same time as his right foot. He kept in step but looked somewhat out of sync and it took some time before it was twigged what was going on. It was hilarious to watch, for he did it with such determined concentration that it was laudable as well as laughable.

Charlie was in Connaught House with us and a couple of years my senior. He devised a very strong catapult and fashioned lead balls to fire out of it. For practice he would set up a floor brush against the wooden panels of the wall and shoot at it from across the room, trying to break the shaft. We enjoyed watching this spectacle. However, the wall panelling was soon shattered into smithereens. He eventually did hit and break the brush shaft. His next ploy was to jump heavily, for he was hefty, from the top of a desk on to the solid wooden floor. He persisted in this for hours until he succeeded in shattering the floor as well. Those boards had probably lasted for 300 years before he came along!

In addition to Charlie's efforts, we used to play a form of indoor rugby, with a great mass of bodies heaving over a ball hidden in the midst, something like the Eton wall game. There were no rules except to try and get the ball and touch the opposing side's back wall. We greatly enjoyed this rough and tumble, but the furniture suffered. We invited teams from other Houses to play us, but those who tried couldn't take the violence of it and soon withdrew.

Each week we had a ration of extra fruit, delivered by a local merchant: apples, oranges and bananas. Sitting at our desks during prep, presided over by a Prefect, we would consume the fruit and hurl the debris at the wastepaper box in the corner. Soon the entire corner, floor to ceiling, was covered in splatters of fruit and juice, which was left there to dry. The Headmaster tried to do something about our vandalism, by installing pictures of historic rugby teams on the walls and a large grey metal filing cabinet in the corner, to discourage our activities. In no time the pictures were shattered and turned backwards against the wall. The filing cabinet was reduced to a heap of creaking metal panels. The janitor, Bert, came along one day to remove it, but when he took hold of one of the side panels, the whole thing collapsed into a spread-out shambles. Most of it was still attached together by a screw or two, so by pulling one, Bert hauled the whole lot of it in a train behind him, out of the door and away to the dump. Eventually indoor rugby was prohibited and Charlie's excesses were curtailed. We took up shove halfpenny on the desk tops and, by pulling several desks together, were able to play a miniature version of table tennis instead.

Charlie, alas, went overboard altogether in the end and was expelled from the school over drinking offences. He went to Canada where it was reported he had got into further trouble. His death was announced in the last School News in the obituary column, which read: 'Phipps, C E. Charles, has died'. Another character was Walton Empey, a Prefect who serenaded us with Irish rebel songs, such as 'Kevin Barry' and 'The Soldiers' Song', the Republican National Anthem, whilst we were supposed to be doing our prep for next day's lessons. He went on to become the Church of Ireland Archbishop of Dublin. He was a good friend of Fred's while at school. Mickey went on teaching in Connaught room and never alluded to the events nor took any notice of the mess. The place was eventually repainted.

Apart from lessons, weekly corps parading and instruction, the usual down town church services continued, followed each evening by a combined service in the School Hall. At this service we invariably sang the hymn, 'Abide with Me' which had been penned by Sir Henry Francis Lyte, an old boy of the school.

We played rugby and hockey in the Winter. We had been known as a fine rugby school, but our success was waning. Hockey was played by a select few and our captain, David Judge, became Irish schoolboys' captain and eventually played in the senior game as captain for his country. Cricket and rowing were the main official Summer sports, not forgetting the team shooting for Bisley. We enjoyed ad hoc sports on the parade ground, such as touch rugby and hockey on roller skates. We had a fine boathouse on the lake shore and a variety of clinker and fine boats for eights, fours and sculling. I played cricket for a season or two, till I had a contretemps with the master in charge of our lot. I had missed a catch and was unduly criticised, so I decided to take up rowing. To get into the club you had to be able to swim four lengths of the pool or 100 yards. I managed this in relays, for though I could swim, it was mainly downwards. I struggled for half an hour with a frenzied dog-paddle, achieved the distance in stages and declared myself able to be let out on the water.

Early training consisted of sitting in fixed tubs at the landing stage to learn the art of blade control and co-ordination of the legs, arms and torso to achieve maximum effect. You then graduated to wide, two-seater boats with a coach sitting at the back. If you were any good you would progress to clinker fours or eights. I was really too small and light for rowing, so was assigned to duties, looking after the outboard motor boat and following the crews as they were berated by the senior coach, who was in the front of the boat. I was useless, ramming into the jetties, upsetting the rowers by getting tangled with the long oars and on one occasion, the outboard motor jumped off its mountings and disappeared into the river just before the West Bridge. Des Gray, a friend of mine for years, spent two or three days with a grappling hook and the motor was recovered. It was dried out and continued to work. I didn't. After we left school I never heard of Des again, except for rumours that he had gone off to teach in Devon.

So as not to waste the manpower, I was stuck in the bow of the second eight. I was eventually made captain of the eight and for three years appeared at regattas in various parts of Ireland. In 1953 we won the IARU schoolboy championship. The first eight, comprised of big fellows on special training diets, spent their time training for Henley, but never achieved much success there. However, my good friend, Paddy Holmes, who was the stroke, went on to Cambridge and stroked the senior eight there in his year, in the Varsity Race.

Paddy was a fine fellow, good-looking, an excellent scholar, well-spoken, friendly and a charming companion. His father was Governor of Ceylon, before it became Sri Lanka, and his English mother, who had married at the age of 16, was a very attractive lady, particularly to us young lads, as she was still in her early 30s when we knew her. Unfortunately, Paddy's father died during his time at school and we were all very sad for him. He returned after the funeral and continued as before in his friendly manner. His mother moved to Ireland, where she took over a family farm near to where we then lived, in the town land of Ballyclare. Paddy and I remained friends after school until he became a geologist, got married and went abroad. I never met his wife. Paddy died tragically in a mining accident, I understand, in Teheran. He was a charming companion, a brilliant scholar and sportsman; everyone who met him confirmed that opinion.

The rowing coach, who was also Housemaster of Ulster and taught French, was another Cambridge graduate. He was very small of stature and had been a rowing cox there, as well as being a leading member of the Masonic Lodge in Fermanagh, where he achieved high office. He was nick-named Titch, had fought with the French Resistance in the war and had received the Legion D'Honneur. This master instilled fear and respect and trained us vigorously. He had known my father when he was in Enniskillen. In my last year, he arranged for a team to attend the European Rowing Championships in Amsterdam. A new course had been built there, called the Bosbaan, and I was selected to go. I had arranged a cycling tour with a friend, Mark Scott, to Belgium and Germany. We would get to Bonn and he would continue up the Rhine to Heidelberg. I would then make my way to Amsterdam to join my fellows for the rowing events. We would stop at Youth Hostels during our trek.

CHAPTER 6

Mark and I started off by steamer from Belfast to Liverpool, then a train to London, then to Dover and finally a steamer to Ostend, where our cycling would commence. Off we went, intending to visit Bruges, Ghent, Brussels and Liege and then to Germany via Aachen, to Cologne and Bonn. Things started well enough till the rain came on. Belgium looked small on the map, but our scheduled daily mileage was proving arduous. We ploughed on and managed the first two stages until things started to go wrong. Heading for Brussels, Mark began to fall behind. We each had panniers on the back of our bicycles. I stopped till Mark caught up. He looked distressed and said that he simply couldn't keep up speed, as his bicycle seemed very heavy. I agreed to swap with him, but on trying to mount his cycle I found it sluggish and unable to freewheel. The panniers had slipped down the frame, impinging on the brake blocks of the back wheel, virtually locking them on. We rectified this and things were easier, although getting even wetter. I was wearing a raincoat and decided that it was time to put on our rubber ground sheets, as I was soaked through. They had been amongst Mark's load, but couldn't be found. They had obviously fallen off somewhere, so we re-traced our steps without success and wasted no more time looking for them.

We continued on and found a good flat road, making things easier. This didn't last long. Some miles later we were flagged down by the police, to be informed that we were on a motor-way - no cycles allowed! We were escorted off and directed to a canal towpath, with directions to get to Brussels by a more circuitous route. This added to our distress and on finding a wayside inn, we decided to indulge ourselves in a good meal. The inn-keeper was friendly and we enjoyed a hefty feed with plenty of good fried potatoes and meat. Sated, we were feeling better and full of bonhomie, till we received the bill. This was more than anticipated, blowing a hole in our budget and dissipating our goodwill.

We were late arriving in Brussels, only to find the hostel full. We were directed to another on the outskirts but by the time we found it in the pouring rain, we were exhausted - and disgusted. It was an annexe to the main hostel and we found a space on the floor to lie down. The facilities were minimal and rats scurried about! It was obviously a converted warehouse, but we had to put up with it. The rain thundered down. We survived that night but re-planned our route next day, heading straight for Aachen. That was a dismal place of heavy industry, smoke-blackened buildings and desolate stretches of railway lines. But the hostel was quite good and we spent a better night there. We carried on re-vitalised, eagerly anticipating our scheduled two days in Cologne and Bonn.

Cologne was a fine city. The Cathedral still showed its bomb damage but was a magnificent edifice. This was in 1955. The River Rhine was splendid, wide and busy with shipping and traversed by inspiring bridges. I was delighted. The hostel here was also excellent, clean and well-ordered and the food was wholesome. We stayed for two days and I was loath to leave. We went on to Bonn. It was quiet and ordered, interesting as the capital of West Germany and the birthplace of Beethoven. Still, I'd preferred Cologne, so we decided to part the next day. I would go back to Cologne for an extra couple of days and Mark would continue on his own to the beautiful Heidelberg. We parted, agreeing to meet up again on the appointed date at Ostend for our scheduled transport home.

By the time I got back to Cologne I'd had enough of cycling, so I went to the station and consigned my cycle by train to Amsterdam to await my arrival there. In the meantime, I had lost my camera somewhere along the way, so never got one snapshot the whole time. I enjoyed Cologne and spent a couple of days seeing around, before boarding a train to Amsterdam, where I arrived in due course. I found a posh hotel and spent the first night there. This was expensive and with the cost of the train for the cycle and myself, I found my resources severely depleted. I decided that the best thing would be to recover the bike from the station and cycle around, as the good burghers were doing, en masse. This would save tram fares and further storage charges.

The railway had been efficient and I recovered my bike without difficulty. The next thing was to find a cheaper hotel, but before that some food. They eat wholesomely but well in Holland, and so did I. I also became hooked on their luscious hot dogs, drooling with juices and deliciously succulent. The cold drink, Chocomel, was like nectar to me and assuaged my craving for chocolate. I found a place to stay for another night, for I had arrived before my school friends and would have another day to last out on meagre funds. Each of our party would be assigned a billet with a Dutch family for the duration of the rowing competition.

I was cycling around without care, observing the sights, when I ran into the back of a Volkswagen car which had stopped abruptly. I landed on its roof. The occupants turned round to observe me scrambling off the back, sliding down the window. They ignored me and drove on. I was left unhurt in the middle of the road, but with a mangled front wheel on the bike. No one took any notice of me, which I thought rather odd. Perhaps it was a common occurrence with so many cycles around. In disgust, I carried the bike back to the station and consigned it to Ostend, to await collection on my return.

This meant that I was now nearly broke. I developed a fever after all the wettings I'd had and the tiredness of the journey. I also had to find a cheap lodging for the night and wondered when I might find my colleagues. I felt wretched and decided to fortify myself with a few stiff Dutch gins, for I'd heard of its reputation. I gulped down the fiery liquid and found a cheap hotel which was full, but they said I could sleep in a bath. Anything was better than nothing so I agreed. The gin was having its effect. I was highly flushed and in a fevered state, so retired at once. In the night I sweated profusely, so much so that I had to get up and discard my soaking pyjamas and wring out the sheet. By the morning when I arose, the fever had gone and I felt invigorated.

I took a tram and was sitting contemplating my apparently desolate immediate future. Looking out as the tram stopped at traffic lights, what did I see but a Ford Consul, driven by our rowing coach, with the other three members of our party inside. I leapt off as the traffic was moving in front of them and was nearly run over. What luck to be so happily reunited! Warm embraces were exchanged all round and I got into the back between two large oarsmen from the first eight, Bill Cantley and Chris Bradley. Paddy Holmes was in the front along with Titch Andrews. We made off to meet our hosts at the Amstel Rowing Club. They were very hospitable at the club and we received our instructions regarding our hosts for the next week. I was assigned to Hans Ingenhose and family, of Nicholas Maestraat, and the others also went to family homes, except Paddy, who was to be billeted at the American Hotel, care of the manager and his pretty daughter, Kitty/ Lucky fellow!

Kitty was at the club and became our companion/hostess/ tour guide for the duration. She was lovely and very friendly to us all. I met the Ingenhose family, who were very nice, and was shown to my room. The rowing was of great interest to them and in the city generally. We were there to represent Irish schools, comprising a rowing four. Russian oarswomen were seen here in Western Europe for the first time, which excited much interest and comment. The Regatta was well organised and we did our bit as required. We were well catered for and enjoyed the week's activities. At the end, I was interviewed by the press and was asked by a reporter what I thought of Dutch girls. My reply was that they were very beautiful and friendly, but a bit heavy in the leg. I guess I was thinking of all that cycling building up their muscles. That evening the main paper showed a picture of me with the caption 'Young Irish Oarsman says Dutch girls are heavy in the leg', thus alienating the entire Amsterdam public instantly. We had a good laugh and the Ingenhoses were amused, if a little taken aback. I didn't return to Amsterdam for many years and then only incognito.

Following the competition, we had a few days touring in rowing boats, through the canals of the northern Netherlands before embarking on our journey back to Ostend. We stayed at farms, sleeping in barns and enjoying good Dutch breakfasts of eggs and cheese each morning. Driving back to Belgium, when crossing the Rhine we were able to stop and make our way down to the river for a quick swim in its waters. When we arrived at Ostend, we parted company and I went in search of Mark, my travelling companion for the journey home. I collected my now battered cycle at the station, we met as arranged and waited for our ferry to Dover. The journey from there was uneventful and we arrived in London to make our way to Euston Station, to take the boat train to Liverpool, to embark for Belfast. We were now both broke and starving. We had to sit on deck for the overnight voyage to Belfast, as we had no berths. The ship was crowded and as we put to sea, the evening chill seized us, felt all the more keenly due to our weakened and ravenous state. A lady on board had a flask of tea and offered us a cup with a single Rich Tea biscuit each. We accepted gratefully and nothing ever tasted better.

Arriving at Belfast Quay, Father and Fred were there to meet me and Mark had his own arrangements. We said our goodbyes and didn't meet again until some 40 years later when Mark, who had gone to Sandhurst Military College, joined the Army and, on retirement, finished back at Portora School, where he had been appointed Bursar. He was also the secretary of the Old Portoran Union and in that capacity he sought me out, looking for a renewal of my membership fee! So began our re-acquaintance.

But back to my school days. I continued in the rowing club and we won regattas all over Ireland with the second eight. I played rugby and for my last two years, was vice-captain of the first XV, playing all the major schools in Northern Ireland and Sligo Grammar and Blackrock College, Dublin, amongst others in the Republic. This meant visits to many places during my rowing and rugby days and I particularly liked Limerick, Dublin and Coleraine. I was also selected as scrum-half for all the rugby teams for which I played during my school years, right from the under-15 team, up through second XV and first XV. This was due to three things: my smaller size, my talent for it and the fact that everyone else avoided the job, for it was too hazardous, in terms of being constantly hammered by opposing forwards.

It was interesting playing in the Winter on the pitches at lakeside. Quite often the end pitch was flooded, due to Fermanagh's heavy rainfall and the proximity of the lake. It was not unusual to be trudging through swampy ground and wallowing in sizeable pools of water. On one occasion after a scrum was collapsed, a submerged body was found face down in the water, almost gasping his last. He was quickly seized and resuscitated and play resumed.

School plays were an annual event. These were always produced by Mickey Murfet but for some reason he never gave me a part, even though I had won the best actor prize at Gloucester House and appeared in the inter-house plays competition, which we won in a production by Mark Scott. Only in one play did he finally give me a small part. In rehearsal I apparently spoke my very few lines with proper dramatic feeling, resulting in my being given a larger role when someone else dropped out. Apart from the odd school concert, there was little other outlet for any other musical talent. Mark and I sang the Gendarmes duet on one occasion and were recalled for an encore. In order to satisfy the thespian aspirations of others, some fellows got together to produce a revue. This was exclusive to seniors and we of the lower ranks were snubbed. Nevertheless, they encouraged us to attend as an audience.

Those selected to perform kept tight-lipped about what the show would contain. However, one chap who could play the piano a bit had been selected to play a Winifred Atwell honky-tonk number. He practiced it every day for weeks ad nauseam. It came the day of the performance and we all assembled in the Steele Hall. The revue commenced and got worse by the minute and when the pianist appeared, we were so sick of hearing him practise that all impact was lost. This chap went on to become a Bishop after school. The sketches drew forth little or no mirth. To liven things up, the producer had the brilliant idea of introducing some community singing. His efforts to get us going only resulted in a few desultory groans and some off-key crooning. To encourage us, a senior prefect came to the front of the stage waving a rolled up newspaper, in a rough imitation of conducting, all the while shouting, 'Sing, sing!' Not having much effect, he leapt off the stage in a rage and hurled himself upon us, tearing up the aisle, beating those nearest him about the head and screaming 'Sing you bastards, sing, damn you, sing!' The result was pandemonium. Years later, this chap became Black Rod and I often smiled when I saw him on television, so soberly carrying out his duties as he paraded his staff of office at the opening of Parliament. In fact, he was generally a most genial and amusing companion.

By this time, Douglas Graham had left the school to seek his fortune elsewhere and was replaced by an Englishman, the Rev. P. Rogers. Fred left at the end of the 1953 Summer term, when he won the school's Athletics Championship against all expectations. He had never done much in the way of athletics but had played rugby throughout and boxed for a while. He won the mile, half-mile and quarter-mile races, establishing a school record in the mile, which stood for many years. He also passed enough exams to achieve the Senior Certificate of Education. Graham had the good grace to congratulate him and present him with the Sports Prize. As Father ran a family business, it was expected right from the start of our schooling that we would go into it. This may not have been our own idea but it was a mind set and nothing was done about it, as careers guidance was non-existent then. Others were destined to be doctors, military officers, lawyers, clergymen, dentists, accountants or other professionals. So that was where Fred went, into business two years ahead of me.

The Rev. Rogers was not popular either with staff or pupils. He had no interest in rugby at all, a passing interest in rowing and no feeling for the culture of the establishment. His main concern was to get as much government money as possible, to support his aspirations for the school. This meant a considerable change in the school's status, which tended to destroy the morale of both staff and pupils. Several long-standing key staff left, including our history master, D A R Chillingworth and his wife, who had taught Classics. They and others went to find employment in Belfast and elsewhere. The pupils, of necessity, stayed on, not wanting to disrupt their education at a crucial time.

Rogers lacked a real sense of humour, as did his wife. She played a more prominent and high profile role in school affairs than had Mrs Graham, who had never interfered. Mickey said nothing. Nevertheless, I was appointed as a senior Prefect under the new regime, along with others of my year. This meant that we dined with the Head at the top table in the school dining room at lunchtimes, where Rogers could feel more at one with us. His wife usually attended as well. He never bothered me particularly and was generally supportive of me.

We continued much as before but change was inevitable as his influence took effect. New projects were started to improve the buildings and to add new schoolrooms and general amenities. Rogers also sought to increase the numbers of day pupils. Some years after I left, girl pupils were introduced for a time but this did not last. All this was 40 years ago and was revolutionary. In the mid-50s, Northern Ireland was reasonably peaceful. The effects of war were now less noticeable. Rationing had been removed, new teachers were brought in, there was less adherence to old traditions but discipline was maintained in a more subtly ruthless manner, not always with violence but with a certain lack of mirth, shall we say. An instance of this occurred in my last year, which, if compared with an event in Graham's time, may illustrate it.

Graham, if nothing else, was a cultured gentleman. He instilled respect and was determined to see that proper manners were displayed at all times. He composed a poem to improve table manners. It started: 'Forks, spoons and knives/ to eat with we devise/ and not to point at neighbours or the skies'. I do not remember the rest but it was a humorous way of pointing out deficiencies, without directly insulting anyone. To increase our cultural appreciation, he brought a troupe of Shakespearean players to perform extracts and a group of female players of medieval musical instruments to serenade us and the famous bass, Kim Borg, to sing opera. Capt. Peter Chirchill, the husband of Odette, the famous wartime Resistance heroine who was tortured by the Nazis, visited the school to lecture to us. He had met her in the Resistance and undergone considerable risks with her.*

Now to the point. Many of the cultural groups were boring, but the all-female players with their assortment of serpents, sackbuts, recorders, lutes and the like, singing madrigal dirges, were the worst. When the end fell off a serpent with a clatter, hilarity broke out. It was not intended to be derisive but was simply a way of releasing the boredom we were experiencing, including the Headmaster, who laughed with us. The concert was curtailed, as much to his relief as to ours.

In Roger's time, by comparison, a pupil had climbed the bell tower and muffled the 'Big Bell' which was usually rung at seven each morning to arouse the school, followed at regular intervals to announce breakfast and then Assembly. When Bert, the Janitor, came to ring it that particular morning, no sound was heard. Bert damn nearly pulled the bell off its mountings in his efforts to make it ring. The perpetrator was sought out and given a severe beating.

At the end of my last term, there was to be a grand concert. A second grand piano appeared on the stage in addition to the usual one, for duets to be performed. Parents and local dignitaries were present. When the performers appeared and began to play, no sound came out of one of the pianos, except some toneless *plink plonk*. It had been wired up so that it would not play! Rogers went crazy but the concert was allowed to proceed once the obstruction was removed. Everyone saw the amusing side of it. Not Rogers! He made the entire school stay in their seats afterwards refusing to let us go till the culprits owned up. No one was allowed to move or utter a whisper. It was like holding hostages, threatening to shoot someone every ten minutes if no one came forward. Nothing happened for quite a while and we were all despairing. If anyone knew who

---

* Although under sentence of death in 1943 she was imprisoned and tortured at Ravensbrtick until April 1945 when she was handed over to the americans by the commandant, thinking that she was Winston Churchill's niece by marriage and would therefore be a good bargaining ploy to save his own skin. He was tried and executed.

had done it, they certainly weren't going to tell. In the end, after a prolonged period, the two culprits gave themselves up. They were marched away and given a vicious beating. This did nothing to improve our opinion of the new Head. Heaven knows what he might have done to Charlie Phipps for jumping through the floor!

Not all was fun and games, of course. Lessons were continuing all the time with homework (prep) for the following day's assessment. Detention or other non-corporal punishments were devised for the truly indolent or incompetent. Cadet Corps parades each week meant having to press your uniform, jacket, trousers and shirt and to spit and polish boots and brass buttons. Belts and gaiters had to be treated with blanco, a dull green colour and brasses on belts polished to a high degree. We were required to mount guard at the opening of the Enniskillen Petty Sessions, at the Courthouse. This meant marching in full regalia, with the band leading us through to the far end of town, opposite the Presbyterian Church. On one famous occasion we had to prepare to go to Belfast, to mount guard along the avenue, leading up to the Northern Ireland Houses of Parliament at Stormont, in honour of a visit by the newly crowned Queen, Elizabeth II. We looked forward to this in a way. The splendid buildings stand impressively at the top of a one-mile straight driveway. A famous racing driver in the early days of TT Racing was once timed driving up at over 100 mph., considered a daredevil escapade.

We were sent by bus to our assigned spot. As usual, everything was done early to ensure plenty of hanging-around time, in true tradition. It was a hot day. We were lined up in ranks in full uniform with heavy rifles and boredom and fatigue set in. It was a serious crime to drop your weapon, whatever the cause, and though we were not at attention it was really arduous. To relieve the monotony, several members of the troop effected swooning fits, collapsing to the ground and being dragged off to lie down to recuperate. This was beginning to happen quite frequently and it finally got through to the Commanders that we should be allowed to relax, at least till there was evidence of the Queen's actual appearance. When the motorcade finally did arrive, we were well in order, saluted arms as the Queen drove by and the whole thing was over in five minutes. Back to base!

Col Halpin was the senior officer. Capt Wheeler was the second in command, joined later by a new master whose name eludes me, but who held the rank of Major. Our Sergeant Major was a real bawler in the traditional manner and kept us in order. Capt Wheeler was of particular note. Not only had he been in the Army but had represented Britain in the Olympic Games as a swordsman and gymnast. His wife was also an Olympic swimmer. For a time he taught art, carpentry and was the physical education instructor, keeping a tidy gymnasium equipped with all sorts of paraphernalia. He was inspiring on the parallel and cross-bars routines. In addition, he built a Pro-scenium Arch for the stage of the Steele Hall and always pro-vided the stage scenery for the plays. In his spare time he organised the swimming in the new pool and trained the youth of the community, who were given access to the pool at certain times. He received an OBE for his services. I visited the school some 40 years after leaving, to find him, in his mid-70s in the gymnasium waiting for the oarsmen to come in for training. 'Ronnie Frazer!' he exclaimed, recognising me immediately and greeting me warmly by the hand. His biceps were still hard as iron and he looked fit and well. We expressed our mutual de-light at meeting again. Alas, not long afterwards he was knocked down by a car and seriously injured. He lingered for some time but never made a full recovery and died some weeks later.

Tom Molyneux was another great character at school. I think he was in Ulster House. Being in the rowing club had its advantages for it gave us access to boats when we weren't en-gaged in official training or races. We could sometimes also have leisure use of the outboard motor, but mostly we had to use ordinary rowing boats and our own muscle power. Tom kept ferrets and would invite some of us to go with him down the Lower Lough Erne, to the famous Devenish Island, where rabbits abounded. He taught us how to net up the warrens before releasing the ferrets down a hole and we would bag as many as 18 or two dozen rabbits on each sortie. Tom could skin and gut a rabbit in a twinkling and we would then roast one or two over a wood fire and make a meal of them. The rest were taken back to school and skinned, one or two being roasted in the school's kitchen by courtesy of the domestic staff and consumed in the locker room, below the Stone Hall. The remainder were sold to a local butcher and the skins disposed of to a dealer.

In 1998, we met again. The Rowing Club had sent out an appeal for funds, to which we had contributed. This was appreciated and those having made donations, were invited to attend the Schools' Head of the River Races, preceded by lunch in the Head's quarters. My wife and I went and Tom was there along with other old rowing colleagues. We were greeted by Mark Scott and then by the new Headmaster of the time, and the Head Boy and his deputy. I am pleased to say that the two young men maintained the tradition of good manners inculcated in former years and my wife and I were impressed accordingly. Mark Scott had greatly impressed my parents years before when he had stayed with us at Ballyrobert and my wife was equally charmed on this, her first meeting with him.

The boys attended us at lunch and we guests reminisced about old times. Mostly this consisted of castigating certain members of staff who had offended us at our time at school. I was amazed at the venom of some of the comments, for old wounds ran deep, but highly amused and I'm afraid I had to concur with many of the sentiments expressed - our school days had not been the happiest days of our lives.

After lunch we left for the Races, which were to commence from the Killyhevlin Hotel wharf, on the Upper Lough, rowing down through the town, under the West Bridge and up to Portora Boathouse. Just before leaving for the Races, it was announced that the new fine eight boat, specially built and purchased for the school, in which this was to be its inaugural race, had been damaged in a crash, whilst on the trailer on its way to the event. The crew had to revert to their old craft, but gave a good account of themselves anyway. The school had several crews entered for the event and Titch Andrews, our long retired coach, then in his 90s, was there. He was still fit as a fiddle and amazed me, as I stood beside him at the race, with his stentorian bellowing of 'Come on Portora!' He died in the year 2000and left £200 000 to the school .

Once when rowing on Lough Erne, I caught a 'crab', that is, I caught the back of the blade of the oar in the water on my way forward to the next stroke. There is tremendous momentum in a rowing eight in full surge, powered by eight lusty fellows. The blade caught a wave, ploughed deeper and I was lifted bodily by the shaft of the oar, which caught me in the midriff with a vicious thud, hurling me out of the boat into the water and bending the rigger. On another occasion, when we were competing in the Belfast Head of the River, our number two, that is the oarsman in front of me in the bow, also caught a crab, but instead of the oar handle lifting him out, it caught him under the chin and knocked him out, laying him flat in the boat. The oar went over his head and trailed alongside the boat, causing some disruption to the oars in front. In confusion, the rest of the crew missed their stroke and began to slow down. I was Captain in the bow and seeing we were near the end of the course, bellowed at the Cox and Stroke to keep us rowing. They responded and we finished the race, achieving second place overall, with our number two still lying on his back.

I used to box, both for the school and in the House competitions. I had some limited success in the school fixtures but usually won in the house competitions, not by science, but by sheer aggression and determination. However, in my last year I was in the final against a big strong fellow, one of the local day boys. He was a pleasant chap and played with me in the first XV rugby team. There was much excitement in the school as our match approached. My opponent-to-be was well-trained at the local RUC gymnasium. In the fight all was going well for two rounds, my usual onslaught seeming to be paying-off. He was bleeding profusely from the nose. I was exhausted, for my fights hadn't usually lasted much longer than the first round. He kept his head and in the last round landed a punch from nowhere, which caught me cleanly, laying me out cold. It was a well-deserved victory and I was carried out to recover in the changing rooms. I had a headache for several days thereafter. I

60

never boxed again nor rowed after school, but did play rugby for Ballyclare 2nd XV for a couple of years.

CHAPTER 7

School holidays occurred after each term, Summer holiday being the main one. In our earlier years Fred and I would return home, which was now in the country at Ballyrobert. Prior to that we had holidays at the bungalow in Millisle, when we were very young. All kids love the seaside and we were no exception. We couldn't swim then, but enjoyed the sea and the beach and being amongst the Summer crowds in Millisle. Father would drive us down and then go back to the city to carry on with his business, leaving us with Mother and coming back each weekend and sometimes of an evening. Tom Frazer joined us quite often and we enjoyed his company. At that time a large open motor-driven boat used to travel from Donaghadee to the Copeland Islands which were just off-shore. We went across once in a heavy swell and enjoyed the thrill, for the boat afforded no protection and was somewhat aged. The Islands boasted only a few cattle and a couple of houses. The boat no longer plies this journey and the Islands seem uninhabited and are of little interest. We visited places like Ballywalter, Ballyhalbert and Donaghadee. Simple pastimes pleased us - fish and chips, ice cream 'sliders' , paddling, rowing boats and clock golf.

One year Father had rented a house at Kilkeel, a fishing village in Co Down, beyond Newcastle, in the shadow of the Mourne Mountains. Newcastle was a famous resort and we spent several holidays there, staying with our Uncle Joe, Father's elder brother. He was Sergeant of Police there and we stayed at his house next to the Police Station and near the public swimming pool. The house was on the sea front and had a lovely walled garden. Aunt Mary, his wife, was a jolly lady who loved bathing in the sea with us, whatever the weather. She was fat and we used to chuckle at her in her swimming costume.

Newcastle had lots to offer - boating lake, miniature golf, beaches, fun-fair and Pierots. We loved the Pierots and we always tried to get on stage with them. A big event took place when the British Olympic champion diver appeared at the local pool and we were entertained to a first-class diving display. We used the pool occasionally, but were quite content with the beach, for which we didn't have to pay. On one stormy day when we used the pool because of the rough sea, I was stung by a jelly fish, which had somehow been washed into the pool by a large wave. It was a very unpleasant experience, resulting in a large angry patch appearing on my left buttock and thigh.

We had a long Summer holiday at Kilkeel and Father and Tom would come down at weekends. The harbour was of great interest, as we watched the catch of herring being offloaded and the girls at work gutting and cleaning the fish, ready for market. Great tubs of discarded guts were to be seen and the stench was appalling. The girls wore large rubber aprons but were covered in fish scales and were very adept at their jobs, working quickly and with good humour. We acquired simple fishing lines wound round a wooden frame. Mackerel could be caught off the pier. Fred and I had no luck in this, but there were several fish discarded by the serious fishermen, who allowed us to take a couple of them home. Rather than admit defeat, Fred decided that we should let them think at home that we had caught them ourselves. I was dubious about telling a lie, but he suggested that we would just not say we hadn't caught them and to be sure to keep our fingers crossed to absolve us from for the subterfuge. The strategy seemed to work, for Tom congratulated us and gave us 6d and the fish were cleaned and cooked for supper - delicious!

At the end of the garden of this rented house was the local cinema. We became friendly with the projectionist, who invited us and our sisters in to see how things worked. Winifred was very young so probably didn't come, but Valerie was as keen as us and we enjoyed seeing the reels being changed and re-wound for the next showing. If the film broke, it had to be spliced and this was demonstrated to us. We enjoyed watching the films for no charge from our vantage point in the Projection Room. This must have been near the end of the war because a newsreel was to be shown one evening of the test explosion of the atom bomb. The family attended in the audience and we witnessed the great mushroom cloud emerging and growing as it climbed into the skies. It made a lasting impression. Two small incidents were impressed on my mind. We used to play a form of bowls on the lawn with large round stones, one of which I inadvertently threw through a window. The other incident was even more unfortunate, when I closed the car door on Father's thumb, which crushed it and burst it, causing him severe pain.

The police force in Northern Ireland carried fire arms, Uncle Joe amongst them, and we were allowed to see and hold his unloaded revolver, which impressed us. Uncle Joe retired early from the force and worked with Father in the business for a while. Uncle Joe and Aunt Mary moved to Belfast, where we used to visit them once or twice a year. He was a great golfer. On other occasions I would go with my father up to visit Aunt Sarah, his only sister, with whom he kept in touch throughout his life. She used to make country butter which she pressed us to try, but I never could stand its strong flavour. Father loved porridge with buttermilk, for which I could never acquire a taste. He also took salt on his porridge, which I never ate. I remember when we were ill once at school, with a flu epidemic, we were confined to the sanatorium which was on the Boat House hill and presided over by a stern, elderly nursing sister. We were forced to have porridge for breakfast. It was lumpy and totally unappealing, but the Matron insisted we eat it. She had a small dog which used to run around outside and I suggested to my fellows that we should throw the porridge out of the window at the back of the ward and that the dog would eat it. It wouldn't! However, it was off our plates. Her suspicions were aroused as to why our plates were suddenly empty and she finally twigged what was going on. Looking out of the window, she was presented with a view of mounds of cold porridge, which even her dog had disdained. It was never served in future.

The hill from the sanatorium stretched down to the water's edge and provided a splendid slope for sledging and tobogganing in snowy winters. Those of us not fortunate enough to have sledges used old tin trays, or whatever came to hand. I acquired an old car mudguard which could accommodate two or three of us, in which we flew and spun down the hill at great speed. With no means of arrest, we often finished in the reeds of the lake which luckily impeded our further progress. Competitions were held to see how many persons could mount one toboggan. The best way was to lie flat and pile up one on top of the other. Four was about the height of it and provided great thrills as the speed increased and the pile gradually toppled off. Apart from someone being hit on the head by a loose toboggan, everyone escaped injury.

School holidays meant that Fred and I would go home and help on the farm. In Summer we would be greeted in the fields, as we came up the lane homewards, Father calling us to get changed quickly, to join them in making the hay. Quite often we would have numbers of villagers to assist, working till late evening with night approaching. We used horses to pull the reaper and had a large horse-drawn rake as well as many hand rakes. The hay was raked and dried and built into stacks, using pitch forks. Someone had to stand atop the pile as it grew, spreading and tramping the forks full into place and ensuring that they were properly layered so as to preserve steadiness and to repel the rain. Hand rakes were constantly in use to gather up the debris.

As work progressed, Mother and my sisters would appear with great pots of tea and piles of sandwiches, which everyone present devoured eagerly. The horses were wonderful creatures. Once the stacks were completed and the field cleared, they would stand to settle for some days or weeks till all was finished in adjoining fields. The hay cart then came into play. This was a flat cart with a large spindle at the front end with a cogged lever and hawser. The cart was tipped up on its hinges and backed into the foot of the haystack or rick, as they were called. The hawser was brought round the back of the rick and secured to the other end of the spindle. By means of the lever the whole rick was then winched aboard, the cart levelling off as the weight adjusted, finally being snapped into position, before being dragged back to the farmyard by the horse. The hard work began again, with several hands forking the hay into the barn. The worst job was having to tramp the hay, pulling it back as far as possible into the barn. As the pile rose, so the heat and dust increased. My eyes would stream and I would cough and splutter. Still, it cured my childhood asthma.

We had four horses. Big Barney was a lovely old shire horse with heavy fetlocks, built sturdily for hard work. Then we had an elderly brown mare and a younger white mare and finally a beautiful prancing chestnut gelding called Juko, full of energy and a pleasure to see. He loved getting into the plough harness and would take off with great gusto, ploughing a furrow. He shared one stable with two stalls with the brown mare. They were fed and watered and a supply of hay was left in the manger. Working horses needed salt, which came in lumps not unlike building bricks in shape, size and colour. These were inserted beside their heads in a slot where the horses could get at them. Juko loved salt and would finish his in an evening, even managing to get his tongue round into the one in the next stall.

The white mare had a foal and they were both eventually sold off together. Big Barney got an uncomfortable abscess in the roof of his mouth and a local farm hand said he could cure it. Calling for a jar of rough cooking salt and boiling water, he took a penknife from his pocket, honed to a sharp edge and sterilised it. He forced the horse's mouth open by holding its nostrils and grabbing the lower jaw, inserted the knife and, with a quick slash, cut into the offending abscess, releasing the poison. He wiped it away with a wet cloth, took a handful of salt and rubbed it well into and around the wound. It soon healed and Big Barney was able to eat comfortably again.

A young lad in the village was called to take Juko to the Blacksmith and I was to go with him. He was very confident and handled the horse expertly. We had a beautiful trap with plush velvet seating. The horse was harnessed and we climbed aboard, closing the dainty little door at the back of the trap and set off. Juko responded with pleasure to the trot, to bring us to the smithy, which was some way off.

I greatly enjoyed seeing the smith at work, just as I enjoy any craftsman expertly toiling. The making of a solid iron, well-fitting, polished and finished horseshoe from a bar of black metal is a pleasure to see. The confident manner in which the smith heated and tossed the red-hot metal about, hammering it into shape, the billows roaring to heat up the fire, the sparks flying, the sizzling as he dipped it with tongs into cooling water, all enthralled me. Holding the horse's leg between his knees, he pulled out the old nails from the hoof , loosening the old shoe and paring off the toe of the foot, like a large toenail, to smooth it off. He then tested the newly fashioned shoe against the hoof, with a strong smell of singeing, returning it to the fire to soften it again, to knock it into better shape. Holes were then punched in it for the new nails. The shoe was then fitted to the foot, the nails hammered in and the protruding ends nipped off with pliers. Finally, the shoe and foot were smoothed off with a rasp, so that shoe and hoof merged into one. All this was completed expertly, the horse accepting it with equanimity.

The horses worked in the plough and harrow, the farm cart, the hay rake, the hay cart, and the reaper. Juko pulled the trap and was often used to take us to church, being left tethered at the gate, whilst the service lasted. On one occasion, we decided to visit Aunt Edith and Uncle Sam at Whitehouse Park. That was about six or eight miles away and along some busy roads of traffic. Father and Mother, myself and two sisters went along in the trap. Juko was very lively, wanting to gallop. Father was no great horseman and we were somewhat apprehensive but arrived safely. Aunt Edith was alarmed for Juko seemed restive and could not be brought into the dainty garden. He remained tied to the gatepost, still in the shafts and was provided with a nose-bag full of oats, to keep him happy. After tea, we left and arrived home safely, but we never repeated that experiment again, much to Aunt Edith's relief.

The horses were eventually sold off except for Juko, for we had by then acquired a tractor. Juko provided rides for Val, Win and Fred, though I did not enjoy riding, as the stretching of the inner thighs caused me too much pain. We all loved the horse but when we were back at school, he was finally sold. He was taken several miles away but could not be contained and somehow found his way back to our place several times. He was eventually tamed and we never saw him again.

We also had a herd of Friesian milking cows. This was a hard job and I did not enjoy the milking, which was done by hand. The milk was collected in buckets held between the knees. The cows' tails had to be tied to their back legs to prevent them swishing and smacking you in the eye, or contaminating the milk. The milk was filtered into large churns, each cow's yield being recorded. The churns, when filled, were put on a hand-cart which could carry four of them and it was pulled down the lane to the front gate at the main road for early morning collection by the dairy. The cows were fed on meal, turnips and hay. We grew large numbers of turnips. These had to be harvested and loaded on the horse-cart. They were dug up, sneaded (that is, tops and tails cut off), then piled onto the cart and drawn up to the yard to be hosed clean. We had a hand-driven slicer, rather like a very large cheese-grater, which was used to cut the turnips into large finger-sized slices, which the cattle loved when mixed with meal. We had one working bull, which seemed placid enough, but you never know with a bull, so we kept out of his way. Calves were born, reared and sold off.

There were some 200 laying hens and chickens were hatched in an incubator, to be reared to pullet size. Some were sold, others replenished the laying stock. Several geese roamed the yard and fields and we enjoyed their eggs, which were large and akin to a hen's egg in taste and texture but of a more delicate flavour than duck eggs. They and the duck eggs, were used mainly for cooking. I had once taken a goose egg to Gloucester House, where it was boiled in the kitchen and presented to me for breakfast on a Sunday morning, much to the amusement and interest of my fellows. We always had a goose for Christmas as well as a turkey, but it was bought from the butcher. We had a flock of about 20 white ducks, one old grey-brown, remnant of a previous flock and one finely coloured drake. The old duck waddled about with the others. One day a flight of wild ducks passed over the back field, which sloped down to the stream, winding its way under the railway culvert. The white ducks all took off, running down the hill till they became

68

airborne and disappeared with them for ever. The old duck remained for some years, laying eggs regularly and wandering about with the geese, which often attacked her. She loved to waddle after us and to have her head scratched, quacking happily, as a cat would purr when content.

The geese would hiss and run at you with necks outstretched, seeking to peck at you. Their loud screeching could he heard over long distances and they made good sentries, loudly proclaiming if they were disturbed at night. We had twin goats, which were lively and lovely creatures. It was almost impossible to contain them. They climbed up onto the roof and would eat anything in sight, including clothes on the line. They had to be tethered in the back field.

As well as turnips and hay, we sowed oats and potatoes, which were harvested in due season, usually in very wet weather and unpleasant conditions, which made very hard work.

At the house there were large gardens to be attended to. By the side of the house was a large apple orchard and at the end of which were the poultry coops and enclosures. Eggs had to be collected and packed in cases, each containing 24 dozen, which were made ready for Gracey's, the egg merchants, lorry to call weekly. The coops had to be regularly cleaned and fresh deep-litter strewn. The hens were able to roam free in the large wire pens enclosing them. The front gardens were laid with paths of crazy paving and flower beds, with a lily pond in the middle and a single beautiful apple tree in its own bed to the left. This provided delicious eating apples. Beyond the flower garden was the vegetable patch of about one-quarter acres where we grew wonderful carrots, parsnips, green beans and peas, cabbage, beetroot, onions, celery and leeks. To the side was the orchard of soft fruits, strawberries, black and red currants and gooseberries and a row of apple trees.

The beautiful apple tree at the side of the garden came to grief. One of the farm hands was somewhat slow of intellect. One morning as Father was leaving to go to town, he issued hurried directions to 'Clear that bush at the corner which is getting out of hand', meaning a large overgrown unsightly bush in the corner flower bed. Father returned home to survey the work, horrified on seeing the ungainly bush still in situ and not a trace of his beautiful apple tree.

The main business of the farm was carried out by the hired farm hands. The pig sties were beside the hen runs and behind the byres where the cows were milked in stalls. The pigs were great animals and loved to be scratched with a stick, grunting happily. The sows would produce litters and the piglets fed with gusto. Their teeth grew rapidly like needle points, which could give the sow considerable discomfort, causing her to move suddenly, with the danger of crushing her litter. This meant that the teeth had to be clipped at an early age, to dull their sharpness. This was done with pliers and the memory of the procedure still makes me cringe, although after much squealing during the operation, the piglets were soon romping around happily, none the worse for their ordeal. Castration was even worse! Pigs were bred to be slaughtered at a certain size and age. The pig killer would be called when required. He was a small, bandy-legged, 'hard wee man', but of good humour. He would call for kettles of boiling water to be ready. Having made sure of a cup of tea before commencing, he would lead a squealing pig from the sty into the yard with a spring hook in its nose attached to a rope. Then, with a swift blow from a sledge hammer to the back of its head, he would fell the beast and quickly rip its belly from end to end with a sharp knife and tear out its guts. Care was taken to preserve the liver, which would be sold later to the butcher. Next he would take a kettle of boiling water and pour it over the inert body. Taking another well-honed carving knife, he would shave off the bristles and clean out the insides, leaving the carcass ready to go to the processors. The whole operation would be completed in a matter of minutes and he might kill as many as ten or a dozen in a morning.

This did not put me off bacon or pork products and Father would have a carcass cured and preserved for our domestic use, providing chops, bacon, roast pork and ham. We never used the trotters, although these were a delicacy, prized by others.

The piglets were lovely creatures and liked to get out to root around in the fields, running about merrily with the bigger animals, quickly ploughing up the sods with their snouts. One such piglet broke a leg, which my sisters tried to nurse, putting on a splint and keeping it in the shed for its protection. Their efforts were in vain and the leg became gangrenous, so I had to put the piglet down. Fred had a shotgun and I decided that the best means of despatch would be to shoot it. It was a sad moment. I let the piglet out into the back field, where it gleefully enjoyed its new-found freedom, romping about on its three good legs. My resolve weakened. Still, the deed had to be done for its fourth leg was hanging by a tendon and stank horribly. Catching it, I pinned it to the ground and put the barrel of the gun just behind its ear and blew its brains out, with a single *coup de grace*. The memory of it haunts me still.

When we were younger I devised a training regime for myself and my sisters. As well as the 'guiders' that I had made for them, in which they pushed me around, I set up an obstacle course, where they had to run, jump over a garden bench in two bounds, first onto the seat and then over the back to the ground, take up a skipping rope and complete 20 jumps, run to the first field, where there were steel scaffolding bars forming a barrier, use one of these to perform a number of straight lifts; then into the field where there was a large stone to act as a shot putt and finally, throw a pitch fork like a spear. We also had good fun down at the stream in the back field, building a low dam to create a paddling pool and catching sticklebacks in jam jars. Pat Symmons, the daughter of my parents' good friends, often came out to study pond life as part of her biology lessons, for she was determined to be a nurse, although she also took ballet lessons and would have liked to followed that calling. She eventually became a senior sister at the Royal Victoria Hospital and advisor on hygiene.

We also kept three cats, amongst them a small white one which produced regular litters, which had to be put down or given away, so as to keep numbers within bounds. One of our young farm hands once drowned a litter in a bag in the river and my sisters never forgave him. The small white cat was a great hunter and would bring in the odd hare, almost twice as big as herself, which she had caught, laying it at your feet with a smug look, as if to say, 'What do you think of that?' At one stage, the number of cats had grown to 17. They were always outside in the barns and fields and would keep vermin at bay, but this was too much. We had a customer from Ballynure, who called each fortnight with a large covered van to collect goods. After loading up he would go into the house to settle up the account, then close up and drive off. It dawned on us one day that the cat population had disappeared, leaving the sole white one. The next time the customer returned and asked if we had been missing any cats. It transpired that, after he'd left us and was out in the country, he'd opened his van door, upon which a horde of cats erupted and took off over the fields, never to be seen again.

Those were the types of activities we were engaged in during the school holidays.

Father had had his name on the list for new cars and after a few years he was able to purchase a new Hillman Minx around 1953. Prior to this time he had been using an Alvis which he had bought some years earlier. It was a beautiful car, low slung with large mudguards and headlamps, wide wheelbase and long bonnet. It was very handsome, with leather seating and he had driven it over the years at great speed. The Hillman replaced the Alvis, which was now somewhat the worse for wear. Mother always knew late at night when Father arrived home, for he invariably tore the garage door off its hinges as he went in, usually hitting the end wall as well, for with its long bonnet, he was not a good judge of the space ahead. We were sorry to see the Alvis go but quickly grew to like the Hillman. Father kept it for a year and then sold it for a considerable profit, for new cars were still in short supply. He then bought a sturdy, second-hand but very handsome Daimler Conquest. This was a splendid motor, with six cylinder engine, twin-carburettors and dual exhaust, in which we thundered around the countryside. It drove splendidly and he kept it for many years.

At this time, Fred was engaged in the business in town, where I was to join him later. I returned to school for a further two years, always going by train and with little enthusiasm, although it was good to see old friends again. I had been appointed a school Prefect and continued to play rugby and to row, as well as appearing in House plays and working towards final school exams.

Following the previous disastrous but hilarious revue, a group of us got together to devise a further show. Seeking out talented people, we asked for ideas and put together a good show in which I starred, singing and doing impressions and appearing in sketches. I was much applauded and my impressions were admired, particularly one of Bert, the school janitor, who had a gammy leg and always stomped about shouting, with his yard brush upturned for a staff. There were plenty of mannerisms about him which gave ample scope for mimicry and he himself witnessed the performance with amusement.

I had many friends at school but many dispersed afterwards and we lost touch. I met some later in Belfast, of course, but there were many fine and outrageous characters whom I would have liked to meet again. Several of my contemporaries become noted doctors, lawyers, army officers and captains of industry, including directors of banks.

I never went to school reunion dinners, except on two occasions. One was in Dublin, coinciding with a Welsh-Irish rugby match. The dinner was outrageous, though fun. A singer had been engaged to entertain us after the meal. God help him, but he didn't have a chance, trying to interest his captive audience with renderings of Victorian ballads and he was howled down. I would have liked to hear him! Instead, one of our colleagues took over at the piano and played boogie-woogie. The other dinner I attended was in London many years later, at the Army and Navy Club, just off Pall Mall, where we were served a dreadful meal and charged exorbitant prices for drinks. Nevertheless, we renewed acquaintance with some rich characters and enjoyed reminiscing, promising to meet again, but never doing so.

CHAPTER 8

And so my schooling finally came to an end. I achieved passes in exams, sufficient to furnish me with the N.I. Schools' Senior Certificate, even achieving some credits, but I vowed that I'd never do another exam, and I didn't. As expected, I was left to join the business, whilst many of my school fellows went on to university. My only ambition at the time was to become an opera singer, for I had found a couple of records in the school library, one of Gigli singing 'Santa Lucia' on the one side and 'Mama Quel Vino e Generoso' from Cavalleria Rusticana on the other, and one of Mario Lanza. These inspired me greatly. At this stage, I must mention the Rev Percy Rogers, for he took an interest in this ambition of mine and encouraged me by giving the name of an old wartime friend in Italy, Signor Bruno Calvani, a sculptor living in Milan, who might be of help if I went there to study, as I intended to do. I was impressed with this show of consideration. Rogers changed the nature of the school but brought many benefits to it for its continued development, although with the succeeding political strife and troubles in Northern Ireland, it ceased to be a boarding school. The Rev gentleman died recently and I last saw him at a function, when he was in his 90s.

Prior to entering the business, I had been sent for work experience in Lewis's of Manchester, an assignment arranged by the school in my last year. It was not my choice particularly, but because the school supposed I was going into business anyway, that's where I was sent. I had lodgings in Salford, a dreary place and went up daily by bus to Manchester. I was directed to the cut-glass department in the store. Meantime, another friend of mine had asked to study British Railways, or whatever their generic name was in those days, for it was before Beeching had devastated them. My friend spent his time being entertained on

74

private trains, exploring the network in comfort. I was set about unpacking cases of cut-glass for display on the departments shelves. The boxes were stuffed with fine wood shavings as protection for the wares and in my enthusiastic discarding of these volumes of packaging, I was inclined to hurl pieces of glass into the air along with the stuffing. I was soon demoted to the Basement, to the counter selling draught excluders, where I might be considered less of a risk! I shared the counter with an amusing fellow from Dungannon, who did not take things too seriously, although his livelihood depended on it.

Next to us on the Basement floor was the music department. Here one could ask for a record to be played or for a piece to be played on the piano, from the sheet music on sale. 'Some Enchanted Evening' from South Pacific was the popular song of the time, sung by Ezio Pinza. I heard it all day every day during my time there, till I was distracted. Ezio Pinza was one of the most famous Italian Bass singers at the Metropolitan Opera in New York and went on to even greater fame and popularity on Broadway in that show.

My digs weren't too bad and the landlady's husband was a kindly man. They had a daughter who invited me to a dance. Her father had tickets one evening for a radio show, recording for broadcast, to which we went with her. The star turn was Ken Dodd, starting out on his career, for this was in 1955. He rather muffed his lines and had to do a re-take. The compere begged our indulgence and understanding, explaining that this was the young man's first broadcast and hoping we would give him another chance. Ken Dodd went on to become one of the country's greatest ever comedians, packing more into one show than many performers put into a lifetime in the halls. In the year 2002 he is still entertaining us hilariously, I am delighted to say.

Although I enjoyed the experience in Manchester, I was glad to return home to get started into the business and farming. I enjoyed the basic physical work, hated being sent on sales expeditions and did not enjoy meeting the Belfast customers at all. I had acquired a certain 'tone' at school and spoke quite well but with a Southern Irish intonation, and was very polite then. Some customers would ask me who the hell I was, for my then re-fined accent offended them and it was a sudden come-down to be launched into a career as a lorry-driver.

Friends of Fred had worked in the business in their school holidays and loved getting down to the docks and delivering goods around the country, which seemed like fun. To be con-fronted by doing it for a living and forever was not such an appealing prospect. Long days spent travelling to all parts of the six counties in all weathers, often late at night, with awkward ill-mannered customers, slow to pay but quick to complain, had a demoralising effect. It was, however, nice to meet our better customers and to do business with them.

Many aspects of the business were interesting and reward-ing. I visited many places of interest, such as the Cregagh or Dromona Dairies and the cheese factory at Magheralin, where thousands of 56lb cheese blocks were stored, stacked six high on pallets in large rooms. They had to be turned over regularly to keep them fresh and despatched in rotation. Visits to the cold-storage to withdraw supplies of butter for re-packaging at Cregagh and visits to sweet factories and the Martin Manu-facturing Company were all enlightening. The Martin Co. was an establishment near where we had lived in Belfast. There they packed such products as cod liver oil, olive oil, pickles - onions, beetroot and mixed pickles, pepper and spices, such as, cloves, nutmeg and ginger. They produced vinegar, made in great vats, brown and white, from acetic acid and bottled, which was all very interesting to see. We had another supplier of vinegar who took a liking to Fred and offered him a job and the likelihood of taking over his business, which Fred declined.

Father had also bought the local Post Office and general store at Ballyrobert with petrol pumps and a large shed, which was let out to a mechanic who repaired cars. Fred and I were not businessmen nor business-minded. We did enjoy the physi-cal aspects, though, having had to start at the bottom driving vans and lorries, collecting tons of sugar, butter, cheese and tinned goods from the docks and off-loading them into the store. The business was moved to new premises on the Mountpottinger Road. This consisted of what had been the

High Sheriff's House and afforded ample yards at the back on which new stores were built as well as a small well-equipped sweet factory. The house had several large rooms and a second yard with further storage sheds. Fred and I worked with other lads in the store. We used to have competitions as to which of us could carry the most and we managed to stagger along with four 1cwt sacks of sugar perched on our shoulders, steadied by the lads who had helped load us up. No wonder I have had a bad back for years! Though I was short, about 5 foot 8 and slight of build at the time, I could grab 1cwt of sugar from the floor and hoist it onto my shoulder with ease. I regularly delivered half a ton of sugar, ten bags, to Desano's Ice Cream Parlour on the Newtownards Road, carrying each bag in turn from the van into the shop and up an iron spiral staircase. I could pick up a couple of tons of sugar at the docks and off-load them into the store in a morning.

Opposite our premises were those of Harkness and Company. They were Hauliers, using horses and carts and had two steam traction engines as well. Their premises stretched far along Mountpottinger Road, behind a facade of houses, where they had large storage capacity and stabling for the dray horses. They were beautiful beasts, heavy, with great fetlocks and harnessed in leather and brass, to be seen daily hauling heavy loads from the Belfast Docks up onto and over Queen's Bridge, back to the depot. Very large loads, such as machinery or great rolls of newsprint, might require the use of the traction engines, huge and lumbering, belching steam and smoke as they trundled up with massive loads. Sometimes two horses were used in tandem, where the load was too much for one. In places, drinking troughs for the horses could be seen and notices were displayed, exhorting drivers to let down the reins and get off the cart.

CHAPTER 9

Belfast Docks in the 1950s were still very busy, with ships from everywhere tying up. The Belfast Shipyard was still busy too and several thousands of men were employed on the Queen's Island, building great ships. As shipbuilding later declined, they turned their expertise to building massive oil rigs for use in the North Sea exploration.

We went to the docks twice a week to collect supplies. It was exciting to see the ships unloading, the mountains of merchandise in the sheds, the porters and stevedores pushing hand trucks piled with boxes, bales and sacks. We had to visit a large sweet factory and we were able to see them at work and sample their wares. Our own small sweet factory produced every variety of boiled sweets, lettered seaside rock, fruit rock, yellow man and toasted coconut logs, which were a great seller and a favourite with our customers.

The place was equipped with every type of machinery necessary for the production. In large copper pans the sugar was boiled over gas-blown ovens - white sugar, Demerara sugar, coarse brown sugar, molasses and syrup were used. The mixture had to be boiled to the exact required temperature, tested by a stick thermometer of heavy brass, which was hung on the side of the pan, in the molten liquid till it was ready. The molten sugar was then poured onto heated steel tables in different quantities, awaiting the various flavourings and colourings to be folded in. There was a moulding machine and a large two-handled machine over which a lump of about twelve pounds of soft, pliable boiled sugar was draped, the handles then beating it up and down, backwards and forwards, aerating it and expanding it, to form the white core for the sticks of rock, or for yellow man, which was made from the brown sugar.

The sugar boiler was the expert. He would apportion the ingredients, according to the product to be produced, adding flavours of mint, clove, aniseed, brandy, varieties of fruit and appropriate colourings. Rock was made with a coating of red sugar. A slab of mint-flavoured molten sugar was laid out and rolled flat on the heated table. A large lump of the whipped sugar was cut to size and laid over it. Letters for the centre were made up of strips of red sugar, laid across the inner whipped layer, a core of white was set on top of these and the whole lot was rolled up within the outer layer, encasing the core and the red strips to form the lettering inside. This produced a fat roll, which was tapered and, with constant rolling, became gradually elongated. When the correct thickness was reached, it was cut off at required lengths, to produce the sticks of rock. This was a work of art, for when the rock was broken straight across, the name inserted, for instance, BANGOR, would be clearly formed and readable. This was taken to even greater refinement when fruit rock was made. In that case, patterns of different colours would be built up, which resulted in the depiction of bees or butterflies, appearing at the core. The yellow man was also whipped up on the machine. Made of brown Demerara sugar, it had a distinctive flavour and was moulded into small cushion shapes, to be sold individually in the shops. Lumps retailed at a half-penny each.

Boiled sweets such as clove rock, aniseed and brandy balls, fruit lumps, striped balls, cough rock and black balls were produced and packed in 5lb jars, for sale to the shop, with a two shilling deposit on the jars, which were recycled. Toasted coconut logs were a fondant macaroon confection, made with fine desiccated coconut and then toasted on a conveyor belt, passing through a large grill-like machine. This was a most interesting to see and our chief sugar boiler was an artist. Several girls assisted in the factory and Fred and I learned something of the processes.

The Milk Marketing Board produced a very fine butter at Dromona. This was very popular and was rationed, as production was limited. Every fortnight we went out there to collect this product, which was a ready seller. Another dairy started production of Golden Cow butter, which also became very popular, even being exported to the Middle East. We still received supplies from New Zealand, of course. Tea had a pleasant smell when the imported crates were opened up. After blending, it was packaged for us elsewhere and the empty tea chests were much in demand by people for storage and fetched around two shillings each. Empty hessian sacks, which had contained peas, barley, lentils as well as animal food stuffs at the farm, were sold to a sack-sorting factory on the dockside at Queen's Bridge. Mother worked in the office with two or three other staff. She would cook lunch for us on a gas stove installed in the room next door. Father had his private office at the back, with a large desk and chaise longue, where he always took an afternoon nap before going out on his business. He slept very badly at night. He and Mother were voracious readers, consuming six books every week from the lending library at Oldpark Road, near where we had lived. Father did much of his reading in bed and continued throughout his life.

Fred acquired an MG Midget car and began to take more interest in the farm. It was decided that we would relocate the business to Ballyrobert as travelling across town every day, after driving in from the country, in ever increasing traffic was making things difficult. A number of break-ins had also occurred at the premises, which caused further upset. So around 1960, Father sold the premises to BP, who intended to build a petrol station there and everything was moved to Ballyrobert. The business was curtailed, for this was at the time when Cash and Carry was the growing trend and the advent of large supermarkets away from the centre was looming. We had many country customers, who we maintained, and business was going on at the cash stores, where Mother took over the running of the Post Office.

I, meanwhile, had decided to go to Italy to study Opera. I had written some time earlier to La Scala Opera House in Milan, detailing my hopes and intentions and asking for advice. I hardly expected a reply but one eventually came - from the Director, if you please! This had to be taken to the Italian Consulate for translation and the letter extended a very gracious invitation to visit the Director, Signor Ghiringhelli, if I came to Milan. Little did I realise at the time that getting to see him was like asking for an audience with the Pope, for he wielded enormous influence.

When I'd left school with this desire to sing opera, I had an audition with Father's old singing teacher, Frank Capper, considered by some to be the best in Northern Ireland. He lived in a large house in Sans Souci Park, off the Malone Road, the poshest part of town. Father came along to the audition. Mr Capper was a very austere man and lived with his sister in great style. He ran a very ordered regime, teaching from early morning to late afternoon, playing the piano himself. He was rigorous in his habits, worked hard, but always took a break to attend the Edinburgh Festival every year. His fees were expensive. His house was full of the finest antiques, paintings and furniture and there was a Steinway grand piano in the large drawing room and several other pianos throughout the house. I can't remember what I sang for him, probably 'Questa O Quella' from Rigoletto and another song or two. He advised me to go and study music for a year, recommending his organist brother as a teacher, and then to return again.

I met Mr George Lilley, the organist who had been the accompanist at Father's concert in York Street Church, a way back in 1939. He was a friend of the family. He was also an organ and piano tuner and was visiting us at this time to tune the piano in our house. He invited me to go to him for lessons, as Fred had had some piano lessons with him sometime before. He was a rare man, slightly eccentric, with a benign countenance. He and his wife lived in a small semi-detached house off the Antrim Road. He was a pianist of great ability, a church organist, though he hated churches and was a bit of a rebel. He was also an inventor and maker of things, could re-wire a house electrically and was a keen grower and propagator of geraniums. I liked him a lot and so began to attend for lessons. It was soon evident that I had no keyboard skills and he was quite happy to teach singing, for he had done some singing himself and so we began.

He had a thorough knowledge of the mechanics of the voice

and the variety of vowel sounds and modulations, and could play any song or aria. He explained to me the shock of the glottis, apparent in Italian singers, but not a good habit to acquire. I was enthusiastic, too much so, and almost immediately, began to sing arias, many of which I knew from records. I learnt them properly with him and have remembered the words and music, French, Italian and German, from that time. He taught me to phrase the Wagner arias from Lohengrin: 'Mein Lieber Schwann' and 'In Fernem Land'. I still have the sheet music with his phrasing markings on it. I was singing such arias as 'Spirto Gentil' from 'La Favorita', with two high Cs. I had a naturally high voice. We practised arias from 'Rigoletto', 'Cavalleria Rusticana', 'Trovatore', 'Faust' and 'Don Pasquale'. He built a 33 rrpm LP record player for me and so I was able to begin collecting Lps, instead of the old heavy and limited 78 rpm discs.

We decided to make a recording. He had a tape recorder, but I could never stand the sound of my own voice on it, so I hoped that a studio recording would let me hear what I hoped I sounded like. We arranged a date at the down town studio of another singing teacher. I decided to sing 'Di Quella Pira' from 'Trovatore', with two high Cs and 'Amor ti Vieta' from 'Fedora', which were short enough to fit onto one side, and a Tosti song, 'Addio', on the other side. The studio and recording methods were still in basic form, recording through a microphone, but directly onto a soft disc, cut by a stylus, as you sang.

Arriving at the house after a cold wet day, out on the van, we went to the studio in the evening. Mr Lilley was a great pianist and with just one take, the pieces were recorded. I had no problem with the high notes, although the choice of arias was outrageous. The record was cut and off we went. It had to be played at 78 rpm, with a trailer needle, because of the tender surface of the disc. I was reasonably pleased with the two arias, but disgusted with the reverse side, so it was goodbye to 'Addio', and I crossed it off with deep scores across the record. I still have the disc, which is now very worn. I was about 19 years old at this time. Some years later at home, I was playing it and, unknown to me, a lady called to see Mother and said to her 'Who's that singer with a fine voice?' I was very pleased.

George Lilley was an extremely talented man. Being an inventor and good at making things, he was doggedly pursued by a fellow inventor, who kept producing ideas for developing perpetual motion. He nearly drove George mad, getting him to construct the contraptions which he had conceived, for George knew that no matter how inventive they were, the laws of physics were against him. He preferred something more practical and stuck to his piano and organ-tuning as well as his music. George was a great fan of Jimmy Shand, the famous Scottish bandleader specialising in Scottish dance music, whom he declared to be the best in the world. He started a dance club at a local hall, rigged up speakers he had made and played Shand's records, whilst the folk danced to his calls. I was asked along but hated it. The participants were considerably older than me but the ladies liked me because I was vigorous. I couldn't stand it any more and flew for my life. I actually met Jimmy Shand in Glasgow, where I had gone to stay with Bill Cantley, an old school friend. We took the August 'Doon the Water' boat trip on the Clyde and Jimmy and his band were performing on board. He was a small, sad, serious-looking man who played the accordion expertly, but without a trace of emotion on his face.

CHAPTER 10

Around this time, I acquired my first car. I had very little money but decided to put an advertisement in the Belfast Telegraph, offering £10 for any car in going order. I received three replies. One said, 'What you want is a go-car, ha ha!' The second was quite serious, saying that he couldn't sell for £10 but had a reliable roadster, which he offered for £17/10 shillings, thinking I might be interested. I couldn't afford that much. The third offered a Morris Match Box, that is, the smallest Morris car produced and asked would I like to view it. I went to see it and although it was in poor condition, having been made in 1935, it did start and drove quite well, so I bought it. Tax and insurance had to be arranged.

I had a driving licence, which could at that time be acquired in Northern Ireland without a driving test. Fred had tried to teach me to drive at Ballyrobert. At that time we had a medium-sized van with sliding doors, which was chosen for my first outing. The only other time I had driven prior to that was to take Father's car, an old but beautiful Rover, to the garage at the cross-roads, where the Post Office and shop were located. No one was at home, so I decided to have a go, got the engine started and crashed into gear, stalling immediately. After several such false starts, I managed to get some forward movement, jerking and revving noisily down the lane. That was easy enough, as the lane was downhill, so I free-wheeled most of the way. Approaching the main road I had to turn off the ignition and shudder to a stop. Seeing the road clear, I started again, jumping and stalling across the road to go up the hill towards my destination. By a series of jerks, stalling and sudden surges, I managed to arrive at the garage, where the mechanic asked me to back the car round to the side. This was an unexpected development and I abandoned the car where it was.

So back to my driving lesson with Fred. Revving of engine, crashing of gears and a repeat performance in the van, got us to the bottom of the lane, whereupon Fred leapt out, by this time in a rage of frustration and terror, running off telling me to get back whatever way I liked. That was my only driving lesson, which taught me one thing - never ask a friend, or particularly, a member of your family, to teach you to drive. I did eventually master the gears and reversing and other rudimentary manoeuvres and with practice in the vans, became proficient.

My Morris Matchbox created considerable interest. It was small, narrow and square with mudguards and headlamps and a temperature gauge on the radiator. It had four doors and leather upholstery. The wheels had very narrow tyres. It drove nicely except when a front wheel got stuck in the tram lines. This was fine if you were proceeding in a straight direction and the lines weren't wet, for turning the steering wheel was no good in these circumstances, as the wheel continued to slide in the groove of the rail, so that when you came to a junction, instead of proceeding ahead as intended, you would shoot off at an angle across the road, according to the direction the lines were taking.

I decided to drive to Enniskillen one weekend to visit the shool. Des Gray would come with me but I would have to meet him at Armagh. There were no motorways then. The trunk road took you through Lisburn, Lurgan and Portadown. Outside Lisburn I was waved down by two fellows requiring a lift. They turned out to be two old school fellows on their way to play rugby at Portadown. I was dubious about lifting them, due to the delicate condition of the car. My kind nature prevailed, so I invited them to sit in the back to preserve balance, which they did, their large rugby forward frames being just about accommodated. Off we went. After some time I noticed something passing us on the inside. Looking closer, I exclaimed, 'Where did that wheel come from?' as it trundled down the road into the ditch. At that moment the car lunged to the left, keeling over with a crunch and a grinding of metal on the roadway, the bodywork lurching from its mountings. We shuddered to a halt, descended and discovered that the rear wheel had shorn off two of the wheel nuts. That seemed like the end.

85

However, I noted that one of the bolts was still intact and found a compatible nut. I instructed the two heavies to lift the back of the car, whilst I attached the wheel which I had retrieved and it was screwed back on with one nut instead of three.

The rear bodywork had moved over to the left, giving the car a crab-like appearance during movement. I thought it advisable that the two friends should seek a lift in something more sturdy, bade them goodbye and I proceeded onwards to Armagh, where I met Des Gray. By use of his dressing gown cord, we were able to ensure that the back door which had been hanging loose, didn't fall open. We proceeded to Enniskillen, the car by that time having covered 80 miles from Belfast plus ten from home without further incident.

The car was the object of much interest at school, everyone wanting to drive it across the parade ground and cricket pitches. We had some fun but I was anxious not to overdo it, for we had the return journey to consider. This we accomplished without incident and Des and I parted for the last time. Arriving home, the car was declared unroadworthy by Fred, who decided to chop off the bodywork and to use the chassis, still with wheels, engine and steering wheel attached, to race around the fields. This worked for a while, till I decided to try running it on paraffin oil instead of petrol. After a few spluttering yards, with billowing black smoke emerging from the exhaust, it chugged to a halt and was abandoned to the dump.

My next car, some two years later, was a 1937 Rover, which had leather upholstery, radio and heater and could achieve 80 mph. Its front right mudguard was severely dented, but it was in running order. I paid £8 for it and had the dent knocked out. With the radio and heater it proved a great improvement in terms of comfort. It had a feature peculiar to Rover at the time, of a free-wheeling device. This enabled you to change gear without requiring the use of the clutch and allowed the car to free-wheel when the foot was removed from the accelerator, thus reducing the engine revs and supposedly saving on petrol consumption. The only drawback was that it removed the retarding effect of the engine, when going down a hill, thus throwing additional reliance on the brakes. I ran it for a year or so, till the brake pads were worn out and the brake blocks were running bare against the discs and scoring them, causing metal dust to form which quickly rusted. This became unsightly. When I short-circuited the radio and the battery went flat, I gave it up and sold it for £2.

Prior to going to Italy, I went with my friend, Barry Quin, to process vegetables at the Baxter canning factory in Lowestoft, to earn some money. We travelled over by boat and train and arrived there, to be told that the vegetable season was late that year and we couldn't be accommodated for a couple of weeks. We couldn't afford to hang around, so made our way to Bird's Eye in Gt Yarmouth. They took us on to freeze peas. The crop wasn't yet ready but we were given a job, breaking up half-hundredweight blocks of peas, frozen the previous season, to fill such an emergency. These were thawed out and then fully processed through the system.

As things weren't yet up to speed, we decided to take a weekend break. Barry had an aunt in Uxbridge and so he suggested we should make our way to London by hitchhiking and visit her, saying that she would make us welcome for a couple of nights. We got to Norwich, which is a pleasant city and I would have liked to have explored it, but we had to press on and somehow got to London in the late evening. We made our way to the underground to take the train to Uxbridge, which is at the end of the Piccadilly Line. The journey seemed interminable and I was apprehensive about arriving so late and unannounced at a stranger's house, without specific invitation. Barry reassured me that we would be welcome. Finally, finding the house, by now in semi-darkness, there was no one at home and the place was locked up and without a light to be seen. This unforeseen eventuality left us somewhat nonplussed. Had we arrived and been refused admission, might have been understandable, but to have come without even determining if anyone would be in, seemed incomprehensible to me. The house stood in a close of four or six substantial properties.

We looked all round the house, back and front, to see if there might be some means of entry, for by now we were exhausted. About to give up and settle down in the back garden, I noticed a small fan-light window, slightly open, on the upper floor above the front door porch. I said that I might be able to effect entry there, if I could reach it and suggested standing on Barry's shoulders to get on top of the porch, which would then make the window accessible, which course we pursued. I was able to release and raise the flap, allowing me to reach down inside and to open the main window. This gave access to the landing and I was able to negotiate my way in, across the cluttered window-ledge, without wrecking the place. Surprisingly, in spite of the very visible means of entry that we had chosen, no neighbours remarked on our noisy activities.

I came downstairs and opened the front door, pleased that there was no alarm to be activated. We found some food in the fridge, consumed it with gusto and, it being by now very late, we decided to go to bed. We selected separate rooms and retired for the night. Some time later, Barry's aunt and uncle returned to find us asleep. Somewhat taken aback, his aunt aroused us. I left Barry to do the explaining. We returned to Gt Yarmouth the next day

Before things got going in earnest at the factory, Barry gave up and went home. We had been staying in nice digs by the riverside, just across from the factory and were well looked after by a Yorkshire lady, whose husband spent his time in a hut in the garden, making things and was hardly ever seen, much to her despair. She made wholesome and tasty dinners and was kindly. I commenced the real work at the factory, working 16 hour shifts, which included night-working.

The peas were harvested in the field and shelled into large skips, which were driven into the factory on lorries. The skips were hoisted up to a machine, where a trap was opened in the bottom of the skip, to allow the peas to descend via a spiral conduit, with running water into a pea-washing machine. The flow had to be strictly regulated, otherwise spillages occurred. In the same way, the pea-washer needed constant watching for great billows of foam could form and envelop you, standing alongside. A substance could be introduced to help control this, but vigilance and manipulation of the controls were the secrets and the substance was extremely expensive and had to be used sparingly. Good peas, that is, of even consistency, bubbled about in the middle of the tank. 'Floaters', as the name suggests, together with any extraneous leaves, floated to the top and were drained off, heavier substances, like any stray stones or grit, would sink to the bottom. The fit peas were then sucked back up, to go through a machine which slightly steamed them to give them a rich green plumpness and sweetness, whence they were conveyed onto shaking conveyor tables. These spread them out, for eye inspection, where girls sat, deftly removing any debris, such as leaves or stalks that might have got through. I tried it, but finished up a quivering idiot and continued as a pea-washer. After the shaking, the peas were conveyed to the packer, where packets were made ready by mechanical means from a flat state, filled, packed in cartons of two or three dozen and then conveyed straight to the freezer. It was an almost seamless, non-stop operation, whilst the flow of peas from the fields continued day and night.

Working at night, it was very cold and tiring. The only respite was in getting away, to trundle out the truck which bore the rejected peas, to the dump outside. Here great mounds of already fermenting peas, exuded a strong odour, but you could snatch a cigarette and lie down on a low wall for a couple of minutes, to rest your legs. The season was extended and I had to move digs. You were able to eat as many fresh peas as we could stomach and I was averse to peas for some time after this experience.

I moved lodgings to a single room, shared by two other southern Irish fellows, who were friendly and we had a few laughs. The bare bulb in the ceiling light, cast a dismal glow over a dingy room and beds, covered by threadbare blankets. I stayed because it was cheap and the pay at the factory was good, especially with overtime. I was able to go to the end-of-pier shows in Yarmouth, but had to find food elsewhere, for we only had the room provided. I was quite glad when the season ended and I could return home, before which I spent a lot of my money on various presents for family and friends.

Back home, I had had a girlfriend who had been two-timing me. She was my first real love and we were both extremely jealous. She would rage and sulk if I even looked at another girl. When I found out that she had arranged another date, when I got to her house to see her, I became enraged and left her a note telling her to go to hell. Well, all hell broke loose after that. I was vilified, castigated, ostracized, criticised and thoroughly maligned by her and her family. Talk about the fury of a woman scorned! I was particularly hurt because I had brought them all presents. This determined me to leave for Italy as soon as possible. It is worth mentioning that I went to her wedding a few years later. My good relations with her family were restored.

I did not go at once to Italy, but continued to work in the business. I was very unhappy, but consoled myself by going out to dances at weekends, particularly to Larne at weekends, where my friend from school, Seigneur McClelland, lived. He was attending the Belfast Technical College, to qualify for hospitals' administration. His parents lived in a nice house just outside Larne on the northeast Antrim coast, a beautiful spot. His father was a dentist, well-known in the town, and his mother was a keen golfer, bridge player and a leading member in the Inner Circle of Women's Rotary. They were very good to me. Seigneur and I went with other friends to the dance at the King's Arms Hotel, which was a popular venue. A few beers beforehand would set us up to release our inhibitions and so, onto the floor. I hated dancing but was a good mover and tireless in my gyrations. Jive and the twist were the rage. I often sang as I danced ,so loudly that the band complained that I was putting them off, for they could not hear themselves. Partners abandoned me, and I was sometimes asked to leave the hall. There was one fellow who came each week and he was so good that the girls queued to dance with him. He was no great example of male pulchritude, but they cleared the floor for him, so exciting was it to see him in action.

We often drank too much and I usually stayed at the McClelland's house and on Sunday we would go to the golf club for a 'hair of the dog', a walk in the air and then back for lunch, with a game of croquet on the lawn beforehand. Mr McClelland suffered a stroke and died about the age of 60.

Seigneur was then working in the local hospital in Larne. He eventually got married to a girl from Port Patrick, whom he had met at the dance. He finished up living and working in Bristol. Mrs McClelland sold the house and moved to a smaller place in Larne, where she still lives and we meet her from time to time. Seigneur had played the pipes in the school band and retained that interest throughout the years, playing occasionally at weddings.

I was fortunate to get tickets to see Mario Lanza, who was appearing for one night at the King's Hall in Belfast. This is a large exhibition hall, generally used for the N.I. Royal Agricultural Show, car show or world champion boxing matches. Many great fights took place there and there were many famous Northern Ireland champions in the lighter weights. Rinty Monaghan, in the 50s, was the most famous and was World Flyweight Champion. He always sang 'When Irish Eyes are Smiling' at his fights and went on to appear in pantomime after his boxing career. Gigli had once performed at the King's Hall, so it was considered a good venue for a large audience. I greatly admired Lanza, particularly in the film 'The Great Caruso', in which he sang many operatic arias with thrilling quality. Alas, I was disappointed. I have never enjoyed such large spectacles and didn't even go to hear Pavarotti in the open air at Stormont, many years later. Frankly, an operatic singer should be heard in the opera house or concert hall, not through a microphone, in a great canopy of a hall or out of doors. He arrived late, came in like a boxer waving his fists in the air and climbed onto the stage, which was set in the middle of the arena. All was that missing were the ropes of the ring. His programme was inconsequential and with piano accompaniment, the whole thing sounded anaemic. It was not long after, that he went to Italy to make his last film, where he tragically died in 1959, at the age of 38. I have many of his records and considered him, when at his best, as one of the most thrilling singers I have heard on record.

CHAPTER 11

In February 1960, I booked a one-way first-class ticket to Milan via London, paid for by the dwindling funds that I had saved from working at Gt Yarmouth. I packed my set of 'The Art of Caruso' records which had recently been issued by HMV on LP, the best transfer from old 78 records ever effected for historical items, along with those '50 Years of Great Operatic Singing', covering singers from 1900 to 1950, all issued under the HMV, Golden Treasury of Immortal Performances label. In addition, I packed much of my sheet music and a few other records and whatever clothes I thought would be useful. The date of my departure was unfortunate, for the first disaster was being told at Nutt's Corner Airport that the flight to London was cancelled, due to fog and all flights were disrupted. I had to go back the next day and eventually got to London to be told that Milan was fogbound and that the flight was cancelled. After waiting for some hours, I was diverted to Zurich, where I was further delayed. I finally arrived at Malpensa Airport, in freezing fog conditions, in the late dark evening. So much for sunny Italy, I thought!

Malpensa lies well outside the city of Milan, so after a long drive by coach, I arrived at the city terminal. Undaunted, I took a cab and asked the driver to take me to an inexpensive hotel. On the way, I decided to have a look at La Scala Opera House and directed the driver accordingly. Like many opera houses, from the outside, it is not too impressive and in the freezing foggy conditions, did not inspire me. At least the driver didn't rip me off and he delivered me to the Hotel Ariston, on Via Torino, within easy distance of the Piazza Duomo and the adjacent Galleria, monument to Vittorio Emanuele II, which leads to the Piazza alla Scala.

The hotel was clean, not very big and did not serve meals, but afforded comfortable up-to-date accommodation. In my eagerness to see all and in spite of the ravages of the journey, I decided to take a walk, without at the time knowing exactly where I was, in relation to the centre and the aforementioned landmarks. Not only that, but when I sought to return to the hotel, I couldn't find it. I had noted its name as Arlston, due to the way the neon sign outside had formed the letter 'I' , which had appeared as ' L' to me. I hailed another cab and asked to be conveyed to the hotel Arlston, which made no sense to the driver, in my Irish accent. We drove around for a while and then I had the brainwave to write it down for him. ARLSTON I wrote and after some puzzlement, it dawned on him that the name should be Ariston and so I was safely delivered.

At the rates quoted for the room, I couldn't afford a week's stay, so I considered my priorities. Somewhere else to stay was important, but the wherewithal was the question. I still had to arrange to see the Administrator of La Scala, but that was assuming less importance for the moment. Having been given the name of the sculptor, Bruno Calvani, by my old Head at school, I thought he might be a useful contact. I had also been advised by our local clergyman at home, the Rev McConnell of Ballylinney Church that the Waldensian Church, an obscure Protestant sect in Italy, might be worth remembering.

Next day I met a fellow hotel-guest, one Oskan M Salih, a fat merchant from Turkish Cyprus, young and friendly. He in turn, introduced to me an Egyptian lady staying there. She was an elegant, sophisticated lady, older than us but very attractive and engaging. We walked down Via Torino together. Heads turned to see this raven-haired beauty and her unlikely companions, a fat swarthy Turk and a fair-haired youthful Irishman. They were each staying for a few days only, but we were great friends. Our perambulations gave me the lie of the land and I was pleased to see the Duomo, Scala and the great Sforza Castello at the end of Via Dante, all within easy reach.

I decided that a visit to Bruno Calvani was appropriate, so I made my way to his address. He was an elderly man, who spoke some English and was most pleasant. From the state of his place, it was evident that he wasn't well off, which he confirmed when he heard of my plight. He was sympathetic, saying he couldn't offer me any job, but took me to a trattoria, where he ran an account and authorised me to use it in emergency, at his expense. I was most grateful but didn't like to impose. However, I did go back alone before the end of the week, just to have a coffee and to contemplate my increasing despond. I heard voices speaking in English, so introduced myself. One of the company was English, who took a great interest and asked did I not know the Sullivans, for they were singers from Australia. This gentleman worked for George S May International, a Canadian company with offices near the Pirelli building in Milan. I should go there and ask for Audrey Verga, who was Ashley Sullivan's fiancee, and that my new-found acquaintance would explain my situation to her. With many thanks and felicitous goodbyes, off I went.

Next day found me at the offices of George S May Intl, a very imposing building. I was directed to the 18th floor, to meet la Signorina Verga. She turned out to be a half-Scottish, fair haired beauty with a friendly manner, but showed initial horror as I went roaring down the plush corridors to greet her. I was always accused of roaring when in fact I was just ebullient and had a naturally loud voice. She hushed me, ushering me into her office. It was decided that I should meet her that night at Giorgio's Trattoria, on Via Foppa, as that was where the Sullivans invariably dined and we would meet. The Sullivan brothers had been sent by their father to study opera with the best teachers in Milan. He had always wanted to sing himself and was a great friend of Peter Dawson, the very famous and popular bass baritone. Like my father, he had to make his way in business, so never fulfilled his dream and determined that his sons would fulfil theirs and his desires. This was unlike my father and indeed mother, who did their utmost to discourage me, in my ambitions.

We sat awaiting their arrival, when they appeared like persons of note. Ashley was short and stocky, looking like a young Marlon Brando; Craig was more slight, but with a jaunty air. Both wore berets in the French artists' style, which I thought a bit of an affectation. Both were well-dressed and looked well fed and at ease with themselves. We were introduced. The waiter made a fuss of them as they ordered their meal. I was forgotten. After some time, they noticed my ravaged look and Ashley, turning to his brother, said, 'Give the poor bugger a dish of pasta, he's starving'. I ignored the insult and seized upon the dish with gusto. Thus began our friendship and we met regularly thereafter. Meantime, I had to find lodgings. I was advised to go to a certain meeting place, where students gathered, to get advice on cheap places to stay and there I was directed to a Pensione on Via Porpora, not far from the Stazione Centrale. I acquired a bed there, in a communal room, with cheap meals available at extra cost, if requested. I settled for a while and met a very nice lad from Venezuela, Rafaele Reyna, who was a tenor studying at the Milan Conservatory. I heard him there in a concert and was impressed with the quality of his voice, when he sang 'Quanta e Bella' from 'L'Elisir D'Amore' by Donizetti.

We became good friends for the duration. Another young fellow staying there, was a young lad on the run from Paris. He was a wild character and spent his time at brothels indulging himself, before the authorities caught up with him and he was deported back home. One day at the pensione, I noted a pair of lovely red shoes attached to a pair of very attractive ankles, descending the stairs. As they came lower, the legs were equally impressive, as the figure and face of a beautiful, blonde girl emerged. Her name was Ursula Magura from Munich and I fell for her immediately. We became friendly and went about together for a short while. She had left home over a broken romance and was unsettled. I begged her to stay, but she wanted to go home again and bade me farewell. She wouldn't give me her address and I never made contact again. I was desolate.

I decided to pursue my invitation to meet the Director of La Scala, as had been suggested in his letter should I ever come to Milan. So I made an appointment to meet him one evening and went to the opera house as requested. Signor Ghiringhelli was most charming and greeted me warmly, speaking in perfect English. He regretted that he was rather under pressure at that moment as Madame Callas was to sing and was creating something of a crisis. He suggested that I should see his secretary to discuss my intentions. That was the last I saw of him, for his secretary, although a charming lady, spoke no English, I spoke no Italian, and our French was mutually inadequate, so I was unable to pursue the matter. Friends were amazed that I had got so near the seat of power.

My need to earn money was now pressing. The Sullivans said that I should try teaching English, which was carried out by many singing students from England, Australia and America, at various private schools. Many executives of business, such as Pirelli, Coca Cola, Rinascenti etc., were required to learn English and several schools provided this service. I applied to the Oxford Institute, where I met the owner, Mr Archer, a pleasant Englishman. He couldn't offer me much due to my total inexperience but said I could take a few classes of more advanced students, who would benefit from conversation and discussion. Also, there was a lady from Venice who came each weekend to Milan with her husband. She required private lessons, for she was going to London to meet the Queen and wanted to know the rudiments of the language. In addition, there was an Italian family, Dr Panerai and his wife and son, who required someone to come to dinner each Thursday and to help their 11-year-old son with his books, for an hour. In return, I would have dinner with them and if they liked me, they would take me with them for the month of August holidays, to their apartment in Tellaro, near Lerici on the Gulf of La Spezia. This all sounded good, so I accepted with alacrity.

Mr Archer became quite friendly with me, for we shared one thing in common - penury. He was planning to sell the school. His wife had left him and he was in an impecunious state, with a young daughter to look after. Things went well. The Panerais were pleasant, she from Varese, he from Piedmont. He was Dr Gino Panerai and worked for Ciba Geigy, the Swiss Pharmaceutical firm. He looked like Gregory Peck. She, Bruna, was a teacher, blonde and beautiful. Her father, a cartographer, and mother still lived in Varese, and I met them several times at their pleasant villa. Dr Panerai's father was dead and I met his mother on one occasion only. Their son, Alberto, was quite big for his 11 years and very bright. He was to go on to become a noted doctor and expert on endocrinology, travelling the world lecturing at conferences. So began a lifetime's friendship and I was assured of a good meal each week, for Signora Panerai was a good and generous cook.

The lady from Venice was a good-looking woman, probably in her mid to late-30s and *simpatica*. Her husband, a businessman, was up for the football and they stayed at the grandest of hotels. She and I would have an hour's English tuition. I had acquired some simple books and made up lessons as we went along. She spoke no English and as yet, my Italian was non-existent. We got along fine and after each lesson, for which I was quite generously paid, she took me to dinner, which cost three times as much as the fee she had given me. So I was assured two good meals each week.

Classes at the school were conducted in the evening. I was allocated a few to conduct, with salary paid weekly. I was encouraged to open a bank account and was issued with a cheque book, not much use, as my limited funds were soon dispersed. I continued to stay at the Pensione meantime and the lessons didn't seem too onerous, except when they got too technical in matters of grammar and syntax. I didn't bother about that.

One day, Mr Archer asked if I would go along to his flat and clear it up a bit. His young daughter was ill and would I please see that she was alright. He couldn't pay me for my trouble, but suggested that I could eat whatever was in the fridge. He explained that he lived frugally. I was happy to oblige. His frugal existence was obvious when I got to the flat and his daughter, who was about 12 years of age, was in bed and looking rather glum. I cleared up as best I could and talked to the child, ensuring that she was all right on her own. She was used to it, but was suffering from a cold or flu and had to stay off school. Remembering Mr Archer's invitation to eat whatever was in the fridge, I proceeded in that direction. It was empty.

Reporting back to him, I declared that all seemed alright at home but that there had been nothing to eat. He regretted this and apologised. He said he often ate very little himself but that

97

it was essential to maintain levels of iron in the blood. To that end, he kept a rusty nail in a jar of water, drinking the resultant murky liquid, which he said, did the trick. He said it with such sincerity that I howled with mirth but never tried it myself!

Through the Sullivans, I began to meet others. They lived in a small apartment round the corner from Giorgio's Trattoria and had a cleaner in each day. Ashley did some teaching, whilst Craig had had some work as a male model, as well as earning money, intermittently, as a wool classer. With their father's allowance, both went to the famous baritone, Ghirardini, for singing lessons, Ashley a baritone, Craig a tenor.

Another Australian, Eric Swinburne, had come over with the Sullivans to study, but had given up singing more or less, to go into the teaching business with Bruno di Matteo. Eric and Bruno were older than ourselves. Eric had had a career in Australia on Radio and on voice-over recordings for advertisements. He had been married to a Greek girl whose father owned waterfront 'joints' in Sydney. Eric was small of stature but very broad and strong and was a natty dresser. His father-in-law had given him one of his toughest clubs to run, to prove his worth and he said he had to eject fellows from the premises twice as big as himself. That marriage failed, but he didn't talk much about it for he had been deeply hurt. He had started his own line of drinks dispensing machines but ran out of cups. He had tried recycling them but they stuck so often, that people in rage wrecked his machines. He then got into the one-arm bandit racket, with a series of gambling machines and found he was making so much money that it became embarrassing carrying it in sacks full of coins to the bank. He spent some time in England and was a Red-Coat at Butlins. He was a fast wit, full of jokes and had a great personality. He had studied *Lieder* singing in Germany and thereafter had travelled to Canada to sell refrigerators. He worked his way back to Australia, stopping on the way at Hawaii, where he became a car salesman. He returned to Australia and spent time on the Sullivans' property, herding cattle and sheep and making fences. He had gone on the drink, had sunk to the depths, but redeemed himself in the gymnasium building up a strong physique. He had served in the second-world war and spent time in New Guinea, where he suffered malaria and other tropical diseases. He was friendly with Sullivan senior, who had made a fortune in elastic during the war and was famously called 'knickers' Sullivan, for he had cornered the market in British production of elastic, before the outbreak of war, sensing that supplies from the Far East and Germany would dry up, once the Japanese and Germans got going in the war.

So Eric decided to go to Milan when the two sons had decided to go there. I once heard him sing 'Ich Grolle Nicht', by Schumann, and never heard such feeling and expression as he produced. He also sang 'It is Enough' from the Elijah, which thrilled me too. On a later occasion on a visit to London he sang the 'Prologue' to 'Pagliacci' and 'Cortigiani vil Razza' from 'Rigoletto', which brought the house down.

His partner in the school, Instituto di Studii Britannico, in Via Dante, right in the centre of Milan, was Bruno di Matteo, a Neapolitan who looked like the 'Capo Mafia'. He called himself Matthews and spoke with an American accent. He had a fine baritone voice and a knowledge of opera. The school prospered and they made a fortune. Other friends were Mike Zacconi, a fine bass and a handsome man. Much later he developed cancer of the throat but survived and I met him in 1980 in Milan, where he was now making his living as an interpreter. Steve Columbo was another, from St Louis, Ohio, who was a good friend and was training as a tenor. He was also very fond of the women and eventually took off with one, finishing up in Australia. There was another fellow called Al from California, who has been a backing singer for pop recordings, but decided to go to Milan to study opera. He was a tall skinny fellow, but a wow with the women and not much of a singer. Bob Haddow from New Zealand was another member of our group. He, also had served in the war and been captured by the Japanese. He had a greengrocery business in New Zealand but decided to go to Milan to study opera. The business continued to afford him a monthly income. He was very large and had a fine bass voice. He used to play a small ukulele with his huge hands and crooned songs. He was amiable when sober, but drink turned him into public enemy number one and he would fight any-body.

I continued with the few lessons, teaching at the Oxford Institute, till Mr Archer handed over to the new owners. They kept me on, eyeing me with some apprehension. One evening I was conducting a class of senior businessmen and women, who wanted to hear of my experiences to date. As you can imagine, with a bunch of friends as described, and my own penchant for the unusual, some of these were quite amusing. The result was that the class was in an uproar of laughter and merriment, when one of the new partners burst in to see what was causing the clamour and I was sacked. This left me in a delicate situation once again and I had only the free meal at Panerai's and the lesson with the free dinner with the lady from Venice to keep me going. I had to get out of the pensione. The Sullivans' cleaner offered me a room in her dingy apartment, for a small weekly rental, which I accepted gladly, though the place smelt and was constantly occupied by her out-of-work husband. I wasn't suited to teaching English anyway.

I had retained the cheque book which the school had organ-ised for me, which proved useful on one occasion. I had never used it and had no balance on my account. However, Bob Haddow and I were out one night, having attended a concert with the others, where Mike Zacconi and Rafael Reyna were singing. We also heard the now retired and elderly Carlo Tagliabue, who had been a famous Rigoletto. He was singing with a new Japanese student soprano. They sang the great Si Vendetta duet from Rigoletto and he, in his 60s, sang so pas-sionately and with such vigour that the young lady was almost struck dumb and looked terrified. Nevertheless, they received rapturous applause.

Bob and I had had too much to drink and of course, he started a fight with some Italians in the street. He came off rather worse than they and our other companions had disowned him for the night, for they had known what his drunken state might lead to. Bob was a frequent guest of the Questura, (Night Police), being picked up on occasions, when in his cups. He became well-known and was well liked there, for he would serenade them with his ukulele in the cells, where he would pass the night and was usually let out the next day. I, in my early innocence, knew nothing of this at the time and volunteered to see him home. On our way, we decided to visit a night club and went in. We were greeted warmly and were ushered to a table, with plush chairs. Two young ladies appeared and sat on our knees, even though we were not pretty sights. Drinks were ordered and consumed. I hesitated and managed to get through to Bob that this was going to cost us money. We made to leave and were stopped at the door with a demand for payment. We were both broke. Bob's first reaction was to fight his way out but I calmed him. I had remembered the cheque book and asked if they would accept a cheque. The answer was 'Yes' and with inordinate cheek I demanded a pen and quickly issued a cheque for the amount, which was eagerly snatched. I don't know whether it was ever cashed or not but I may still have an unauthorised overdraft. I would like to think, however, that the clip joint itself was clipped. We escaped and spent the night in the park, where Bob had collapsed and fallen asleep, half on the path and half on the grass. I shivered on a bench.

We all became friendly in Milan with a visiting American tenor called Leonard Del Ferro. He had come to Milan for auditions at La Scala and to further his international prospects, having already caused a stir in America. He had been featured in Time Magazine, the article complaining about why the Metropolitan, New York, was having to import so many foreign tenors, when they had their own ready-made in the shape of Del Ferro. He was a genial character in the traditional short-statured, rotund-figured mode of the operatic tenor, and with a good personality. Women loved him, although he was no beauty. He had made useful contacts already and with auditions at La Scala, his hopes were high. However, at a crucial second audition, being short, he was wearing up-lifts to increase his height. The stage was raked, that is sloped, adding to his concerns and perhaps he was too ambitious in his choice of arias, for he wanted to impress the incisive quality of his voice by singing Otello, Verdi's great masterpiece. This is the pinnacle of Italian tenor roles, usually only undertaken by singers in their later years. The great Martinelli had only assumed the role in his 50s, although noted exponents have been Del Monaco and Domingo, who each sang it from early on and throughout their careers. A modern day young Otello, already acclaimed in Italy, is the Argentinian, Jose Cura. Caruso was preparing for the role in 1921, when he died at the age of 48 before ever singing it. He recorded some notable extracts, in particular, Si Pel Ciel, with Ruffo.

Del Ferro was therefore not at his best on the day and did not secure a contract. He went on to make a career in Europe nevertheless and had sung with Callas, performing the role of Arturo with her, in the 1959 recording of Lucia di Lammermoor, with Ferruccio Tagliavini as Edgardo and Piero Cappuccilli as Enrico Ashton, an august cast. The mezzo soprano in the role of Alisa, companion to Lucia, was Margreta Elkins, an old Australian girlfriend of one of the Sullivans. The conductor was Tullio Serafin, who had been instrumental in encouraging Callas and Sutherland in their forays into the coloratura roles of Donizetti, Rossini, Bellini and other great 19th century operas. Serafin remained active into his 80s and had also guided Rosa Ponselle in the 1920s and 30s. He declared that he had known but three miracles of singing, Caruso, Ponselle and Tita Ruffo. Del Ferro went on to become a professor at the Amsterdam Conservatory.

Another friend was Piero Francia, a baritone, who had sung at La Scala and is on record in Un Ballo in Maschera, in the role of Renato. He lived in Asti with his aged father and a sister, where they had a small vineyard producing Barolo wine. He was also a man of business. His father had been a chef in Argentina and they now ran a local restaurant and Piero also ran a launderette. He was a man of gargantuan appetites and gross appearance. He sadly died at the age of 54 from pancreatic cancer, only finally marrying his fiancee of many years when on his deathbed.

It was decided that I should get down to some more serious study of singing. I should go in the first instance to an old gentleman called Casari, a composer who made a living by instructing singers in the rudiments of interpretation and in following the conductor's beat. He had written several operas including 'Una Notte con Cleopatra', which was never produced, but he was ever hopeful of getting it heard and thought that some of his pupils might one day perform it. He was an elderly gent with one yellowing tooth at the front and bad breath and had I been able to afford it at the time, he would have taught me much that would have been useful about operatic tradition and interpretation.

I was then introduced to the once renowned tenor, Nino Piccaluga, who was born in June 1890, near Milan. From early photographs he appeared as a fine looking slim gentleman, unusual for tenors, with a reputation with the ladies, which is not so unusual. He had gone to South America in his teens, where he became assistant to the FIAT representative, a wealthy Italo-Chilean. He shared a pensione in Santiago with a tenor who encouraged him to take up singing. He was drafted back to Italy to join the army, but before that he heard Caruso at the Buenos Aires Teatro Colon, which determined him to become a singer. He described Caruso's voice as 'like a shower of crystal cascading throughout the theatre'. Others have described Caruso's voice as 'liquid gold wrapped in velvet'. Piccaluga eventually sang at La Scala, under Toscanini's direction, but was always overshadowed by Toscanini's favourite tenor, Aureliano Pertile, who said of him that he sang as if he were his son - just like himself. Piccaluga made his debut in Novara in January 1919 in 'Manon Lescaut' and at La Scala in 1922, with his wife, Augusta Concato, in 'Il Tabarro'. Puccini had wanted the more experienced Amedeo Bassi in the role and did not know Piccaluga. However, on hearing him at rehearsal, after one difficult passage, Puccini jumped to his feet, crying out 'Si, si, si, va bene! Va bene cosi!' Although virtually self-taught vocally, after studying briefly with Giuseppe Borgatti, a noted tenor, he was soon dismissed with the words, 'I have nothing else to teach you'. He had a very large repertory and was quick to learn his roles. He created several world premieres of operas and sang in Cairo, Buenos Aires, Barcelona, Madrid, Lisbon, Rio de Janeiro, Santiago, Valparaiso, Alexandria, Nice, Monte Carlo, Budapest, Prague, Riga, Berlin, Frankfurt and Amsterdam, as well as all over Italy. He toured Australia and New Zealand with Melba and N America with the Columbia Grand Opera Company. He performed works by Verdi, Mascagni, Puccini, Zandonai, Mule, Moussorgsky, Catalani, Giordano, Wolf Ferrari, Boito, Meyerbeer, Bizet, Leoncavallo and many more.

Like many singers, he had led an extravagant life and due to ill health, he'd had to curtail his career at the outbreak of the second world war in 1939. His last performances were at the famous La Fenice in Venice and the Grande in Brescia. He was in his 70s when I met him. He had a few pupils to augment his income. His method was simple. Singers are always aware of their throats, to the point of neurosis. They gargle and spray them, take potions and lotions, pills and lozenges, worry constantly about colds, draughts, diet, allergies, hoarseness, tiredness and what not. *'Fa niente la gola,'* he would say - just keep it open. To illustrate he would let off a sustained high C, inviting you to look down his cavernous throat, whilst emitting a piercing tone. This was akin to the dictum of the great Russian bass, Fyodor Chaliapin, who said singing was only educated yelling, but most singers weren't educated. Many years later, Pavarotti likened singing to howling, saying he often arose in the morning with no throat, no tone and no hope and had to spend time getting the voice into position by 'howling' till tone emerged. The great tenor Franco Corelli, whom I saw at La Scala in the 70s, was so paralysed with nerves that he dreaded singing and was physically sick, so much so, that he curtailed his career, saying he was not made for singing. If he sang well he was up all night with excitement, if he sang badly he would be up all night worrying about it. He couldn't stand it. Chaliapin frequently wanted to cancel, saying he was unwell and locking himself in his room. 'What about the performance, maestro?' they would ask. 'No good!' 'What about the audience, what about the orchestra, the music, the contract?' All to no avail. 'What about the money?' Ah yes! He would sing after all. Piccaluga was understudy at certain times, taking over at short notice if required. Sometimes Gigli would indicate an unwillingness to sing, due to some indisposition, all pleas unavailing, until he would ask 'Ma chi canta?' 'Piccaluga,' would be the reply, whereupon Gigli would recover miraculously, saying, No, no, no, I will sing, for he knew how popular and able was his rival.

I could only afford a few lessons with him and he often took me to lunch afterwards, for he was friendly and kindly. He had other pupils and one day a large-framed, smiling and amiable tenor of a peasant background, came along to the studio for an audition with an impresario, which the Maestro had arranged for him. Selecting the dramatic recitativo and aria 'La Vita e Un Inferno All Infelice' from Forza Del Destino, he launched into it with piercing tones so loud that I had to rush from the room, my eardrums tearing, whilst the diminutive impresario covered his head in his arms, pleading, '*Basta, basta!*' ('Enough, enough!'). I don't know whether he ever got a contract, but he would have filled any large theatre and out sung the loudest orchestra.

I had a similar experience with Ashley Sullivan who was a good baritone. He and his brother had moved to a new larger apartment, in Via California. It was a very bright, marble-floored place and very resonant. Ashley often during the day, when not teaching or singing, would lie in bed reading, smoking and drinking Coca Cola. A visiting pianist from Belfast, George Gibson, had arranged to meet me, so I brought him along and Al, Craig and myself were having a song or two with him. Ashley came in and started to bellow so loudly (I don't recall the aria) that I had to rush out onto the balcony and close the window. George carried on unabashed. He may not have shattered glass but he shattered my hearing. The decibels created by a trained operatic baritone have been likened to a jet engine taking off, and the tenor, Tamagno, could be heard in the street outside La Scala Opera House in performance. Someone once said of Mario Lanza, that he had a voice that would crack glass or turn milk! In an early broadcast, a well-known Danish tenor, anxious to be heard by as large an audience as possible and by his friends in England, sang so loudly that he shattered the microphone.

However, loud singing is not always required and a smaller, well-produced voice, can be heard at the back of the auditorium, provided that the orchestra is not too loud. Big voices are generally required for dramatic operas such as 'Aida',

'Trovatore', 'Otello' and most Wagnerian operas, but they all have their soft passages. Nevertheless, it is thrilling to hear a good tenor high C in 'Di Quella Pira', ringing out above the orchestra and chorus. The Italians refer to this as *squillante*. It is said that Richard Strauss, in rehearsing the great mezzo- soprano Schumann-Heink, whom he didn't like, in 'Elektra', shouted at the orchestra 'Louder, louder, I can still hear her!'

CHAPTER 12

In spite of my impecunious state, I was somehow able to visit La Scala from time to time, to hear some of the great singers of the 60s. I heard Del Monaco in Carmen with the great mezzo, Giulietta Simionato, Tito Gobbi and Giuseppe di Stefano in La Boheme, Franco Corelli in Trovatore, Malaspina, Flaviano Labo, Bergonzi, Capuccili and many more. Sometimes great singers can be disappointing. Not all can be at their best every night but also, records can often flatter them, so that actual live performances can be disappointing. On the other hand, bigger voices such as Del Monaco, do not always sound so well on record but are heard at their best in the theatre. Records do not always do justice to the bigger voices, whereas smaller or lyrical voices can sound great.

Tito Gobbi was the singer who impressed me most in the theatre, sounding exactly as I had hoped to hear him. Many of his records were also wonderful. I had long admired Di Stefano and his early records were wonderful examples of bright, pure, lyrical singing. However, on the night of Boheme, he was having vocal difficulties and did not impress. He was a great tenor, but undertook more dramatic roles, than was perhaps wise and his career was somewhat curtailed. His records with Callas and Gobbi are legendry. I met him one evening in the Biffi Scala Restaurant and he kindly gave me his autograph. He looked rather sad and bored. The other great trio of rival singers, who were on the major full operatic recordings, were Del Monaco, Renata Tebaldi and Ettore Bastiannini. His recording of La Gioconda is exceptional, particularly the aria, O Monumento. He died of cancer of the oesophagus in 1967, at the age of 45, a tragic loss of a great Verdi baritone. Del Monaco sang the role of Otello over 400 times in his career and was buried in his Otello costume. Tebaldi was a delight and created many fine recordings.

Ugo Benelli was another tenor who greatly impressed me, both by his singing and his lively stage performance in 'La Sonnambula' in Dublin and 'L'Italiana' in Algeri at La Scala. He was a *tenore de grazia*, whose voice could make La Scala ring and he had a long and distinguished career. Another such tenor was the Peruvian, Luigi Alva, great in Rossini and Mozart and a fine comic actor as well as singer. He had shared a pensione with the Sullivans in Milan in the late 50s whilst he was studying at La Scala Opera School. Callas was to sing the role of Rosina in 'Il Barbiere' and wanted a good tenor but one who was not too well known, for she wanted to shine. Alva was auditioned and selected, making his Scala debut with Callas to great acclaim. He went on to a noted career and founded Peru's Opera Company.

I needed work. I continued to enjoy the weekly visits to the Panerai family and their generous hospitality at the table, and the weekly lesson with the lady from Venice and her lavish dinners at the hotel. However, I had only another few private lessons to sustain me. I met a Dutch fellow in the pensione, who was staying a short time. He was amusing and spoke good English, but his language was dreadful and he must have learned it in the trenches. He knew of an Italian who was married to a Dutch woman and living in Amsterdam. He had a chicken hatchery at Nuova Milanese, on the outskirts of Milan and we sought out the address and made contact with the Foreman. The boss was in Holland but would be back in a week or two. His business was hatching chickens in incubators, rearing them and exporting them to Holland. I was invited to go to the hatchery to work there till he came back. I set off on foot, for I couldn't afford the tram fare. Those particular trams went beyond the city boundaries, able to run on railway lines to outlying districts. I got to the terminal and enquired the way to Nuova Milanese. I was advised by an official which tram to take and I set out. He followed me, asking how I intended to get there and when I said I intended to walk, he kindly gave me the fare, so I was able to ride there.

Prior to that I had visited the Waldensian Church, to seek advice on the prospects of work amongst the parishioners. There was no hope in that direction but the Pastor gave me a meal ticket for the Salvation Army, entitling me to a meal each day for a week. I visited their establishment and tried one of their offerings. Hungry as I was I just couldn't stomach it and when they came round me singing hymns, I escaped. I have continued to support the Salvation Army, for they are one of the charities I feel sure that veritably do good and are seen to do it.

So I arrived at Nuova Milanese and was put to work with the incubators. We had those at home, so I was not totally unused to the functions, although this was a large business with many incubators, in large, very warm sheds. The trays of eggs had to be rotated and the eggs turned at frequent intervals to ensure their even warmth so as to maintain favourable hatching conditions. For my time until the boss returned, I would be fed and given a bed, but no pay or guarantee of employment, till he would decide my fate. This was good, although the work was long and arduous and extremely tiring, due to the heat as much as anything else. There were two other pleasant chaps working and we got on well.

I developed a violent toothache and they took me to the local dentist, who diagnosed a bad abscess at the root of an eye tooth. As a temporary solution, he bored up through the tooth to let the poison out. He packed the resultant hole with cotton wool soaked in strong antiseptic. This gave me great relief from the agonising pain and I went back to work.

The proprietor returned after a week and was sympathetic but couldn't offer me permanent work. He gave me 50,000 lire for my work done, which in 1960, I felt was generous. So we had to part company and I returned to Milan and my dingy lodgings, to take stock of the situation. I had the 50,000 lire, a cheap room, very little income from teaching, but was reasonably assured of food, for I had a line of credit with Giorgio's Trattoria and two free meals weekly, with a firm promise of a month at the seaside in Tellaro, with the Panerai family and very little else.

I met a girl who worked in the Law Courts and added her to my list of pupils. One day at the Courts I met a Czech girl and we became friendly. I invited her to meet me at the Sullivans' apartment at Via California, so that I could introduce her. She arrived first, for I was walking there and arrived quite late, which obviously annoyed her, even though she had been made welcome. She had encountered both Sullivan brothers, as well as Eric and Al. Knowing their lasciviousness, I suppose she was lucky to survive till I arrived. They were all agog! To make up I invited her to attend La Scala with me for a performance of 'Madama Butterfly' and so the date was set. I acquired tickets in the second tier and awaited her arrival at the theatre. As if to get her own back, she arrived late, full of apologies of course, but very nicely dressed. I was flattered but annoyed too, for the tickets were quite dear and we had to watch the first part of the opera standing, until a suitable break allowed us to get to our seats, so we had a reasonably good evening. The romance, however, was short-lived and I don't remember her name!

Our favourite pub and meeting place was at the Quadrante, just off Piazza Duomo, where Craig Sullivan, Eric, Bob, Steve Columbo and I used to congregate at times. Ashley had his own affairs to deal with, for he taught English regularly, and he had a fiancee, Audrey, and he therefore avoided most of our excesses. The Sullivans continued their vocal studies with Ghirardini, and Ashley performed in La Traviata as Germont Pere in Milan, where he had quite a success. Craig was able to produce a recording of part of the performance, Ashley giving a good account of himself in the aria 'Di Provenza, il Mar' to rapturous applause. There are many 'schools' of singing, that is, methods according to the ideas of the Maestro di Canto. These vary extremely but the Sullivans never tired of telling everyone that Ghirardini's was the proper method, poohing poohing all others. This is all very well but the trick is to find a method and teacher early in a singing career, suitable to the particular attributes and aspirations of the pupil. Many careers have been blighted by the failure of a maestro to detect and cure faults in vocal technique at an early stage and once bad habits are adopted they are very difficult to eradicate. Great singers are not necessarily great teachers. The very great baritone, Tita Ruffo, who had a splendid natural voice and an illustrious career, although only very basic training, suffered vocal difficulties later on. Af-

110

ter retirement from the stage he had been encouraged to teach. Such was his fame, that he could have commanded high fees. He refused, saying that, as he had never learned to sing, he would not dare to teach and pass on his own bad habits.

It is also interesting to note of the great baritone, Mattia Battistini (1856-1928) hailed as one of the great singers of the Golden Age and referred to as 'King of Baritones' and 'Baritone of Kings' and the 'Gloria d'Italia', that he said in his 70s, that he thought he had finally mastered the art of breathing. So, technique of vocal production, breath control and careful nurturing of the voice, allied to good health, musicianship, hard work and an element of luck are essential to success.

Many methods were taught. One teacher would insist on placing the voice forward in the 'mask', another would say it was an affair of the nose and some would advocate singing on the chords, others to sing from the chest, use the head voice, breathe high, breathe low, sing from the diaphragm, sing on an open throat and so on. Caruso, when asked how to sing, is reported to have said that it was like going to the lavatory - in the one instance you pushed down, in singing you pushed up.

I heard many stories of many teachers' methods. One had pupils yapping like dogs, for he said that dogs had perfect production of sound, able to be heard over long distances and untiring. Another made pupils wear clothes-pegs on their noses, so that they could better sense the vibrations of tone in the cavities of the head. One famous American soprano's maestro would have her lie down and he would stand on her diaphragm and make her sing in that position to strengthen her breath control. Ashley came upon a teacher, who said that he had found the secret of vocal production. He would only reveal his technique provided that the pupil would swear on the Bible never to divulge the secret. Ashley agreed and the teacher stated that the secret of great singing was in the arse, not singing through it, though some might as well try to, but controlling it by the gradual clenching of the buttocks and forward thrusting of the pelvis, as the singer ascended the scale. In many cases, fortunes are spent by would-be singers, in pursuit of acquiring a technique, when in fact, a simple approach most suited to the individual, allied to careful selection of roles to be studied and concentration on phrasing, musicianship and posture, would more usefully serve both singer and audience.

One night at the Quadrante, where we had imbibed liberally of 'Birra alla spina', a pleasant Italian beer served from the tap, Bob got aggressive, his invective addressed to me. He launched a physical attack. We had often been involved in argument, but this was the first time he had ever gone for me. I was quick to react and we were soon at each other, crashing about the bar. Our friends separated us and the bar staff begged us to quit the premises. Outside, it was agreed that once and for all, Bob and I should be allowed to fight it out. I was 5 foot 8 inches in height, Bob a towering 6 foot 2 inches and several stones heavier than me. Marching into the road full of purpose, I was all for fair play and mindful of our mutual interest in singing, suggested that there should be no attack on the throat or the genitals, otherwise no holds barred. This was agreed and as I was ahead, I received a mighty thump from behind. I turned to defend myself. I was wearing a shirt and tie, so naturally the first thing Bob did , was to seize me by the tie and try to strangle me. So much for fair play! I was outraged at this lack of sportsmanship and went wild. I launched a vicious attack, hurling blows upon him, as he ripped off my shirt. He went reeling backwards and fell full length on the street, I on top of him, continuing to pound at his head, which I was now able to reach. There was a lot of blood. While this was on going on in front of the gathered on-lookers, windows of the upper storeys of buildings were opened and a salvo of light bulbs was launched upon us, crashing to the roadway and exploding, accompanied by irate shouts for us to desist. Finally I was dragged off Bob, both of us covered in blood. As I stood up my trousers fell down round my ankles, the only things now covering me, being my underbags and my tie, still tightly knotted round the back of my neck.

Bob was dragged away and I was helped to tidy myself up and to make my way back to my lodgings. At that time, I had moved from the cleaner's house for failing to pay my rent. She had commandeered my belongings against future settlement, so it saved me the bother of dragging cases around. Steve had found me a temporary place to stay with a friend, a lovely girl, who was not particular about rent, as my stay was to be short-lived. It was some way out from the centre of town, so by the time I got back it was late and I had little time to rest, for I had to be at the hotel in the morning, it being Sunday, and the day appointed for my weekly lesson with the lady from Venice. I washed and donned what fresh clothes I had with me and started from the city on foot, so as not to be late for the appointment. My hostess (I couldn't call her landlady) on rising, noted my absence. On investigation, she found my discarded ripped and blood-stained shirt and was about to call the police, thinking I had been brutally attacked. She was able to contact Steve, who put her in the picture, so nothing occurred.

Following the lesson and my usual hearty meal, I decided to go down to the Quadrante to see if any of my friends were there and found Craig, Eric and Steve, who welcomed me with relief and a pint. Discussion of the previous evening's events was inevitable and the bar staff were apprehensive. It was decided that Bob and I should be kept apart if possible. However, he telephoned to say he was coming in and asking if 'Irish' was there. They tried to discourage him from coming to the bar but he insisted. When he appeared, the staff disappeared under the bar and our friends tried to keep between us. All were amazed, as we greeted each other with a handshake and enjoyed a drink together. The Italians were unable to believe what they had seen and relieved that their bar was safe.

Having been ejected from the cleaner's house and my belongings being impounded, I had spent a night on a park bench - not pleasant! I decided I would go back to the pensione at Via Porpora and try my luck. Finding an open window I climbed in and took a spare bed and went to sleep, arising early and escaping by the same route. The second night I returned and was comfortably asleep, when a late guest arrived and was shown into the room by the Padrona, to find me snoring in the visitor's bed. Pandemonium broke out, a bravura performance by the Padrona to equal anything on the operatic stage. Police were threatened, the whole place was awoken, when my old friend,

Rafael Reyna appeared and calmed the situation. A collection was made and the bed paid for and I was allowed to stay for the rest of the night, but banned thereafter. That was when I had moved to the temporary lodgings with Steve's friend.

Meantime, my tooth abscess had re-emerged and I was in agony. I had to find a dentist, who said that I needed immediate penicillin and gave me four phials of increasing strength, to be administered by injection over a period of days. To get this done I was directed to the Red Cross, where this was kindly administered to my buttocks. The pain subsided and I returned to the dentist, who said that he could not save the tooth. The poison being drained had left it loose in its socket and it was easily withdrawn. I had already lost some upper back teeth, victims of my over-indulgence in sweets and chocolate, so I had a partial denture. The gap left by the newly missing tooth, looked somewhat grotesque, so the dentist attached a temporary false one, a garish white hue, not at all a match for my own. I'm not sure that it wasn't, after all, more noticeable than the gaping space. This served me for some time till it fell off. Unable to afford to go back for further treatment and at least, being free from the violent toothache, I had to put up with my embarrassment.

Meantime I was still meeting the Panerai family and the time for the Summer holiday was approaching. They had a friend, a Countess, who wanted the walls of her bedroom washed down in preparation for redecoration. If I would do it she would give me a meal and a hot bath, which I sorely needed, for I was by now staying with Bob in a small attic apartment with few amenities. This was near the Stazione Centrale and not far from Via Porpora. I accepted gladly and started into the work full of good intentions. Washing walls is a thankless task. You think you are doing well as you see the water in the bucket getting blacker, as you rinse out the cleaning cloth, until you stand back to observe your handiwork - a mess of streaks and patches, only serving to show up the true filth of the walls overall. An even coating of grime is not noticeable, until the contrast makes it obvious. Taking pity on me, or because of the frustration she was feeling at my poor efforts, she told me to desist and to take

114

a bath, while she prepared the lunch. I was much relieved and did as she bade me, afterwards enjoying lunch. Before my departure she gave me a pair of her husband's very fine pigskin shoes, which I used with pride, till the soles became so worn, that I was wearing holes in my socks, they being the only thing between my feet and the ground.

It was July and I was staying with Bob, where we enjoyed the hot sunshine on the roof of the building and meeting our friends from time to time, at the bar in the Stazione. This is a good meeting place and a very impressive building. We also used to meet down town in the Galleria, the great monument to Vittorio Emanuele Secondo, which links the Piazza Duomo and the Piazza Alla Scala. This is a great shopping arcade, with a splendid silversmiths at the centre, opposite the famous Biffi Restaurant, where we sat watching the world to by, often seeing great singers passing, some of whom greeted us affably. Next door was the wonderful Alemagna shop, purveyors of delicious cakes and other goodies. The Galleria is in the shape of a cross, with towering glass domed roofs and mosaic pavements. In the centre, at the crossroads, so to speak, is a depiction of a bull, surrounded with ornate mosaic decoration. It is supposed to bring you good luck, if you can spin round full circle, on the heel of one foot implanted on the bull's testicles. That part of the pavement is well indented from the efforts of successive hopefuls, over the years. We all had a go and my right heel was eventually worn out from my frequent tries. To the left arm of the Galleria, you found yourself in the great record shop 'La Voce del Padrone' (HMV). In the 60s it was famous for classical and operatic records and had a large photograph, showing Caruso, Chaliapin and Ruffo together, at the height of their fame, and the only time they were ever pictured together. It hung there for many years but now the shop is totally different and has given way in great measure, to pop music. During that time the favourite song was 'Volare', by Domenico Modugno, which was played incessantly on radio, juke boxes, television and by street buskers. This was as bad as my time in Manchester at Lewis's when I could not escape 'Some Enchanted Evening'. Opposite HMV is the Telephone Exchange with many phone boxes and general information for the public. Other shops, a travel agent and restaurants, are to be found and the Galleria is a major tourist attraction and meeting place.

I decided that I would go to the Arena di Verona, to see a performance of Aida. This meant a train journey from Milan and a ticket for the opera, which started around 9 p.m., leaving the option of returning in the early hours of the next day. Fools rush in, so I made off on my own, got a cheap return train ticket and arrived in Verona. Next thing was to try to buy a ticket for the opera, which could only be acquired from a tout. We had our own contact in Milan for La Scala but in Verona, I had to take my chance and was lucky to find a ticket which gave me access to the top tier of the amphitheatre. Amongst the cast were the famous Simionato, Antonietta Stella, Carlo Bergonzi and Giangiacomo Guelfi. I took a hurried supper prior to the performance and wended my way to my distant seat on the ramparts. Aida is a great spectacle and the Arena gives scope to its grandeur. The Grand March scene was memorable, with a host of torch-bearing extras, emerging from the bowels of the stage and at every level of the background tiers, whilst the chorus and cast on stage, were accompanied by horses and chariots. There were no elephants as is sometimes the case. The whole evening was memorable and I returned to Milan broke but content.

The Panerais lived at Via Vittadini, in an apartment, part of a corner block. They decided to move to another, larger apartment, on the third floor across the quadrangle. I helped them to do this over a period of days. They had a large collection of books and encyclopaedia and a very large impressive bookcase, which had to be dismantled and reassembled on the other side. There were no lifts at that time, so that meant a journey down three flights and up three flights of stairs, carrying loads of books and household items. The new apartment had a corner position giving views across Via Vittadini and to the park beyond and where Mrs Panerai still resides.

CHAPTER 13

It was finally time to go to Tellaro. It is very hot in Milan during August and there is a general exodus to the seaside and to the mountains. Tellaro is a small village perched on the rocks, not far from Lerici, which is a sizeable seaside town and a popular resort, noted for its fish restaurants and is on the Gulf of La Spezia. Spezia is in the province of Genova and is a famous port and naval dockyard. It is a sea bathing resort, where the poet Shelly was drowned in 1822. Genova and Pisa are not far away and Camogli, Santa Margarita and Portofino, popular seaside resorts, are nearby. The famous British actor, Rex Harrison, had a castle at Portofino, which also boasts the famous Hotel Splendido.

The Panerais had a small house in the village, overlooking the picturesque harbour below. The weather was glorious and I was assured of comfort and good food for the duration. I continued to assist Alberto with his books for an hour after supper and Dr Panerai expressed an interest in improving his own English but often fell asleep as I talked. Mrs Panerai did not and still does not, speak much English, although she and her husband were proficient in French and German.

I am not much of a swimmer but with the clear blue Mediterranean sea and the fine weather, I spent long hours in the water with Alberto and his mother every day. Dr Panerai was sometimes away on business, but we were able to travel around by car quite a lot all together. This gave me the opportunity of savouring the delights of Portofino and Santa Margarita, playgrounds of the rich and famous. We visited Spezia and Genova, climbed Carrara Mountain, famous for its white marble, which is exported all over the world and served as a medium for the sculptures of Michelangelo and other great artists. We visited the quarry, where Dr Panerai's friend was the site engineer and we had lunch. I can't remember their name, but he and his wife had a pretty daughter, Alessandria, a bright and affectionate child, who took an immediate liking for me. I met her ten years later and she remembered me. She had been married but her mother had died tragically when she was still young. We visited Pisa and explored the sights. We sampled the pleasures of the various dishes in a restaurant in Lerici, prepared from the local fish catches. Very memorable, was the frutti di mare hors d'oeuvres and swordfish steak grilled and drizzled in olive oil and lemon juice.

We visited the Cinque Terre, a noted wine growing district, where Dr Panerai had some old wartime friends. He had served in Russia and related stories of how many of his companions had died in the cold there, many of them very young, who hadn't the stamina to survive, whereas the older men had been toughened and inured by harsher living conditions and survived. He often wept at the sad memories.

The area could only be approached by train, as there were no roads at the time. We dined at a friend's house and he produced a prize possession, a gallon jar, which he had managed to retrieve from the Americans during the war. This was filled with wine, which the three of us consumed at lunch, making for a riotous afternoon. We visited the beach, where a great sword fish had been landed by a local fishing boat. It was enormous, with a massive sword protruding from its upper jaw. It had been sliced open and a cascade of fish of all sizes, some whole, some partly digested, poured forth. Some of these in turn, were slit open, cascading their own stomach contents and yet again, others were slit. It was like a group of Russian dolls, each opening up into ever smaller ones inside. We returned to Tellaro, tired but with happy memories. Another day we visited Florence. I have been back many times but the first sight of the great Duomo, the Forte di Belvedere, the River Arno and the Pontevecchio, made a lasting impression. Even in those days, the traffic was a problem in the narrow streets, but it is a city which can be explored easily by foot, affording many wonders within a small area. The Duomo, the Forte, the Pitti Palace, the bridge and river, the markets, the

Uffizi Gallery and its great Renaissance treasures and of course, the restaurants and shops, with their profusion of local goods, leather, wood, marble and bronze sculptures, shoes, boots, handbags, tooled leather ornaments and boxes, clothing and pottery, class and china, all of great beauty and inventiveness, were all truly inspiring. Also, spectacular, were some of the massive sculptures of Michelangelo in the streets and everywhere, were artists depicting the scenes in water colour and oils, their work for sale as they produced it.

The weather continued fine and hot and I was enjoying cavorting in the sea. Earlier in April, I had been in the park in Milan eating oranges. April is a dangerous month, for in spite of the sunshine, the air is thin and it is much colder that one imagines. I contracted a chill and some kind of infection to the right of my throat. This had affected me badly, causing severe tiredness and lassitude, with which I struggled for years. I never had it diagnosed but I supposed it to be some form of glandular fever. I had a naturally high voice and used to surprise my colleagues, laughing on a high A Natural, but I often suffered severe bouts of catarrh and sore throats. The good sun and sea water of Tellaro, worked wonders for a time and the throat and sinus cavities were well rinsed out and the voice was loud and clear. One day when the Panerais were all away, I shut myself in the house and practiced singing along with some of my Caruso records, which I had brought along. I sang several arias easily and without inhibition. When the Panerais came back and parked their car on the main road at the entrance to the village, they were accosted by residents as they walked through, enquiring who was the great singer in their house? I was very pleased at this second-hand compliment but played it down, as I was secretly rather shy and didn't want to be pressed to sing in public without accompaniment. That is something I never do, for it is never satisfactory, except perhaps in certain types of folk singing and I even abhor having to sing at parties, with indifferent pianists.

Finally, the holiday came to an end and we returned to Milan. I stayed again with Bob, where we virtually starved. On one occasion we only had an onion and a carrot to share and one pot of tea leaves, which were boiled until they became blanched. This was getting nowhere and my desire to study singing properly, was not going to be fulfilled like this. I could have taken up English teaching more seriously, like so many other foreigners had done in order to survive. However, I decided I would return home and pursue my ambitions by other routes. In September, I managed to get a one-way ticket for surface travel by boat and train to go back to Belfast. During my time in Milan I had many friends and shared some interesting experiences. I had acquired gifts of a suit of clothes, a pair of shoes and sundry other articles and was even given a suitcase to carry them all.

CHAPTER 14

So I left Milan with a great deal more than I had arrived with. A large number turned up at the Stazione Centrale to see me off and so we embraced and I left. I was to return many times to Milan in the future and many of my friendships survived the years. Bob Haddow went to London, joined the D'Oyly Carte Opera Company, as a chorister and toured America with them. He was subsequently seen, playing 'heavies' in TV productions and we lost touch. Ashley and Craig Sullivan continued their singing, appearing in Turkey, Greece and Bulgaria, where they met the British baritone, Peter Glossop, who won a competition there. Ashley's fiancee returned to Scotland, as she couldn't get a resident's permit to stay in Italy and he eventually married Cecilia Ferrando, a lovely girl, whose mother was Argentinian, her father an Italian, who had died after the war from the effects of gas. Craig married a TV presenter, of Sicilian and Russian extraction and as already mentioned, Steve Columbo disappeared to Australia and was never seen again. Eric Swinburne married a ballerina and they had a son, but the marriage did not last and he continued in business and voice-over recordings. Ashley achieved several successes and was signed up for various contracts to sing. His father died and against his express wishes, he and Craig returned to Australia for the funeral, intending to come back to Milan quite soon afterwards. However, offers to sing in Australia and New Guinea delayed their return, which meant that Ashley lost his opportunities to pursue his contracts in Italy. Craig went on to study with a gentleman called Brentegani, and we shall meet him later. Dr Panerai died in his early 60s and Alberto and his mother continued to feature in my life until this day. Mike Zacconi still lives in Milan, where he survived his cancer operation and has a successful business in doing translations. Bruno di Matteo contin-

121

ued with Eric for some years, till his death, leaving one daughter. No one knows where exactly his money went to but he had enjoyed an extravagant lifestyle and he was a man of eccentric genius and sympathetic personality and was generous. Returning home, Fred met me at the Docks and the first thing I had to do was to get my tooth fixed. I helped in the business and on the farm for a while but set about finding a job. I hadn't a lot to recommend me to prospective employers but tried several avenues. During my travels around Carrickfergus, with the van, I used to see a travelling library, parked along the back road near Knocka Monument, the driver sitting comfortably in the sunshine, reading, whilst one or two clients searched his converted single-decker bus for volumes to borrow. It seemed like a nice racket. Seeing an advertisement in the Belfast Telegraph one day for a travelling librarian, I applied to the Belfast Corporation Library for the post.

I was asked to attend an interview. What qualities or qualifications did I have for the post? I was asked. Thinking of my familiarity with large commercial vehicles, I replied that I thought I would be able to drive a bus, which wasn't considered quite enough. I had even gone so far as to ask an eminent friend to give me a recommendation, which he refused, as he felt I wouldn't be suited to the post; rather did he put it that the post was not suited to me. Either way, he was right and I never ever asked anyone in the future to use influence on my part.

I sought career guidance at the Recruitment Advisory Service and was interviewed by a very nice lady. After some pleasantries, we got down to business as to prospects, aspirations and abilities. Finally, she asked what I would really like to do. I suggested 'diamond cutting'. My imagination had been fired after reading 'Diamonds are Forever' and I liked the idea of becoming an expert in gems and in achieving fame as a sought-after cutter, fashioning fabulous stones. She fell off her seat and when she composed herself she suggested that the jobs she had on her lists were below my expectations and bade me a fond farewell.

I applied for, and was offered, a job as a sales assistant in an electrical warehouse. However, I had planned a trip to Milan and told them this, asking if they hold the post for my return, in a week or so. Their needs of my services were more urgent and the offer was withdrawn.

In 1961, an advertisement appeared in the Belfast Telegraph, for staff with British European Airways, to work as Traffic Officers at Belfast Airport, which in those days was called Nutt's Corner. I replied and was selected for an interview, which was conducted by the Station Superintendent and his deputy, the Senior Traffic Officer, and was grilled for a while: Why did I want the job, what did I think it would entail, what were my thoughts on shift work, how would I act in a crisis, what were my ambitions? I answered as best I could with as much enthusiasm as I could muster, all the while restraining myself from screaming that I needed the money, which was most on my mind. They were not unkind at the interview and it was only after I had concluded and gone away to await the verdict, that I realised on reflection, that the questions had been astute and quite reasonable. I received a negative reply and was not offered the job. I was somewhat disheartened, but some weeks later, the same advertisement appeared which came as a surprise, as jobs were hard to come by in N Ireland and they had had many applicants first time. So obviously they had been very selective and demanding in their required standards. I applied again, with a determined and positive tone, was called for interview and felt more confident, remembering the pitfalls of the previous meeting. The same two gentlemen were the interrogators, accompanied by the Personnel Manager and I showed my enthusiasm, which had some effect, for I was offered a position, at a basic wage of £9.12s per week, plus overtime, with pension and holiday entitlements. An added bonus would be discounted staff travel, to be granted after a year's satisfactory employment.

The job was as a Traffic Officer, working shifts, mainly at the airport but occasionally at the town terminal. Uniform would be provided after a probationary period to be worn on all occasions thereafter. The airport, Nutt's Corner, was affectionately called 'Crackers' Bend' by the long-serving staff, for they said you had to be crackers to work there. It was six miles from where we lived; indeed the airport beacon could be seen at night from our house, as it swept the surrounding area with its beam. The town terminal was situated in Glengall Street beside the Grand Opera House and within the complex of the main Great Victoria Street railway station. The trouble, of course, was how to get there. The company provided a crew car, which went only as far as the city limits. That meant that I had three miles to go to get to Glengormley, the nearest pick-up point, or six miles across country direct to the airport. At the beginning, I resorted to bicycle for the early shift, riding to Glengormley, much of the road uphill and in high winds, to meet the Crew Car. If a van was available I would use it direct to the airport.

Four basic shifts were worked to cover the 24 hours, with an additional early shift in the Summer, starting at 6 a.m. I therefore had to work alternately, early, late and night shifts and this was the worst aspect of the job for it was most disorientating. Being a small but busy station meant that all aspects of the ground running of the airline, had to be covered, on a rota basis. The main duties of the Traffic Clerks were: -

PASSENGER HANDLING: Duties included meeting and despatching flights, conducting the passengers on and off the aircraft, receiving and delivering the 'Ship's Papers', that is, documents relating to the balance, loading, take-off and landing weight of the aircraft and the numbers of passengers aboard. Assistance had to be given to women and children and the invalided. Wheelchairs, for instance, might be required, or carrycots for infants ordered in advance.

TICKETING DUTIES: Issuing and amending tickets, charging for excess baggage, upgrading and so on and accounting for the day's takings at the end of shift were carried out. Accuracy was demanded to the last penny. This often incurred dealing with irate passengers, at very busy times and I hated this aspect of the job.

LOAD CONTROL: This entailed the compilation of 'Ship's Papers'. Load and balance charts had to be prepared regarding numbers of passengers and everything on board by weight, fuel requirements, load distribution, actual take-off and esti-

mated landing weights at destination, taking into account estimated fuel consumption during the journey and contact with
Head Loaders, Pilots, Air Traffic Control, Engineers and Cargo
Officers, and the check-in desks had to be maintained. Time
was of the essence, for as the passengers checked in, baggage
was weighed and numbers of men, women and children accounted for by average weights, adjusting loading instructions
according to projected load as against actual and advising the
loaders where the baggage and cargo should be stowed. In
some cases, passenger distribution had to be dictated, where
there was not a full load. As check-out time approached, specified as 20 minutes before published take-off times, late passengers had to be accounted for and any late cargo distributed. I
enjoyed this aspect of the business very much for I had an aptitude for it and had good rapport with the Head Loaders and
Engineers. Mutual difficulties could arise where the weight of
the load could be accommodated, but distribution to achieve
balance would be complicated by bulky rather than heavy loads,
unable to fit into specified holds. This required a quick decision
for redistribution to be effected, so as to meet take-off time
and the safe balance of the aircraft in flight.

CHECK-IN: Passengers would be dealt with at the counter, recording their numbers, male or female, weight of baggage, issuing of excess baggage dockets to be paid for at the
ticket counter. Constant flow of information to Load Control
was essential for all was done manually in those days, without
the quick calculations of today's computers.

OPERATIONS: The Operations Room displayed a large
wall-mounted blackboard, showing all in and out scheduled
flights. Stated times of departure, estimated departure and arrival times and actual times were displayed with information on
weather conditions, constantly updated by the Met Office, coach
schedules from the town terminal and so on. Met reports were
delivered to the Captains of the flights and fuel information
was relayed to the Engineers and estimated and actual times of
flights relayed to destination stations. Phones rang constantly,
with incoming info and queries, all very hectic at busy times and
worse, if diversions or cancelled flights occurred.

The station was run on strict lines with minimal absenteeism, no tolerance of error and a pride in our turnround times of aircraft and our good record of timely departures. In Summer, many charter flights would be handled, often throughout the night. The main day's business came in tranches, around 8 a.m. to 10 a.m., mid-day to 2 p.m. and 5 p.m.to 9 p.m., with mail flights in and out continuing during the night. The day to day running was the responsibility of the Duty Officers and the Loaders and Engineers had their own hierarchy. We were paid weekly, with overtime in arrears.

The place abounded with characters. We were not overburdened unnecessarily with political correctness in those days and friendly rapport existed between male and female staff and everyone could have a laugh. We were a night-stop centre, so we met many of the crew and a friendly atmosphere prevailed. I struck up friendship with a number of night-stopping air stewardesses. Many came from Manchester, for it was another main operations centre and I often went over there for parties. There was one girl I was particularly fond of, from Cheadle Hulme, and we went out together several times, when she stopped over in Belfast. I had met her at a party in Manchester, where I was ranting about something which a haughty Welsh girl had said. This amused the other girl who had observed the contretemps and she calmed and pacified me and we became friends. She invited me home to meet her family at Cheadle Hulme. The house was impressive, in a nice area and I met her mother, grandmother and brother. Her father had been in the textile business and had died. She came from an old Manx family and often went to the Isle of Man, where she still had connections.

I was invited to dine with the family and we had roast chicken for dinner. The brother was the usual English Public School product, mannerly, but a little haughty, well-spoken and seemingly, bored. Her mother viewed me with suspicion and was obviously not overcome with my natural charm, whereas, her grandmother took to me instantly and we got along fine. The girl and I remained friendly for a time, but she remained reserved and I was greatly upset when we finally parted. She had an old boyfriend in the Isle of Man, so I suppose that was where she went.

126

I had a couple of other girlfriends who night-stopped in Belfast from time to time and I also met them in Manchester at parties. Another girl from London, invited me to dinner at her flat somewhere near Kew Gardens. When I arrived, the door was opened by her husband, somewhat to my surprise, for I had known nothing about him. I was invited in and we had a pleasant evening together with an invitation to come again. I didn't.

One of my good friends at BEA was Jim Frame. He was a good-looking well-built fellow of about my own age. He reminded me of Burt Lancaster, for he was a body builder with a fine physique and an amiable smile. He was very attractive to women, although he was married and had two children. He invited me to join him in weight-lifting classes, at the gymnasium of Buster McShane in Belfast. Buster had been an Olympic weightlifter, representing Northern Ireland in the Games. He was also a good friend of Mary Peters, who won the Ladies Pentathlon in the 1974 Games in Munich. She is now Dame Mary Peters. Buster and his brother, ran the Gym together and Mary Peters opened her own fitness clubs. I joined and was made welcome by the McShanes and was warned not to do too much at first, till the muscles became accustomed to the various exercises that I was given to do. Jim was well practiced in the varieties of lifts, bench presses, squats and so on and had a fine, though not grotesque physique. He kept trim, for he wasn't trying to be Mr Universe. What I also liked about the Gymnasium was that operatic music was played whilst we exercised, rather than the bland and annoying musak, played incessantly in other establishments, popular at the time. I thought I was pretty tough and fit, after all my rowing and rugby-playing and my ability to toss cwt bags of sugar and other products around, onto my shoulder from ground level and able to carry them up flights of stairs and on and off lorries. I was therefore surprised the following day, to feel the aches and pains in muscles I hadn't known existed, from the relatively simple exercises with which I had started and so I accepted the wise counsel of my instructors in future. There was a pleasant atmosphere in the club and as I became more adept, Jim remarked how, already, my general musculature was improving. I had one unfortunate occurrence when practicing the squat, when I lost balance slightly and allowed my torso to lean backwards and I felt something give in my lower back. I had not slipped a disc but the pain was intense and so I had to be careful.

Jim and I remained good friends, even after I left the airline and years later, he went to South Africa with his family, where he got a good job in the travel business, but died of a heart attack at an early age and so passed a legend.

Buster McShane, who lived in some style in a castle, tastefully furnished and which was once featured in a magazine article, also died tragically, in a car crash, at an early age and was grieved by all for he was a well-liked and respected figure.

I was sent on a course to London along with another friend, Joe Hawkins, who was married and had a young daughter. The course was run at Hatton Cross and we had been assigned lodgings in Hounslow for the two weeks duration. The weather was freezing and we had to get to and from the course by bus, standing in long queues morning and evening. The lodgings were also freezing. We had the use of a small dining room with a dim glimmer from a 25 watt lamp and a feeble oil stove gave up more smell than heat. The evening meal and breakfast of a basic kind were provided and we had separate bedrooms. It was so cold, that I used to take a hot bath before retiring and then dress in pyjamas and overcoat, before going to bed, to shiver until morning.

Joe's wife was expecting another child and he hated being away from her at that time. For some odd reason, we were not allowed to go home at the first weekend, but were entitled to take a free flight to any European destination, as part of our flight familiarisation programme. Naturally, Joe was bemused by this, for the birth of his child was imminent. I never found out why this rule pertained, but we decided to go together to Paris to see a few sights. The trip was not particularly memorable, for Joe was subdued in the circumstances. We did a bit of a pub crawl, after seeing the sights. Everywhere we went, the cry of 'service Monsieur, service', was heard, each time we bought a drink. I eventually got fed up with this, for we had graduated to ever more seedy establishments, as the evening wore on and I did not see the need to be giving tips all the time. I exploded and in my basic French, told them to clear off and stuff their 'service', much to Joe's amusement and the horror of the bar staff. I was to visit Paris on two subsequent occasions, where I had more adventurous times to relate. The course was interesting and we met some very nice people, especially the girls, who were very friendly. Joe really made a hit, but of course his marriage state precluded any involvement. At the end of the course, we had to sit an exam and I received a good report. Joe's second child was born during his absence and he rushed home, where all was well.

Because of the varied shift pattern, you would often not see particular friends for a period of weeks unless you were assigned to the same roster. Nevertheless, we had a certain clique and would go drinking together on occasions. We were paid weekly on a Thursday and that was the signal for us to get together and hit the town, those of us without family responsibilities. The shift work was exacting and so we were glad to let off steam. It was not unusual to be out all night, particularly if there was a party somewhere. On one such occasion, I was out all night when I had been assigned to duties at the town terminal, for the early start at 6.a.m, when I had to be there to open up. Passengers would be arriving for the early check-in for flights to London. I had no keys with me and was unable to get home and back in time to acquire them. What was I to do? I went round to the terminal, to find a number of passengers already waiting for the place to open. I decided that I had to get in somehow and remembered that there was a small glass-panelled door at the back which was never used. This led to a short corridor, giving into the main lounge. There was nothing else for it, but to break a pane and unlock the door to get in. There was nobody about at the back, so I put the plan into action, shattered the pane and was able to open the door by the inside catch, only to find that there was another locked door at the end of the corridor. Too late to go back, I broke the pane in it and luckily, found that there was a key in the lock on the inside and I was quickly in. To cover the evidence of my break-in, I pulled a large armchair across the door, opened up the front main doors to admit the passengers and commenced the check-in.

To add to my embarrassment, one of my colleagues, still much the worse for wear after our night's excesses, wandered in. Stretching himself out across a row of seats, he fell noisily asleep. I carried on dealing with the line of passengers, affecting indifference. Suddenly arousing from his slumber, my friend ambled up to the counter and stood grinning at me, before slumping across the desk, his head resting on my check-in sheet. Without batting an eyelid and in spite of the startled look of the passengers, I quietly pushed his head to the side, whilst requesting the next passenger's ticket and carried on till all were attended to and the coach was ready to depart for the airport. The Duty Officer was to start at 8 a.m., by which time things were beginning to get busier for the various flights, departing up till 10 a.m. to London, Liverpool, Manchester, Birmingham and other destinations. Soon after his arrival, a passenger came forward from the end of the lounge where he had been sitting, complaining of a strong draught. I carried on with my work as the officer went to investigate. On pushing back the strategically placed armchair, my handiwork was revealed, so I had to come clean and own up. He was a very pleasant and efficient colleague, never stumped by a problem and was a good contact man. Once the passengers had departed and after suitably reprimanding me, he set about the solution. He knew a nearby glazier and so called him and repairs to the two doors were effected and the debris was cleared up. I was eternally grateful to him.

He was a great character and most helpful everywhere. He was always sympathetic to nervous travellers and would take them aside to talk gently to them, restoring their confidence and allaying their fears. He could also humble the awkward and offensive customers. One particular ruse he had, was in handling a pompous female traveller who arrogantly complained vociferously, because her baggage had not arrived from the airport. She made an unnecessary scene. He had an old suitcase in the office, full of tatty underwear and clothing, which he produced for this unduly pompous person's inspection. Opening it he withdrew a pair of worn corsets and a soiled bra, holding them up for all to see and asking loudly, if these might be the articles she was looking for. She had little to say after that, especially as it was discovered that she had failed to claim her bags on arrival at the airport.

Another problem we encountered was the illegal parking of cars behind the terminal building, preventing the coaches from getting round to take on passengers. He kept a porter's baggage trolley, which he would lever under the back of such cars and heave them out of the way, ensuring if possible, that the driver's door was left inaccessible against a wall. We often howled with laughter at his antics. He was a great community person. Some old ladies in his neighbourhood, were being constantly molested by youths in the street at night. He dressed himself up one evening in a old shawl and skirt and hobbled out with a large walking stick. Sure enough, he was approached by the taunting remarks and gestures of the unruly youths, whereupon he leapt into action and chased them down the street brandishing the stick, in hot pursuit.

Another of our colleagues had a rented house in Belfast, where parties were often held. Very often there would be poker played. I was never interested so never played but I was watching as a game progressed, when an interloper, not a member of staff, struck one of the girls, in response to some remark about cheating. She was a popular and friendly girl. I was outraged and remonstrated with the lout, whereupon he thumped me. We set to and I repeatedly punched his head. Catching me round the neck, he pulled my head forward, bringing his knee up into my face with some force. I went down, the blood pouring out of my nose. He then set about kicking hell out of my kidneys. He was dragged off and I got up and found my nose was broken and I was bleeding profusely. I cleaned myself up and felt my nose grating, as I wobbled it. I stuck it in the middle of my face and left it to heal. I have had a deviated septum ever since. I had not known my assailant and it turned out that he was a professional light heavyweight boxer, employed as a bouncer at a well-known dance hall and he was a judo expert.

He appeared at the terminal where I was working the next day, to apologise and invited me for a drink. He was sporting a vicious looking black eye where I had punched him. He showed a genuine concern for his actions, in the undue use of his acquired skills. I refused his offer of a drink for I was at work, so we shook hands and that was that. I had not intended to get involved in a fight and was more careful in future.

Word got out of course and I, with several others at the party was reprimanded by our boss a few days later, for being involved in such a scene, albeit in private. We expressed our apologies and my nose healed up, without apparent outward distortion. I only ever got involved in two fights thereafter, one at the airport with Jim Frame, for no apparent reason, but we beat hell out of each other for a while and called it quits. I was involved with another colleague years later.

Whilst on the subject of fighting, I might add the following anecdote. Prior to joining BEA and just after my return from Italy, I attended a Boxing Tournament at the King's Hall. One of the bouts was between a local man and an Italian. Now, the boxing ring is about the loneliest place you can be, before engaging in a match. You shiver with cold and nerves and wonder why you ever got involved. When your bout starts, you warm up quickly enough, but with each successive round, you get more and more tired, till it becomes an effort just to keep your arms up. Such was my personal experience anyway and it compares with the feeling many opera singers experience when going on stage. So, thinking of the poor fellow away from his home in Italy and because of my recent fond memories of Milan, I thought that I should give a yell or two of encouragement to the Italian. No sooner had I done this, than a big fellow in the row in front, leapt up and punched me on the head. He was dragged down luckily before a riot ensued and I cheered for the home side thereafter.

I was therefore surprised one day at BEA to hear one of the Duty Officers, talking about the time he was at the King's Hall and had thumped someone. Sure enough, he was the one who had been my assailant on that occasion. He was a burly big fellow called John Pollock and we became quite friendly and often had a laugh, when recalling this and other adventures.

CHAPTER 15

In August 1962 a batch of new recruits arrived at Nutt's Corner to join BEA. I did not meet them immediately due to the shift pattern I was on. One day I was introduced to one of them, a young lady, petite with red hair, neatly attired in a two-piece grey suit, with a dainty shoe and ankle. She was called Elsie Bunting. She gave me a somewhat quizzical look as we shook hands, seeming slightly serious. I paid little attention to her, not knowing at the time that I was meeting my future wife. That would be some time later and I thought nothing more about the encounter. I only learned afterwards that her female colleagues had warned her to look out for Ronnie Frazer, for he was a terrible shouter who terrified them all.

It was a while before I met her again, when I was assigned to teach her and her colleagues about Load Control. She told me years later that I was merciless with them for they showed no aptitude whatever and could not grasp even the rudiments of what was required. I also had to accompany her on Passenger Handling duties to and from the aircraft. On one occasion, a distinguished elderly gentleman in splendid camelhair overcoat and using a walking stick was, on crossing the tarmac, unsteadied by the blast of another aircraft's engine which was starting up. He stumbled and fell. He was brought inside and a full incident report had to be completed. I had to deal with him for he was shaken and indignant. He turned out to be an eminent cellist, who had come to perform in a concert at the Ulster Hall with the Ulster Orchestra. In stumbling, he had staved his thumb with his cane and thought that he might not be able to play. I chatted with him and showed interest in the music, asking him if he knew the great Pablo Casals. In fact, he was a great friend of Casals; we finished up chatting amicably and I was able to arrange for a car to take him to his hotel and to ensure that his expensive coat was suitably cleaned. As far as I know the concert was a success and there was no more about it.

Passengers also had to be escorted to the aircraft, which might entail taking special parties out first, or helping mothers with small children, reporting to the air steward or stewardess of any special needs. Elsie Bunting was extremely efficient, patient and good with people. She had worked for several years for the Singer Sewing Machine Company in Belfast and, much against their wishes and her father's counsel, decided she needed a change and so had joined BEA.

To get to and from work more easily I bought a two-stroke moped, to travel directly from home to the airport. This cost me £15 and I bought it from a man living in the Ardoyne area. It had pedals and could be started by setting it on a stand and quickly pedalling whilst manipulating the throttle. Once running, the gear could be engaged and off it went. It was extremely cold riding this machine but the deal included a set of riding gear, being rubber trousers and coat. These were very good but on very cold days, I had to pad my front and chest with newspapers. Often I would arrive at work frozen stiff and would not thaw out till lunchtime. Still, it was better than riding a pushbike to Glengormley to meet the crew car. It went quite well, was economical and I never thought of taxing or insuring it. There was one drawback - I frequently fell off it. Either the roads would be icy, or in good weather, on the country roads, I would skid on patches of horse manure and come crashing down. I was never seriously hurt, due to so much padding, but the moped suffered. The exhaust fell off. Then the clutch broke and to get going, I had to put it in gear, push it, running beside till the engine fired and then leap on, for I could not disengage the gear and off it would fly. Then the number plates, head light and mudguards fell off and finally the brakes failed. The only way to stop was to throttle right down and chug to a halt. In emergency I had to drive into the ditch.

It kept going for quite a while and served me well. It was also fun riding across on the fields on it. Occasionally I would have to ride it into Belfast, for an early start at the terminal. One afternoon coming home, it ran out of fuel on the main Antrim Road. I dismounted and parked it against the kerb and set out in search of fuel. On my return to the spot, there was no sign of the machine, so I gave up and took the next country bus home. On the way up the road I looked out as we were passing the police station, only to see my moped sitting at the front of the building. I thought of getting off and claiming it, but remembering the state that it was in and my lack of necessary documents, I decided to leave it for the moment. I would return in the night and quietly remove it I thought. On further reflection, I abandoned this idea, for police stations were heavily guarded even in those days before the major troubles and so I abandoned the moped as well.

My next immediate need therefore was for a mode of transport. Near where we lived, on the way to the airport via Templepatrick, before the major M2 and airport roads were built, was a second-hand car dealer recently set up in business. Though I was earning a reasonable wage I never had a penny to my name each week, for I spent it as it came in. So I bought an old 1937 Ford Popular, with running boards and front mudguards and mounted headlights, for £25. It was pretty rough but went very well and had a very reliable, though basic four-cylinder engine. It had no heater and the roof leaked, but it would start in any weather and was reliable. This served me for a period and was a great improvement on the moped.

Another friend was a rare character. He had been at BEA for some years before I joined, but had had a period of illness, which had left him very thin and pale. He had red hair and a straggly red moustache and a pallid complexion with clapped in cheeks. He was stooped and his chest seemed to cave in as well. He smoked a pipe and was always covered in ash, all down the front of his uniform. He would sit during quiet periods with his legs entwined in a knot, smoking and filling in football pools, for he ran a syndicate for Zetters Pools. He was a kindly soul and very helpful to all but he was a demon with the ladies, unable to let one pass without either commenting or fondling. He worked in Load Control with me and once complained in tears to the Duty Officer that he could no longer work with that fellow Frazer, for he shouted too much. He was well known by the stewardesses for he would come up the aircraft steps to deliver the ship's papers for the flight. The pilot had to peruse them and sign them in triplicate before take-off. Any stewardess at the top of the stairs, could expect to be embraced, along with a leering grimace. How he got away with it I don't know, but they all took it in good part and laughed it off. He was well-known, everyone liked him and made allowances for him.

He surprised us all one day, by announcing that he was getting married to a Swiss girl from Zurich. Her father had an expensive leather goods business in down town Zurich and she was a pleasant lady. I don't know how or where he had met her, but she came to live in Ireland with him after the wedding, so I met her then.

A number of his colleagues were invited to the wedding in Zurich. It turned into a riotous occasion and we heard many outrageous reports of the event. A cine film had been made of the proceedings by one of the guests and an evening was set aside at the airport for us all to see it. It was hilarious. The cameraman must have been drunk, for all we saw were flashes of sky and trees, alternating with rows of people's legs and feet and not a recognisable person in it, not even the bride and groom. I never laughed so much. However, the marriage turned out well and they had a couple of children. I did hear, several years after I had left and was working in London, that my friend had died, but I don't know exactly when and at what age.

Meantime, I got to know Elsie Bunting and asked her out for an evening, to a dinner and dance at the Wellington Park Hotel on the Malone Road. I turned up at her house in the old Ford car. She appeared dressed to kill and looked somewhat startled when she saw the state of the car. Off we went. It was a lively evening and we met several people we knew but when it came to dancing, we were not at all compatible, my style quite unsuited to Elsie's hesitant steps and demure approach. Overall the evening was a bit of a flop and I left her home without further ado, thinking that was that.

With three or four colleagues, I decided to go to a party in

Manchester and set off for the weekend. The party went well and I met a large attractive blonde girl and we got quite friendly and we enjoyed the party. Unfortunately, fog set in and when it came time for us to return to Belfast, flights were cancelled. It was imperative for us to get back, for we were all on duty the next day. So we decided to take a taxi to Blackpool, where we hoped we might be able to get on a Silver City Airways flight. I had never been to Blackpool and looked forward to the trip. When we got there the weather was atrocious and it seemed to be the most miserable place ever. Nevertheless a flight was going to Belfast and we managed to find places. The plane was an old Dakota, seating about 36. BEA used to fly these aircraft. They were very reliable but slow, propeller driven and not pressurised, so had to fly at a relatively low altitude. We took off in the driving rain and swirling mist and were just able to discern the famous tower through the gloom. We were amused, when the stewardess stood at the front and made her announcements without tannoy and with the roar of the engines, she was almost inaudible. Of more concern, was an apparent leak from the roof, as a trickle of water appeared but we arrived safely to report for duty.

BEA were still flying a number of Dakotas when I joined. Indeed, Father had taken us on holiday to the Isle of Man, when I was about 14 years of age, in the Summer of 1951 on one such aircraft. That was a great novelty for myself, brother and sisters, for we had never flown before. We stayed in the Grand Hotel on the seafront at Douglas. Joe Loss and his band were the resident attraction at the dance hall and I enjoyed listening to the big band sound and seeing the large ballroom awhirl with gyrating bodies. We toured the island, saw the Laxey Wheel, sampled Manx kippers and had some sent home to us afterwards and rode on the horse-drawn tram along the promenade. It was quite a happy occasion.

A couple of weeks later, I decided to ask Elsie out again. We decided to go to the cinema but instead finished up going for a drive and things began to look more promising. By the end of the evening we were getting on so well, that it was the start of a four-year friendship and we went about everywhere together. Marriage was never mentioned, except by other people embarrassingly asking,'When's the big day?' and similar irritating remarks, which if anything, made us the more determined never to get married. To make up for missing the pictures on that occasion, I decided to take Elsie to the Ritz to see Dr No, with Sean Connery as James Bond. My old school friend, Barry Quin, who had been to Bird's Eye with me, asked if he could come too!

Just after my return from Milan and before I joined BEA, I enlisted as a pupil with Mr Frank Capper for singing lessons. He charged high fees for weekly half-hour lessons. Everything was done in an orderly manner. You arrived on time and went in and the previous pupil went out without ceremony. You had your half hour and that was all. Capper's method was to place the voice forward, as if 'singing through the eye of a needle' , from the bridge of the nose. First of all he tested me for solar plexus and diaphragm strength. With rowing, I had built up great strength in my solar plexus. Putting me against the wall, he placed his fist in my midriff and levering himself against the grand piano with his other hand, he pushed with all his strength, without making any impression. Next, he stretched his hands, fingertips together in a V shape and pushed his fingers into my midriff with all his might, again without making any impression on me. He was impressed. Support of the breath in singing is very important. However, freedom of the throat, allowing the breath to pass over the vocal chords, with space in the mouth, for the tone to resonate in the head cavities is equally important. This method of enormous pressure of the diaphragm against tone through the nose leads to bad habits of 'squirting' the voice. My voice was naturally high and didn't need this approach at all. Of course I didn't realise this early on and carried on as instructed. I suffered constant bad throats as a result. This method may be successful for singers who concentrate on Lieder or such composers as Benjamin Britten, but for Italian opera the voice needs to be opened up to allow it to rise above the passaggio, in the case of tenors around F or G, otherwise the voice tightens and the tone becomes hard. I continued with Mr Capper for a couple of years but felt frustrated and left, for I considered that I was making no progress at all.

On a visit to Milan some years later, I was taken to meet a lady, Signora Lerario-Grassi. She had been a repetiteur at the San Carlo Opera in Naples and had set up as a coach, in her Milanese villa. She was quite famous and Mario Del Monaco was a particular friend, who went to her to rehearse from time to time. Her room was padded, not because singers are mad, though often the case, but because the noise from screaming opera singers, without padding to absorb the decibels, would eventually damage the hearing irreparably. She put me over a few scales, quickly interrupting to push the voice down, quite contrary to my previous method and not dissimilar to what Piccaluga had been telling me. Having placed the voice, she then asked me what I would sing. I suggested an aria from Mascagni's opera Iris - Apri la Tua Finestra. She had a very large bookcase crammed with scores and took it down immediately. Adopting her method, I sang the aria with abandon on an open throat to such good effect, that a tenor waiting outside, rushed in applauding me. He was preparing to sing at the Arena di Verona. Eric was with me and he rushed out to Elsie who was in the next room, exclaiming, 'Did you hear that?' Lerario-Grassi was highly pleased. I then sang the duet 'Solenne in Quest Ora' from La Forza del Destino, with Eric, to our mutual satisfaction. This was one of our favourite party pieces. I was only able to go to la Signora two or three other times, for I couldn't travel to Milan every week. On a subsequent visit back to see F Capper, for we had remained friendly, I sang for him and his response was 'What has happened to you to effect such improvement?'

That was some years after BEA and when I was living in London. Meantime, Elsie and I carried on meeting and going to places together and we were preparing to move to a new airport terminal at Aldergrove, which was the military airport used only by the RAF. Nutt's Corner was a series of one-storey buildings and was becoming inadequate for the continuously growing traffic which it had to handle. A major event occurred in February 1963, the year of the 'big snow'.

We had arrived on a Monday for the late shift starting at 2

p.m. Snow had been forecast and was already falling, as the early shift prepared to go home by crew car into Belfast. It came on very heavily and the outgoing crew car got stuck in a snow drift halfway down the Black Mountain. The passengers were able to trudge to the safety of a country pub, unable to move further, as the snow continued to build up. At the airport, all flights were abandoned as drifting snow built up to the height of the telegraph poles, and it covered the terminal buildings. We were also marooned. Somewhere in the car park, my old banger was buried in six or eight feet of snow. There were about ten of us snowed in.

With all flights suspended, there was little to do, or which could be done. Luckily all of the passengers had been despatched on the lunchtime flights. Some of the canteen staff were still around, so we were able to get food while it lasted. The Duty Officer had the key to the safe, so we were able to get an advance on our pay and the barman was marooned with us. He kept the bar open according to official rules, adhering to opening and closing times. Thus we were supplied with that diversion, now having the wherewithal to pay for drink consumed. We were fortunate that heat and light remained in operation, so we began to enjoy the new-found leisure to avoid boredom setting in. The early shift members were not faring so well, marooned as they were in a small country pub with few amenities. After two days we received telephone calls for help, for their drink and food had run out. They were sitting on the beer crates, lacking enough furniture to afford any comfort. The main cry was for food supplies, even though they had drunk the pub dry by this time as well.

The Airport Commandant, not a BEA man, whose dwelling was on the airport complex, suggested that he would ski down the mountain, taking supplies from the canteen, if he could get a volunteer to go with him. One big fellow volunteered, saying that he could ski. It turned out that he had had only one skiing holiday in his life and had very limited ability in that direction but he did not mention this. Finally kitted up and laden with food supplies, the two started out from the back exit of the terminal buildings. The Commandant reached the

141

front end but there was no sight of our colleague. Not wishing to waste further time, the Commandant decided to go ahead leaving instructions for the other fellow to follow on. Snow began to fall again but the Commandant was quite expert and arrived at the pub bringing relief to the beleaguered. Meantime, his companion had managed to get beyond the airport perimeter but was floundering. He managed to get to a phone box on top of a hill where he was marooned, exhausted and unable to go on. He phoned for help. The situation was serious but at the same ludicrous and hilarious. He was given directions by someone who knew the area well, how to get to a nearby farmhouse and safety. This was only the start of a series of ridiculous events.

Some of the engineers were also marooned and were servicing an aircraft in the hangar. One of the chaps fell off a wing and broke his arm and was in need of medical attention. A helicopter sent to collect him crashed in the snow, luckily without loss of life and another was despatched. It managed to land, but when the door was opened, it blew off in the blizzard. However, in spite of this mishap, the injured man was loaded aboard and taken safely to hospital.

We continued to drink at the bar, card schools were constantly in action and our own food supplies were running low. In spite of the situation, the barman stuck rigidly to his code of regulations, dispensing liquor as required by his customers. The only concession he made to breaking his rules, was that he drank plenty himself and was often plastered. He would lock up the bar at night, pull down the shutters and subside behind the bar into an inebriated slumber. It was hilarious in the morning at opening times, to see a hand fumbling up over the counter followed by the appearance of a bedraggled head, peering blinkingly around as the body gradually emerged. So opening up, it was back to business.

We were able to dig our way to the outside and get across to the runway, which was not so deeply piled with snow, due to the fact that, being open territory, the snow had drifted across and not piled as it had against buildings and hedges, where it was above the height of the telegraph poles. Eventually it was

142

possible to get a snow plough to begin clearing one of the runways and fire engines were able to run up and down, helping to disperse the slush. Somewhere across at a local farm, a funeral was taking place and it was a startling sight to see from a distance, a coffin apparently drifting across the snow, for the pall-bearers were moving below the line of sight, in a trench which had been cut in the deep drifts. I can see it yet, for it was like something out of a 'Carry On' movie. It was pleasant in the open air and interesting to walk down the middle of the runway, right to the perimeter fence. We were beginning to get a bit bored by now and with less than ideal sleeping conditions, the situation was becoming less amusing. We were beginning to stink for want of clean clothes. The Duty Officer, who lived in the vicinity, decided that he would try to make his way home on foot. We had reports that he had suffered a heart attack from his exertions and had to seek assistance. Those reports turned out to be somewhat exaggerated and the suspected heart attack was merely over-exhaustion.

Elsie and her friend, Annabel, offered to wash the men's shirts, which was gratefully accepted. They collected them off us, leaving us in our underwear, whilst they washed them with soap and water in the basins of the Ladies Cloakroom. There were several other amusing and outrageous events which modesty prevents me from relating. Suffice to say that some reputations were ruined forever. Some good came of our ordeal, for with the bad weather throughout Britain, many football matches were cancelled. Our pools syndicate expert was able to take advantage of this and by clever selection of permutations, was able to cover all eventualities and ensured a win on the Zetters' weekly pools entry, netting us £28 for each member of the syndicate, which was gratefully received, considering that it represented almost three weeks wages. We were able to be relieved on the Friday afternoon, having been incarcerated since the previous Monday and the crew car came to remove us. We hoped for and expected to be given a few days off, but the management insisted that we should report for our early shift start on Sunday and refused us any overtime allowance, saying as we had done no work (there wasn't any to do), in the circumstances, no allowance would be made for our enforced 24 hour days on the premises. My car remained buried under the drifts, so I suggested to Elsie that she should stay over at her sister's house in Glengormley and that I would collect her there for the early start on Sunday, using the large van which would be better to negotiate the prevailing road conditions.

Things had meantime been equally difficult at home but with the tractor and a lot of effort, they had been able to forge a way down the lane to the main road, where the snow had been opened up, leaving it still piled high on each side, so that you were driving through a chasm. It took several weeks to thaw out. When I went to collect Elsie early on Sunday morning, I was unable to reach the house and had to carry her on my shoulders, through the drifts to the van on the main road. Some of our exploits featured in the BEA News, circulated throughout the airline and even today, forty years after the event, people still talk of the 'big snow' and the things that happened at the airport.

CHAPTER 16

The next major upheaval was to move to the new, modern terminal at Aldergrove. New aircraft had come into service in the shape of the Vanguard, a large propeller driven aircraft, capable of carrying over 200 passengers and increased loads of cargo, in its capacious holds. These gradually replaced the Viscounts which had superseded the Dakotas, which were by then phased out. Aldergrove was a great improvement in terminal facilities and general working conditions. However, such was the pace of increasing traffic, that already the buildings were inadequate and a continuous programme of improvements and additions took place for many years, culminating in a modern international airport, capable of handling all types of aircraft, including Concorde and even Air Force One, when Clinton, the US President visited the Province, to encourage the move towards peace, after 30 years of conflict.

At Nutt's Corner we had met many celebrities passing through. Elsie met the heavyweight boxer, Sonny Liston, a giant of a man with enormous shoulders, accompanied by a number of minders. In spite of his reputation of being a mean 'hombre' he responded pleasantly to her when she asked for his autograph, which he was pleased to give, asking her to be patient, saying, he 'wrote awful slow'. Helen Shapiro, the young pop singer with an even greater entourage, came through. Frankie Vaughan, Wilfred Pickles, the Beatles and many others passed through, having appeared in shows in Belfast. I was particularly interested to meet a group of professional wrestlers, who were frequently seen on TV. Tournaments were often held in the Ulster Hall, which I attended occasionally, and it was amusing to see them all together, laughing and friendly, considering the maulings they had been giving each other in the ring the previous evening.

On 21st Dec.,1961, I dealt with the hangman, Albert Pierpoint, who that day had carried out the last hanging in the UK. His victim was one Robert McGladdery, who had killed a lady called Pearl Gamble. Throughout the trial, he had protested his innocence, only admitting his crime at the final moment. I had mixed feelings but had to do my duty at the Ticket Desk and was surprised to see how unconcerned Pierpoint looked, chatting amiably with his associates, whilst relishing a gin and tonic. Pierpoint was also used for hangings in the Rep of Ireland, till their government decided that if they couldn't hang their own criminals, then the death penalty should be rescinded. Thus public hangings in the Republic ceased before the laws in Gt Britain were changed and hanging was abolished.

Pierpoint was returning to his home, a pub called 'Help the Poor Struggler', which he had run since 1946 and where he died on 11th July 1992 at the age of 87.

Another interesting celebrity, was the American comedian, Lenny Bruce, notorious for his lewd shows. The Home Secretary had banned him from entering Britain to perform his one-man show, for his material was deemed offensive and degrading. To get round this ban he had come in through Dublin in the Rep of Ireland and travelled up to Belfast intending to take a flight to London, for there were no immigration or border controls to prevent him from crossing that way. A direct flight from Dublin to London would have entailed Customs Clearance. At the last moment, at the airport counter, he asked to send a telegram of apology to the Home Secretary, hoping to change his decision and to let him in to fulfil his contract to perform. His plea was refused and he was deported on landing in London.

Sammy Davis Jnr was another interesting character who appeared with his wife and only one piece of baggage, a brief case containing $10,000 which he said he always carried with him.

The move to Aldergrove had a subduing effect. The town terminal was closed and all operations were transferred to the airport, with a new, frequent coach service to and from the city. This meant that the Town Supervisor had to work at the airport, which he didn't like so much. Several of the 'characters' had left and a new regime took over. It was no longer 'Crackers Bend' and a new sense of purpose seemed to prevail. Air traffic continued to grow, the airport continued to expand and UK operational procedures had changed, resulting in fewer night-stopping crews. New Shuttle services were introduced between Belfast and London, with very cheap rate flights operating more frequently, making use of the large capacity Vanguards. The Comet aircraft had been introduced, bringing us into the jet age.

Elsie and I were now going steady and she had a calming influence on me, for she was eminently sensible, level headed and efficient, as well as being popular with her colleagues. Whilst at Nutt's Corner she had been amused if a little irked, when meeting Manchester flights, at being asked by various friends, if Ronnie Frazer was on duty. This did not spoil our relationship and we often laughed about it. I was frequently required to help out at the business which, with working different shifts at BEA, meant that I had little time or energy for many extraneous pursuits. Elsie had no lack of her own admirers. A couple of flight captains had the temerity to phone her at home, to be told curtly by her father that she already had a boyfriend and would not be interested. This greatly embarrassed her when they mentioned it to her.

Whilst we lived at Ballyrobert we used to go to the local church at Ballylinney, where the Rev McConnell was the minister. He became a great friend of us all. Father acted as relief organist and sang in the choir and was appointed an Elder of the church. In the early days, the regular organist was George Gibson, already mentioned when he visited Milan. He was a fine musician though not a great accompanist and he taught the girls piano lessons. He was eccentric but could play anything in any key, even though his ability as an accompanist was limited by his super sensitivity as a musician. Singers take particular liberties to express themselves in phrasing, rubato and rallentando. He kept strictly to the composer's notes and time signature. The Rev McConnell had also been a pianist and in his youth had gone weekly by boat to Liverpool for lessons. He composed music and was a writer and he and Father would go once a year to a spa at Crieff in Scotland. He often attended parties at our house and with him and George Gibson, Mother and Father, who by this time had taken up the violin, and Fred who was having trumpet lessons with a member of the Ulster Orchestra, we would make lively music. Valerie and Winifred were good singers, who often performed duets at church when they were children. Val was a mezzo and Win a high soprano in the Galli-Curci mode. She was encouraged to take up singing and could sing a high F with ease. She wasn't interested for she said that she didn't want to grow into a fat lady, her idea of an operatic soprano. Valerie was a pianist and in her later years, she became President of the Monterey Opera Company in California, where she still sings in the chorus.

The Rev McConnell was a character. He came from a Ballymena family, where they had had a boot and shoe factory and he was of independent means. He served Ballylinney Church for about 40 years and never took his stipend, donating it instead to the good works of the church. He lived in the large Manse on Hillhead Road outside Ballyclare, shared with an elderly housekeeper, Miss Steele, who was a devout member of the Plymouth Brethren sect.. He treated her as an equal and she often accompanied him on visits to our house. When visiting him at the Manse, he would usher you into the kitchen when her back was turned and ply you with a couple of quick shots of whiskey from a bottle secreted at the back of a cupboard. He would often, with a twinkle in his eye, condemn the purchase of Sunday papers, but always came round on a Monday to collect ours which had been discarded. He drove an old Austin Ruby and I would pass him on the back road on my bicycle for he never exceeded 20 m.p.h. He was kindly to us all and I still have his written reference, which he gave to me before I went off to Italy. When he eventually died of a heart attack, we were all greatly saddened.

Val and Win went to the local Ballyclare High School which had a fine record for academic achievement. Val became Head Girl and was determined to become a doctor. Nothing would dissuade her and she insisted on going to Trinity College, Dublin, for which she was fortunate enough to achieve a scholarship. She went on to become an eminent Consultant Paediatrician in America. Winifred went on to Queen's University, Belfast, where she took her degree and became an Archaeologist. She took a job at the Ulster Museum and became Curator of Ethnography. She was to publish widely in archaeological and historical journals. She produced written and illustrated catalogues of the museum's collections and her latest book, 'Exploring the Spanish Armada', was produced by the O'Brien Press of Dublin, in October 2000.

Fred, being older, didn't take much to do with us and had a few friends of his own. We all attended church for Father and Mother were regular church goers and there was quite a lot of social activity, which we joined in occasionally. There would be such events as Beetle Drives or concerts, where ladies would 'do recitations', sing or show lantern slides. There would always be supper served, but many of the sandwiches were not palatable. Trifles and cakes would be consumed with gusto. There were some very attractive young ladies in the congregation. Everyone was encouraged to join in such activities as Treasure Hunts and Charades. It was noticed that the piano in the church hall was sounding sluggish and there was something of an odd smell around it. On taking off the front panel, it was found to be stuffed with mouldy sandwiches.

Father had allowed the local football team to use one of our fields, at the Belfast Road entrance, which was used as their home ground and matches were played there. This was at the back entrance to the farm which we used when going on foot to the Post Office. One Saturday, when returning home, Mother and I were surprised to be stopped at the gate and asked for an entrance fee, as a match was in progress. The official was somewhat embarrassed to discover that this was our field, for which they had free use themselves.

Nearby was the Lisnalinchey Horse Racing Course, where we went to the point-to-point races annually. Tom Frazer always came, for he loved a flutter. It was a popular venue, attracting a large crowd and it was difficult to get parked. Local farmers were able to take a charge for parking in their fields, which to me sounded like a good racket. I liked the horses and the races when in progress, but there always seemed to be too much time wasted between them. I could not make head nor tail of the betting, but Tom always had a good tip and could work out odds and winnings instantly. The favourite spots were by the jumps and people would cross the track when races were in progress, to get a better vantage point. I remember vividly, when some horses had passed, a fellow ran across below the high jump. A following horse landed on him and I heard the sickening crunch of his skull as the horse's hoofs smashed into it. He lay there while the blood gurgled from his mouth until the course was cleared and the ambulance men came. They carried him off on a stretcher, under a blanket, leaving a blood-stained patch on the ground.

The Dundrod Grand Prix racetrack was not far away, over towards the airport, down the Seven Mile Straight by Clady Corner and round by Dundrod Village. We went once, but the noise was deafening and the smell of engine fumes and burning rubber and the cars screeching round the corners, caused me such discomfort, that I never expressed a desire to go again. In addition, the effort to get there through the dense crowds and the difficulty of getting parked and then out again, were the clinching factors. It was a popular venue, attracting the greatest drivers and it operated for several years.

The farm next to ours was owned by the Bamfords. I think he was Major Bamford, but I never saw him or his wife. They had a daughter called Valerie. She was a blonde beauty, who rode a white horse and she was a magnificent sight as she appeared at the Post Office shop, where we used to help out as children. She was much admired in the community and she eventually went away to be married.

The Ballyclare May Festival was held each year and lasted several days. It offered various types of entertainment and activities. Horse and goat trading took place and stalls sold various goods and homemade products. Competitions were held. A large lorry trailer was used as a stage and children might get up and dance or sing. Onion eating contests took place, with fellows stuffing their mouths with raw onions, the tears streaming down their faces, to see who could consume the most in a short time. Likewise, scone eating contests took place. Wheaten scones, dipped in syrup, were hung on a string. The scones had to be eaten by contestants, with their hands secured behind their backs. The syrup dripped all over them. Usually, at the first bite the scone would fall off the string, resulting in the participants grovelling around on the stage, trying to finish them off. The messiest game of all was the greasy pole. A telegraph pole was plastered in axle grease and erected. Contestants would try to climb up the pole to try to snatch a prize from the top. Very few made much progress upwards as they embraced the pole, being immediately covered with the black grease. Eventually, a group of three or four lads were successful, by climbing up one on top of the other, to reach the top before collapsing. It was all good 'clean' fun!

The Music Festival was also held, though I don't recall if it was around the same time. Certainly, we used to go to it. This attracted entries from many areas, for competition in solo singing, operatic and oratorio singing and there were competitions for various types of instrument. The solo singing usually included one set piece which all competitors had to perform. Mr Symmons attended once and asked for his money back for he objected to paying to hear the same song sung over and over again. This brought perplexed frowns from the attendants, but of course it was a joke. I attended to hear the operatic class which was free choice of item to be sung in the original language or in English. A young lady called Mary Bell sang 'One Fine Day' from 'Madame Butterfly'. I was used to hearing it in Italian, but her English rendering was most beautiful and the clearly enunciated words remained in my memory, so pretty were they and so delightfully performed. That was at least 40 years ago.

Fred and Bobbie Alexander, a part-time farm hand, tried several farming initiatives. One, was the bright idea of going around local farms, near Christmas time, to purchase fowl, which would be plucked and prepared for sale to local butchers. I was assigned as the chicken plucker and set up the operation in the lower byre which was free. Much of the herd had been dispersed by this time and only a few bullocks were grazed for slaughter. There was not a ready supply of fowl to be had, but a few scrawny hens were brought in and I set to work, plucking them in a welter of dust, feathers and fleas, till my eyes and nose were streaming and my asthma recurring. Thank goodness, this was soon curtailed when, after one particularly fruitless sortie, they were offered one lame, bedraggled bird, by some old farmer in the outback. Fred's accomplice, a man of the sod, said 'Sure ye wouldnae thow yon tae a gru' ('Sure you wouldn't throw that to a greyhound'). So the venture floundered and I was saved further indignity.

Fred had acquired a Triumph TR 2 sports car and took great pride in it. I was allowed to drive it occasionally but I didn't like it, for it was not a good road-holder in my opinion, being too light at the back and hard to control. In frosty conditions one night I tried to negotiate a sharp bend, with a down-hill slope, on a road outside Larne. The back skidded and I hurtled backwards through a wire fence into a field and was saved by a telegraph pole just inside, which brought me to a sudden halt, thereby probably avoiding having my head sliced off by the wire strands of the fence. This left a large dent in the back of the car. I was able to regain the road and visited my friends at Drains Bay before returning home. This was just before I went to Italy. Unknown to me, the number plate had fallen off the back, in the field. It was handed into the police, who later turned up looking for the owner of the car. Fred admitted that it was his and when asked who had been driving, told them it had been his brother. 'Where is he?' they asked. Fred told them I had gone to Italy and when they asked when I was coming back, he said I wasn't, so they went away.

Some time later, Fred had a serious accident while going down the Antrim Road towards Belfast. Just before Bellevue, he skidded violently and smashed into a wall. The car was bent double and completely wrecked. Fred and his passenger were injured, his companion sustaining broken ribs. A picture of the mangled wreck appeared in the evening paper and made head-line news. The injures were not fatal, but it was a salutary lesson and the end of Fred's involvement with sports cars.

Fred decided to leave the business to seek a more satisfying career. He consulted Col Halpin back at school, for guidance and advice on career prospects with the Army. He enlisted and trained at the Army School of Physiotherapy from 1959 to 1962. He served in Germany for a while. On rejoining civvy street, he became District Physiotherapist for the South Birmingham Health Authority and was the first to achieve a Doctorate for his thesis on the care of the elderly. He was a member of the Chartered Society and achieved BA Hons and PhD degrees. His book 'Rehabilitation within the Community' was published and he lectured widely to the medical profession, writing frequently for the medical and physiotherapy journals: a fine record considering his poor showing at school and a worthy rejoinder to the Head's criticisms.

Father had suffered severe back pains for a number of years and was finally diagnosed as having kidney trouble in 1957, when he was taken to hospital. He had a very large kidney stone removed, which was given to him in a jar to take home. He kept it for some time, a gruesome reminder of the years of pain. It was at that time that he decided to withdraw from farming and to disperse the livestock, to let the land for grazing. With the business reduced, due to the impact of cash and carry and the advent of supermarkets, it was now more manageable, having moved to Ballyrobert. He decided to sell off the Post Office and shop, at the cross-roads, although Mother advised him to sell off the farm instead and to transfer all operations to the other business at the shop. She suggested extending the house there and thus, have a wholesale/retail outlet and dwelling altogether. With hindsight, that would have been the better option, but Father was not easily persuaded. His health seemed to have improved and so I had joined BEA, helping out with the business as required, although several employees remained.

Elsie and I spent a good deal of our spare time together. My old car was giving trouble. It had survived the 'big snow' all right, but the roof which was soft padded and covered in waterproof fabric, had lifted at the edge during the storms. It eventually blew off, unwrapping the folds of padding material underneath. Elsie had to use an umbrella inside the car. The passenger side door was also tied on, for the hinges had given way and the driver's side running board was flapping. Nevertheless, we decided to take a trip to Enniskillen to meet my old House Master, who had retired to a bungalow on the outskirts of the town. We arrived in the vicinity and passed the house of my old History Master, D A R Chillingworth, who still worked at the school. I took the opportunity to visit him first. He was pleased to see me and approached the car to be introduced to Elsie. I was just shouting 'Don't touch the door!' when he wrenched it open and it came away in his hand. He stood for a moment, looking mildly surprised, with the door in his hand and without a word, he handed it to me and helped Elsie from the vehicle.

The last time I had seen Mickey Murfet, I had travelled up with my friend Barry in a Rolls Royce. It was actually his father's car. He was blind, so Barry always assumed control of the family car. When he was at school they had an official chauffeur. Barry's father was Senator Quin, a senior partner of the accountancy firm, Stewart, Blacker, Quin & Knox. He was also a barrister at law. He had invited me on one occasion, to lunch at Stormont with the Northern Ireland Prime Minister, Capt Terence O'Neill. It was very interesting to sit in such august company and to sense the power of authority exerted by the head of government, as he sat there, surrounded by his acolytes. I never entered Stormont again till years later, when I performed in a concert there in the Great Hall with the Castleward Opera Company. It is an impressive building.

Mickey was delighted to see Elsie and me and we were to meet him on future occasions in London, when we were living there. Barry and I had visited him several times before and he was always glad of the company, for in retirement, he was quite bored. He had even visited Milan on one occasion when I was there and entertained me to lunch at Biffi, which had been another welcome free meal.

The old Ford had been very reliable, starting in all weathers and had twice survived being buried in snow, for periods of over a week at a time. It did need a little help in starting in winter, for the battery was flat. I used to park it at night, under the awning between the main barn and the byres. On early mornings, I would have to push it backwards up the yard, often with Mother's help and then run it down, to jerk it into gear and into life. It would often freeze up. To warm it up and thaw it enough to be able to turn the engine, I used to soak a rag in paraffin oil and light it under the sump. When I had it started I would put the burning cloth on the front of the radiator, which drew the flames through the engine. This began to create leaks in the radiator, so I carried a five gallon can of water all the time, to replenish it. Eventually, some of the wiring insulation melted, causing difficulty with the electrics. The driver's side headlamp had also fallen off and was swinging loosely by the electric wiring, against the mudguard, I decided to get rid of it and sold it for £1, to a local lad who had plans to use the engine to drive a power saw. I then bought a neat little Austin Ruby for £50. It was a sturdy bus and comfortable, but came to a sticky end when a friend crashed it and it was written off. I returned to the bicycle, but eventually bought a Ford Consul for £80, which was a beauty, with a reconditioned engine and it seemed almost luxurious.

During Fred's time in the Army, he met and married a nurse from Edinburgh, called Nina. This was about the time when the Danish pop singers, Nina and Frederick, were at the height of their popularity, so Fred and his wife had to put up with a lot of obvious remarks. They lived on Shooter's Hill in Woolwich and Fred worked at the Arsenal. They had a daughter by this time, Deborah, and I visited them by a roundabout way. I had met a lady and her family at the airport ticket desk. They were on their way to Vienna, to join her husband who worked for the Atomic Energy Commission. In course of a pleasant conversation, she invited me to visit them there. I decided to take up this invitation and arranged a ticket to Vienna via London. The flight from Belfast was delayed due to weather conditions, so I hadn't time at London to make my connection to Vienna. I abandoned that venture and went instead to Paris, on a flight just about to leave.

In Paris, I stayed at a hotel on Boulevard des Italiens, near the great opera house and I decided to see the sights and enjoy some French cuisine. It was the opera that attracted me most and I acquired a ticket for a performance of Rigoletto.

The Paris Opera House was designed by the architect, Garnier. It has a commanding presence in the Place de L'Opera, created by Baron Haussmann, under the instructions of Napoleon III and opened in January 1875. It is one of the most splendid opera houses ever built with an imposing exterior and beautiful interior, with wide marble stairways and balustrades, leading to galleries displaying many sculptures of famous singers and composers, painted ceilings and magnificent chandeliers. The auditorium has a capacity of 2131 and boasts the largest operatic stage in the world. Alas, it has since given way to a modern monstrosity, built at the Bastille. I was unaware of it, but the ticket that I had acquired afforded me a seat in the front row of the stalls, beside the conductor's elbow, where I was able to read the score as he turned the pages. I found myself surrounded by the cream of the audience, all attired in evening dress. I have no idea what it cost me. I made acquaintance with a gentleman from Canada, who was sitting beside me. He was on his own, as his wife had been taken ill and so we had a few drinks together, during and after the opera. The performance was notable for the baritone's assumption of the very taxing role of the jester and I enjoyed the tenor's bright tone as well. At the final curtain, when the cast appeared to take their bows, I startled audience and conductor by calling out loud 'Bravo' for the baritone. He heard me and with a gratified smile, bowed in my direction - even the greatest singers hunger after praise and appreciation. The rest of the audience looked at me askance, their applause being more muted.

I had not intended staying long in Paris, but my short visit was curtailed, by the ' Je ne sais quoi' , of the French cuisine in which I had indulged. I succumbed to a severe bout of gastro-enteritis. I managed to survive the trip back to London, but couldn't think of waiting and going on to Belfast, so made my way to Woolwich to stay with Fred and Nina, where I lay exhausted and drained for two days, until I felt well enough to go out. Fred was at work, so Nina, baby Deborah and I, drove around, visiting Lewisham market and doing the shopping. Fred had a small Austin A35 estate wagon, which was easy to drive and easily accommodated the pram and we had a pleasant couple more days together before I returned to Belfast.

CHAPTER 17

In 1963, Fred was posted to Munster in Germany. Nina, by now with a daughter and a son, Andrew, did not care to go at the beginning, so she and Fred bought a house in Belfast, at Newtownbreda and Fred went on to take up his job in Germany. I helped Nina to get installed in the new house and she and the children accompanied me on journeys in the big van to Bangor, Newtownards, Donaghadee and other seaside towns, as I went about my business deliveries. The children loved playing at Ballyrobert, till Nina decided they would go, after all, to join Fred in Munster.

Elsie and I were going about together and we would take Valerie to Dublin for the start of each term at Trinity College. Valerie loved it there and enjoyed the social scene, meeting the best of Dublin society, whilst successfully completing her medical studies and we all had pleasant times together.

At this time, I was getting very fed up with working at the airport, what with the exacting shift work and the apparent lack of prospects, so I decided to leave BEA. This decision was also hastened by the fact that Father had suffered health problems. I was required to help out more in the business. Father had been rushed to hospital, with apparent kidney failure and an operation was required. The extent of his ailment was never fully disclosed and instead of removing a kidney, as had been suggested, he was sewn up again and came home in a few days. It is worth noting that the ambulance left him off at home on a cold day and the house being empty, he had to clamber in through a window to get in. When we came home, we found him sitting in his overcoat, working at his desk. He seemed to recover.

I tendered my notice at BEA, which was reluctantly accepted by the boss. He regretted my leaving, saying that I had proved valuable and shown great promise. He proposed to recommend my transfer onto the Management Training Scheme in London for my ability had been noted on the course. I was flattered of course, more so, as I thought that he didn't like me and this came as a pleasant surprise. However, my mind was made up and I left in August 1963. Elsie too, had been less than happy there and she left three or four months later to take up a position with the Norwich Union Insurance Company in Belfast, where she became the manager's secretary and was highly regarded.

Winifred, meantime, had been working during holidays as a waitress in a hotel in Belfast. After school, she went to Queen's University Belfast and during two summer breaks, went to France as au pair, with a family in St Coeur. They referred to her as Brigitte Bardot, for she was petite, curvaceous, pretty and full of determination. Like the Panerais, the family she stayed with took her around to visit some of the beautiful places in France. Elsie encouraged her to take temporary work with the Norwich Union, where the manager offered her a permanent job with good prospects for a career, which she declined, as she had already determined to become an archaeologist.

Our visits to Dublin continued. Ashley and Cecilia were married in August in 1964 in Milan and they spent their honeymoon in Southern Ireland. Ashley Sullivan, although a third generation Australian, was more Irish than the Irish and he wanted to research his ancestors from Cork, a difficult task, as there were hordes of Sullivans and O'Sullivans, over the decades and centuries. Cecilia wasn't so keen to spend her honeymoon visiting churchyards, graves and public record offices. We went down to Dublin to meet them and along with Valerie, I took them for lunch at the Gresham Hotel, which was very grand in those days. It was located very near to Nelson's Pillar, a major landmark in the city, which, being a reminder of British rule, was a prime target of the IRA, who blew it up in the 70s. That completely changed the character of the centre of the city to my mind, removing one of its most notable sights. Cecilia wasn't feeling too well and Valerie was able to administer a potion, which quickly relieved her discomfort. Ashley and Cecilia went on their travels around County Cork and he eventually wrote a book about the Sullivans and the Kings of Hibernia, tracing the Sullivans back to the Pharaohs in Egypt.

A famous tenor, John O' Sullivan (1878 to 1955), was from Cork. He was noted for roles in William Tell, Les Huguenots, La Juive and Otello and was famous in Paris and Milan in the 20s and 30s. He claimed to have sung the role of Arnold in William Tell, one of the most exacting of all tenor parts, more than 200 times. James Joyce was his great champion and wrote on his behalf to the Editor of the New York Herald, challenging the noted tenor, Giacomo Lauri-Volpi, who had been hailed in the role in L' Opera, to a competition. He claimed that Lauri-Volpi had cut out half of the role, particularly the hardest parts and that Sullivan would match him in singing the entire role, as written by Rossini. He said that this had not been accomplished, except by himself since Francesco Tamagno had performed it at the turn of the century. Sullivan was noted for his very loud high notes. Joyce is said to have created a furore in Paris in 1930, after O' Sullivan had sung one of the difficult arias, by leaning forward from his box, shouting (in French) *Thank you God for this miracle. After 20 years, I have again seen the light.* The only record I have of O'Sullivan is the 'Esultate' from 'Otello', which I can only describe as 'fierce'.

He was very fond of the drink and was sometimes pushed on to the stage, shouting   'What opera am I in and what are the words?' Apparently, he disappeared from the scene in the 30s, along with a Spanish baritone, making their way to Cuba, where they had heard that the rum was cheap. Ashley talks of him with great affection.

Valerie graduated in 1965 and joined us in a trip to Munster in July to see Fred and family. Fred met us at Dusseldorf Airport and we spent a pleasant few days in Germany, visiting Arnhem and other places of interest. Valerie returned to Belfast and Elsie and I flew to Milan, were met at the airport by Dr Panerai and we all went to Tellaro. We stayed at a new hotel, recently built in the village, beside the new church and spent some time visiting the old haunts and dining with the Panerais at their home, as well as visiting the famous fish restaurant in Lerici.

We returned to Milan to stay at the hotel Ariston for a few days, by which time the Sullivans had returned from Camogli. We went to their apartment for dinner, where we met Mrs Ferrando, Cecilia's mother and one of her cousins. We met Craig and Eric, visited our old haunts, but avoided any major incidents or contretemps.

Fred had taken the A35 with him to Germany where he bought a new Morris, so he decided to give the Austin to me. In January 1965 he drove it over with his family and met Elsie and me at Heathrow Airport. He was going back to Germany and Nina and the children were flying to Belfast. I suggested that they should drive with us, for I was taking the car back to Belfast and intended to drive to Stranraer, to take the steamer back to Larne. Nina thought it better to fly for they had already had a long drive from Germany. This was a lucky decision. The weather was bad, flights were delayed and Heathrow was in chaos. They eventually got on a flight and Elsie and I started off, to drive to Stranraer.

There were no motorways then, so without maps or any particular plan, I headed north, aiming for Manchester and Carlisle, where I knew to turn left for Dumfries and Gretna Green, on the way to Stranraer. The journey was about 400 miles. The car wasn't going too well, running on three cylinders most of the time and burning oil. The weather was foul but my determination was undaunted and we kept going. We reached Manchester and drove through it in a fog following a corporation bus, which took us in the direction of the main road going north. We did stop for a meal which cheered us up, for we had got very cold as the heater was ineffective. I pressed on into a blizzard which was starting. Carlisle was still a long way off and I had intended getting an early sailing the next day. The car was sturdy, though the engine was worn and I was determined to keep it going at all costs, whilst it still functioned and I was prepared to drive all night. The snow was quite serious and Elsie thought that we should try to find somewhere to get a bed for a few hours. By now we were in remote countryside and though we did find a place, our knocking was in vain. No one appeared to let us in so we strove onwards for a while. We then decided to stop, to try to get a little sleep in the back of the car by folding down the seats and making as much space as possible. Fred had given me a bottle of brandy for Father, so I opened it and we had a few slugs to warm us and to cheer us up. We tried lying down under a blanket, but the cold defeated us and we couldn't get a wink of sleep, so we started off again.

Disaster struck, not through mechanical failure, but by stupidly running out of petrol, in heavy snow, at the top of Shap Fell, as remote and elevated a place as you could find. There was a small village nearby and I made my way there in the hope of finding fuel. It was after midnight. I found a petrol pump outside a shop beside which was a telephone box. The proprietor's name and telephone number were displayed over the shop front, so I called and received an answer. I explained my predicament but the swine wouldn't come down to open up. I couldn't believe the meanness of the man. The snow was deep and still falling, we were freezing and the place was remote. I cursed and ranted for a while until I warmed up a bit and my brain again took over. I decided we should try to thumb a lift down to Penrith, for there were heavy lorries passing in the night. We had luck and after a time succeeded in getting a lift down the steep road in a large tanker lorry, to a petrol station, where I got a gallon can of fuel. We then had to wait to get a lift back, but as lorries were stopping at the station and cafe, I was able to talk to the drivers and found one who would deliver us back to the abandoned car. It was now well wrapped in a thick covering of snow. We thanked him and I poured the petrol into the tank, cleared the windows, primed the carburettor and finally got the engine started.

We started off again going to Penrith on our way to Carlisle, first of all, replenishing the tank and topping up the oil. The Austin proved its robustness as we travelled on still burning oil and firing on three cylinders and in the cold dawn, passed through Gretna Green. My right foot was frozen, my ankle bent to the angle of the accelerator and I refused to stop till we got to Stranraer. When we arrived, I had to lift my leg off the accelerator and hobble into the terminal to purchase tickets for the next sailing. We made it home to Belfast without further incident. The journey was achieved without maps or planning and in the depths of a severe winter, driving all night.

The car proved its worth. Father had the engine re-bored and the brakes attended to. It became a valuable asset to the business for with the seats folded down, it was as good as a small van.

John, our farmhand, had brought us a dog that had sustained a severe injury to his front leg from a reaping machine on another farm, where he was about to be put down. Valerie put a splint and bandage on the leg, which healed satisfactorily, although it had a permanent bend in it. He was a black and white mongrel collie, which Valerie named Spot and he became a lively and loving companion. He was allowed into the house in the country.

One evening I had invited Elsie to supper at Ballyrobert. My parents were at a concert and Mother had cooked a chicken for us, leaving it covered on the kitchen table. We arrived looking forward to a tasty chicken salad, but could find no trace of the bird. Spot was noticeably quiet, lurking sheepishly under the kitchen table. He had eaten the whole bird, leaving not a trace of it, only a clean dish. Incidentally, the first meal that Elsie had prepared for me when we had been going together for a time, was a tasteless disaster, which did nothing to improve our relationship. She perfected her culinary skills and we have enjoyed her tasty dishes ever since.

Later in the year Father decided to sell the farm, to move back to Belfast, much to Mother's and my delight. We had never liked country dwelling. It was almost full circle for he bought a house on the Cliftonville Road, not far from where we had lived before and Father bought premises in Conlon Street, off the Old Lodge Road, comprising a house, yard and large store at the back, where we installed the reduced business. The house was converted to storerooms and an office. What a pleasure to be back in town, with a bus stop at the door, the business and town centre within walking distance, with past pursuits to be taken up again. The new dwelling was a large Victorian house on three floors, with sitting room, dining room, kitchen, scullery and pantry downstairs. There was a fine large drawing room on the first floor with a bay window, affording Mother great pleasure, sitting looking out and seeing the people passing, commenting on their mode of attire and style of walking. There were five bedrooms and a kitchen upstairs, for the previous owner had a tenant, who stayed with us for a short time. The house came with two pianos, several large and fine sideboards and other articles. Each room had a fireplace, those in the main rooms being of sizeable marble construction with mantelpieces. We had it decorated and Mother's own piano was installed in the downstairs sitting room.

We had brought our faithful dog with us and the white cat was installed in the business premises where she settled in happily. The dog was completely at home in the new house.

I decided that I wanted to get away from the business now that things were settled. I wanted to make some sort of a career for myself and thought of going to London to seek employment and to make a complete break from home. I had been suffering devastating toothache and was taking painkillers for a time. I was thoroughly depressed at my lack of prospects or progress. Several of my colleagues had already resigned before I left BEA. Joe Hawkins became the agent for Weetabix, another friend had gone into insurance, Annabel had gone to work in Gallagher's laboratory, one had died and others had dispersed elsewhere. Dai Madden, another friend and I, had got so far as visiting the Canadian Consulate, to discuss our prospect of emigrating to Canada. After due consideration, we didn't pursue the matter and I left before him. He did leave some years later, went to Spain and set up Paddy's Bar in Sitges, got married and finished up back in England with his wife, running a hotel up North. We all thought that he would never have married for he had had many girlfriends, was charming, with a great line of chat and a Triumph sports car. He had seemed destined for the life of a bachelor. He died.

To earn some money to get to London, I got a job in the textile engineering firm of James Mackie & Sons. They employed a large workforce in their factory and foundry on the Springfield Road. They were specialists in the manufacture of their own patented spinning machines. It was known as a sweat shop, with poor pay, long hours and rigid discipline, but they employed a great many people of all sorts in unskilled jobs. Their fitters and machine makers were, of course, experts. The fitters were sent all over the world to install the firm's machines. It was a most famous company, which had survived wars, depressions and the political strife of Northern Ireland and always resisted all strikes. Their machinery was renowned worldwide and they had a virtual monopoly of the linen industry through the efficiency and ubiquity of their flax and jute spinning machines.

I was engaged to work in their Bought Goods Store on the Springfield Road, just off the Falls Road and not far from The Royal Victoria Hospital. Work hours were 7 a.m. starting to the sound of a hooter, to 4 p.m., with a short lunch break. Basic pay was low, but overtime could be worked if you could stand the pace. If you arrived late, you would be admitted up to 7.15 a.m., a quarter hour pay docked from your wages, any time after which, you were locked out and lost a day's pay. If you were late more than twice in one week, you would be turned away for the day. Bought Goods were everything brought in, which the company did not make itself and included a wide variety of nuts, bolts, screws, washers, ball bearings of all sizes, grinding wheels, springs, rivets, split pins and so on. These had to be received, unpacked and stored in great 'bins' - racks of deep, steel containers, into which were shovelled tons of washers and loose nuts and screws. Steel shelves to the ceiling carried packets of screws, ball bearings and other packaged material.

Steel washers of every size, doused in grease to preserve them from rusting, were delivered in skips, to be loaded with a large coal shovel, into the bins. Ball bearings had to be unpacked but retained in their heavy greaseproof wrappings and stacked on the shelves. These were items of fine engineering, mostly coming from Germany in crates and in all sizes, from the very tiny to nearly a foot in diameter. Packets of Allen head and Philip head screws were stacked as well. Grinding wheels were stored at another factory further up the road and occasionally, you could be selected to go there to unload them from lorries, to be rolled into store and stacked up. These were huge 'wheels' of granite or sandstone, up to six feet or more in diameter and were very rough on the hands, particularly in cold weather. I had the temerity to ask for some gloves and was ridiculed.

The foreman was a little Hitler, determined to get the last drop of blood and sweat out of the workforce. You got no rest and were timed going to the toilets, where you had to sit on the lavatory, surrounded by low walls, so that another spy could time you and report back, if you were too long about your business, or if you went too many times. Our little Hitler took pleasure in making me brush the floor. This was better in a way than shovelling washers or other duties, for it gave you the opportunity to get out of the way at times and sit behind a storage bin or climb up on top and lie on your back close to the ceiling. The shop floor workers and fitters' runners, would come to a counter of the goods store, to collect supplies of our wares, according to the requirements of the machines they were building. Varied orders such as six rivets, two dozen Allen screws, 12 washers, numbers of nuts and bolts in every variety, had to be counted into small hessian sacks. If you weren't quick about it, they would shout abuse at you, for they were on piece rates and any delay held up their production. In addition, orders for spares for machines installed abroad, would be received via the Accounts Office, on dockets listing the required items. You might get an order for one screw or nut, or another for 30 different items in different quantities, all to be tied up in the same small sacks and labelled for despatch. In a peculiar way, I quite enjoyed aspects of the job and the camaraderie - a common foe unites! I also had the opportunity to visit the shop floor several times, to see the machines being assembled, in their different degrees of completion. A visit to the foundry, was like a visit to hades. It was like a subterranean hell, with gaunt workers, bare armed in singlets or others covered in protective overalls, their white faces streaked with soot and dust, others in goggles or visors, pouring molten metal from the furnace, sheets of flame erupting and cascades of sparks flying, as the gurgling metal was poured into moulds, everyone sweating in the intense heat and from his efforts.

I worked with a variety of fellows, mostly very decent, in their own rough ways. Amongst them were some sensitive souls and some amusing characters. One was a double bass players in a jazz combo, who would frequently be absent and it was noticeable that these occasions coincided with his appearances on TV. There was a local show called 'Scene Around Six' and he and his colleagues would be seen, backing such singers as Julie Felix, who was famous at the time. He also appeared on religious programmes. He was an amusing and likeable character, but often indulged in too much Guinness and would appear the worse for wear when he came in. Naturally, he missed a day's pay whenever he was off, but he would return to work always with some fatuous excuse for his absence and totally without embarrassment. In any case, this afforded extra overtime to be worked, by those of his colleagues who were more resilient. One such, was a small man, who complained constantly of the state of his health but who would work as much overtime as was available.

He had worked for the RAF in aircraft maintenance and suffered from a skin complaint, brought on by his using dope to coat the fabric of the aircraft. This had resulted in him losing most of his skin and having to receive specialist treatment, by being submerged in baths of liquid paraffin. He had recovered after prolonged treatment, but still had complications which required frequent checks. Where he got his energy from no one knows but when he wasn't working, he would be out around the streets on his pools round, collecting his clients' stakes for the week.

I was friendly with another chap who loved opera and we exchanged views and opinions, enjoying talking about various singers whom we admired. I had no recordings of Caruso in Gounod's Faust and he gave me an LP which contained two excerpts, one a duet, Il se Fait Tard, with Geraldine Farrar, and the aria Salut Demeure, both sung in the original French, which was pleasing for many well-known Italian tenors recorded these items in their own language. The record also contained interesting items from 'Aida', 'Les Huguenots' and two rarities, Quando nascenti tu', from 'Lo Schiavo' (O Escrivo) by Gomes, a Brazilian composer and 'Deserto in Terra', from 'Dom Sebastien, Roi de Portugal', by Donizetti. In return I gave him an LP of Carlo Bergonzi, which contained the famous aria 'Quando le Sere al Placido', which he particularly wanted. I would say that Bergonzi's rendition of that aria was the best on record. These LPs were produced well before the advent of CDs.

The factory was quite near to where we lived and I used an old van for the journey of a mile or so to work. This meant, that as soon as the hooter went for us to stop work, we would rush out and half a dozen of my colleagues would leap into the back of the van, to be transported to their homes around the Shankill Road. Two or three of them would invite me for a Guinness in one of the existing side street pubs. During the troubles of the 70s and 80s, many of these pubs were blown up. In the case of my colleagues, a Guinness meant several pints but my limit was two, which set me up for a good dinner when I got home. One of these companions had a great interest in brass bands and he invited me to attend a major competition in the Ulster Hall, where several well-known bands would be playing, to be adjudicated by a prominent figure in the field. I believe the adjudicator on that occasion, was the famous Harry Mortimer, leader of and player in his own 'All Star Brass Band'. These competitions were taken very seriously, the winners vying for a place in the national finals.

To preserve impartiality, the adjudicator was housed in a high enclosure, so that he could not see which band was performing and could only mark their anonymous efforts by reference to their sequence of appearance. I surprised my companion at the end ,by nominating the eventual winner, he asking how I had done it. I was no judge of brass bands per se, but judged them as I would a singer or instrumentalist, on their purity of tone, sensitivity, legato and general clarity and their precision in ensemble.

An interesting sideline to my very short time working at Mackie's was my meeting a fellow, who amongst his other outside activities, worked as a driver, delivering customers' cars back to base after servicing. One of his jobs was to drive the car of P Rogers, the Headmaster of Portora, to Enniskillen.

This was a rare low-slung sports saloon, an AC it was called, which my colleague enjoyed driving. Naturally, he was somewhat surprised to see a former Portora Royal School Prefect, vice-captain of rugby and lover of grand opera, working in such a 'hell'. Mickey Murfet, my old Housemaster, would have revelled in the knowledge, considering his former disdainful remarks "He did it with his hands."

Mackie's was a tough regime, but they treated junior members of their own family equally harshly. They had to serve their time on the shop floor, learning the business from the bottom. They designed, patented and built their own machinery and dominated the market in flax and jute spinning for many years until the man-made fibres produced by Courtaulds, ICI and British Enkalon, virtually obliterated the flax and linen industry. It was an interesting experience working for them and I met many friendly and pleasant companions. When I left, they gave me a box of chocolates and cards expressing good wishes. Knowing of my intention of going to London, they gave me the names of their friends over there to contact, should I need assistance in finding employment. I remember them with nostalgia and learned much from them and admired them for their fortitude, in facing their daily grind.

CHAPTER 18

It was finally time to go to London. Once again, I bought a one-way ticket, this time 'steerage'. I had enough money to stay for one week in the YMCA, just off Tottenham Court Road, a week to find employment and alternative accommodation. I visited the nearest 'dole' office, to ensure that I was properly registered and documented for employment. The young lady who took my particulars was from Londonderry. When she asked what had been my previous employment and my reason for leaving it, I told her Mackie's and that I had left of my own volition. She regretted in that case, that I would not be entitled to any allowance. On reflection, she said she knew of Mackie's reputation as a sweatshop and didn't blame me for leaving, so would authorize dole relief payment, as appropriate at the time. I thanked her kindly, but said that I did not come to go on the dole, but simply to see that my cards were up to date, for I was in London to seek permanent employment and wouldn't presume on the taxpayer, in the circumstances. This was probably rash of me, for I was virtually broke and any pittance would have been useful. However, having started at the bottom in Mackie's and gone downwards, I was determined to make my way, for I felt that if I accepted handouts, I would never get anywhere.

So I set about seeking a job and visited several employment agencies, many of which abounded at the time. It was always the same: nothing suitable, can't help you, try elsewhere! I went to one of the foremost and well advertised agents. After filling in their forms and the interviewer had read them, he regretted in rather condescending disparaging tones, that I had no experience. I exploded and upbraided him roundly. What did he think I was, some peasant from the bogs, some drop-out non-entity? I reminded that I was an educated person with a considerable working background, whereas he was nothing but a cypher, a glorified clerk, simply placing typists with companies who were crying out for them. What right had he to call himself an employment agent, wasn't it his job to find out what other positions were available and to do a bit of work for his money? I snatched the papers from him and tore them in shreds and stormed out, satisfied with the startled look on his face.

Halfway up the Tottenham Court Road, I found a smaller agency and went in. I was interviewed by a young man with a marked Cockney accent and a down to earth approach. He searched his records and selected a few prospective employers and called them by telephone, emphasising my good points and stressing my varied attributes. I was impressed by his keenness to sell me and allowed him to do his job, without interruption. Finally, I was asked to attend an interview, with the engineering firm of Babcock & Wilcox, whose offices were on the Euston Road and within walking distance. They were looking for a clerk in their Purchase Control Department. The mention of my previous experience with Mackie's in their Bought Goods Store, must have impressed them!

I went for the interview and one of their senior men, Mr Strickland, had a chat with me and showed interest. He explained the nature of the firm's business as being heavy engineering producing boilers for power stations. The clerical position on offer would entail working in their Purchase Control Department, with responsibility for ordering spares for power stations. It was explained that each major power station had a budget of £1m for spare parts. These had to be ordered from various suppliers as the need arose and requests were received from the site engineers. The orders had to be priced from the prospective suppliers' catalogues and chased up, to ensure timely delivery. Price changes had to be noted, for it was inevitable that prices were always going up. I showed interest, my previous experience with nuts, bolts, screws and so on being emphasised and I was offered the job at £12 per week, with canteen facilities on the premises and holiday entitlements. Mr Strickland insisted on showing me round the office, where I met a dozen or so staff, destined to be my future colleagues. Most of them were middle aged to old, except one, who was nearer 40, with a care worn look. As we went round, my guide explained the other sections of the large office, including a group at the end, called the urging section. This was explained later. Pulling aside some large filing cabinets, mounted on rails, revealed an old chap, snoozing in a chair. Mr Strickland explained that this was Fred and that he was getting on a bit, so they tended to leave him alone. This was a distinctly different attitude from my last employers. I said that I was ready to start immediately and it was agreed that I should report at the beginning of the next week. Now I had to seriously look for new lodgings, for the YMCA was full and there would be no possibility to stay there, after my allotted one week for I wasn't even a member after all.

Conditions there were spartan but no worse than boarding school and cheap meals were available. Over the coming days I called at several letting agents and scanned the papers for somewhere to live within my meagre price range. I made several phone calls and began to understand what discrimination must feel like to the oppressed, being made to feel like a criminal on the run. Eventually I approached an agent in Camden Town, advertising a room to let in North Villas at a weekly rental of £2/10 shillings and presented myself there. They requested references and evidence of permanent employment plus a week's rental as deposit, to be held till I moved, which would be refunded if I proved to be a satisfactory tenant. In addition, rent would be paid weekly in advance.

I went to look at the room, which was a little more than a box room at the head of the first landing. It contained a single bed, a tiny hot plate, one kitchen chair and a small table and electric meter. Shared bathroom and toilet facilities were provided on the next floor. However, the house was well maintained and the room was clean, so I agreed to move in the next week and paid my deposit. The good thing was that it was situated more or less within walking distance of Babcock's offices and there were launderette facilities in nearby Camden Town. I quickly grew to hate it, but it served its purpose.

The letting agents, F Scott Ford, were less than pleasant. One day I had forgotten my keys and applied to their offices for the spare set, which was handed over with a very poor grace, by a snivelling clerk. The same happened some weeks later, except that they wouldn't release the keys this time and sent me away. My first reaction was to put a brick through their windows, which I resisted. What to do? My keys were locked in the room, but I needed access via the front door as well. I couldn't hope to kick them both in. Then I had a brainwave. There was a basement flat, accessible by a side set of steps and I had exchanged pleasant words with the elderly lady tenant before now. I approached her with a request to climb through her back window, which gave access to the down pipe of the bathroom, which also passed by my window. Luckily it was slightly open and being of a sash type, would be easily raised. The lady agreed and so I performed my breaking and entering routine again and gained access by climbing up the drainpipe to the window two floors above.

The job proved rather boring but my colleagues were pleasant and offered to show me the canteen. They explained the machinations of the office and were generally helpful. They soon learnt of my straightened circumstances and my lowly dwelling. There wasn't a lot to do, which I found to be tedious. The older gents would play Bridge at lunchtime and spent a good deal of the afternoon analysing their every move. I became friendly with the younger chap and we went to the pub for lunch a couple of times but he couldn't even afford a pint and a sausage, for he had two children and travelled up from somewhere in Kent or Essex. His wife was a nurse.

He was always tired, often slumped over his desk in the afternoon, a result of being bored I thought. On enquiring as to his feeble state, he explained that he had a night job, loading Mothers Pride bread lorries, hence his fatigue. He was a marvellous caricaturist and he could draw ,in full face and form, with detail, a picture of anyone he knew, from memory. He showed me some of his work.

I encouraged him to seek employment in that field, or at least to submit some work to the papers or periodicals and explore the possibilities of making some money to augment his earnings. He had tried, he said, and bemoaned the fact that he could never think of captions to accompany his drawings, so never got an opening. I am sure, with an interested manager or agent, he could have used his talents profitably, but I don't know if he ever did. He presented me with a picture of myself when I left, only a photocopy and I would have liked the original to frame it, but he never released any of his originals at that time. Another photocopy that he gave me, was one of the 'Three Freds', being two former employees and old Fred, previously mentioned, walking together one behind the other, as if in some stage routine, with brilliant attention to detail. I still have them.

Another colleague, but from the 'urgers' section, was a rabid socialist. He hated stockbrokers and those who dealt in or owned shares, working himself into a frenzy in condemning them. He was equally vehement about Royalty and the aristocracy and those with inherited lands. His favourite story was of the Lord who had been asked how he had acquired his lands and estates. He said that he inherited them from his father. How had he acquired them? From his father and so on, back to his ancient forbears. And where did they acquire the lands in the first place? Oh, they fought for them was the reply, whereupon he offered to fight the present owner, for possession forthwith. I used to howl with mirth! The urgers' job was to chase up the dilatory suppliers, for lack of specific spares would be a problem for the power stations, holding up their production and development.

So far so good. I was employed and had established my credentials and was living in a miserable, but affordable room. By avoiding any luxuries, I could keep head above water. My visits to the launderette in the evening were about the only social activity I was able to indulge in. I had one other contretemps with the landlord's agents. I had put an Irish shilling in the meter on one occasion. When it was emptied a month or so later, I was summoned to their offices, like a criminal on remand and accused of the heinous crime, reparation being demanded at once. I was astounded at their pettiness, for the pound sterling and the Irish pound were at parity in those days and it would have been of no loss in the end. In any case the equivalent value today was a mere two and a half pence.

Aspects of the job interested me. Several of the products I had handled in Mackies, were amongst the items I had to order. I learnt something of the various power stations, coal-fired, oil-fired and emerging nuclear power stations, such as Hinkley Point and Sellafield, then being built. Such items stored as spares, included, seamless tubes, grinding balls, and sprayer plates. These were all specialist products. Grinding balls were large steel balls, used to pulverise coal to a fine dust, which was forced like a gas into the boilers, under pressure and fired, creating great heat. Sprayer plates, manufactured to a fine tolerance were used to spray oil through in a fine mist, just like the coal dust, to be ignited. It was of interest to learn that these sprayer plates had been invented by a man in Croydon, working in his garage. They were of such fine quality and precision that he became a major supplier to the industry.

The power station boilers were massive affairs, manufactured at the company's works at Renfrewshire. I never got to visit them but they covered a huge acreage and Babcock's had installed their boilers all over China, Australia and Latin America.

One of my older colleagues was the son of the company's former Chief Engineer in China and the Far East. He had been brought up there but was sent to school at Oundle. He was an inveterate Bridge player, with little interest in anything else. He had married a Russian lady, a virago from Vladivostock, who hounded him, often pestering him at work on the telephone. His response was always a mild 'Yes dear'. His father was 92 years old and insisted that he would play tennis with him every weekend, much to my friend's annoyance, for he was rather stout and totally out of condition. Another older man, married to an Irish woman, used to come to work with liver pate sandwiches, forced on him by his domineering wife. He always gave me these sandwiches for lunch and whilst I was glad of them, I found them much too rich and indigestible.

At weekends, I would wander about Central London, unable to afford even to go to the Cinema, but enjoyed the many street entertainers who performed in those days. There was one old boy who dressed as Admiral Nelson and did a shuffling tap-dance, while singing through a toothless mouth, a drone of a tune, in time with his dancing. He looked feeble but I saw him in London as late as 1999, still shuffling , but not singing. There was a famous band, called the Happy Wanderers, who marched up and down Oxford Street, playing traditional jazz. They were great, but gradually dwindled over the years, to two only and finally disappeared. Another act, was the sand-dancers, dressed as Egyptians, doing a shuffling dance on boards bestrewn with sand, to recorded music. One played an oboe in a wailing manner, to which was attached a string coming out of a basket. As he played Eastern-like snake-charmer music, so he raised the instrument, drawing up from the basket, a tatty brassiere, like a snake emerging.

One day, I came across a fellow singing opera. He had a good voice, of a fine robust quality and was singing some well-known arias, such as E Lucevan le Stelle and Vesti la Giubba. His Italian was of mixed quality, but the tone was good and I took a great interest in his method of voice production. He ignored me, as I prodded his stomach and gently felt his larynx, just as he ignored an American, who was busy recording him, with a cine camera and a tape-recorder. I never found out his name, nor would he tell me much, except to say that he had also been a boxer. He may have been the once famous Jack Doyle, who had gone to America vowing to fight like Jack Dempsey and to sing like Caruso. Critics at the time, reported instead, that he had boxed like Caruso and sung like Jack Dempsey. He became a celebrity and was much lionised by London society, at one time. I never confirmed my suspicions of the street singer's origins, but remember vividly his rich ringing tones, albeit with his invented phonetic Italian. He certainly spoke with an Irish accent.

Elsie and I had been going together for four years and had a good relationship and I telephoned her when I could and wrote quite frequently. It was often difficult to find a public phone box that was working in Camden and when you did, there was usually a queue at it. We decided that she would come over in April for her birthday, which fell on Good Friday and that we would take a trip to Oxford. The weather was intensely cold and before she arrived, I succumbed to a stomach disorder and felt wretched. We decided to abandon the trip to Oxford and instead, booked into the Kenilworth Hotel at Russell Square. This was a wise move and a good night's sleep in comfort did wonders for me and I made a quick recovery. We had a few days in London together and saw the sights. I decided to propose to Elsie that we should get married. She looked at me in some surprise, as if I had lost my senses, having put the moment off for four years without a hint of it. I admit that my prospects weren't great and I had little to offer her at the time, but she finally agreed and so we set about making arrangements and setting a date for the wedding. She returned to Belfast to make the announcement there.

My next problem was where to arrange the wedding, for we both wanted a proper church ceremony to make it meaningful and in deference to both sets of parents, her father being a Church of Ireland Lay Reader. I abhor weddings in Registry Offices, which seems like a meaningless formality. The Rev McConnell had mentioned at some time, the Rev John Stott, Rector of All Souls Church in Langham Place, so I sought him out. All Souls Church is a beautiful building, designed by the architect, John Nash, famed for his town planning and fine terraces in London. The Church sits beside the BBC Headquarters and the Rev Stott was already famed for his preaching and recorded sermons. I did not know this at the time. I made an appointment, explaining my desire to get married in the Church, to which he graciously acceded. However, there were barriers. I would have to publish the Banns, which meant residing in the Parish for a period of about a month. I was advised that this could be arranged, if I could move to a flat, which the church maintained for short lets, for such purposes. This was just off Goodge Street and convenient to Tottenham Court Road and I seized the opportunity to avail myself of the offer. I arranged to leave North Villas at the appropriate time, retrieved my deposit and with great joy, vacated my room.

The flat's greatest asset was its convenience, for it was otherwise pretty basic, but provided a sizeable room and a small kitchen, with bathroom and toilet facilities in the yard below. It was a great improvement on the miserable place I had just left, although a bit dearer to rent. I announced my forthcoming wedding at the office and my colleagues made a collection and presented me with a very useful electric fan heater, which served us for many years and which I gave to my nephew 35 years later.

I was very pleased and grateful for the help from the church and decided I would go regularly and also join the choir there, to show evidence of goodwill. I never liked organised religion, but I went morning and evening, every Sunday and never missed a choir practice. There was a magnificent organ there and the organist, Clark Bedford, was an American, who took a great interest in my voice, often saying that I was singing up a storm, when we performed Bach Cantatas and rehearsed for the Christmas Oratorio. He was a great organist and accompanist and had been a repetiteur at the Metropolitan Opera in New York and he encouraged me to sing solos. Several singers from the Metropolitan Opera, passing through or singing in London, called to visit Clark Bedford and sing at the Church, which was a great thrill for me. One, in particular, was the baritone, Calvin Marsh, on his way to sing Simon Boccanegra, in Geneva. He sang for us. The acoustics of the church were very good and his resonant baritone, flooding the place with glorious sound, was memorable. A few staid old ladies tut-tutted, disapproving of such an uninhibited display in church, which increased my enjoyment. He was a very pleasant man and talked to me, taking an interest in looking down my throat, to reassure me that it was in good order. I never met him again, but I have him on record, as the Herald in Lohengrin, recorded in 1965, with the Boston Symphony Orchestra under Erich Leinsdorf and it is a fine example of his singing. Another baritone, whose name I can't remember, was good enough to sing the duettino from 'La Forza Destino' with me and commended me for my efforts. As previously mentioned, this was a favourite duet for Eric and myself.

We sometimes were required to broadcast on the BBC World Service and a very pretty young lady, who worked in the BBC sound archives, also sang in the choir. She invited me to visit her place of work, which I would have loved to have done, but the occasion never arose. It would have been exciting to hear recordings of some of the great historical performances stored there. The choir was invited each year, to perform at the Whitchurch Festival, which made a pleasant day out. We also had our own orchestra and they and the choir, are now quite famous. We had our moments in 1966/7 of course and I took part in the Bach Christmas Oratorio with them.

Clark encouraged me, by introducing me to a singing teacher, Madame Capiani, who had a studio in St John's Wood, but lived in Tunbridge Wells. She was a Grande Dame of the theatre ,of an imposing presence. She has been a singer, but suffered diphtheria early in her career and an operation had damaged her vocal chords, bringing her career to an untimely halt. I visited her at the studio in St John's Wood during a lunchtime break. She had a companion who travelled with her and who was the accompanist. I elected to sing M' Appari, Tutt' Amor from Marta, an aria much favoured by all the great tenors. I gave a good account of it, which excited and pleased her and she immediately asked me to attend for lessons at her home in Tunbridge Wells each weekend. I had neither the means nor the wherewithal, to travel there and pay for lessons, at the time and only went once. One of the ladies in the choir, a soprano, who also sang solos, invited me to go to meet her teacher, who was the daughter-in-law of the great Elizabeth Schumann. We went one evening and I chose to sing the aria, 'Dai Campi, Dai Prati' from Boito's 'Mefistofele'. My companion played and I sang it quite well, except for a little squeezing of the B flat, towards the end. The teacher commended me, but suggested that I should sing on the 'chords'. This was quite contrary to what I had been taught by F Capper, who had insisted on singing through the nose and so I did not feel happy that her method would suit me. It was only some years later, when I had had advice from Lerario-Grassi in Milan, that I learnt the error of my ways. My hasty decision not to go to the teacher in London, was probably one of the most stupid mistakes I ever made, leaving me to pursue my bad vocal habits for some time, making it all the more difficult to overcome them later.

Meantime the Banns were published and an announcement in the Belfast Telegraph made known the fact that Elsie Bunting and Ronald Frazer were to be married in London, at All Souls Church. Elsie's father provided the money to entertain 20 of her friends and her sisters, to dinner at the Midland Hotel in Belfast, joined by Winifred, where they all had a jolly time. I had a dish of mince beef stew in my lodgings, which was about all I could cook or afford. The wedding date was set for the 29th September 1966. The ceremony to be conducted by the Rev John Stott, Rector of All Souls Church. Clark Bedford would play the organ and as well as the Bridal March, would also play the Widor Toccata, as we left the church.

Both Elsie's and my own father were unwell and would be unable to come over. Father had been in hospital, receiving treatment for high blood pressure, but seemed in good spirits and I was able to go to Belfast a couple of times before the wedding and Elsie managed a visit to London on a Bank Holiday. The film, Dr Zhivago, was premiered at the Odeon Cinema, Leicester Square. We went and enjoyed it greatly. She stayed with her friend, Rene Scott, a model, at her flat in Hans Crescent in Knightsbridge. As the Banns had been published and not challenged, I had to leave the temporary accommodation near Goodge Street and look for another place to stay. I finished up in a room above Nick the Greek's Cafe in Camden Town. The room was much larger than that at North Villas, but a deal seedier. It contained two single, metal, army beds, each covered with a thread-bare blanket. I was the only occupant and the only washing facilities amounted to a 'jaw-tub' under the stairs, with cold running water. The rent was £5 per week, with breakfast and dinner included, from Monday to Friday only. There was a constant smell of fried food. Nevertheless the meals proved to be substantial and tasty. Breakfast was a large fry of bacon, eggs and sausage, with bread and tea and dinner was either roast pork, beef or lamb, with gravy, potatoes and tinned peas or carrots and I considered them very good value. Elsie visited me there once and was horrified.

I said that I was the sole occupant, which was the case for a while, but had been told that there might be someone else to share the room sometime, and it was so. Eventually a young Irish fellow was brought in. He was a pleasant enough lad and his sister, whom I met, was a respectable looking girl from Galway, a nurse at one of the London hospitals. He had come over to seek employment and was to sign on with a firm of road builders. I didn't exactly welcome his company, but he was no trouble really, except that his feet stank.. I told him to wash them but he said that he had no soap, so I provided it. Then he had no towel, so that was provided too. I saw little of him and I was buoyed by the fact that it wouldn't be for long anyway.

I had been over to Belfast, after the engagement, to buy the ring. I had already told Elsie to look around and select anything she might like. We went together to Corrys in Royal Avenue, one of the leading Jewellers in Belfast, where we agreed on her selection of a fine diamond cluster, in 18 ct gold, which opened some eyes when it was displayed. It emptied my bank account. We had decided on a quiet wedding and would invite only 12 guests, as neither of our parents were coming and because of our delicate financial state. To make it as convenient as possible, I booked a suite at the St George's Hotel, right beside the church, for the reception. A friend, Terry McNeilly, would take the photographs, as well as bringing the cake over from Belfast at the due time. Elsie's mother baked the cake, which was iced beautifully by her friend.

Meantime, Elsie had been negotiating a transfer with the Norwich Union, who arranged for her to take a job after the wedding, at their offices in St James's Street. Obviously she could not expect a job of the same status as she enjoyed in Belfast, but at least it meant secure employment, as a Secretary/ Typist. The other advantage was that the Norwich Union had flats to let in various areas of London and although quite expensive, we would manage with joint salaries, mine rather meagre at the time. We accepted an offer of a flat in a new purpose-built block, in Cromer Court, on Streatham High Road, almost opposite the railway station, which would afford Elsie easy transport to Victoria to get to work. I would use the bus, so things were progressing in that direction.

Back at my lodgings, things weren't too bad. At least I was eating heartily and being nearer to Babcocks meant that I could save on bus fares and always walked to work. I sometimes chatted with the Irish lad. One day he asked me if I had ever been in jail. I was somewhat taken aback at this direct question. Why did he ask I enquired. He said he had been in Mount Joy jail in Dublin. He also said that anyone who thought the experience might be worth having, was quite mistaken, for it was terrible. His uncle had been there at the same time and he had seen him crying with the cold and misery of it all, 'so don't kid yourself,' he said, 'if you thought of trying it.' I didn't, but enquired as to why he had finished up there. 'I tried to kill a policeman,' was his reply. 'Oh really,' said I, 'and how did that happen?' He related the following. His brother had been working in Canada and had returned with a large American car which he allowed him to drive around County Galway. One night he was out and espied a policeman on his bicycle and decided to drive over him. He had had a few drinks, he said, and his aim wasn't too good, so he had only hit him a glancing blow, knocking him into the ditch. He stopped the car and went back   to finish him off with a knife, but the policeman had overpowered him and thus he was arrested, put to trial and committed to a spell in jail. I could only laugh and expressed my amazement at his matter of fact attitude. He had vowed, however, that he would do everything to avoid crime and jail, in future.

So the time of the wedding was nearing. An old friend of Elsie and her family, Mr Ivan Flack, who had lived for many years in London, would give her away. Fred and Nina would come down from Catterick, where they were now living. Fred would be Best Man. Winifred would come over from Belfast, along with Annabel McDowell, who would be Bridesmaid and they would stay in a hotel together. Terry McNeilly would be over anyway staying with friends at Bushy Heath. He would deliver the cake, attend the wedding and take the photographs. Terry had succeeded George Gibson as organist, at Ballylinney Church and was a frequent visitor at Ballyrobert. Alberto Panerai was coming from Milan with his friend, Antonio, to stay for a while in London. Rene, the model, would come and Clark

Bedford and his wife, Sandra, would also attend. The Rev Stott was unable to attend the reception, due to his heavy commitments, but one of the curates came along to even up the numbers.

I paid a visit to the hotel to discuss the menu and other arrangements. I selected consomme, followed by roast duckling and braised celery, with roast and new potatoes, with creme caramel and petit fours to finish. Sherry was to be served before the meal which would be accompanied by Chablis. Elsie meantime had been arranging her trousseau. She had selected a dress in crepe de chine, of fashionable short length and a coat in guipure lace, all in ivory white. A cloche hat to match and a small white bible with an orchid attached and high heeled shoes in fine white kid completed the outfit. The lady guests would be dressed fashionably, the men in grey suits, with buttonholes. Annabel, the bridesmaid, would be in a pale blue crepe de chine dress, designed and made, by the lady who also fashioned Elsie's ensemble.

We had by this time, agreed the terms for the rental of the flat in Streatham. It had two bedrooms, a hallway, bathroom, kitchen and lounge/dining room and being recently built, was up to date in all respects. The gas heating was fired by a boiler in the hallway and conveyed heat through vents which blew hot air throughout and was an effective form of heating. However, it was somewhat temperamental and required attention from time to time. Downstairs in the flat below, were the caretaker and his wife and in the courtyard was a row of garages, which could be rented at extra cost. The surrounding gardens were maintained by the company and the whole block was just off Streatham High Road, behind the Norwich Union Offices and beside the ABC Cinema.

We had no furniture and purchased a new double bed in the Bon Marche in Brixton, a branch of the John Lewis Partnership for £17. The caretaker lent us an old armchair which had lain in the garage for a while. It was wretched looking but serviceable. He also lent us a rickety table, which appeared to have been lying in a field, such was its condition.

CHAPTER 19

On the morning of the 29th September 1966, Elsie and I were married. Everyone turned up in good time, the church was splendid, the organ ringing out as Elsie and her escort entered the church. Fred and I were in position at the front, as Elsie and Ivan Flack approached in their finery. Ivan was very smart in a dark suit and Elsie's outfit was a real hit, matched by Annabel's as she followed behind.

The ceremony was soon over and we withdrew to have photographs taken on the steps of the church. Everyone looked well and the sun shone on a glorious day as Terry got to work with the camera. Rene had turned up in a beautiful pink Dior coat, with a hat to match. The coat was cut a good six inches above the knee and she created quite a stir in this latest fashion, which saw the advent of the mini skirt. Alberto fell for her at once and they had a couple of good days together, before he had to return to Milan. Rene had not realised that he was only 18 for he gave the impression that he was in his 20s and he had the air of a man about town.

We walked across the road to receive sherry at the hotel before lunch, which was served by two waiters in the suite of rooms allocated to us. They had been opened up into one sizeable area giving a pleasant and intimate feel to it. The meal was delicious, the duckling being particularly succulent and beautifully served, well complemented by the tangy taste of the Chablis. Nina declared it to be the best day out she had ever had and Alberto was so impressed by the roast duckling, that he ordered it for his own wedding some years later. That is another story to come.

Before leaving the hotel I requested the bill for I wanted to pay it there and then. I was told that they would send it on to be settled later, but I insisted, for I had a wad of notes in my hip pocket which would not be there when we returned from our honeymoon. This caused them some consternation and running about, till a bill was produced and I peeled off the required number of bank notes to settle it. After the reception, Fred drove us down to the empty flat, to change and to collect our baggage, before taking us to Heathrow Airport, for our flight to Paris. There we said goodbye and off we went.

Arriving in Paris, a taxi, driven by a madman, took us to our hotel, which was conveniently situated in the centre and near to the opera house, as I had requested. It was comfortable but old and creaking and the plumbing was antique, which proved a source of embarrassment, for the 'je ne sais quoi', of the French cuisine struck me once again and I had to make frequent use of the bathroom in the night, which caused a great clatter and gurgling, each time the chain was pulled. We enjoyed some tours around the city by coach and on the river in Bateaux Mouches, which gave us fine views of the many bridges on the Seine as well as the Sacre Coeur and Notre Dame Cathedral. We paid two visits to L' Opera, to see La Traviata and the Ballet Coppelia and one visit to L' Opera Comique, another fine building, to see Il Barbiere di Siviglia. At L' Opera two American women sat behind us, one with her feet on the backs of our seats, legs apart, showing her big drawers, whilst breaking wind, as well as talking during the performance! I have experienced difficulties at other times with people at the Opera. They cough and talk a lot, some laughing at inappropriate moments. Once at Covent Garden we were at a performance of Massenet's 'Manon' and sitting beside a man and his wife. He sniffled and snorted and creaked his seat, till I asked him to desist. We were sitting in side seats in the balcony. I leant forward a little, to see better, whereupon he touched me on the arm as if to pull me back. I said when he stopped snorting and sniffling I would ensure I would not encroach on his line of vision. The opera was rather boring anyway, so I said to Elsie that we would leave at the first interval. As we were descending the back stairs, who should we see but our tormentors, furtively leaving as well. We passed on without comment, laughing inwardly about the absurdity of the situation.

Paris was beautiful and we enjoyed it very much, in spite of my gastric indisposition, which was not so severe, as the previous time I had been there and had had to seek rest and recuperation with Fred and Nina at Woolwich. We returned to London and the empty flat with the prospect of work the next week. Our next purchase was a gas cooker and we made do with the bed, the one armchair and the table, till we gathered our resources. Curtains were the next priority, for although we weren't overlooked, the bedroom required some privacy. Carpets were not so important for the moment, as there was parquet flooring throughout the flat.

There was a very fine department store on the Streatham High Road called Pratt's, which was also part of the John Lewis Partnership. They stocked a good range of fine furniture and kitchen and bathroom appliances. We acquired a fine sofa bed with two matching armchairs and a set of Mackintosh dining furniture, as well as another double bed for the spare room. We acquired these items piecemeal for I vowed never to be in debt and the flat became comfortable and elegant. The dining furniture sat at the end of the large sitting room and the sofa bed sat along the other end wall, surmounted by a fine watercolour, which I had bought years earlier in Belfast. It was by E St John and depicted a scene of Lake Maggiore. Eventually we got a fine large Indian carpet, with beautiful colouring on a white background, to set the room off, stretching across the centre. It was beautiful and of excellent quality.

The caretaker and his wife were helpful and kindly. He was an older man and a divorcee. She was something of a lady, much younger, and very well-spoken. They had met during the war when she took a job on the buses, where he was a driver. She had been an Olympic sprinter and was very attractive, but both of them had a fondness for drink and I avoided any involvement, for I had abandoned my drinking habits entirely. Nevertheless, they kept the place in good order and would have done you a favour at any time.

Elsie started her new job at Norwich Union in St James's Street, where she quickly showed her ability and worth. She became friendly with a beautiful French girl from Marseilles, a real stunner, married to an Englishman, who was a rare character and I could write a book about him alone. We all became quite friendly and we visited their flat at Crouch End, they in turn visiting us on occasion. I continued working at Babcock's, but was less than settled, mainly because of the dull routine and with little to do, I began to feel under employed. I was unable to do much about it for the moment until we would be properly settled.

I bought a small car which was useful for getting up to church on Sundays, when the public transport was not so reliable. It was very cheap, in the tradition of my previous vehicles. Although not quite such a wreck, it was useful for short journeys to Croydon and North London where we had friends.

We had become friendly with a young couple of our own age, almost as soon as we moved into the flat. She was a blonde Danish beauty and he was a public school educated Indian, whose family were in Kenya. They were called Raja and Lise Pradhan and they had a pretty little daughter called Kirsten. He was an Accountant and she had a temporary job as book-keeper with Cosy Cars, whose office was next door. On the floor above us was a Jewish lady, Mrs Heller, and she was also very friendly with us. Opposite us, across the landing, was a couple whom we rarely met. He was a jazz trumpeter and was often away playing in a band on board luxury liners. She was a friendly blonde but kept much to herself. I continued singing in the church choir and Elsie and I went each Sunday, where we met many visiting Americans. On rehearsal nights, Elsie would come up with me and spend the time with Sandra Bedford, the organist's wife, and we met the American Ambassador's Secretary there, who later came to dinner with us.

We had not yet got a telephone installed, as we considered it less of a priority than getting furniture and other essentials. We made use of the public telephones at the station across the road and frequently called our families. Father had been unwell on and off over a period and was in hospital. Mother assured me that he was alright and did not wish me to come over for she was keen to see me settled in regular employment. Father was able to visit Fred in Catterick, where he was still living. The children were at a private school there and wore a brown uniform. Deborah had red hair and every time they visited us, people took her to be Elsie's child, because of their similar colouring. She was a lovely little girl and both she and Andrew thought I was great fun and we got along fine. So far, Father had not been to see us in London and we looked forward to the time when he and Mother would be able to come over, now that we had good accommodation.

Valerie had gone to spend her post-graduate year in Toledo, Ohio, and there she met her husband-to-be, Mr David Barnes. He was an Englishman from Blackheath, who had also been a medical student at Trinity College, Dublin, where she had ignored him. Being somewhat lonely in Toledo, they started to go out together. He had joined the British Army, which had put him through college. At least they shared a common interest in medicine and were company for each other.

One evening I said to Elsie that I was going to telephone to enquire how Father was. I went over to the station and called Mother, to be told that Father had died on 14 December 1966, the day before my call. Mother had sent us a telegram which we had not received. I was devastated and prostrated with hurt and grief. I howled with remorse and shook, dropped the phone and rushed back to the flat, to give Elsie the terrible news. All my hopes of seeing him again and showing him that I was at last settling down were shattered and it was the greatest sorrow and blow that I ever suffered. We set about making arrangements to go to Belfast for the funeral. I went to work to break the news, asking for time off to make the journey, which was granted willingly, the same in Elsie's case, and we set off for Belfast. Valerie came immediately from America, accompanied by David. Fred and family came from Catterick. We were all able to stay with Mother, who was bearing up well, but the business had to be seen to and couldn't just be left to the staff alone.

It was decided that Father should be buried in Red Rock, where he had provided a grave with granite surround and head stone, for his parents and where he had been born. The grave was in the churchyard, where he had been organist in his youth.

The coffin was brought home and we were able to see my father one last time. Fred and I spent a little time with him, regretting his early demise at the age of 61. Fred recalled that when he had been over to see him in Catterick, he had dropped his briefcase when leaving, exclaiming that he'd had a sudden weakness in his arm, which on reflection, Fred said was evidence of a slight stroke. He reproved himself for not taking note at the time and doing something about it. We all had our reasons for self-reproof and regret. Father had always had his suits tailor-made and took pride in his appearance, with hand-made shoes and he always wore a Homburg hat, like Churchill. He was dressed in his best suit and I touched him one last time and felt the terrible chill of death. I wanted to feel the width of his larynx, for it has always interested me that he had had a fine, natural, easily produced, high tenor voice. I am sure he wouldn't have minded my curiosity for, apart from an expensive education, a desire to sing was the only legacy he left me.

The funeral took place on 17th December, on a bitterly cold Winter's day, in a snowstorm in the windswept cemetery at Red Rock after a short service in the church. Tom Frazer had come with us, along with some other friends, others having attended at the house, but unable to accompany us on the long journey to Armagh. Afterwards, we repaired to Aunt Sarah's house, where we had a lively gathering and renewed acquaintance with some of our cousins, uncles and other relatives, but I was glad when it was all over and we could return home.

Father had enjoyed an interesting life, filled with music and had seen his four children well educated. He had been President of the Northern Ireland Wholesalers Association, which was a considerable accolade by his peers who had voted him in. On a number of occasions I had had to represent him at functions. On one occasion I met a delegation from the Irish Milk Marketing Board, at a dinner in the Midland Hotel. I met the head of the delegation and we had a lengthy evening together into the early hours, during which he expressed his interest in me as a good prospect for a position with them in the Republic. I was flattered but did not pursue it. On another occasion, I had to attend a function at the Harbour Master's Office, after which we toured in his launch, around the Docks and the Shipyard. This was a wonderful experience, seeing the massive cranes, Hercules and Goliath, as they were affectionately called, at close range. It was also awe inspiring to see the great hulks of ships rising from the stocks, in different stages of being built and to see the huge dry-dock which could contain the largest ships afloat.

Father was much respected in business, in the church and in the Philharmonic Chorus where he had been a member for nearly 30 years. If he had a weakness, it was his simple generosity and he never pressed any of his customers during hard times, for payment of outstanding accounts. He had an artistic nature, was of considerable erudition, a great reader and an interesting companion. He and Mother enjoyed their life together, sharing their love of music and the church and supporting us in our vicissitudes, as we came to terms with life. He always said that he wanted to live rich, not die rich. I think that he achieved both.

Mother was a widow at 58 and had a business to contend with, as well as the large house. She always regretted having Father buried so far away and he was the last and only member of a large family to be buried at Red Rock with his parents. Several of his brothers had emigrated to America. I was up at Red Rock recently and the grave is in good order but with only three names on the headstone, those of himself and his parents, whom I never knew. Mother insisted that I return to London to get on with my work. She decided to wind up the business and Fred was able to stay to help her in this. Winifred was still living at home.

I returned to work immediately and my colleagues were surprised to see me so soon, as were Elsie's at Norwich Union. But that was the way of it and it was best to get on with living. After Christmas, when Mother had freed herself of the business, she came over to stay with us for a couple of weeks and continued to visit us two or three times every year, till we finally left London in 1995.

Mother decided to keep busy and sought employment, settling finally, for a job as a receptionist in a busy medical practice, with four doctors, at their surgery in Albertville Drive, which

190

was within walking distance of home. She loved it and worked there till she was 81. When she started, Belfast and Northern Ireland were still relatively peaceful. Little did any of us suspect, when we moved to the Cliftonville Road, that 30 years of devastation were to follow. We went home as often as possible throughout the years and stayed with her there. Winifred got married in September 1967 and we all attended. Valerie had got married previously, in Toledo, and she and her husband attended. We did not like him. Mother was criticised by Uncle Joe for having Winifred's wedding so soon after Father's death. We thought that a ridiculous sentiment and although he came to the wedding with Aunt Mary, his wife, we never saw them thereafter. Mother had enough grief and worry to contend with, without unwarranted carping criticism. Such are petty family squabbles!

The wedding took place at Ballylinney Church, conducted by the Rev Young, successor to Rev McConnell. Fred's two children were there, Deborah dressed in a long blue velvet dress with flowers in her hair and Andrew in a kilt, acting as page boy. They looked a picture. George Gibson played the organ and as guests left the church, I sang two items by Handel, 'Where' er You Walk' and 'Silent Worship'. Several people remarked how much I sounded like my father. The reception was held at the Wellington Park Hotel, where I had taken Elsie on our first date. Food was placed before Andrew, who was about four or five at the time. He screamed, beat his head on the table and ordered it to be taken away. He was eventually pacified with a dish of jelly.

Winifred married Peter Glover, whom she had met at University, where he had studied Engineering. He worked as an aeronautical engineer, for Short Brothers and Harland, the aircraft manufacturers in Belfast, now owned by and called Bombardier, a Canadian company. They lived with Mother for some time at Cliftonville, until they bought a new detached house at Stranmillis, near Winifred's place of work at the Ulster Museum and their first son, Christopher, was born. Peter's father, who had been an Army Major ,died and we attended his funeral. Peter decided to take over the family home, on Ballyrobin Road, near Aldergrove Airport. He rebuilt the house, greatly enlarging it but maintaining much of the original. He and Winifred and family moved to stay with Mother, whilst the building was going on, having already sold their house at Stranmillis and Mother welcomed the company.

CHAPTER 20

After a year, I had got fed up at Babcocks, in spite of their friendliness, for I hadn't enough to occupy me. I sought other employment and was interviewed for the Civil Service, where I was duly offered a job. I tendered my notice at Babcocks, who regretted my leaving and the fact that they had not been able to offer me more to do. One of their senior executive engineers had invited Elsie and myself to lunch one weekend at his house in Kingswood, Surrey, where we had met his wife and daughter. We enjoyed a pleasant afternoon with them in a very large garden and he was keen for us to remain friends. I had received nothing but kindness with the company and left with expressions of goodwill from my bosses and colleagues.

I was appointed to a position of Clerical Officer in Naval Personnel Division One, in the Old Admiralty Building in Whitehall. This sounded very grand, with such a good address and in the same building was the Lord of the Admiralty, Lord Louis Mountbatten. I had to attend an Induction Course before I joined. This took place at a large building in Earls Court, where we had the modus operandi of the Civil Service explained to us, emphasising our non-political status, our role being to serve whatever party was in power. Terms of employment and various rules and regulations were explained, including the arbitration procedures and our rights thereunder. I remember thinking that a greater emphasis of the employer's rights might have been appropriate.

I reported for duty at Whitehall as directed and met the Principal, Mr Nigel Nicholls, a young man of excellent manner and bearing, who finally directed me to my place of work, in one of the smaller offices within the building. This room was occupied by three ladies and one man. I was to replace him. Miss Cooper was the Senior Clerical Officer and the other two ladies were of similar lowly rank to my own. The gentleman I had come to relieve had resigned his position and was leaving the service. He was sitting at a desk, empty but for a rolled umbrella, a watch placed beside it and a book of ancient Greek, which he apparently read for pleasure. The only other thing on the desk ,was his feet. He leapt to greet me, saying "Welcome Ron, now sit down here till I tell you about the job." I was impressed by his manner and the fact that he had taken the trouble to know my name. The first thing he had to tell me, was that this would be the worst job I would ever have. However, he said that meantime it would pay the rent, but that I should start looking for another job immediately. This did not sound promising. He was politeness itself and told me my range of duties, which seemed interesting enough. My main concern would be to administer the affairs of Naval Officer Cadets, during their time at the various colleges at Dartmouth, up to the rank of sub-lieutenant. I looked forward to getting on with it. We parted friends, my mentor and I and he left, to pursue some private business affairs. Miss Cooper, I think, was relieved to see him go and she made a fuss of me. She was somewhat older than the other two, all unmarried ladies. She smoked incessantly and sniffed a lot, spreading a lot of cigarette ash over her desk and papers, but she was quite chatty and not at all threatening, but had a certain air of authority. The other two ladies were quite quiet, but one became quite chatty as we became more familiar, the other remaining more reticent. The more friendly of the two, showed some interest of my background and previous employment. She had a twin sister.

The office was comfortable but plain and the whole building was nicely placed, at the top end of Whitehall, beside the Whitehall Theatre and in front of the Horse Guards Parade Ground, with views across to St James's Park and The Mall. There were canteen facilities for lunch. I could get to work either by 159 bus, or by train to Victoria and walk along to the office. I could also take a tube train for the couple of stations to either St James, Park or Embankment on the Circle or District lines. In the good weather of Summer, bands would play in the park and there were lunchtime concerts in St Martin in the

Fields Church. In a hall in Lower Regent Street there was a pianist, who, over a period of weekly concerts, was recording all of the Beethoven Piano Sonatas. He was great and played on a piano once owned by the renowned Myra Hess.

One of the best bands I heard in the park, consisted of pipes, brass and wind instruments. One memorable item they performed had a lone piper approaching through the woods, playing a lament. As he came nearer, the band took up the refrain with increasing crescendo as the piper mounted the stage where they were sitting and the full sound of pipes, wind and brass instruments was thrilling. There were also lunchtime concerts at Charing Cross Embankment Gardens. The police band was particularly good, with a fine solo tenor, singing operatic arias. Another band had Russian singers, one of them a former diva, of formidable voice and physical girth.

I must say that I was not entirely devoted to operatic music, but enjoyed a wide variety of instrumental works, particularly for piano, the violin or clarinet. I preferred classical music but was equally thrilled by the like of Acker Bilk and his emotive clarinet, or Stanley Black with his Latin American rhythms and his dextrous piano playing. I greatly admired Liberace and his boogie-woogie and his showmanship. I love virtuosity in any field of music, enjoyed traditional jazz and big band sounds, such as Glen Miller, Joe Loss and Billy Cotton and the great bands of the 30s. I admired Frankie Laine, Dean Martin, Elvis Presley, Guy Mitchell, Frank Ifield, Alma Cogan, Jo Stafford, Anne Shelton, Nat King Cole, Les Paul and Mary Ford, Al Jolson and the Big Band singers and many more. Ruby Murray was thrilling in her simplicity, with clear tones and diction. I never liked Frank Sinatra, although he spoke highly of the aforementioned Ruby. Nor did I care for Tony Bennett, though I admired Al Martino greatly and thought Bing Cosby's early recordings were very fine, with good legato and tone, but his voice spread in later years and, to my ear, he seemed to sing off pitch, getting away with it by lazily sliding around the note. Sinatra may have been great, in terms of phrasing and timing, but his tone of voice was unremarkable. The same might apply to Tony Bennett, although his theme song 'I left my heart in San

Francisco', was moving. Of the pop groups, I most admired Queen, with Freddie Mercury and I was indifferent to the Beatles, although 'Yesterday' and 'Hey Jude' were great songs. Elvis Presley was the greatest. Shirley Bassey was a genius and so was Judy Garland. I don't like the raucous quality of much modern popular music, such as Reggae, Rap, Heavy Metal, Hard Rock. I never heard the Rolling Stones, didn't like Cliff Richard, but found Barbara Streisland very pleasing . The Andrews Sisters were terrific on record and they had a great accompanying band.

At the Civil Service, the work I was given to do was very basic and there was not much encouragement to show initiative. Of necessity, everything was done to a prescribed format and became very routine. I am constrained by the Official Secrets Act, so cannot go into detail, but suffice to say, the company was pleasant enough, as was the general environment. I was able to acquaint myself with the Archives, which stretched below the offices in the underground basement. In my researches, for instance, of prizes available to the various students at the colleges, some of which had been donated with complicated trust funds, I had the opportunity to go underground. I could go from the Admiralty Building along to the Admiralty Arch, come up above ground and cross the Arch on the upper level over the Mall and descend again into the bowels, before re-emerging to ground level back at the office. I was able to read old copies of The Times dating back centuries and to refer to old documents of historical interest. I did take it upon myself, to complete an analysis of turnover of recruits to the Navy, to determine why so many left, for what reason and at what stages of their training. This proved useful and I was asked to prepare 20 collated copies of my findings, for a Conference of Admirals and other senior officials. One thing that particularly annoyed me at the time, was the general running down of the Navy, as I always had a great admiration for that force, the backbone of Britain's military strength for centuries. Dennis Healey was the Minister of Defence then and I blamed him personally. I suppose that was naïve of me, but I always regarded him with suspicion ever afterwards. One day a Middle Eastern Head of State was visiting London. He and the

Queen, rode up Whitehall together in the Irish State Coach. I was at the gate of the Old Admiralty as they passed and Her Majesty, inside the brightly illuminated coach, turned and graced me with a beaming smile. It was like the sun coming out and I felt a warm glow, as I went back to work.

Of considerable interest were the various personalities I encountered. Miss Cooper was of note. She told me she had had an unfortunate accident when younger. She had slipped or fainted in the bathroom, smashing her mouth against the lavatory bowl. This had left her with a slight disfigurement to the upper lip, giving her a rather severe look. As I said, she smoked incessantly, with cigarette ash everywhere. She wrote a very fair hand, but left her papers streaked with ash, as she swept it away accompanied by a sniff. She made her own dresses of silk which hung down to her mid-calf, below which her legs were purple, the result of her over-indulgence in smoking. When preparing to go home she would produce a large powder puff and plaster her face liberally, surrounded by clouds of cough-inducing dusty powder. She would then don a beautiful fur coat of excellent quality, which left about four inches of her dress hanging below its hem and off she would go. She often discussed this coat and told me how she had bought it. The assistant in the shop had looked at her with disdain and she told how she had put him down with a snort, as she displayed evidence of her well-to-do status. She was unmarried, but talked fondly of her nephews who were good to her and stood to inherit her worldly possessions. We often talked at length and I caused her and her colleagues no end of merriment, with my stories of my experiences and my exuberant behaviour. She was always very nice to me and to my wife on the phone, should she ever ring me at the office.

My other immediate colleagues were diverse characters. The one who was a twin, could be chatty and friendly. I would meet her at the traffic lights sometimes at Trafalgar Square, on my way to work and we would greet each other and walk over together. During the day she would talk to me, as happened naturally. On other occasions, I would meet her and greet her and be ignored, as we crossed the road and I wouldn't get a civil word out of her all day. I eventually concluded that she wasn't the person I thought she was, but probably her twin sister, on occasion, sent to work for the day in her place.

The other younger lady also smoked and was of a nervous disposition. She hated to leave the room, if asked to go across the corridor to another office. She lived with her parents and her brother in a council house. They all had cars and she complained constantly about the Council, because they had failed to repair a cracked window. I used to think that a little self-help would have solved the matter simply and cheaply.

I met other members of staff in offices across the corridor. Most were pleasant, some showing interest in music, which gave me something in common with them. I dreaded having to go to the Typing Pool, presided over by a somewhat truculent 'lady', who showed a marked reluctance for any work to be carried out, particularly if it was urgently needed. After much cajoling and obsequious pleadings the work would be done, with many reminders of how busy they were and with much important work inundating them. I, being of the most lowly of clerical grades, was made to feel my place. On the other hand, I did pass Lord Mountbatten in the corridor one day, who recognised me as a human being.

In sequence of seniority, above Miss Cooper, we had a Higher Executive Officer, a lady of bustling appearance and manner. She was absolutely dedicated to her work, exercising her control in a rigid manner and seeking efficiency from those below her. We had our contretemps from time to time, but she had the grace to acknowledge that I was right on one occasion on a matter of principle and we almost became friendly, without her losing her formal air.

The department was presided over by the Principal, Mr Nigel Nicholls. He was a young gentleman of the first order and was most gracious to me, particularly as he had a great interest in music. He was a member of the famous Bach Choir. On learning of my great interest in opera and knowing that I lived in a flat, he offered to arrange a room for me in the building after hours in which I could rehearse undisturbed. At the time I was involved with an Opera Workshop, run under the aus-

198

pices of the Inner London Adult Education Authority in Tooting, South London. I had joined this group in 1968 and we
rehearsed weekly. That, with my involvement with All Souls
Choir and weekly rehearsals there, meant that I was well enough
accommodated with two Sunday services in addition, but greatly
appreciated the kind offer of a rehearsal room.

Mr Nicholls showed a great interest in All Souls and in the
work of the group, which was organised by the Tutor, Mr John
Chapman, who lived in Streatham. He was a rare character. He
had been in the Army and was stationed in Naples for a time
during the war, where he had been able to get behind the scenes
of the famous San Carlo Opera.

There, he developed a great interest in operatic production.
He had been a bass singer with a group of Russian Balalaika
musicians and dancers, but his interest in opera took precedence
and he was determined to pursue that line. He was a very fine
accompanist and could play anything set before him, as far rang-
ing as a simple but beautiful Bellini aria, or such as 'O Don
Fatale', Princess Eboli's great aria from Don Carlos or something from Boris Godunov, by Moussorgsky, the Prologue to
Pagliacci, or Rigoletto's great outburst 'Cortigiani vil Razza' from
Verdi's opera.

After the war he had taken a job with NAFFI as Entertainments Officer, which was his steady job. He ran the Grand
Opera Workshop, a Light Opera Workshop and a solo singing
workshop. When he wasn't engaged with those, he taught privately at his home in Streatham, as well as keeping a number of
lodgers. He had married for a second time, a lady considerably
younger than himself, who had a fine mezzo-soprano voice.
They had one daughter, also a nice singer. He had two sons by
his previous marriage, both characters in their own ways, much
as that of their father. One was a revolutionary poet who had
attracted attention with his work, some of which had been published . I didn't ever read any of it but it was, by all accounts,
outrageous and obscene and he led his own Bohemian existence. The younger son ran off to Turkey and became enam-
oured of a Turkish 'princess', whom he wished to marry. He
had to seek parental assent through the Consulate, for he was

199

under age according to Turkish custom. The marriage went ahead and the young man commenced to make a living as an artist, also selling other works of art on commission. Painting was something that his father had also taken up. Often, when he was at the piano giving a private lesson at home, he would be playing an aria such as Salut Demeure, which I used to rehearse with him, and his gaze would drift across the room to where one of his nearly completed paintings stood on an easel. He would continue to play, with his legs comfortably crossed, his mind concentrated on the painting, but never missing a note of the music.

Each season, the group would perform a concert, consisting of operatic excerpts, solos and ensembles and would also include an act from a major opera, all performed with piano accompaniment, but in full costume. Our first concert in May 1968, consisted of Act 2 of Carmen and I was assigned the role of Don Jose, which gave me the opportunity to sing the Flower Song, to the Carmen of a lady from Ewell called Beryl. We had a fine Escimillo in a young Welshman, Keith Rotchell, who lived in Norwood. There were several very fine voices amongst us and the rest of the concert gave everyone an opportunity to sing an aria or two.

Keith opened the proceedings with the Prologue from Pagliacci and other items were included by Gluck, Mehul (Champ Paternels, from Joseph, sung by me), Donizetti, Mascagni, Puccini, Verdi, including O Don Fatale, Dvorak and Mozart. The Miserere duet from Trovatore, with chorus was also performed.

In 1969, we were joined by a fine bass baritone, John Stevens, from Tooting. He was an electrician but had been trained to sing by the great Heddle Nash and had the finest of voices. He had been offered work by the English National Opera, but his wife did not encourage a professional career, preferring the more stable income from his regular work. In our concert that year, he performed the Prologue in rich and sonorous tones. Keith had gone on to study elsewhere.

The main items of the concert were the scene from Act 4 of Rigoletto - Sparafucille's Tavern, including the aria, La Donna e Mobile, and the great quartet. John sang Rigoletto and the Duke was sung by Edward Robinson. Part two of the concert consisted of Mimi's death scene from Act 4 of 'La Boheme'. I had the small part of Colline to fill in. In the first half, I sang the duet 'Prendi L'anel Ti Dono' from 'La Sonnambula', with Margaret Phipps and the aria 'Ah si Ben Mio' from 'Trovatore'. The highlight of the evening, was a scene from the Italian Girl in Algiers, by Rossini, notable not so much for the singing, which was good enough, but for the surprise that was in store for us all, the audience in particular. Isabella was sung by Beryl, I sang Lindoro, John was Taddeo and Christopher was Mustafa. Beryl appeared half naked, draped in a gossamer wrap. She wasn't exactly slim and without warning or at rehearsals, she had inserted a large glittering jewel in her navel, emphasising her protruding belly. Chapman, at the piano, was so taken aback, that he nearly fell off the stool. The audience, which included Mother, my wife, my sister, Valerie and her husband, who had come over from America, were convulsed. David and Val had to disappear behind their seats, howling with mirth and Mother and Elsie were prostrated with laughing. We somehow managed to finish the performance, but Beryl was quickly hustled off stage before further indignities were perpetrated. Other items by Verdi, Rossini, Gounod, Weber and Puccini were soberly performed.

We performed a 'Continental Evening' concert in the Summer. I was assigned to sing Italian songs. A flamenco singer and dancer were imported from Spain. Others sang French and German songs. The audience sat at tables, where food of the different countries was provided and this was a very successful evening, when I was recorded on video performing a song by Tosti, - 'A Vucchella. John Chapman also produced his light operas at the Stanley Halls in South Norwood, with orchestral accompaniment.

In 1970 we performed works by Thomas, Puccini, Ponchielli, Saint- Saens (duet from Samson and Delilah, myself as Samson in a ridiculous looking long wig). John Stevens sang Eri Tu, from Ballo in Maschera. Other items were from Aida, and Ballo, (me as Riccardo, Beryl as Ulrica). I performed the cathedral scene from Tosca Act 1, with Jean Hewitt. I sang Vesti la Giubba, from Pagliacci and was called for an encore. This was followed by the mad scene from Lucia, sung by Margaret Phipps. Mavis Skinner sang 'Antonia's Romance' from the 'Tales of Hoffmann'. She had the sweetest soprano ever heard, but was extremely nervous. She could have been another Galli Curci, with proper guidance and confidence.

We finished with the Prison Scene and final trio from Faust. I sang Faust, John Stevens was Mephistopheles and a newcomer, Priscilla Flanders, a beautiful girl from South Africa, was Marguerite. The audience demanded an encore of the great trio, with which we obliged.

That was the last year we were together. John Chapman decided to retire. He left his job, sold the house and everything in it, and moved with his wife and daughter to Minorca, where he set up a property agency and was engaged for two days each week, as a music tutor at a prominent university on the mainland of Spain. John was one of the most interesting characters I have ever met and his retirement was a great loss to us all. Someone else took over the group, but he was inept and so I left.

John Stevens joined a troupe of Russians, billed as The Russian Balalaika Players and Dancers, with Ivan Stepanov - Bass. John eventually took them over and was in future, billed as Ivan Stepanov, and his Russian Balalaika Players. He booked the Albert Hall, where Elsie and I went to see him in concert. He sang and looked magnificent in his Russian outfit of fur hat, Cossack costume and long boots. One of the most beautiful items was his rendering of Lara's theme, from Dr Zhivago, which, with the haunting tremolo of the instruments, created an unforgettable sound and everlasting memory.

During the interval, I was amused to hear people behind me talking, saying how good these Russians were and only they could produce such fine bass singing, as displayed by Ivan Stepanov. They commented further on how well he looked in his Cossack costume. I was very pleased and refrained from interjecting that they had, in fact, been listening to an electrician from Tooting, called John Stevens.

One of the good results of belonging to the workshop group was our introduction to the English National Opera, where a number of us were engaged for several years, as extras in productions, most notably in Don Giovanni and Carmen, both excellently staged over several seasons. Carmen provided a colourful spectacle, with bright costumes, large chorus and lively movement. We were each fitted out with our respective uniforms, mine being that of a Chulous (who assist in distracting the bull and in clearing the ring of dead carcases at bullfights). The costume consisted of a grey suit and elaborate tunic, knee-length boots, a large brimmed hat and ruffled shirt and carrying a whip. We appeared in the last act, for the main procession to the bullring, all very lively musically and in stage movement.

This was a popular and well-mounted staging, in the traditional manner. We were paid each evening after the performance by the stage manager. Years later I saw a production of Carmen at the Coliseum, when it was set in a Mexican junk yard, the stage littered with scrapped American cars and a large heap of rags and Carmen was stabbed with a stevedore's hook, writhing in death on the front of one of the cars.

In our production, where Don Jose has joined the smugglers, a gun is fired at him as he approaches their hideout for the first time. Usually I was at the other side off stage, as a stage hand in the wings fired the actual gun, to create a loud report, in keeping with the actions on stage. I usually remembered to put my fingers in my ears, for the noise was fearful. One evening, I was at the wrong side of the stage and forgot about the gun, as I was watching the scene. Nothing but a flimsy back-drop separated me from the rifle, as it went off alongside me. I was deafened for a week and left the theatre that night, with my ears ringing and in a daze.

Accidents often occur on stage. One evening during a performance of Don Giovanni, a large heavy wooden music stand fell from a minstrels' gallery above the stage, striking the lady stage manager a severe blow to the head. She yelled out and collapsed and was carried off injured. She had to give up her post eventually. She became a News Reader and was seen for a time on London TV.

One Saturday evening, Fred and his wife were staying with u, having driven down from Birmingham. Fred drove me to the theatre for the performance and was able to come back stage with me. As the time of our entry came near, it was noticed that a couple of our colleagues were absent. I grabbed a costume and told Fred to get quickly dressed and to follow me on, simply embracing a few of the female crowd of orange sellers and the like, on his way across the stage. The performance was completed successfully and Fred was able to collect his pay for that evening, much to his delight.

In Don Giovanni we were dressed as monks, in heavy cowls with pointed head gear completely enclosing us, with only slits for the eyes like the Ku Klux Klan. A large Madonna figure had been fashioned, to be carried by us on a litter, across the stage to the tomb of the Commendatore, Donna Anna's father, who had been slain by Don Giovanni. With the heavy cowls, our line of vision was severely restricted and we had to manoeuvre this large and heavy litter out from the side wings, through a narrow passage between the scenery and shuffle in our long cloaks, to the appropriate spot, before setting it down at the same time bending to one knee beside it. First of all, with difficulty and much creaking of scenery and mumbled curses, we emerged from the wings and made our way across the stage. We managed to set the heavy apparatus down with difficulty, trying to keep our feet from getting entangled in the hems of the long cloaks. When it was time to rise again, it was found that the litter had been set on top of the folds of the hem, making it impossible to rise to our feet, till released, which could not be done as the thing was too heavy to raise from a kneeling position. This necessitated much straining and pulling of the cloak, whilst others who were less trapped, tilted the statue, making for a very undignified exit. This was soon abandoned by the Producer and instead, we were issued with spears or crosses, to carry on to kneel with them around the tomb and the statue of the Commendatore.

I was privileged to meet the famous soprano, Rita Hunter, a lady of considerable girth, who sang the role of Donna Anna. She also had a fine career singing Wagner. I have her on record along with Jessye Norman, in Weber's 'Euryanthe', a fine recording. The tenor for a couple of seasons, as Don Jose in Carmen was David Hughes, who had been a pop singer in the 50s/60s, but who made a successful career in opera, later. He was down to earth and friendly and would come off stage exclaiming 'What a fucking way to make a living!' He died tragically of a heart attack, on stage at the Coliseum, just at the end of a performance of 'Madam Butterfly'. Another great singer, the American baritone, Leonard Warren, died on stage during a performance of 'La Forza del Destino', in 1960, at the Metropolitan Opera New York.

We were finally released from our employment at ENO by the new management, in accordance with the dictates of the actors' union, Equity, for we were not members. It has been a good experience and I met some well-known singers and found most of them to be pleasant and appreciative of praise as appropriate.

CHAPTER 21

Meantime I had left the MOD, much to Mr Nicholls' chagrin. He regretted my going, saying that I had a good future ahead of me. My immediate needs were greater and I had to say that what I was earning was simply not enough, even to pay the rent of the flat where we lived. He and I discussed the possibility of my moving to Scotland, to the Naval Submarine Base, but I decided against that. We were only able to afford the flat, as Elsie was working and she was reluctant to leave London. She had seen an advertisement in the newspaper, for staff at Midland Bank in the City and encouraged me to apply. The salary offered was considerably more than that I was then receiving, but the main attraction was the offer of house mortgage facilities at two and a half per cent, after a probationary period. Banking, per se, had no attractions for me whatever, but I swallowed my pride and applied. I had such difficulty in completing my CV as required, due to the previous varied nature of my non-existent career to that date and after patching it together, I swore I would never move jobs again, should I be successful at the interview.

I was interviewed by the District Staff Superintendent at Bucklersbury House, in Cannon Street, who told me that the bank was run very much on Civil Service lines. This was not very encouraging, but I said nothing. As it turned out, the Chairman of the bank at that time was Lord Armstrong, former Head of the Civil Service. I did not know this! It was quite some time before I was advised of the outcome of my application and interview. In fact, I had to telephone the Personnel Manager to see what was going on. He prevaricated to some degree, indicating that their investigations were as yet incomplete, but not damning me outright. Eventually I was offered a job in the Overseas Branch of the Bank at 60 Gracechurch

Street in the City of London and was engaged to start on 4th June 1968. Overseas Branch, in its entirety, employed some 5,000 staff and bore no resemblance to my previous conception of Branch banking.

I was summoned by Mr Nicholls, who had received a request for a reference from the Bank. He was rightly outraged, as he had had no prior intimation of my desire to leave the Service and it was at that stage that we had our chat, which nevertheless ended amicably. We shared a mutual regret at my going for I had otherwise been well treated. He agreed that my situation, working with three staid spinsters was not the most exciting assignment for a young chap. The ladies gave me a little present and I gave them a cake and pastries, for a little celebration when I left. I went back a couple of times to visit them and used to send Miss Cooper a Bank diary at Christmas each year. One year I wrote to her inviting her to visit us and received no reply till much later, when her colleagues wrote to me, regretting that she had died from cancer. They had eventually opened her mail and so were able to contact me, to afford me the sorry details. Thus ended my connection with the MOD.

I hated the Bank so much that I didn't take their mortgage facilities, for that would have tied me up too much and I didn't think that I could stay there. In fact, I was to stay for nearly 28 years and eventually progressed, as we shall see. After three and a half years, I succumbed to the temptation of the mortgage, for house prices were rising, along with our rent and I thought we should get on with it. I borrowed £6,400 and had to make up the remainder to buy a house at £8,000 in Culverhouse Gardens, Streatham. This was a nice, semi-detached house, with a small front and a decent back garden, with a lean-to garage at the end. This was in 1972 and negotiations were protracted, aggravated by a postal strike.

Whilst we were still living in the flat, several events worth listing occurred. As already mentioned, I had bought an old car, an Austin A.35 which served us for a time, till it came to grief at Lambeth Station, when a driver coming through the lights from the left at the junction, ran into me. Within minutes a tow truck appeared, with a tout offering to drag my wreck

207

away. The police did their bit and the matter was left in the hands of the insurers, but I was able to limp the car home, with the front wheel jammed against the undercarriage and the bent mudguard. It lay abandoned at the flat, till I got a breaker to take it away for nothing. I had hoped to get something for the remains, he on the other hand, wanted me to pay him for removing it. We remained without a car for some years thereafter, which was a relief to Elsie.

One Saturday afternoon, Elsie had gone up Streatham High Road with a friend from Belfast who was visiting us. Going up the road, who should she meet but Ashley, Cecilia and Eric, wandering around hoping to find us. They had driven over from Milan without our address, but knew that we lived in Streatham, so had come down in the hope of seeing us. It was a pleasant reunion and Ashley and Cecilia stayed with us, whilst Eric stayed at the East India Club in the Strand. We spent some days together, wandering around the West End, for Cecilia loved the shops, Harrods, Peter Jones, Harvey Nichols and Fortnum and Mason. She wouldn't hear of shopping at Marks and Spencer in those days and sought only the best cashmere and other merchandise.

Eric was very interested in my singing and would give advice on vocal technique. We became absorbed, as I practiced the aria "Come Ruggiada al Cespite", by stopping on traffic islands in the middle of Regent Street, as I tried out the high notes, with Eric directing me as to the proper approach and placing of the voice. The others were hugely amused and the passers-by were astounded. Eric and I were oblivious. He stayed on with us for a couple of days after Cecilia had left. We were able to have a rehearsal with a young friend, Rosemary Barnes, from New Zealand, who was studying piano at the Royal Academy. She had joined our opera group briefly, as a repetiteur, where she had made an excellent impression as an accompanist, but she didn't get along with the tutor and had left. She had taken rooms in Streatham where she did some coaching, much to the outrage of other residents, who had to put up with the endless caterwauling of aspiring opera singers. She ignored their protests. She had a magnificent Bluthner grand

208

piano and was a terrific sight reader. She went on to become a repetiteur and assistant conductor at the ENO. Years later she returned to New Zealand, to take a position as head of the music faculty at Auckland University.

I worked in association with Rosemary for some years, till she moved to Hampstead Garden Suburb, where she found more understanding neighbours and amenable accommodation. Nevertheless, she was to move many times thereafter, always with her piano, till she bought a flat in Ladbroke Grove, where she settled till she left London permanently.

She also became assistant conductor with Opera Rara and in 1993 invited me to a recording session of the opera 'Medea in Corinto' by Mayr. This was recorded in the Henry Wood Hall, where I was welcomed by the conductor of the Philharmonia Orchestra, David Parry, and the Director, Patrick Schmid. I met members of the cast, including the outstanding Rossini tenor, Raul Gimenez (we heard him in the Barber of Seville at Covent Garden). Another noted American tenor, Bruce Ford, was there, along with the bass, Alistair Miles, and I heard them both several times since then at Covent Garden. The soprano in the title role was Jane Eaglen, a fat lady indeed, with a voice to match, now noted for her Tosca and Wagernian roles and she is world famous. Several other well-known singers made up the cast. Bruce Ford was a very pleasant chap and we had lunch together, with Rosemary, in the canteen below the main hall.

The recording was a most interesting experience and lasted all day. I eventually went home at 9.30 p.m., whilst they were still at it. The leader of the orchestra was the violinist, Warren Green, who had to perform a long introduction and obbligato to one of the soprano's arias. This was a tour de force, but his music fell off his stand several times. He recommenced each time, with equanimity, to complete the difficult piece, which was most thrilling. Jane Eaglen's voice was so powerful, that even in the large hall where I sat in the balcony, I had to cover my ears, so as not to be deafened. I eventually bought the full recording.

In 1970 we were in Milan. Ashley and I went to visit Nino Piccaluga, now in his 81st year and in poor health. He had retired to the Casa di Riposo, endowed by G Verdi in 1898, as a home for old and invalid musicians and singers. At Verdi's death, his Will gave all his author's rights in Italy and abroad, from all his operas, to maintain the home, where he lies alongside his second wife, the soprano, Strepponi, in the Chapel there. A great monument to Verdi was erected in the grounds.

Piccaluga was frail and lying in bed, but he greeted us fondly and we chatted for a while. He then kindly signed an LP album of some of his greatest recordings for me, inscribing the cover with the words 'Al caro amico Ronald Frazer, con ringraziamento'. He was well looked after and content, amongst friends and former colleagues, many of them famous names. We said our goodbyes and left, as a group was heard singing the most famous of the Verdi's choruses, 'Va Pensiero', in homage to their benefactor. Piccaluga died about a year later.

Ashley was often engaged in events in Milan, such as the British Week, Anzac Day and the Australian Trade Fair. He also made sure that he was at the British Church, when HRH Prince Charles and Princess Diana visited Milan on one occasion. He wasn't particular about which church he belonged to, Protestant or Catholic, and would probably have even joined anything, if it had suited his purpose.

During our current visit one lesser advertised event took place. This concerned the Irish Saint Columbanus (543-615). He was an Irish Misssionary, who had lived and studied in Bangor, County Down. He founded monastries at Anegray, Luxeuil and Fontaine. He was expelled from Burgundy and preached in the Rhine region and in Switzerland. He went to Milan in 612. He died at Bobbio, in the Appenines, where he had founded a Monastery. His festival is held there each year. The town of San Colombo, in Lombardi, perpetuates his name.

Ashley had hit on the bright idea of combining the St Patrick's Day celebrations on 17th March with those at Bobbio. He contacted Aer Lingus and they agreed to fly a consignment of shamrock from Dublin each year. Ashley would collect it at the airport in Milan and transport it to Bobbio, where a joint celebration would take place. We went with him that year. The weather was foul, cold, snowing and windy. We attended a service in the Crypt, joining lustily in the singing of the hymns. The collection plate was being brought round as we sang and I put my hand in my pocket to extract some money. Grabbing my arm, Ashley urged me, 'Don't make a move, it won't cost you a penny!' I was bemused.

After the service, we were invited, as dignatories, to meet with the senior Priests and the scholarly Abbot regaled us with the whole history of Columbanus. Elsie doesn't speak Italian and mine was sorely strained. After about an hour of this peroration, we asked to be excused. It was a Sunday, but shops were open in the main street of the small town and Elsie ended up by buying pairs of boots and shoes. We had been invited to a local restaurant for lunch and made our way there, to meet with the delegation. We were treated to a sumptuous lunch, with the finest of wines and were each given a medal in a velvet lined box. Altogether it was an interesting day, in spite of the cold. I thought that we had been done proud for the sake of a bunch of shamrock.

CHAPTER 22

In late 1969 I was suddenly taken ill in the night with violent pains in the right side. I was rolling around the floor, ashen faced and shivering in agony. The emergency doctor was called. He immediately diagnosed kidney stones and gave me a shot of morphine there and then, which calmed me and eased the pain. An ambulance was called and I was swiftly taken to St James's Hospital in Balham, to the Urinary Ward. I received excellent treatment and with the help of drugs and pills, the stones were eventually dispersed. I was afforded a small cubicle in the ward, which gave a measure of privacy and I was well looked after , particularly by a pretty black nurse, who paid me a lot of attention. When Elsie visited me, she demanded to know who she was and seemed not at all pleased to learn that she was my wife.

The ward was mainly occupied by elderly gentlemen, walking about with tubes hanging out of them, some of which would fall out, spraying the floor and anyone nearby, with urine, or worse. There was always a terrible racket during the night, like buckets of cutlery being poured out on metal draining boards. On one particular night the noise was even worse and the whole place was disturbed. On enquiring next day what had been going on, I was told that a patient had died in the ward. So as not to disturb us, they had decided to ship him out of the window, rather than wheel his body through the length of the ward. A team of horses dragging a hearse couldn't have been worse than the noise they actually caused, in their concern for our sensitivity.

There was one younger fellow there who became friendly. He said he had 'come by' a load of Welsh roofing slates, which he could let me have at a reasonable price if I wanted them. I regretted that I didn't actually have a use for them, but wished him luck in his dealing.

Each day we were offered a choice of menu and had to enter our orders on a list. One old gent was hard to please, so the nurse took the trouble to explain the choices available. She suggested sweet breads for dinner, whereupon the old geezer shouted out, 'Not bloody likely, I don't want none of them sheep's bollocks!' This speeded my recovery and I was soon home again.

I suffered subsequent pain, as the fragmented stone came out in pieces, over a week or so, but have mercifully been free of problems since then. The hospital was eventually closed, but not before I had to go again, in 1972, for a tonsillectomy, which I will describe later.

Elsie had decided that she would re-join BEA and on 25th March 1968 she left the Norwich Union. She was engaged by BEA as a secretary in Advertising in their offices in Cromwell Road. This reinstatement afforded us the previously held privilege of discounted staff travel, which we had enjoyed when in Belfast.

Another, more terrible event occurred in 1970. Lise, Raja and their daughter, were planning to visit Lise's parents in Denmark. Lise and Kirsten accompanied by a friend, went on ahead by boat from Harwich to Ebsjerg, leaving Raja to fly over later. On board, Lise went below decks to attend to the baggage, leaving Kirsten, who was about three years old, with the friend on deck. She notice that the ship was slowing and heard a commotion above. On re-gaining the deck, she found the ship coming to a halt and people in a state of agitation. Kirsten had been by a window looking out to sea. She came to an opening and fell overboard and was swept away. It was not till several days later that her little body was found in the North Sea. The tragedy was reported in the national newspapers. Our first intimation of the disaster came from the wife of the Caretaker at the flats. Everyone was horrified and a major enquiry was instigated. Lise and Raja were devastated and we were hardly able to speak to them when we met them later. Her parents had come over to stay with them to lend solace. Almost a year later, they had another daughter, Rikke, who filled a terrible void in their hearts and lives. She is now a beautiful girl and the mother of two daughters. Lise and Raja then decided to go to Brussels, where Raja would take up employment in 1971, about the same time as we were moving to our new house and they stayed with us the night before they left.

Craig Sullivan had come to London, to do auditions at Covent Garden, where they were very impressed with his spinto tenor voice. They went so far as to arrange stage auditions for him. He bcame very friendly with the secretary there. She lived in Wimpole Street. He was not offered a Contract but was invited by Richard Armstrong, of the Welsh National Opera, to audition for them and was offered the role of Radames in Aida. His teacher in Milan, had latterly been Maestro Brentegani, and we were to meet him later.

Craig came to stay with us at the flat, which we were preparing to vacate, the incoming tenant was the son of a well-to-do Egyptian. He readily agreed to purchase our carpets and curtains, but we retained the large Indian rug, of which we were so fond. We had been negotiating the purchase of Culverhouse Gardens and had given our notice to the Landlords.

The future tenant was a bit of a playboy, but seemed decent and friendly. He asked if he could leave his huge fridge-freezer, full of food, for a while, till we were ready to vacate the flat. We agreed and so installed it in the spare bedroom. This didn't give Craig much peace as it intermittently came on and off during the night, making him shudder each time, he said.

Craig's Aunt and Uncle from Australia were visiting London and with the exception of Elsie, we all arranged to go to Birmingham to hear Craig in his appearance in Aida there. He drove us up in his Ford Taunus, which he had brought over from Milan. Fred, who was living in Birmingham, joined us at the theatre. Craig was to drive us back to London after the performance. He made a good job of the daunting role, although his B flat in the opening aria, 'Celeste Aida', was somewhat strained. This is a notorious hurdle for any tenor, who has to come on cold and virtually start the evening with this demanding piece. Craig always complained about his throat but the performance went well, after which we repaired to a local night club, for a few drinks. There we met some of the members of the chorus. Craig quickly got involved with one of the young ladies and disappeared.

We were left stranded, after midnight, in Birmingham and the aunt and uncle, who were elderly, complained bitterly. Fred came to the rescue and invited us all to stay at his house, which we gratefully did, somewhat to Nina's surprise. We took the train to London the next day, the uncle muttering the whole way, that he would strike Craig from his Will, immediately he returned to Australia.

I arrived back to be greeted by Elsie in a very bad mood for she had been unaware of the change of plans, as we had not wished to phone her in the middle of the night. We went out shopping together. On our return at lunchtime, who, but the bold Craig, was waiting to greet us, cheerily waving to us as we came up the drive, totally unabashed. Elsie soon changed his mood and roundly upbraided him. The Welsh National Opera were impressed with Craig and encouraged him to learn La Forza del Destino and Ariadne auf Naxos. He did not pursue the matter, but went back to Milan. He reappeared in London, with his brother-in-law, selling exclusively designed jewellery to the top jewellers in London. They carried a large case full of samples with them, which had to be chained to the wrist, for the contents were valued at £20,000. I said that I hoped that they were insured and Craig replied that the jewellery was, but they were not. They had some success with such houses as Graff, Asprey, Kujinsky and others, but Craig quickly tired of this and went back to Milan. Meantime, Craig's singing teacher, Maestro Brentegani, had come to London, to introduce a young soprano to the musical scene. He stayed with Lord Harewood, Head of ENO, but came twice for dinner, when Mother was staying with us. He was charming, nattily dressed and wearing winkle-picker shoes. Mother was taken by his gracious manner. He addressed her as Donna Winnie and my wife as Donna Elsie. He spoke no English, Mother no Italian, but with his clear enunciation and precise delivery, he seemed to communicate with her quite well. We laughed as we watched them engrossed in conversation. After dinner he remarked, 'Squisito!', smacking his lips contentedly. I presume he meant the meal!

We had moved to our new house in May 1971. I had borrowed the maximum allowed from the bank, being £6,400 and had to find the difference of £1,600, plus enough to cover conveyancing and solicitor's fees. Somehow we made up the remainder and the purchase was completed. The house was owned by a gentleman, who had retired from the DoE. His main hobby was sailing his ocean-going yacht off Burnham-on-Crouch. His wife was from Northern Ireland and hated sailing. He was a quiet man, she more garrulous and she took a liking to me, probably because I made a fuss of her cat. We met it in the sitting room when we first called to negotiate terms for the purchase. I took it in my lap for I genuinely like cats, although they can start me wheezing. Well, this one sure did that, for it was moulting hair at an alarming rate and it stank, for it continued to break wind as I caressed it. I didn't like to be too abrupt in hurling it from me. It was important to keep on the right side of the vendors, for house prices were rising alarmingly and we didn't want to spoil our chances of acquiring this attractive property. The house was pleasant with a bay-windowed front. It contained a sitting room, dining room, hallway downstairs and three bedrooms and a bathroom upstairs. The garden was in excellent order, but the front was surrounded by a high thick hedge and two trees stood along the front gate, so that the house was very secluded. The attached neighbours were three elderly spinster sisters. We only learned later from them that they had hated their neighbour, who apparently crept down the back garden on hands and knees to avoid them. He, on the other hand, had not mentioned his aversion to them, but the reason for the thick hedge became apparent on hearing that news. The house on the detached side, was occupied by a chemist, who worked for Boots, and his wife, who turned out to be very friendly.

The floors downstairs were laid in oaken parquetry and each room had a fireplace, all very cosy. They offered to sell us their carpets and curtains, which we declined, for we would have thrown them out. Culverhouse Gardens was a pleasant avenue, mainly of semi-detached houses, but with a large private clinic, at the top end and a doctor's surgery two doors up from us.

On moving in, I went and introduced myself to the neighbours. Len, the chemist, and his wife, Phoebe, made me welcome as did the three ladies on our attached side, who invited me in. They expressed their interest in music and when I mentioned my own involvement, they looked forward to our coming. They were quick to tell us of their opinion of their previous neighbours, as mentioned above, which made me wonder why, as they had been more than pleasant to us. I said nothing for the time being.

The first thing I determined to do was to knock down the wall between the sitting and dining rooms, so as to accommodate the grand piano I was determined to buy. Also the two downstairs fireplaces would be removed and central heating would have to be installed. The front hedge and a large bush at the front window would have to go and the two trees at the gate would require severe pruning.

Money being scarce for the moment, I set about the jobs that I could do myself and commenced to pull out the hedge. I had tried cutting it down first, but found that I could more easily up-root it, piecemeal, which I did by degrees, trailing the debris round to the back, via the communal entrance which served the rear of our row of houses. The old girls applauded my efforts, for the hedge had impinged on their light for too long and they welcomed the open aspect. Later on their approval was to turn to resentment, when I decided to burn the pile of hedge and tree prunings, at the end of the back garden. This was going well for a couple of days, till I set fire to their garage. Horror! Needless to say, I offered to put the damage right, which luckily wasn't extensive and they benefited from a new door to their garage. Our neighbourliness continued to deteriorate thereafter and I then began to realise why the previous owner had been reduced to crawling down his own garden to avoid them.

I had been suffering from bad throats for years and had pestered our own doctor for some time. He usually dismissed me and was more concerned with the state of the stock market and talking about opera, than the state of my throat. He was always genial, of Maltese extraction and he had a house in Eaton

Square. He was very friendly with Elsie and myself.

He prescribed a spray on one occasion. My wife went to the chemist to collect the prescription, who asked what was the matter with her husband's foot. She said there was nothing wrong with it, but he had a very bad throat. The chemist replied in astonishment that the prescription was for a foot spray. This could have been a severe case of 'foot and mouth', had I used it.

The sore throat persisted and when I had a particularly bad eruption from the right tonsil, the doctor, on looking at it, explained that my tonsils were rotten and should be removed forthwith. This was what I had been suggesting to him for years. He arranged for me to visit an eminent throat surgeon in Harley Street. The surgeon was called Alfred Alexander, an Austrian, whose great passion was opera, about which he wrote books. He was a character. He told me he had removed the tonsils of every type of singer from famous pop stars to top opera stars. He was on call to Covent Garden and often had to treat stars preparing to go on stage. Alexander lent me a copy of his latest book 'Operanatomy', priced £2.85, when printed in 1971. He agreed to remove my tonsils the next day. I said I couldn't come then, for I was going to Hong Kong. When would I be back he asked. In a week, I replied, whereupon he said to come in the day I arrived back. When I enquired how much the operation would cost, he asked how much could I afford. I explained that I was with PPP. 'Well, find out how much they will afford and let me know how much more you can pay,' was his reply. I found that PPP would allow £300 and on being told this, he again asked how much more I could pay. I said, nothing, whereupon he said he would take PPP's offer anyway.

CHAPTER 23

We had decided to go to Hong Kong since Elsie had re-joined BEA. BOAC which was still a separate entity at that time had offered us a staff interline trip for a very reasonable price, which we readily accepted. It is worth mentioning that two other friends and colleagues of Elsie's at Norwich Union had left simultaneously to join airlines. Marie Claude had joined Air France and Janet Sexton was successful in becoming a long haul stewardess with BOAC.

Though we had no funds, we decided to go ahead with the Hong Kong trip anyway for it was too good an opportunity to miss. The trip was memorable. First impressions were over-whelming. We were installed at the Hyatt Hotel on Kowloon and a number of inclusive tours had been arranged for the party we were with. A young Chinese lady by the name of Rose was assigned as our guide throughout and she was the essence of charm and efficiency. Everything was different and the whole atmosphere excited us.

We visited the Floating Restaurant, The Chinese Opera (very noisy), took the Star Ferry to Hong Kong Island, visited Happy Valley Race Course, rode on double-decker trams around the island and were taken on the funicular railway. Back on Kowloon, we visited the New Territories, which took us right up to the Chinese border and afforded us views into mainland China. We visited a drug rehabilitation centre. We went to a Night Club and dined sumptuously at Hugo's Restaurant, the gourmet restaurant of the East at that time. We bought many items of brass, jade and silk, lamps, paintings and ornaments. Merchandise of every type abounded and the Chinese were keen to strike a bargain. I had a suit tailored and Elsie had many items of clothing beautifully made. Everything we did was a revelation and we enjoyed the whole trip greatly, especially with the efficient organisation and Rose's cheerful companionship.

The day before we were to leave, we saw the Queen Elizabeth I ocean liner on fire. It had been undergoing refurbishment in Hong Kong Harbour, to become a floating university. As we flew out next day, we passed over the smoking wreck, now lying on its side, witnessing the great ship's demise. The hulk was later used in a James Bond movie, as part of the secret operations' quarters of M.

When I returned from Hong Kong, I was admitted to a ward in St James's Hospital for the tonsillectomy. I was the first of some 20 cases the surgeon was dealing with that day, most of them on the NHS. The job was quickly done and I was returned to my bed. When my wife arrived to see me she found me ashen-faced, with blood drooling from my mouth and she feared I was near to death. She was assured that I would survive. My throat hurt like hell and next day I was given cornflakes, followed by kippers, for breakfast. I had been expecting jelly and ice cream to soothe the pain and when I enquired where it was I was told that such food was an old fashioned remedy, and that the roughage of the flakes would help to cleanse the throat. When I ate the kippers, the saltiness doubled the agony. When Elsie phoned to enquire how I was and was told I had just consumed cornflakes and kippers, she asked were they sure they had the right person, for I had seemed near to death the previous evening.

The surgeon came to see me and said that I could sing that evening if I wished, for the tonsils had nothing to do with the voice and that the vocal chords were not affected. He did say, however, that he had had to dig deep for there had been a long-established abscess at the root of the right tonsil, which must have been causing me agony for years. This confirmed my own, previously held opinion.

After leaving hospital I arranged a follow-up consultation and to settle the bill. Alexander pronounced me fit, asked me how I had found his book, had I read it and did I like it. I replied in the affirmative, whereupon he asked me would I like to buy it. I said I wouldn't, so he said, 'Ah well, you can keep it anyway.' We said our goodbyes and I never saw him again.

Craig met a young English lady in Milan and eventually split from his wife and came to England with her. Her family ran a pub in Lyme Regis and she introduced Craig to the licensed trade. They became Landlords of a pub just outside Exeter, called the Nags Head. They eventually got married and decided to have a marriage blessing in church in Lyme Regis, to which we were invited. Eric had joined Craig and Irene at the pub, where he worked for a while and Craig's mother, who had left Australia and come to London, in hope of Craig finally pursuing his operatic career, stayed with them there. Elsie and I went down for the ceremony and met the in-laws. After the ceremony, we repaired to their pub for refreshments. Eric had driven us over from Exeter, in his beaten up, left- hand drive, VW Beetle, but got too drunk to drive us back. I had to take over. For the first time in my life I had to contend with a left-hand wheel, with a gear shift that wouldn't stay engaged, unless held in permanently, with Elsie and Mrs Sullivan on board. Eric stayed behind to be brought back later with Craig and Irene, who would be returning for the next day's work.

We made the journey slowly, jerkily but safely and went to bed. The noise of the juke box in the pub below, was making the floor tremble and we had a restless night. Next morning we found Eric, lying inert on his back on a small camp bed at the back of the pub. He was able to raise one eyelid, muttering that death was near and immediately fell back into a deep trance. He came round later and was able to get moving as we began bottling up for the day's trade and generally tidying up the pub.

We stayed for a few days and helped in the pub and Eric and I joined in one of Craig's musical soirees, where we entertained the clients with songs and arias, along with other artistes. We also performed a concert at the British Legion Hall.

On returning home our next priority was to get the wall, between the sitting and dining rooms, removed and we sought estimates from builders. One old fellow was ready to start immediately, at a price considerably lower than the others and we got quite excited. He proposed inserting a wooden cross beam and would do the work himself and remove the rubble. Had he gone ahead, the whole house would probably have ended in rubble, for his suggestion of a wooden cross beam in place of a main load bearing wall, was almost criminal, as we subsequently learned from the local council surveyor's report. Luckily, when we had said that we would be seeking the necessary council permission for the alterations, the old boy disappeared.

We went ahead with another genuine builder and the work was completed satisfactorily. Len, next door, asked if we would keep the rubble for foundations as he intended to construct a new brick-built, double garage, to accommodate his car and a small caravan which he had bought. We foolishly agreed and we were left with a huge heap of rubble in the back garden with no sign of it ever disappearing. Goodwill can soon disappear when dividing fences or partitions are under discussion. He wanted to remove part of our dividing fence, which I agreed to, but he also suggested knocking down a hut which was behind my garage and between it and the fence. I drew the line there, for it was useful as a workroom and preserved my line of demarkation. We didn't fall out completely, but our patience was further strained as we were greeted by the heap of rubble with no apparent sign of its being used. With much urging and our own physical help, this was eventually accomplished and his garage was built.

We had a pear tree in the back garden which was prolific in its production of fruit. Len was a wine-maker and requested any pears which we didn't want, which was most of them. They required storing till about Christmas, wrapped in newspaper, in the attic, until they achieved an eating consistency. They were initially very hard, but when ripened they were lusciously sweet and pleasant to eat but we were glad to get rid of them. That was until he had us in one evening to sample his wine, which he had made from the pears. Its sweetness would have poisioned you and it had a kick like a mule. We declined his offer of a couple of bottles to take home! He also made beer, which was even worse, and I thought later that a couple of bottles would have been useful, when I was doing the interior redecoration, to help with the paint stripping.

The central heating was the next requirement and we engaged a local firm to carry out the work. This made an awful mess, for they had to cut chases into the walls to accommodate and disguise the piping. This meant removing the picture rails and the subsequent repapering and decoration of the entire house, which I did myself. Meantime, I had tackled the kitchen for it was somewhat shabby. I retiled parts of the walls and fitted laminated boards on the main wall. A new sink and taps, cooker and fridge completed the transformation. We paid for the work as we went along and things were progressing nicely. Everything we could save was being put towards the refurbishment. The release from paying a high rent and the low-cost mortgage payments, made things manageable.

Elsie's mother was able to visit us from time to time and enjoyed meeting our friends. Her father did not enjoy travelling, so never visited London. My mother continued her visits. She loved the shops and spent entire days on Streatham High Road, whilst we were at work. She loved clothing and shoe shops, of which there were plenty. One fashionable ladies' outfitters shop was owned by a Jewish gentleman, who lived at the top of our road, and there she bought several garments. Mother always assessed towns visited, by the quality of their shops and would dismiss my question of how she had liked such and such a town, by saying they were useless for there wasn't a decent shoe shop in them. This, in spite of places being of historic or scenic interest!

Fred had moved to a house in Dundee where he was employed as a physiotherapist, at the local hospital. We visited him there, flying via Edinburgh, where he met us. That was in June 1972 and it rained the entire time we were there and it was intensely cold and windy. We visited Stirling, Perth and other places. We had a party one evening and met some friends, colleagues and neighbours, but the cold overwhelmed us and we were not sorry to escape back down South.

With the alterations, we decided that carpeting throughout was necessary and we proceeded in that direction. The Indian carpet fitted nicely into our bedroom at the back, which afforded us the morning sun from the south facing garden. The front bay window room was maintained for guests. It was a pity to have to cover the nice parquet flooring downstairs, but it was all or nothing.

I had been determined to acquire a grand piano and in September 1972 I bought a reconditioned, Alison Grand, with a splendidly re-polished solid mahogany case. It had been restrung and completely restored. It was of unusual heart shape, rather than the general bow shape of most modern grand pianos, with double lids, hinged at the middle, and referred to as a butterfly piano. It had good tone and cost me £340 nett, for cash, which included a discount of £45 off the original asking price. It was a beauty and served me for 32 years and came with me to Ireland on my retirement.

The piano was installed in the centre of the room and Clark Bedford came down to try it out for he was looking for one for himself. He pronounced it of good tone and action and we performed a few arias together. Clark soon afterwards resigned from All Souls and was invited to join Welsh National Opera in Cardiff, where he became part of the music staff of the opera company. He remained with them for about two years, till he returned to America to take a position in one of the State universities. I was sorry to see him go for he had given me much encouragement at All Soul's Church.

The piano afforded me great pleasure. I do not play very much, but with Rosemary and other connections with the ENO, I made friends with another repetiteur, David Sutton, who lived in a flat on Streatham Hill. We often had musical parties. One memorable party was attended by Craig Sullivan and Piero Francia. They had driven over with a consignment of Piero's fine wine, which he hoped to introduce into England. They arrived just after the party had started. A couple from Covent Garden, a baritone and his wife, a soprano, arrived and James Holmes and his wife, also a soprano, from the ENO, also came. James went on to be a Conductor and achieved renown. One unexpected, but very welcome guest, was a fine bass baritone, Sean Rea. He was over six feet tall, bearded, and handsome. Lise and Rikke came as well, for Raja had left Brussels to take up a good position in Detroit, which Lise couldn't stand. Her little girl asked Sean if he was a giant. He sang superbly and with two sopranos performed the delicious trio from 'Cosi Fan Tutte Soave sia il Vento' - exquisite! Sean then sang a solo, in the Paul Robson mode, 'Just a Wearyin' For You', to great effect. He was a dentist, specialising in orthodontia, but he went on to join ENO and appeared with them as a soloist in several works. I heard him a while later in Belfast, as one of the villains in Ballo in Maschera. The baritone from Covent Garden sang Eri Tu from that opera and he was also a fine accompanist, playing for me to sing 'Quando le Sere al Placido', from Luisa Miller. Many other solos and ensembles were sung, but Piero showed us all how to do it. James accompanied him in the 'Largo al Factotum' and the 'Prologo', sung with panache to great applause. Craig followed with the Death of Othello, 'Niun me Tema', from Verdi's great opera.

We went on into the evening till the ladies next door asked us to desist. Piero then offered to make us spaghetti, all the party food having long been guzzled up. He took over the kitchen and every available pot and pan. By the time he had finished producing a large bowl of pasta, the walls and sink were streaming with the 'debris'. It was a very memorable party. I had been out one lunchtime from the bank and had bought a splendid powder blue, linen, silk-lined suit.

I was so pleased with it that I kept it on and came back to the bank still wearing it. As I went through the office, everyone was agog and someone asked me if I had left the ice cream van outside and could I give him a 'Neapolitan'. I wore that suit for the second and last time at the party and have a splendid picture of myself, David Sutton and Zed, a Polish tenor (we could never pronounce his name), who was Rosemary's boyfriend, grouped together. The suit was a real beauty, but not practical, for I was embraced several times by ladies and it finished up smeared with lipstick. I had worn it with a pink shirt.

Rosemary had also brought a New Zealand soprano with her, from Germany, where she was permanently engaged, she was called Marie Sutherland. She gave us a rousing rendition of the Hungarian Czardas, from 'Die Fledermaus' - wow! Rosemary and Zed sang the great duet 'Tu Qui Santuzza'. Another (non-singing guest) was Ivan Flack's friend, Charles (Berg) Martyn. Ivan had died about a year earlier and Elsie had attended his funeral. She had known both Berg and Ivan for many years and Berg was the Queen's hairdresser. He had been unable to attend our wedding for he had been on a tour with Her Majesty at the time. He travelled abroad with her for many years. On one occasion, in Canada, the Royal train stopped at a remote halt and he descended to stretch his legs. The train moved on without him and he made headline news when his predicament was revealed. We remained friendly with him and he retired at a late age to live in Poole in Dorset, where we visited him. He had been honoured by the Queen and he died in his early eighties. Over the years he had always sent us a Christmas card of the Royal Household, which we have kept .We visited Berg at his home and dined on pheasant, shot at Sandringham, by HRH Prince Philip.

Altogether there were 30 people at the party and Elsie had prepared and served all the food herself, whilst everybody else happily guzzled it, along with the drink.

I was in the habit of buying clothes or shoes and keeping them on after fitting in the shop and having my discarded items packaged instead. I once bought a pair of shoes at Russell & Bromley's and was very pleased with them. I kept them on to go home. When I went to pay for them and asked for my own shoes, the young lady replied that she had put them in the bin! I promptly asked her to retrieve them.

During Craig's earlier time with us in London, we had gone to a performance of Adriana Lecouveur, by Cilea, at the Camden Festival. We were accompanied by the Covent Garden secretary and Craig's aunt and uncle. This opera boasts a particularly beautiful tenor aria, 'La Dolcissima Effigie', the famous 'Ecco Il Monologo' for the baritone and Adriana's aria 'Io son l'umile Ancella'. The soprano, as I recall, was Mila Andrew and the tenor an emerging Kenneth Collins, who went on to an international career.

We met the great diva, Eva Turner, one of the greatest Turnandot's of all time. She had sung at La Scala with Toscanini in the 1920s. When we met her, she was in her early 80s and spoke with great clarity and authority and enthusiasm. She had been noted for her clarion voice and high sense of the dramatic and she was equally famous in Italy, London and America. She died in 1990 at the age of 98. In her later years, she had taught at the Royal Academy of Music and was a frequent visitor at Covent Garden. She had often sung with the great tenor, Giovanni Martinelli, who had also lived into his 80s and who praised her highly. He died at the age of 84 in 1969, his last performance being as the emperor in Turnandot at the age of 82, in Seattle.

The next job with the house was to renew the bathroom fittings and appliances, the original basin and bath were of heavy cast iron, excellent in quality, but dated, along with the old high flush lavatory. We selected a new suite in Avocado Green, which was installed. It was a mistake, for we had been persuaded to buy a fibreglass bath tub, which, although of good appearance, it creaked a bit when full and was easily scratched. I undertook the retiling of the walls and floor myself.

At the beginning of my employment with the bank, I was selected, along with a number of other recent recruits, to do a special one-off job at the New Issues Department, in Austin Friars. Companies launching a shares or rights issue would advertise widely. This would attract large numbers of would-be purchasers, who either filled in forms in the newspapers or forms received by direct mail. We were assembled in a large room in which broad tables had been brought together to form a large working area. It was explained to us that messengers would soon be delivering volumes of these orders to us. Our job would be to remove the contents from the envelopes, ensure all the documents contained were kept together, which might include an order form, a letter and a cheque. It would be essential to ensure that these were secured together with a pin, not a staple, or a paperclip, for subsequent splitting and processing by the Securities clerks. We had had an induction programme on joining the bank and I had been very impressed by the young man delivering the lectures. It turned out that he was a hockey player and well acquainted with my old school friend, David Judge, the Captain of the Irish team. This young man spoke well, was well dressed and looked like a Banker and made my future prospects seem quite encouraging. I was therefore unprepared for the shock that awaited me in the New Issues section. The doors suddenly burst open, messengers appeared with large suitcases, the contents of which were dumped before us on the tables. They grew to a mountain and I laughed hysterically. I began to think I might have been better staying in Mackies, to shovel washers, or on the farm shovelling manure.

I was still not settled in the bank, although I was now tied in by their generous mortgage terms. I had started in the old Currency Reconciliation Section, where I was assigned the job of maintaining the ledgers of the bank's accounts with Irving Trust, Chase Manhattan and First National City Bank, in New York. Midland was known as the 'Bankers' Bank' and was once the biggest in the world. We were one of the 'Big Four' Clearing Banks (Midland, Lloyds, Barclays and Nat West) and we had 33,000 agents abroad.

Our job was to maintain and reconcile the foreign currency accounts we held with banks abroad. These reflected all movements of currency, whether Foreign Exchange Deal settlements, Currency Payments to or from abroad, Documentary Credits, Bills of Exchange, Securities Dealings and so on. This incurred mountains of incoming payment advices, credit and debit advices and up to 20 ledger pages a day, for the bigger banks. I stuck at it and worked two hours overtime on three nights a week, for there was a constant backlog of work. Urgent reconciliation was essential to guard against loss, fraud or interest claims for late payments. I was constantly amazed at the amount of paper to be dealt with and the amount of correspondence to be entered into. I was quite good at the job, but kept shouting 'Get me out of here, I can't stand this any more!'

I was given an unexpected rise and thanked the management, who were equally surprised. I was eventually moved to the Currency Disposals Department. This was even worse for it was more hectic. The paper continued to come in sacks and the phones rang constantly, with clients looking for urgent payments and other enquiries. Payment Orders were received by mail and telex, from all over the world expressed in foreign currency. You might get hundreds of payments from German Banks in Deutsche Marks or from French, Italian, Dutch, USA or any country expressed in their own currencies. Worse still, any of these orders might be expressed in a currency other than that of the originating country, where third party cover was put up with their foreign agents for credit to our own accounts in that currency with our agents. This added to the pitfalls of the job in ensuring that the correct disposal took place with the correct rate of exchange applied, should the customer require the sterling equivalent. Large amounts had to be advised to the Foreign Exchange Dealers Department ensuring correct cover details were given, so that they could manipulate their foreign exchange balances within their prescribed limits. Correct recollection of the ledger entries depended totally on this being given appropriately, as well as ensuring that the correct amount of money was paid away. I don't wish to bore the reader further with these technicalities.

In spite of my abhorrence of this work, I did well and was put in charge of a section. I was then promoted to supervise the Customers Currency Accounts Department and became Group Chief, CMHA (Customers Money Held Abroad Accounts). This was complicated in those days, by the exchange control regulations imposed by the Bank of England and Government edicts. Only approved companies or foreign nationals, were permitted to hold such accounts and rigid control was enforced. I had to complete the weekly and monthly statistical returns to the Bank of England, which entailed listing all the Bank's foreign currencies, expressed at an agreed rate of exchange, held under countries of origin and various other categories. The department was also responsible for the London Dollar and Currency Clearings. This afforded a mechanism for member banks and their agents, to exchange certain currencies through London, in bulk, without the necessity of settling each individual payment separately by cover abroad. Final settlement of aggregated totals were agreed at the Clearing House and nett cover payments to agent banks abroad were used to reconcile all participants' totals. Currency Control Regulations were eventually removed in the early 80s, which resulted in an explosion of currency accounts, including the introduction of the Euro. I made a good impresssion in this department and was promoted to Senior Supervisor to create a Currency Control section in my old Reconciliation Department, to ensure more efficient pursuit of outstanding items and queries, and to save endless correspondence with banks abroad. This was a mighty undertaking. Senior management had placed great emphasis on this work and I had two other supervisors assigned to me and we made a good start. The main frame computer had been installed at Gracechurch Street, taking over three entire floors and we had already been moved to Suffolk House at Upper Thames Street.

We had some rare characters in the department I had already worked in. One fellow in the Reconciliations was a jazz pianist, who basically came to work to rest as he was often out on late gigs. Another was a property landlord, more interested in that than the work of the bank. These people used to annoy me intensely, for it just meant more work for the willing. I had a good friend in the Currency Accounts Department. He was in charge when I first joined them. He was a very clever Welshman, erudite and able to recite Shakespeare, as well as being well versed in music, but he was eccentric. A bachelor who lived in a rented room in South Croydon, he was a whiz at the Bank of England figures, having been trained as an accountant, though never completing his exams. But he was lazy, leaving me to do most of the work. A good deal older than me, he had been in the Navy and served in Australia, where he had been Paymaster in Sydney, responsible for the ship's payroll. Once, when the entire ship's crew was assembled for payroll, he had to announce that he had lost the keys of the safe and couldn't pay them. All hell broke out and he was put on a charge and confined to barracks over the weekend. Part of his mandate was to control the ship's rum ration and having access to it, he and his fellow detainees, raided the stocks and drank the lot. He had once been jailed on St Patrick's Day in New York, where he had also met Dylan Thomas, who invited him for a drink. After drinking together all day, Dylan had said to him, 'Well now, boyo, let's get down to some serious drinking!' They finished up paralytic and were arrested for causing a riot in a bar and were incarcerated. He used to regale me with these stories and it gave me many a laugh. For many of the years that I knew him, he never took a drink, preferring tomato juice whenever we went to the pub. I now understood why! He was a great raconteur, but only when not prompted. If asked to relate stories he would withdraw, but left to his own, he would recount the most hilarious experiences. His sister was a music teacher and like most of the Welsh, he had an interest in music himself.

He was never smartly dressed and often wore a shirt with a large singe mark on the collar. One day he appeared in a better suit than usual, on which I remarked. He replied that he had bought it in a jumble sale for four pence. He had been suffering headaches and sought his doctor's opinion, who could find nothing wrong and suggested that he might need new glasses. The optician tested his eyes and questioned where he had got the glasses he was wearing, for they were of quite the wrong prescription. Eric said that he had found them on a train and had been using them for about a year! One day he came to work, hobbling on a stick. He complained of his discomfort throughout the morning. At lunchtime the manager sent him home, saying he wasn't much use in his condition. He beat a hasty retreat but returned ten minutes later to say that he had forgotten his stick. He was later observed running across London Bridge to catch his train, the stick under his arm.

At a late age, he decided to get married and sought to purchase a house or apartment. Property prices were soaring in the mid-eighties. He would have three or four properties under offer at the same time, watching developments to get the best deal. He liked the look of a place at Seaforde, owned by a lawyer, who entered into an agreement with him that he would hold the property for him, whilst he pursued the financing, but that the price would rise by a certain percentage each month, till completion. The house was near a cliff and an added complication was that the cliff kept disappearing in chunks. Each time he visited the property, the garden was getting shorter, whilst the price was getting higher. I was amazed at his pursuit of this, being as he was an accountant and mean with it. Eventually, nature and good sense prevailed and he withdrew before the house disappeared with the cliff.

In the end he married a lady whom I never met; she was a bit older than himself. She sounded like a lady on the telephone. I had something of an irascible reputation, because of my constant shouting 'Get me out of here!', and hounding of lazy and incompetent staff. The first time this lady phoned to speak to him, I took the call, but of course had no idea who she was. I was quite polite, but she later complained to him, asking 'Who was that fellow bawling at me on the phone?' Before the wedding, our Welshman took us for a drink at the local pub, The Bell, a famous free house, small and dingy, but still standing in spite of the massive regeneration of the City all around. The landlord was a Freeman of the City, presumably for services rendered to the 'thirsty' bankers and solicitors. He kept to soft drinks. As is the usual custom in the office, collections are made to celebrate such events. He had asked me, some weeks in advance, to avoid this if possible, for he didn't want any embarrassment. Later, on second thoughts, he said that as it was probably inevitable that a collection would be made, could I ensure that a clock was bought with the proceeds. This was done and off he went. He eventually did buy a house at Seaforde, but only went home at weekends, continuing his bachelor lifestyle of doing overtime, and maintaining his room in Croydon, where he only had a bed and a chest of drawers, which was stuffed with old personal statements of his own account.

I was moved out, as mentioned, to initiate the Control Section and was replaced by a bright young man on special management stream for quick promotion. After about 18 months on the Control Section, it was decided to move the entire Currency Reconciliations to Sheffield. The bank had taken premises there, at much lower costs than in London. In addition, the South Yorkshire Computer Centre was being installed, to accommodate the bank's entire and growing, mainframe operations. This meant that I was facing redundancy, for I did not wish to go to Sheffield, for more than one reason. We, all those not destined for Sheffield, were then expected to hand over our jobs to new staff, brought down from Sheffield, giving them instruction ourselves, as we saw our jobs disappearing. This caused some ill will, needless to say, but I kept out of it. Eventually it was decided to reinstate me as Group Chief, back in the greatly increased Currency Accounts Department. With the removal of Exchange Control, a huge influx of requests to open accounts occurred and further computer driven initiatives were being pursued. I replaced my earlier young replacement, who was destined for higher things. My old mentor and friend had been removed to another department, for he had outlived his usefulness in his old job.

At that time the Currency Accounts and Currency Disposals Departments were under the joint management of a manager and assistant manager. The assistant manager had been recently installed. He had been in the bank for years and lived opposite us in Culverhouse Gardens. I had managed to avoid him till then. I was appointed Manager's Assistant under him. He and the manager were housed in a glass panelled office. I sat outside it. Eventually, another Manager's Assistant was appointed as my deputy. He was a chap from Dublin, Bill Tuohy. In those days, management appointments were made by the Personnel Department, before the advent of internal advertising of available positions, when people could apply to be considered. The Senior Executive had expressed some misgivings about me, which he confided to Bill, for he thought there might be trouble, as I was a Northern Protestant, whereas Bill was from the Republic and was a Roman Catholic. Bill was outraged, though amused and only told me this years later. In fact we got along very well and became friends, not least because we had our new boss and found mutual support, in contending with his dictatorial approach. Religion and politics were never mentioned in the bank and were not an issue.

One day, I was accompanying my 'boss' around the office, when I tentatively suggested an alternative solution to something he was proposing. He turned on me, saying, 'You don't suggest anything. I am the Assistant Manager, you are only the fucking Manager's Assistant!' The staff were taken aback. I agreed with him, telling him that he was absolutely right and returned to my desk without further comment. Next day he was all over me, inviting me to dine in the Senior Managers Dining room, saying I would meet the Senior Executive there. I declined, needless to say, but he persisted for some weeks, till I eventually went, very reluctantly.

The department was split from Currency Disposals and I was promoted to Assistant Manager to the ever growing Accounts Department. He was appointed Manager and so we had to share the private office. Prior to that, I had been sent to oversee the Sterling Ledgers Department, with a view to organising its amalgamation with our own operation. It was run by a lady who had been in that department for 42 years. She refused to speak to me. There was only one other chap amongst 32 females, in the department, where he was a clerk, who was also completely ignored. One day he made a good suggestion, which I relayed to the lady manager. Her retort that they didn't speak to him and considered his opinions of no consequence. I quickly arranged for his transfer to another department and some years later, he became a Senior Manager himself.

In the Sterling Department was a young Nigerian girl, purported to be of royal lineage. She was a law onto herself, often absent, late and lazy. She was not unintelligent and was very attractive and though a pain, was quite likeable. One day she appeared to faint in the middle of the office floor. The lady manager was on holiday and I was in charge. I didn't over react, but told one of her colleagues to call for the nurse, as she appeared not to revive. Meantime, my senior manager from the then amalgamated Disposals and Currency Departments came over to see me. He was an amiable gent, rather stout and a bit clumsy. Coming in, he noticed the inert body on the floor and simply stepped daintily over it. This was most amusing, not only for the situation, but also for the delicate way he stepped across, for he more usually knocked things over. He sat down beside me and casually enquired what was wrong with her. He was unmoved and on leaving, he stepped over her without a glance, as he left. The nurse arrived and pinched the young lady's ear lobe, whereupon she immediately leapt up, evidently

234

'cured'. I howled with mirth. She left the bank shortly afterwards, thank God.

I was able to effect many major changes to that department, resulting in its reduction from 30, to 12 staff, to be amalgamated with us at Suffolk House. I had given up with the lady manager and told her that I would be pursuing my own initiatives whether she spoke to me or not, saying it was a matter of no concern to me, whether she helped me or not. I went on holiday for a week and when I returned, there was a card on my desk, inviting me to her leaving party, which I gladly attended. She did have a knowledge of music, which was the only thing she would ever discuss with me. We had a large party for her leaving, attended by many other managers and staff, in deference to her long service.

I returned to my new appointment as Assistant Manager of Currency Accounts, which continued to grow. After a time, I was promoted and appointed Manager of the Sterling Clearing Department. Here I took over from my former sparring partner, who had been my supervisor in my early days in Currency Disposals, where our rows were legend. He was of volatile temperament like myself and we had had endless shouting matches, usually resulting in my being 'carpeted'. He took early retirement but we remained friends and he ever afterwards insisted on sitting with me at the Annual Reunion Dinners held for previous managers of Overseas Branch, which had been, for some years now, called International Division.

I was now a full Manager, responsible for a department undergoing re-organisation, to include the installation of new cheque clearing computer systems. This department was responsible for all cheques and bankers' payments, drawn on International Division by its agent banks and commercial customers, as well as those issued by ourselves. In addition, all repatriated sterling travellers cheques from abroad, were processed and accounted for. This amounted to millions of items annually and the sterling, paper based, town clearing, accounted for £9.1 billion daily, as well as the three-day cycle of the general clearing. Large numbers of cheques and payments had to be processed in a short time, to meet the daily deadline of the

235

Clearing House and effect final settlement at the Bank of England. It was hectic.

I forgot to mention that I had served for a while, in Inland Payments Department as Assistant Manager. This was similar to Currency Disposals, but dealt only with sterling payments, which amounted to £71 billion daily. The department was also under major reorganisation and the bank had employed an American company called Productivity Management Inc. They were a bunch of hatchet men, whose main aim was to achieve major cost reductions. Their last assignment had been in a chicken processing factory and their idea was to implement similar streamlined proceses in the bank, where every piece of paper should be handled only once, proceeding to the next stage of production until it reached the end of the line for final action, just as chickens were brought through the door, strung up, had their throats slit, were plucked, gutted, decapitated and their feet removed, passing on to processing and packaging, in one constant stream of successive actions. This was a hell of a time for we were going through major computer systems development at the same time. The new manager there was a young man destined for greatness. He appreciated my support and we achieved much. In fact he had previously been the manager of the Sterling Clearing Dept some years before.

In Sterling Clearing, I also had to arrange the amalgamation of currency cheque processing from Leicester, with our own systems. That department was responsible for the processing and collection of cheques drawn abroad, which were despatched daily to drawee, banks by courier. This function didn't fit easily with our sterling-based operations and mainly served the domestic branch network, as well as our foreign bank customers.

236

CHAPTER 24

The pace of change was rapid throughout the bank and a new Chief Executive was brought in from America, to replace the former CE, Herve de Carmoy, a French aristocrat, who had been brought in to turn Midland around, following its disastrous sally into American banking, by its purchase of Crocker National Bank in California.

The new CE, Gene Lockhart, and his Deputy, Andy Hanges, visited me. I was told that I had ten minutes to say who I was, what we did and what I needed him to do to help. He stayed for three-quarters of an hour. One of the big problems was the Town Clearing, paper based and open to fraud, delays and interest claims, for missed deadlines. I suggested that we should look to automating this, with a view to running it down completely. To do this, CHAPS (The Clearing House Automated Payments System), being developed for Sterling Payments, could be utilised and settlement effected thereby. I had had two Oxford graduates attached to me for a few months, who were on a fast management stream. I had already assigned them a project to get rid of Town Clearing. They had laughed, saying it couldn't be done. My own Senior Manager, Head of Operations, had said the same. 'Very well,' I told them, 'treat it as a joke, enjoy it, but do it!' I instructed them to research other countries' systems, American, Scandinavian, French, Swiss, German, but to come up with ideas. They were to look at CHAPS and the needs of the Securities Department, for they were one of the main opponents to the proposal. Write me a Paper and enjoy what you are doing I said. They did a good job and after leaving my department, they quickly went on to management positions in the bank, one being posted for a term, to Austria.

I mentioned this paper, which was very comprehensive, to the Chief Executive. Turning to Andy, he demanded. Did you know this? Where can I get a copy? I'll get it for you, I said. I'll get, he said. He became chairman of the CHAPS and Town Clearing Board and in a year or so, we achieved our objective and the Paper Town Clearing was disbanded, after over 200 years of operation, and the process was automated.

In the meantime, my old friend and former mentor from Currency Accounts had been languishing in Documentary Credits Dept. He had renewed his fondness for drink and had met a number of solicitors, who frequented The Bell at lunchtime and he decided to take early retirement. He approached me again, asking that I should try to avoid any collection for him as was the usual custom. I agreed. Some days later he came back, having thought about it and said that, as it was probably inevitable that a collection would be made, could I ensure that they did not buy him a clock, for the previous one presented at the time of his wedding, had never worked satisfactorily and had rarely been out of the repairers. Some days later he again approached me, having had second thoughts, and asked if I could arrange for a gift cheque instead, which would be preferable, for he had an outstanding electricity bill to settle. He got it.

I saw him from time to time after his retirement. He had met another retired bank manager, who had never had a drink during his working life. He had found a liking for liquor and declared it was his intention to drink as much as he could for the rest of his life, as he enjoyed it so much. He and my friend joined forces and I read of his death some years ago, a happy ending I hope. I regretted his passing, for he had said that he was the one friend he had had in the bank.

We used to hold annual evenings for the appointed officers, when managers would entertain their assistants at the Cafe Royal or, more latterly, the Porters Tun Room. One night at the Cafe Royal, after a fine meal, we were approached by the Head Waiter to see if there was anything else we required. One of my managerial colleagues asked if they had any custard cream biscuits, to which he knew I was addicted. This caused howls of laughter and confusion to the waiter.

The changes being brought about by the computer were now rampant. Major developments were taking place in every quarter. To keep up with this and to increase our managerial effectiveness, the bank encouraged us to go on courses at their Training Colleges in Betchworth and Oxted. Some of these were very intensive, some may have seemed irrelevant at the time, most were quite enjoyable and whatever our thoughts may have been, much of what I learnt had some bearing on my development and decision-making in future years.

The major problems were always to do with staff management, whether from an operational point of view, in relation to distribution of resources and ensuring fair reward for ability and application, or personal problems, ethnic awareness or equal opportunities. Resources were often strained through lack of staff, as business increased, or lack of essential skills as systems and processes constantly changed. With technology rampant in the 80s and huge demographic and cultural changes taking place, departments were merged, down-sized (an unpopular word throughout the bank) and new types of business or governmental legislation had to be accommodated.

Apart from in-house training at our Centre at Mariner House, the first major course I attended at Betchworth College, was an Executive Course attended by senior management figures, departmental managers and lower ranking management supervisors. This gave me a good view of some of my senior colleagues, some of whom were already in high appointments. In most cases they were an amenable bunch and we all let off steam after hours, with much raucous fun in the Billiards or table tennis rooms and, of course, the bar. Many years later, I met one of the most senior members of the course, who was now a higher Executive. He was guest speaker at one of our Cafe Royal soirees and spoke profoundly on the gold situation and financial matters generally. I met him during the evening and said that he probably did not remember me, but that we had attended a course together some years before. He looked at me and said, 'Oh yes, you were that noisy bugger down at Betchworth, weren't you?'

During a three weeks course at Oxted College, we were put under intense problem-solving and pressure situations, to contend with crisis management. We were split into teams repre-

239

senting different departments of the bank, involved in some way or another, in a common business problem. Sent to different rooms, each section was given sets of incomplete information, statistics, targets and so on, all of which together would give the total picture and afford solutions. Our task, with the aid of 'runners' between groups, was to furnish or seek information from each other, within a deadline, as our individual sections' deliberations, revealed gaps in our available data. This had us like nervous wrecks, but many years later I was confronted by a crisis situation, to which there seemed no solution.

We had suffered a complete black-out in the building, at the crucial Town Clearing time and our back-up generator failed simultaneously. We therefore had no computer machinery to process the cheques and payments, no electricity even to use adding machines and were in semi-darkness. We got no sympathy from the Clearing House, whose rigid rules stated that all work must be delivered, outsorted, listed and agreed, before presentation to the drawees at the House, and within the official deadline. Everyone was panicking when I suddenly went very calm and the situation on the course came back to me. Even though our syndicate on that occasion had failed to achieve a good result, I remembered our mistake and the one essential dictate - gather all the facts, take decisions, then act. I applied this technique and with the help of staff from adjoining departments to act as runners, I assembled small teams with clear lines of directions on what to do and we achieved the clearing deadline by presenting manual listings, corresponding with bundles of manually outsorted cheques and with the runners, achieved the deadline. That, of course, wasn't the whole picture, for tidying up afterwards and ensuring that all customers accounts, debit or credit, were correctly accounted for, required the individual expertise of even the lowest clerical grades, who responded excellently.

I was fortunate on other occasions, when I took major decisions which had good results. These same principles still applied, id est, assess the problem, gather the facts, assess resources, decide priorities and take action, with clear directives to those carrying them out.

I attended several courses in later years, which concentrated on resource management skills, which came into play later, as my job and areas of responsibility changed and grew. One particular course I attended was at an establishment near Aldershot. This concentrated very much on man-management skills and lasted for three weeks. There were some very bright and eager graduate managers attending. One of these was very serious but he could play the piano and accompanied me on several evenings in entertaining our colleagues to songs. We had some amusing times and I also told a lot of outrageous jokes as part of the entertainment. At the end of the course I was presented with a tutor's tie, in recognition of my entertainments contribution and the general enjoyment of the course.

An amusing incident occurred during the day sessions. Each day one of us had to introduce the guest speaker and at the end of the day another had to offer a vote of thanks. A colleague of mine in the Payments' area failed to arrive on his allotted morning, to give the introduction and he only appeared an hour later, dishevelled and embarrassed. To add insult to injury, the next day when he was to give the vote of thanks to another speaker, he started off by forgetting his name. His career was short lived.

CHAPTER 25

We, of course, found time for holidays during the year. As Elsie had re-joined BEA, we had the opportunity to travel at reduced staff rates, so we made frequent visits to Milan to keep in touch with friends there. More particularly, we had the opportunity to take advantage of 'Interline' packages, just like the previous trip to Hong Kong. We took up an offer from Cathay Pacific Airlines, which afforded a tour and accommodation, to Singapore, Hong Kong and Thailand, so off we went.

First stop was Hong Kong, to meet staff members of our host airline. We stayed at the Hong Kong Hyatt on Kowloon and met up with members of other airlines' staff, making up the group. We saw the usual sights of Hong Kong and bought loads of unnecessary items. I particularly enjoyed the Star Ferry, which, for a few pence, would transport you across the bay to Hong Kong Island. This afforded us a good view of the hulk of the QEI, still lying on its side , where it had been burnt out on our last visit there. The party consisted of people from several nations. Our host's representative was Amy Yuen, who was our guide. She visited London on one occasion and stayed with us. Some years later we were to attend her wedding in Hong Kong. Another young and very pretty Chinese girl became friendly with us and she invited us to meet her family at home. This was in a high rise flat in the densely populated district of the island. Elsie and I were treated royally and fed sumptuously. On leaving, our young hostess presented me with a book. It turned out that she was a Jehovah's Witness and next day she invited me to a meeting. By that time, I was already on my guard and was able to gracefully decline. This did not dent our friendship, for the present anyway.

We went on to savour the promised delights of Singapore. I found it beautiful but boring. Raffles Hotel seemed to be rather seedy and tired but I enjoyed the cable car ride which afforded good views. The most memorable thing was the outdoor restaurant area, where every type of Oriental cuisine could be enjoyed at reasonable cost, freshly prepared before your eyes and washed down with Tiger beer.

Thailand proved to be much more exciting. At first sight, driving in from the airport, you would think that you had arrived in a poor third world country. The city, initially, seemed shabby. The hotels were magnificent and we were installed at the Hyatt Rama. However, it was the people, the variety of shops, the traffic and bustle and the great interesting sightseeing that made the place memorable.

It happened to be my birthday, which our guide announced at dinner in the hotel. Somehow people find these things out, which irks me, for I prefer to remain aloof on such occasions. Everyone showed interest, so I decided that I would provide wine for the party at the dinner table that night. Many of those present had never sampled wine before but they took to it readily and became quite boisterous, somewhat to the surprise of the hotel staff, not used to such overt displays of emotion. My heart missed a beat when I later discovered that the wine had cost me about £30 a bottle, of which we'd had several and this made a large hole in my budget. At the end of the evening, I was seized by a young Japanese girl, who pinned me against the wall, kissing me feverishly, to the amazement of my wife and her husband. They stood helplessly by along with the other astonished members of the party. I was not at all averse and it almost made up for the indulgence in the over-priced wine. Of course, her passion could not continue.

Next day we were up early for a trip by boat up the river and through the forest canals, to the floating markets village. We went in those long boats, driven fast and expertly by the Thais, propelled by long-shafted outboard motors as seen on occasions in James Bond movies. The young lady, her ardour now, no doubt, dampened by a hangover and replaced by embarrassment, sat some way away, unable to meet my eye and we never spoke again. The previous evening's interlude was not referred to by anyone else. The floating markets were very interesting as was the trip through the jungle, with houses on stilts coming right down into the water's edge, adults and children bathing in the river, washing their hair and cleaning their teeth. The water looked brown and turgid, but we were assured that it was clean and safe. Certainly, the locals suffered no ill-effects and I was able to eat whatever came before me with impunity. Salads and fruits and drinks with ice cubes in them, caused me no discomfort. This was far from the case on a trip to India some years later.

We visited the temples and palaces, saw aspects of Thai village life - elephants at work, Thai boxing and dancing. We were amazed at the wood carving, bronze smelting and moulding, silver beating, umbrella painting and silk making factories. We returned by rice barge and were plied with Thai whisky, which made me very jolly but frowned on by some Europeans travelling back with us. We also saw the delights and horrors of the Pat Pong night life, where inhibitions are abandoned and shameless pleasure is rampant.

Elsie visited a designer and tailor. She described what she wanted, and beautifully tailored clothes were delivered to the hotel within hours, in the exact European style she had requested.

We returned to Hong Kong before our eventual departure to London and home. My young Chinese Jehovah's Witness had not given up and pressed several tracts on me, before bidding us farewell. I never saw her again, but some months later, I was horrified when a couple of young ladies of the same persuasion, came to our door to proclaim their ministry. I was more forthright on that occasion in expressing my lack of interest in their doctrine and ushered them off the premises and out of my life.

Trips to Milan were taken as a matter of course. On one memorable occasion we met the great British baritone, Peter Glossop. He had been introduced to us in London by Ashley Sullivan. He and Craig had got to know him, when competing in a singing competition in Bulgaria, which Peter had won. Peter had worked in a bank in his early days, I think he told me it was Nat West. He had joined the chorus of Sadlers Wells Opera, attained leading roles and in 1964, was understudy to Geraint

Evans, for the role of Rigoletto at Covent Garden. The papers at the time, reported that Evans was having difficulty at rehearsals and suggested that Glossop should go on instead. Evans (later Sir Geraint) was a great singer and made a splendid Falstaff in Verdi's last great opera. He excelled in Mozart and other German operas and in some buffo Italian operas. 'Rigoletto' is of a different order altogether.Glossop performed on the opening night at Covent Garden and created a furore. He was immediately signed up for La Scala, where he became famously popular. The London performance was broadcast on BBC radio, which I heard.

That same year, the great Welsh soprano, now Dame Gwyneth Jones, emerged and she and Peter were invited to appear in the famous show, Sunday night at the London Palladium. They sang the stupendous duet from Act IV from Il Travatore, which I was delighted to see and hear, on TV when it was broadcast. Dame Gwyneth was a beauty who went on to an illustrious career in Wagner and Verdi operas. Ashley said he heard her as one of the best Turandots ever, in Italy. Elsie and I heard her at Covent Garden, in La Fanciulla del West, around 1994, when she was 58 years old, still beautiful and depicting the character of Minnie. This portrays a young girl of 18 and is a very tough role, which she had delayed in assuming till then for it was so demanding. This was in spite of having sung Verdi, Wagner and Turandot for years. She was so good, that we paid to go to see her again in the same opera.

We had been entertained by Peter's wife, Joyce Blackham, the noted mezzo soprano, at his fine house on the Bishop's Avenue in Hampstead. I had met Peter along with Ashley, for a couple of games of squash at Wembley. Peter was popular in Milan, not just for his voice, but also for his idiomatic Italian. The Italians are very critical of foreigners' singing of their language, so he scored on both counts.

He was to sing the role of Renato in Un Ballo in Maschera and gave us his two complimentary tickets for the performance, which found Ashley and myself sitting in the Presidential box amongst other noted guests. I was overwhelmed by the whole performance, especially in the last act, where the tenor,

Riccardo, having been stabbed by Renato, lies dying. The chorus and cast together, sing the finale, starting like a gentle tuneful hymn, the tenor pleading forgiveness for his assassins and declaring Renato's wife, Amelia, to be pure, although in love. He asks the assembly for their blessing as the chorus rises to a great crescendo, the sound surging across the footlights and over the auditorium, like a great tidal wave, seeming to press you back in your seat, gasping with the beauty and gloriousness of the music. I weep when I hear it on record even today.

We went round to see Peter afterwards, walking across the vast, now deserted La Scala stage, to the back and up to the dressing rooms, where Peter was already standing in his underpants, wiping off the grease paint and bawling for a 'bloody pint', for he liked his beer. Having downed a couple of pints, he took us to dinner at a restaurant, near the theatre, to conclude a memorable evening. We next saw him some years later, at his 60th birthday party, in Devon, where he had retired to live. The party was held at the pub run by Craig Sullivan and his wife, in their restaurant. We dined on Sea Bass, Peter's favourite.

On another occasion, in Milan in the mid 70s I was out with Eric. We were passing La Scala, where Trovatore was being performed. It was already underway and the great Franco Corelli was singing Manrico. I expressed my regret to Eric that we were not inside the theatre. He told me to bide my time, for the patrons were emerging for the first interval. We mingled with the crowd and Eric passed a few lire notes to the doorman, gaining admission to the third or fourth tier. It is quite usual for standing patrons to occupy places at the rear of each tier and so we joined them. Eric is a short chap and I was amazed and amused by his antics, as the show progressed, when he angrily ordered the paying public to stand aside, so that we could see the better.

At the next interval, we were approached by a gentleman from Austria. He had heard us speaking in English and was interested to know if we knew the great British baritone, Peter Glossop. We assured him that we knew him well and he engaged us in enthusiastic conversation. Finally, Eric growing tired of this, suggested we move on, whereupon our new found companion seized me by the arm, saying that he had something to give me. He pressed various pamphlets into my hand. Imagine my horror to discover that they were tracts proclaiming the Jehovah's Witness message. Would I ever escape? We beat a hasty retreat. I must have been contaminated in Hong Kong, for that was not the last time I was to be approached by those, propounding that faith. Even as late as 1999, in the town of Antrim, I was again accosted by two pleasant looking young ladies, of the same persuasion.

Elsie and I attended a performance of Verdi's Don Carlos, a long opera lasting well into the early hours, for they start at 9.30 pm in Milan. However, it boasted young Placido Domingo in the cast. I don't recall the other stars but it was a fine performance. Elsie was bored, so I last saw this opera in Chicago with a friend and in spite of its length, enjoyed it very much. We also attended a performance of Verdi's 'Macbeth', with Piero Capuccili and the great American soprano, Shirley Verrett - (Carter), who had developed from a mezzo, into a dramatic soprano. This is a great opera musically, follows Shakespeare reasonably faithfully and has several show stoppers, for both soprano and baritone, particularly in Macbeth's mad scene, when Banquo's ghost appears, and in Lady Macbeth's sleep walking outburst as she sings 'Out Out Damned Spot!'

We attended Albert Panerai's wedding in December 1977. In Milan, Dr Panerai installed us in a hotel. On the eve of the wedding Elsie, Eric and myself, were in town and Elsie did her usual search for boots and shoes. Elsie and Eric went off together, leaving me to find my way to Ashley's flat, where we had been invited for dinner. I was well home and had finished dinner before they got back for they were unduly delayed with Christmas traffic. Eric and I were to go to a fashion show that evening, where Craig Sullivan was performing songs in cabaret during the proceedings. Elsie had stayed behind to get ready for the wedding. We were already late when we set out and another car crashed into us on the way. Not much damage was done, but the bumper of our Wolkswagen was ripped off on one side and was bent out like a lance, in front of us. After a chase through the streets, we arrived near the venue and parked the car. When we arrived at the show, it was over and the models were in the back changing room in various states of undress, as we mingled with them. They were very friendly and beautiful. They embraced us fondly, Eric jumping up to get at one of the taller ladies who had taken his fancy. Craig wasn't too pleased that we had missed his singing, but we set off together on foot to a local all-night cafe for something to eat and drink and we ended in a piano bar, where I sang the Rose of Tralee.

I was to sing at Alberto's wedding next day in Varese, so in the early hours we set off to find Eric's car. We had forgotten where it was parked and had to give up the search that night. We later spent two days searching for it. I went back to the hotel, arriving about 4 a.m. I blundered into the room, slid on a rug on the polished floor and landed with a thud against the wardrobe. Elsie awoke, propped me up and left me there till I came round. We were to be driven to the wedding by Alberto himself. I was in no fit state to go at all, never mind sing, but I was knocked into shape by the time Alberto arrived. It was a snowy, freezing day and when we arrived at the church in Varese, we met other guests and awaited the arrival of the best man. It turned out that he had crashed his car on the way so we had to proceed without him. He arrived later. The organist, an elderly lady, did not feel inclined to play. She said that the organ was not performing well in the freezing atmosphere, so I was honourably relieved of my obligation to sing.

We went to the restaurant on the shore of Lake Varese, where the larger portion of the premises had been set aside for our use. As at our own wedding, Alberto had ordered roast duckling, but it was cooked in a totally different manner from ours and didn't have the same succulence. The wine flowed and the company was merry. Some motorbikers arrived and seeing a juke box in the corner, plugged it in and started playing loud music. Dr Panerai, senior, approached them requesting that they desist, as the restaurant had been booked for a private party, whereupon he was struck by one of the revellers. To a man, we all rose and went to his rescue. A free-for-all commenced, everyone trading blows and wrestling with the aggressors. Panerai's noted gynaecologist friend seized one of them, encircling his neck in the crook of his arm, and hurled him bodily across the room. With a clunk, the biker hit a large, old-fashioned cast iron radiator and shuddered to the floor. The ladies were screaming and spread out around the walls to avoid the melee, which by now, was like a scene from the John Wayne, Lee Marvin, movie, 'Donovan's Reef'. A Christmas tree went crashing over, scattering the debris, as other bodies scuffled on the ground. All the while, a little man over at an end table, sat eating his lunch, watching eagerly as he continued to shovel food into his mouth, never missing a bite, intent on the action. The chef appeared in his tall hat, a big fellow, bellowing and brandishing a meat cleaver, ready to do murder. The police arrived, the situation calmed down and leaders of each party were taken outside to give an account of things. No charges were pressed, but the bikers were ordered off and away they went. We got back to eating and everyone had a good laugh, the old grandmother saying this had been a good omen for a successful marriage, citing some previous occasion when she had witnessed such a spectacle.

The bride was a young lady called Bianca, a Botanist, and writer of books on the subject of trees. Both mothers were teachers, so the relationship had been brought about. Alberto went on to become an eminent Endocrinologist and they took a large apartment in the street adjoining Alberto's home. They had two daughters and we attended a dinner party at their apartment one evening. There were two Nobel Prizewinners present and two other aspirants in that direction. The guests were of different nationalities, including Mexican and Japanese. Quite memorable. The Mexican insisted on singing songs, accompanying himself on the guitar. Quite dreadful.

Alas, the augury as predicted by the grandmother at the wedding, was not fulfilled and Bianca and Alberto separated, but they remain on speaking terms and we met them and the girls on several occasions since. Both girls were very pretty and showed considerable academic qualities and social graces, particularly Sylvia, the first born, who was able to accompany her grandmother to London when she was 11 years of age and to act as her interpreter. They stayed at the Cumberland Hotel and we were able to take them to such places as Hampton Court and Simpson's in the Strand for a roast beef lunch.

We had already moved to a new house when they came. In 1981 the bank allowed staff to renegotiate mortgages after ten years, thus giving the opportunity to move up-market and to borrow more money commensurate with current salaries and rising house prices. We had decided to move and put the house up for sale. We found a large detached house in De Montfort Road, Streatham. I determined to go for this, for I always wanted space and, in particular, detachment from other neighbours. The house had been owned by a Scottish doctor, a Consultant Chest Physician at St Thomas's. He had died and his widow wished to sell as her family had moved on.

The house had a small front garden, front and rear garages and a pleasant rear garden. It stood on a corner. It had a large hallway with fireplace and a fine stairway. Downstairs was a large dining room, a sitting room, breakfast room, kitchen and pantry. Upstairs there were four good bedrooms, a bathroom and separate toilet and a large attic, where I was able to instal a full-size table tennis table. House prices were rising rapidly and properties were not long on the market, but house moves are never without problems.

CHAPTER 26

Whilst in our first house, I had acquired the collecting bug. We had come across an antique shop in Streatham Village, run by George Nichol and his partner. They had two old shops adjoining each other and sold a variety of bric a brac, some good antiques and paintings and items of interest. The first item I bought for £15 was a small bonheur du jour, a small writing desk of unusual, but attractive design in very poor order. I set about restoring it and it turned out very well. This started my hobby of furniture restoration, which gave me pleasure and relief from the cares of banking. This continued throughout my years in London and we became friendly with George and his wife. George was a most interesting character as were others in the antique business, who met frequently in his shop on a Saturday morning, to talk, deal and drink tea. We sold our house and bought No 1 De Montfort Road. The move was welcomed by the spinsterly sisters, by now reduced to two, for the eldest had died. We were also pleased to get away, not because of any particular unpleasantness, but to have the relief of knowing that I could freely indulge my musical pursuits without interference. Also, Len and Phoebe had sold the year before and we were not happy with the new neighbours on that side.

We had much to do at the new house. Although it was beautiful it was somewhat old-fashioned, though with some interesting original features, such as bells in the rooms, to summon the maid from her quarters in the kitchen area. It was painted internally in sombre browns and much varnish and with threadbare carpets and linoleum. Because we were in a chain of moves, our purchasers were slow to complete, but we persevered and moved in August 1981. There was only partial central heating so we engaged the same plumber to instal new

251

heating and a downstairs loo, in what had been a butler's pantry in the smaller hall off the main one. He was a good plumber but with a fondness for drink. All rooms, including the main hallway, had fine fireplaces, which we kept in situ. He installed a gas fire in the hallway with coals that glowed realistically and added a nice perspective to the house on entering. I did all the internal decoration myself, but engaged George Nichol to extend the attic a little. I was able to use the stair carpets, which were the only ones worth keeping, on the stairs up to the attic, approached by its own door off the landing and there was enough to cover the entire attic floor wall to wall. We had carpets laid throughout the rest of the house, except for the dining room, which had a fine, loose, carpet of 15 ft square on the floor. I replaced the surrounding lino with parquet flooring.

Now I had a place to relax, make music, two garages to work in and a pleasant easily managed back garden, where I could work on antiques in good weather. The back of the house was completely covered in wisteria, which gave a magnificent display twice each year. George and I had table tennis sessions each week in the attic, until the ceilings below began to show the strain. I replaced the table with a three-quarters billiards table and we resorted to snooker thereafter. This also gave endless pleasure to myself and other visitors.

Our first trip to America had occurred in 1973 whilst we were still living in Culverhouse Gardens. We went to visit my mother's elderly cousin, Mrs Edith Kort, and her husband, who lived in Newark, New Jersey. She was very wealthy and had married Neil Kort, a Dutchman, against her family's wishes. He was in government and rose to high office in the Department of Employment. Edith (nee Wright) was my mother's cousin on her maternal side. Grandma had been called Hannah Wright before marriage. Edith and Neil were frequent visitors to Europe and had stayed with us at Ballyrobert. They loved travel which his work often entailed. During the war they had sent us food parcels, thinking we were in dire straits. They were in fact very generous.

We were met at Kennedy Airport and driven to Newark in a new Cadillac, which Neil had purchased for the occasion.

They already had a Pontiac and a Studebaker. They lived in a fine house which they had divided in two, affording accommodation for their daughter and son-in-law on the upper floor and they occupied the lower quarters themselves. They were keen to introduce us to every conceivable relative, however distant and they fed us huge amounts of food at all times. So we were driven around in the Cadillac to visit relatives and friends and fed like Sumo wrestlers, at famous restaurants. At a visit to a turkey farm, we were each served half a beast to eat. To keep our strength up at home, a large fridge was constantly stocked with every type of fast food available. We groaned.

Neil was an organist and pianist and his grandson was the organist at the magnificent Newark, Roman Catholic, Cathedral, which was a nice ecumenical arrangement, for he was Protestant. I had the pleasure of singing with his accompaniment from the organ loft in the vast confines of the magnificent building. Only the best of materials had been used to build the church and artisans from the countries of origin, had fashioned the Italian Carara marble, carved the Indian teak and sculptors from wherever, had carved the granite and sandstone used for the main fabric.

Neil was an accomplished painist and played for me at home. I sang arias and as I was singing, Edith exclaimed, 'Gee, he sings in Eyetalian'. She arranged for a friend to take me to a matinee performance at the Metropolitan Opera house. She was a patron of the Met and had two permanent seats in the circle. The opera was Carmen, with Marilyn Horne in the title role. She was one of the greatest mezzo sopranos ever, excelling in Rossini coloratura, as well as heavier roles, such as Delilah and in works by Wagner, Berg (Wozzeck) and Handel. The tenor, James McCracken, was Don Jose, Escamillo was Robert Massard and the conductor was the great Leonard Bernstein. This became a famous recording.

During the interval, I was taken downstairs to the art gallery and museum. On display, were many pictures of the great singers of the Golden Age, who had sung at the Met. I began to comment to my companion on the various artists displayed, Melba, Caruso, De Reszke, Sembrich and so on. Soon I had a trail of people following me and I responded to the occasion and soon had a crowd around me as we proceeded along. That is one of the nicer traits of the Americans, their thirst for knowledge and information and I enjoyed their enthusiastic appreciation. I could have passed a hat round at the end! I thanked my hostess for the occasion and sent her a note on my return home, enclosing the autograph of Giuseppe di Stefano that I acquired in Milan, by way of thanks.

Our hosts hardly ever allowed us out on our own, for Edith deemed New York to be too risky. So we were driven up to see some of the sights, including Wall Street, because they thought that I was interested in Banking - huh! I had bought a new suit for the trip and looked very well, (I have photos to prove it), but one of my shoe soles fell off, so for a while I was lent a pair by Neil. I decided to go and buy a new pair, whilst we were up town. Neil was a large tall man, and his shoes were size 14, I normally wore an eight. The assistant in the shoe shop greeted me, took my order and asked my size, looking at my feet. My response of size eight please, caused him a momentary jolt, for my feet looked like a circus clown's, and he must have thought I was a joker.

Edith's daughter, Jean, and her husband, Danny, had two sons. Steve we had already met, but Bob was a pilot with the USAF, and we never met him. A terrible tragedy happened some years after our visit, when Bob was murdered in Florida by a drug-crazed lunatic.

We met a young second cousin, a beautiful girl, Terry, who was a super person. Her mother was also a beauty and her father a fine-looking man. He was a fast talking insurance broker, who amused us by his enthusiastic listing of his products and business. It is to my regret that I never met them again for they brought light and pleasant relief, from the continuing round of visits to other ancient and distant relatives, who were of no interest to me whatever.

Neil and Edith had visited London and had lunched with us at Culverhouse Gardens. They were overwhelmed by the house, with Elsie's tasteful decor, and the grand piano. Other furniture I had restored looked very well and they thought our house very grand, which pleased me, for I didn't want to be considered the poor relation, for ever.

We had been to Birmingham to visit Nina, Fred and family. We came upon a junk shop, which was closing down and in the window, was a tattered, double scroll-ended Victorian couch. Inside were two other couches, in similar condition, but of different design. I would have liked them all, but I could see the particular possibilities of the scroll-end, when it would be renovated. I purchased it there and then for £20. I had no means of getting it to London and Fred and Nina refused to have it in the house. The shopkeeper wanted rid of it for he was clearing out. In the end, he had a brainwave. He knew of an upholsterer, who would re-cover it for us and deliver it to London, as he frequently went there. The shopkeeper agreed to hold the couch if we would arrange for the upholsterer to collect it. We did this and agreed to have it re-done in olive green leather, with deep buttoning to the back and arms, for £82, delivered. When it arrived, it was beautiful and it has had pride of place in our houses ever since. That was one of the pieces on which I had no work to do.

I was not at all settled in the bank, in spite of my ability and likely progress. I decided to try for an audition at Covent Garden, with Elsie's agreement that, if successful, even in attaining a position with the chorus, I would pursue a career in that direction. This was about 1972. I was called and sang 'Deserto sulla Terra' from the first act of Trovatore. This required some force but caused me no trouble and it is quite short. I was asked to sing something else, which I think was 'Questa o Quella' from Rigoletto. I was not offered a job, but a while later, Craig's friend, the secretary at Covent Garden, on noticing where he was staying with us, said that she remembered that name and address and recalled my audition. Searching the records, she said that I had received a favourable report, with the comment that I had a good big voice and would be a prospect for the chorus. I was sorry to have missed my chance, for it would have at least have given me employment in something I liked and might have led to other things.

I had not given up singing by any means, singers never do,

really. It is like a disease, worse than unrequited love and is an ambition that pursues you forever. I, nevertheless, determined that I was unlikely to make a living in that direction for it requires much more than a voice to succeed, as well as great energy, determination and luck. Most of all, musicality is required for conductors are now very demanding on singers and expect them to have an ability to read music, like musicians in the orchestra. So I set my ambitions aside to continue my very demanding job in banking but retained my interest in opera. I was fortunate that David Sutton lived nearby and we were able to have weekly rehearsals together. I also worked with Rosemary at the ENO from time to time.

In 1980, I was asked to audition for Jupiter opera, for the tenor role in a proposed production of a short opera called 'A Capital Transfer'. This had been written by a young composer, Kenneth Platts, as a commission for the Nottingham Arts Theatre, which had run out of funds and so was offered to Jupiter Opera. The Artistic Director was Cyril Summers, who was a teacher and sometime singer, at Covent Garden. He was a translator of libretti, who also produced operas, including Ariadne Auf Naxos, at the Curtain Theatre in East London. The libretto for a Capital Transfer, was by Beverley Cross, librettist and playwright, who had completed three libretti for the composer Richard Rodney Bennett and had collaborated on such West End musicals, as Jorrocks and Half a Sixpence.

I auditioned with the aria, 'Elle ne Croyait pas', from Mignon, with Cyril accompanying me. He expressed his approval, saying it was nice to find a tenor with good line and resonant tone. He engaged me for the tenor role of the proposed opera. It was a difficult role to learn, being in modern idiom, with difficult harmonies and high tessitura. The role concerned an eccentric octagenerian millionaire and his desire to avoid death duties by first marrying his son's fiancee, then divorcing her with a large settlement, so that the son could inherit without tax. As you can imagine, it was entertaining and didn't go entirely to plan as was revealed in the action. There were only three principal singing roles and one of a waiter, on stage. The other two were established professional singers.

David finally knocked the music into me and we performed our world premiere at the British Council Students Centre, at Portland Place, W1, to an enthusiastic audience. I received the thanks and congratulations of the composer. Cyril encouraged me to continue with Jupiter Opera to sing Fenton, in a proposed production of Verdi's 'Falstaff', but other things intervened.

We had friends living in Redhill and we visited them from time to time. They were from Downpatrick and Elsie had been friendly with them since school days. The husband was a senior Civil Servant in the DOE. He was posted to Gibraltar as Crown Property Agent and we flew out to stay with them, in 1984. They were accommodated in Loquat House, once the maison de plaisance of a former Prince of Wales. This was very grand and Gibraltar was a pleasant enough place, with good weather and some sights to see.

It was rather old fashioned and I felt that it looked as Tooting High Street might have in the 1950s. We explored the Rock and the Dockyards, drove into Spain, the road crossing the colony's airport runway on our way, just like a railway crossing, with automatic gates to keep you back when aircraft were landing. Our host was responsible for the airport and all other government installations. The Rock has large caves throughout and we were shown through the main caverns, where there is a concert hall, the sounds echoing loudly in the large spaces. We had our photos taken with the Barbary Apes.

The highlight of the trip was an invitation, graciously extended by the Governor and his wife, Sir Peter and Lady Terry, to take lunch with them at Government House. We were greeted by Lady Terry and she invited my opinion of a grand piano, installed in the main dining room, where we were to dine. It was an old Steinweg, that is, an original German-made piano, now the Steinway Company of America. I am no pianist, but gladly tried it out, found it to be of good tone and action, and essayed the first part of the aria 'M'appari Tutt'amor'. That was fine, but the Governor was now coming and my recital was hurriedly brought to an end. I declared the piano worth keeping, but requiring a good tuner and some slight modification of touch and movement generally.

I was seated next to His Excellency, a most charming host, who engaged me in lively conversation, particularly on banking matters. The Colony had only recently opened up off-shore banking facilities, such as those afforded on the Isle of Man or Channel Islands. Our conversation turned to the Midland Bank and its initiatives to attract customers of high nett worth. He was interested to know how the bank was getting along under the exectutive direction of Herve de Carmoy. I mentioned his penchant for videos and of being interviewed. He had recently brought in management assessment procedures, with pay related to output and management by objectives. These were initiatives which were giving us all headaches at the time.

A video had been produced, of an interview by Brian Redhead, who had asked about these initiatives and their beneficial impact on the bank's cost-saving measures. He then asked de Carmoy, what was in it for the managers, if they successfully applied them. De Carmoy hesitated briefly and replied, that they would keep their jobs. We both howled with mirth at this unfeeling attitude. The Governor had a busy afternoon, for some junior ministers were with us at lunch, so he made his excuses and bade us farewell, leaving us in the care of his wife.

Lady Terry kindly showed us round the grounds and chatted amiably for a while, before we had to reluctantly withdraw. Our friends, Trevor and Suzanne Fulton, who were with us, kept in touch with the Governor and his wife ever since. There was a very sad sequel to Sir Peter's tenure, during which he had been involved with the fracas over the shooting of IRA suspects in a thwarted raid on the Colony. He had retired, but eventually the IRA found him and raided his home, when he was severely injured. He survived his fearful wounds. He was one of the nicest people I ever met.

On return to England after their tour of duty, our friends bought a large ground floor apartment at Canford Cliffs near Poole and overlooking the bay at Bournemouth, in anticipation of retirement. No sooner had they moved there, than he was posted to Rhinedalen in Germany, where they were accommodated on the British Army base, in a fine detached house. We were able to visit them there and drove to Holland and Frankfurt, but generally found the place rather dull.

Whilst they were away for a number of years, they encouraged us to use their magnificent apartment at Canford Cliffs, to let it be seen to be occupied. We spent several very pleasant holidays down there, on occasion accompanied by Mother. She loved Bournemouth (plenty of shoe shops) and the general ambience. We were able to visit Poole, Weymouth and Portland Bill, the latter reminding me very much of Gibraltar or Tooting High Street. It was like stepping back a generation or two, as you crossed the spit into the area and I very much enjoyed going there several times. I almost bought the head of a whaling harpoon, a mighty chunk of metal, for sale in a junk shop, but Elsie prevailed, saying that if it came into the house she would go out.

I loved Weymouth, with its busy harbour, long beach and excellent fish restaurants. When I retired, I wanted to buy the Harbour Master's house, which had been advertised for sale at the time. Once more, Elsie's good sense prevailed.

On a visit to Milan in 1983, we met Dr Panerai and his family again. He asked us would we like to go with them to Florence the following weekend. They had a friend there, Varo Cioli, who had retired from his post as a Director of the Uffizi Gallery and had bought a farm, with vineyard, at Grassina, in the hills outside the city. Each year he held the Vendemmia, the vintage, and people congregated to harvest the grapes. It was arranged that we would stay at the house of his friend, Priscilla Bayard, which was situated in Florence, by the walls of the Forte di Belvedere. This is a magnificent medieval structure, affording splendid views of the huge Duomo and a panorama of the city of Florence. Priscilla's house was a treat, both inside and out. She was an English lady, who had been married to an American General and was now living alone in Florence.

The farm at Grassina was a short distance from Florence in the hills of Tuscany, affording beautiful views of the olive groves, the slopes and their Cypress glades, vineyards and terracotta tiled roofs, nestling in the hills. On a late Summer's evening, you can hear the singing of crickets and the odd shot of a hunter after game, or the cries of delight as children frolic in a far-off swimming pool. It is a delight to sit there in the garden, surveying the scene, drinking last year's vintage and sampling the home-produced fruit and nuts, pears, apples, grapes, figs and pickled olives. This, followed by a dish of spaghetti, the sauce liberally laced with the home-produced olive oil, followed by ham, salami and air-dried meat, with luscious tomatoes.

Each year, about 30 friends and acquaintances would assemble to complete the harvest, around the first week in October. Grapes were cut in the field, pounded into plastic bins and loaded into the truck, to be transported up to the yard where the machine was made ready to crush them and syphon the wine into large vats, cleaned out since the previous year to receive the current wine production. There it would remain for a few months, before decanting into demi-johns and then bottled under Varo's own label. Many interesting people came each year. We met an American millionaire, who had made a fortune selling dressed crabs. He had discovered the masses of crabs, easily caught off Florida and devised a special sauce which he franchised. Crabs were cooked and doused in the sauce and sold widely, orders often being received for buckets of dressed crab to be specially flown up to New York or Chicago, for dinner parties. His wife was a photographer and sent us some fine shots she had taken. He was very interested in the 60s singing idol, David Whitfield, whose famous record of Cara mia Mine, topped the hit parade and made him rich. I sang it for him and he was thrilled with my high note and talked about it for years afterwards, when he used to send us Christmas cards. We met Horace Gibson, Head Master and Founder, of the famous American School in Florence and the Art Master, Kevin McIntyre, who produces beautiful artwork designs for fine china as well as paintings.

We met members of the Kuwaiti Royal family, most notably, Princess Dina, a seven or eight year old child, who was at the American School and two of her aunts, one, the beautiful Princess Fatima. Kevin designed china for her. Princess Dina was a very bright child and everyone loved her. She grew into a beautiful woman and I saw pictures of her years later in Harpers Bazaar, amongst the jet set. We also met a gentleman who had a Swiss chateau and another who had made a fortune importing Guernsey tomatoes into England. We met medical doctors, a sculptor from Germany, a Maori Prince, the American Consul, who was a young blonde lady and many more interesting characters, not least the Princess Vippy, from Thailand. We continued to go for the vintage for about 18 years, until a severe back operation put paid to my exertions there. We remain friendly with them still and visit Priscilla, Varo and Janine, a Swiss girl whom we met the first time and who has been a friend ever since.

Alas, three years ago, Varo's only son, Carlo, died of cancer at the early age of 50 and Varo's wife died of shock within days of the funeral. Priscilla and Janine visited us several times in London and both have been to Ireland since I retired here. We met Priscilla, Horace and Kevin in London one year, when they took an apartment at Portobello Road and we joined them there for the 4th July celebrations. We had a great night and met other interesting characters. We still go to Florence but not for the Vendemmia and often stayed at one of the flats owned by Varo, which was rented by one of the Kuwaitis who rarely used it.

Janine moved to a beautiful new apartment at Piazza Donatello. She visited us for a week in 1997 and she loved it here in Templepatrick where we live. Shortly afterwards she suffered a near fatal car accident and we went to stay with her in Florence as she recuperated.

We had been several times to Thailand, but on one memorable trip via Hong Kong for Amy Yuen's wedding, we stayed at the famous Oriental Hotel in Bangkok, then reputed to be the best in the world. Indeed we saw the Queen of Thailand and members of her family there. A fellow passenger on our flight out, hearing that we were to stay at the Oriental, insisted that we should visit the nearby Cha Cha's Indian restaurant. The proprietor and his restaurant were justly famous and had been featured in Time Life Magazine. He has served as aide-de-camp to Lord Mountbatten, Viceroy of India, and had later gone to Laos, where he married and set up a restaurant. He had to flee, so settled in Thailand, where he quickly built up a reputation for the very best of Indian cuisine. We enjoyed an excellent meal there.

An amusing incident occurred at the hotel. We were invited for evening cocktails by the manager, an Autrian gentleman. We were announced as Mr Frazer, a Banker from London and his wife, Elsie. A string quartet was playing Mozart in the Gallery above us and the guests were introduced to each other, bankers, doctors, potentates and so on. I fell into conversation with the manager's very attractive but older secretary, a lady of mild oriental appearance, attired in a beautifully tailored silk suit. She was quite charming and we were getting along fine. She asked me if I had my business card with me, which I reluctantly produced for her. As she read it -'R A Frazer, Manager's Assistant, Currency Accounts, Midland Bank' - her face fell and I seized another cocktail. The card referred to the time which I related earlier, when my Assistant Manager had called me his 'fucking manager's assistant'. Had it referred to me in my previous title as Group Chief, she might have been better impressed. I continue to laugh at both episodes even today.

We bought a load of bronzes and ivory carvings, from a Thai lady, an Antiques Dealer. Many of the items were recently made, but very well disguised 'antiques' and of considerable beauty. We became quite friendly. On subsequent visits I decided to import a consignment of her merchandise to England, with a view to starting a business. They duly arrived by surface transport and I sold most of them, but retained a few choice pieces, some of which I later sold in Ireland. With the difficulties of transport, costs and import duties, profit margins made it not worthwhile, so I abandoned that idea.

The items I purchased when in Bangkok were delivered in huge cardboard boxes to our room at the Oriental. We were horrified at the size of them, so we unpacked the lot, surrounded by billows of polystyrene stuffing and packed them into manageable suitcases. We managed to get them back to London with difficulty.

On one other trip, we visited the northern capital of Cheng Mai, where the Summer Palace is situated, to where the Royal Family goes at the height of Summer. We enjoyed the clearer, cooler air, away from the awful bustle and horrifying traffic of Bangkok. The foothill villages were very pleasant and the girls up there are most beautiful, being of much finer features than their southern cousins. Nearly everyone smoked in the village, even small children. It was very peaceful there, as chickens and black pigs scuttled about, while the children played and the adults lazed. We suffered a severe thunderstorm and the lights failed in the whole area, but no real harm was done, though we were without power all night.

We stayed several times, at the Siam Inter-Continental Hotel, set in 22 acres of ground in the middle of the teeming Bangkok. There used to be a craft industry carried out in huts on the estate, particularly that of stone and wood carving. I bought an exquisite soapstone, carved head, of the finest workmanship and I wish I had a few other pieces of that craftsman's work. The last time I went there he had gone.

We once took a trip to Amsterdam on a KLM interline package. This included a visit to an Indonesian restaurant, for a meal of 40 dishes, many of which utilised coconut and I found them to be rather on the sweet side. A vist to the Blue Note Night Club, afforded supper and a floor show, the highlight being a young, scantily clad female in a cage as a feathered bird, slowly and erotically fluttering to death, as she tried to escape. She was like the dying swan, generally danced to the Carnival of the Animals by Saint Saens. It was a good and lively evening.

We then had a visit to a diamond cutting and polishing workshop. This did not fill the romantic notions that I had once harboured, of being a crack diamond cutter myself. A row of men in overalls sat in a basement, working grinding machines carrying out their tasks. A boat trip on the Amstel and the canals, rather like the Bateaux Mouches on the Seine, completed our free treats.

We had an unexpected encounter with the Queen of the Netherlands, when we visited a fashionable shop. We noticed this elegant fur clad lady and the certain, aloof deference of the staff. We could only look again rather pointedly, as we realised who she was. No one made a fuss and she was perfectly at ease in her surroundings, but was an imposing presence.

Lise and Raja and their new daughter Rikke, were living in Brussels, and we visited them there for a few days. I was familiar with Brussels from my earlier trip, of which I have a snapshot of myself drinking coffee in the Grand Place, taken by my rowing colleagues. We enjoyed the night-time activity in and around the square, particularly as several of the pubs had pianos and where people were singing opera. I sang 'Amor Ti Vieta' from Fedora and enjoyed chatting with the other performers. We sampled the strong beer, the rich chocolate and cakes and heavy meals at restaurants. They are nearly as gluttonous as the Germans. Lise also provided us with nice meals at home.

They stayed for some years and then returned to England to live at Boulter's Lock, where we used to visit them, after Raja returned from Detroit. They then moved to Burnham Beeches, where they still live. We had a great evening with them at the Danish Club in Knightsbridge, to celebrate their 25th Wedding Anniversary. What a lively evening it was, with lots of food, beer and slivovitz consumed. I actually hate liquor, for its main effect is to make me want to sleep, but often I was compelled to partake of it. I rarely indulge these days and for years, never had a drink at the bank. I get plastered now and then, each time swearing never again, for I suffer violent headaches and remorse. On one occasion, Elsie had gone to Belfast to visit her mother who was unwell. I was left to fend for myself, not a good idea. I returned home from work feeling very tired. To make things easier for me, Elsie has left some boil in the bag cod, in parsley sauce, for me to prepare supper. I decided to have a couple of cans of lager to relax before eating. I put the fish on to boil and settled back to enjoy the beer in happy anticipation of the food to come.

The next recollection I had, was of a persistent, piercing sound driving through my head and the awful stench of acrid smoke. As my thoughts rallied through the gloom, I realised that I had fallen asleep and that the noise was emanating from the T V, which had ceased transmission for the night and the screen was blank. The room was full of dense smoke and the hall and kitchen ceilings and walls were blackened. The bottom was burnt out of the pot and there was no vestige of the fish and only traces of frizzled plastic, to indicate that anything had been in it. The whole house stank and it took weeks before the smell disappeared and days before the walls and ceilings were cleaned and redecorated. I usually resort to a cheese sandwich and a cup of tea when left on my own now.

We remained friends with Lise and Raja and will be meeting them again soon. Lise is now a grandmother and will celebrate her 60th birthday when we are next in London. Lise is a lovely lady and when we first met she was a young and beautiful blonde girl. Like ourselves, she and Raja were not very well off when we first met. Lise was charmingly naïve, but decided she would seek some part-time work. She advertised: 'Young Danish Female seeks Employment, anything considered'. You can imagine the flood of replies she had to that! Anyway, she got some work as a book-keeper, with the local Cosy Cars office in Streatham.

CHAPTER 27

I have suffered severe backache throughout my life. This could come on at any time, even the simple action of bending over the basin to wash my face could cause a sudden spasm, resulting in a low back pain, which gradually spread right across, locking me in a stooping position. I used to walk about crouched over like Groucho Marks, for I had a moustache then. My ungainly gait did not attract sympathy, rather did it evoke ribald comments. I never sought treatment, except occasionally, when visiting my brother, Fred, in Birmingham and he would take me to his Physio Department, to put me on traction. In some cases he would also treat me by manipulation, laying me on my side and suddenly twisting my torso, causing a crack in my back, resulting in relief, as the offending vertebrae were realigned. Usually, I hung from the banisters or lintel of a door, to stretch myself and wiggle the lower limbs and hips, to try to creak back into normal position. Fred had given me a halter which went round the neck and head and which had a rope attached over a pulley with a weight at the end. I used this contraption by hooking it to the lintel of the kitchen door at the end of the hall, to stretch my neck. Elsie, unaware of this, returned home one day and on opening the front door, was confronted by the sight of me slumped in a chair with my back to her, apparently attempting to hang myself. She let out a yell and I nearly choked as I suddenly jerked upright. I abandoned the contraption thereafter.

This indisposition, as well as causing mirth to others, had an amusing consequence one Christmas time. Valerie and her husband, David, and their children were coming over from Canada. They worked and lived in Saskatchewan, where they operated a medical clinic and flying doctor practice. David was to stop off in London to stay with his parents, whilst Valerie and the children would go on to Belfast. We went to Heathrow to meet them and were joined there by David's parents. There was some difficulty at Terminal 4 with their baggage. It was David's fault, for instead of booking their baggage through to Belfast, he had insisted that it be off-loaded in London, so that he could extract what he wanted there.

The delay caused the staff at British Airways Terminal 1 to fill the seats allocated to Val and the children, as they hadn't shown. When they finally arrived late at the Check-in for Belfast, they were told that their seats had been re-allocated. A row ensued. My back was severely bad at that time and I was leaning across the check-in desk for support. David adopted his usual arrogant approach and Valerie was, reasonably, in a state of agitation. David's parents added to the fracas. Only Elsie remained calm and I had told the check-in girl that she was removing the wrong flight coupon from Valerie's ticket. The poor girl was becoming distraught, till Elsie ordered us all out of the way.

She showed her British Airways ID pass to indicate that she was on the side of the check-in girl. The girl asked who on earth were all these people, to which Elsie said she didn't really know, but they were connected to the husband. 'And who was that fellow with the moustache, leaning over my desk, telling me I had taken the wrong flight coupons?' the girl asked. Elsie's response was to say that she had no idea for she had never met him before in her life!

The matter was finally resolved and Valerie was able to continue her journey on to Belfast. We got rid of David and his parents and went on home, Elsie shaking with relief after the trauma and upbraiding me for my involvement. I wasn't too pleased either, at having been disowned!

When I first joined the Bank, I travelled up to London by bus, via Brixton, Elephant and Castle and Borough High Street, over London Bridge on the way to the City. I couldn't believe the hordes of people crossing London Bridge from the station on the south side. A dense stream of shuffling humanity, scurried along towards the Monument and Cannon Street. My first thoughts were that something special was taking place, and that everyone was hurrying to it. Next day it was the same, so I realised the hell I was entering and became one of the damned

It was an interesting time, however, for London Bridge was to be replaced. The existing edifice was sold to an American, who had plans to re-erect it at Lake Havesau and to create a theme park around it. The story is that he thought that he was buying Tower Bridge, a much more ornate and distinctive structure, instead of the rather ordinary, five-arched, plain granite, structure, that was London Bridge, further up the river. Still, he was buying history. I continued to travel up by bus and was fascinated as the work of dismantling and re-building was carried out. The bridge never closed. Each major stone was numbered and only one side of the bridge was closed to traffic, which was reduced to two single lanes on the other side. A super-structure was erected, which carried a cradle, to support under the existing arches, as they were dismantled piecemeal, each numbered component being loaded into barges in the river. Once dismantling of the one side was complete, construction of the new bridge began, with pre-stressed concrete sections being delivered and inserted like huge bricks of a building set.

Once completed, this new side was then opened to traffic and the same procedure was adopted, to remove and replace the other, till completion two or three years later. This is a simple illustration of the way it was done and gives no real idea of the enormous planning and logistics, concerned with the work carried out, never mind the awesome task of transporting the dismantled old bridge and its re-erection in America. It was fascinating to see the work progress each day and large photographs of the works, showing the proposed and completed stages, were displayed for the public, to keep them informed of what was going on. The new bridge turned out to be a very plain affair, of simple design, but efficient in its use.

The whole City went through enormous changes during my time there, as skyscrapers replaced traditional buildings everywhere. The old fish market at Billingsgate, was replaced by a new building for Citibank. It is said, that the fish smell never left it. Nat West erected a huge tower, the tallest in London then, near the Stock Exchange. All along the river and around

Southwark Bridge, new construction replaced the old. Cannon Street Station saw major re-development, as did places around Gracechurch Street and Leadenhall Market. Midland Bank Head Office, at Poultry and Princes Street, a Lutyens building, survived, but major reconstruction took place around it, up as far as the Barbican. Across the road in Cheapside and Queen Victoria Street, total reconstruction took place.

The whole of Docklands was redeveloped, with a massive reconstruction around the Isle of Dogs, Tower Hamlets and Canary Wharf. There, a new City was built, creating a concrete jungle of skyscrapers and office buildings. The Canadian consortium which carried out the project, went bust and many of the buildings were slow to attract tenants. Today the area is a major relocation site for banks and has become a major, thriving banking and commercial centre, with many expensive apartment blocks, constructed around the river shores. The Thames Barrier, an engineering wonder in itself, had already been constructed, down river, past Greenwich, to control the tidal flows, to prevent as far as possible, the flooding of London. By the 1980s, Midland Bank was fully involved in what had originally been Project 1970, when the emerging, major computerisation of banks had started rather slowly, but was now advancing apace and causing mass redundancies in the banking world.

Elsie and I visited Rome for a short holiday. Elsie had suffered migraine attacks over the years. No sooner had we arrived than she suffered such an attack. In these circumstances her only resort was to have a day in bed, in a darkened room with a cool cloth soaked in vinegar, across her brow. She usually recovered from these attacks overnight and would appear rejuvenated the next day. Rome was very hot and the hotel room was poor. We managed to take a tour of the city, to see the ancient wonders. I felt revitalised by the atmosphere of the city, as well as the good weather. In Italy, they say Milan earns, Rome spends and so I enjoyed the relaxed approach to life.

We sought out the opera house and had difficulty in finding it. The area it was in didn't look too salubrious and I noticed a queue in a side street, which I thought was probably to do with the labour exchange. Further investigation revealed that the queue led to the opera house, rather undistinguished from the outside and tucked away in a remote corner. We bought tickets for a matinee performance of Il Trovatore. Inside the house was quite fine, rising in five tiers to the upper amphitheatre.

I don't recall much about the performance, except that the tenor was Carlo Cosutta. Although born in Trieste, he had spent his early life in Argentina, where he emerged as a lyric tenor, eventually turning to dramatic roles and was noted for his Otello interpretation. He fulfilled his reputation, by blasting us with a massive high "C" in Di Quella Pira, sounding out like a trumpet above chorus, orchestra and the whole company.

Elsie's indisposition continued, so we curtailed our visit and returned to London.

In December 1976 Elsie had to undergo a major operation and we were fortunate to be able to book her into the Heron Clinic in Belfast, to be operated on by the eminent surgeon, Mr Graham Harley. I took two weeks holiday to go over with her. She was operated on, on the 15th December and was released from hospital on Christmas Eve. I had stayed with Mother during her sojourn in hospital. At the time, Belfast was being devastated by bombing, looting and arson attacks. Much of the public transport was curtailed.

In the Cliftonville Road area, many outrages had occurred. A petrol station had been bombed, as were the football ground, the Co-Operative Supermarket, a hotel and an old people's home. Manor Street, leading to the Oldpark and Crumlin Roads, where Mother worked, had been devastated, many houses in rubble or vandalised and bricked up. There were no street lights. Throughout the troubles, Mother had to rise early and walk through this devastation to get to the surgery where she worked. Bomb scares were frequent and she had to leave her bed in the night on occasions, till the area was cleared. Attacks on the surgery had also occurred with one of the doctors being beaten and tied up during a raid and one of the receptionists was hurt. Mother had been lifted bodily from her bed one night, by the blast of a nearby bomb which blew out her front windows and her front door. Soldiers would sometimes lie in her front garden, which could attract rifle fire and bullets had shattered a window and lodged in her roof on another occasion.

Whilst staying with her, I had to traverse Belfast on foot, to the Clinic on the Falls Road. This meant walking through the devastation, to get round the 'peace barrier', across Oldpark and Crumlin Roads and wending my way through a maze of derelict back streets, where the empty unlit houses were eerily blacked out, or bricked up. I never saw a soul and it was pitch dark and I only encountered one mangy dog one night. No one believed that I had done this night after night, not only because of the condition of the areas through which I passed but because of the uneasy juxtaposition of the Shankill and Falls Roads, strongholds of the opposing factions.

On one of my sorties up the Falls, I was attracted to a shop near the corner of Grosvenor Road, which was flying the Tricolour and other banners, denoting the Republican cause. I was wearing a fine camelhair overcoat, known as a 'British Warm'. That, with my moustache, probably made me look like an Army type. I never thought of this but made my way inside the shop to see what was going on. They were raising funds for the Republican cause of course, which would have been evident even to an idiot, but my curiosity was aroused and I felt no animosity to anyone. In hindsight, this was very foolish, for the Loyalists might have shot me for going there at all, never mind what the Republicans might have done, for encroaching on their hallowed ground. People were known to have disappeared without trace, or bodies found mutilated, on waste ground. I was aware of uneasy stares and I experienced a sudden frisson. I dropped a coin in their collection box, to show my goodwill and lack of any threatening intent and beat a hasty retreat.

I collected Elsie on Christmas Eve in a hired car. In the grounds of the hospital, a lady drove into me and wrecked my door. Although it was a minor accident, her elderly passenger made a great show of moaning as a hostile crowd gathered around. Even though it was the other driver's fault entirely, I made no argument and we exchanged insurance details and I got away as soon as possible to collect Elsie and get her home to her parents' house. Elsie had to stay on to recuperate and I had to return to London to work after the Christmas break, although my boss at the time, Mr Pickles, had been most conciliatory, telling me I could stay on with Elsie. I didn't want to take advantage, but greatly appreciated his kindness. She made a good recovery and was back in London and to work within a month.

Mother remained defiant, but had to sell up about 1983. Her good neighbours on both sides had already left the area. The first to leave some years earlier went to live in Dublin and the new neighbours were not so amenable. Her other friendly neighbour died and her house had been left empty. It was vandalised and finished up as a bricked-up, partly burned shell. The final straw for Mother, was a series of robberies which she suffered. She usually went to Winifred's for the weekends. An elderly lady across the road, who was 92 and lived alone in a huge house, was looking out of her window at 2 a.m. one night, to see a couple of lads walking up the middle of the road, carrying Mother's dining table. On another occasion, she had been staying with us for Easter. On her return, she found her home had been burgled again and some paintings and clocks were stolen. On the third occasion, she was in the house alone, when she was surprised by burglars, who had broken in in the middle of the night and she saw them off the premises. She decided she'd had enough.

She was lucky to find a buyer of the house at a ludicrously low price and she moved to Winifred's in the country for a time, until she tired of the monotony. She returned to a flat in Belfast, where things were more exciting. It is interesting to note that her house was occupied by 50 people after she left it. The whole episode reminded me of scenes from Dr Zhivago, when the family home in Moscow was taken over by the revolutionary vandals.

Mother retired from the doctor's surgery at the age of 81 and took an unpaid job in the Oxfam Shop in Chichester Street near the Belfast City Hall. She suffered several hold-ups whilst there and only left, at the age of 87, when the place was burnt out.

CHAPTER 28

Back at the bank, I made major decisions in the Sterling Clearing Department and was successful in reducing costs without redundancies and accommodating additional growing business. The bank was creating 13 major, centralised, operational and processing centres throughout the country. The London centre was to be housed in a new purpose built building, in Southwark, south of the river, right opposite St Paul's Cathedral. It was built alongside the river and the site of the slowly emerging, new Shakespearean Globe Theatre, which was being built by Sam Wanamaker.

Ours, was to be a state-of-the-art building, fully computerised and able to accommodate over 1,200 staff on five floors. Andy Hanges, Operations Director, set up a team of 'office engineers' called Production Control Analysis (PCA), to look at various operations and to suggest major amalgamation, relocation and other efficiency and cost-cutting procedures. All managers were sent on a protracted course, to develop resource management skills. I considered my main resources to be staff, space and computer time , all very costly and requiring efficient application for best results. I, along with some others, was assigned to the first eight-week course to be run by the firm of Ernst & Whinney, the bank's auditors, at Betchworth. The course was enjoyable but extremely tiring, keeping us working into the late evening and under pressure. The leader of the PCA team was a young Jordanian lady, a graduate and extremely bright.

We were divided into syndicates and the course covered management techniques in terms of staff motivation, problem solving, lateral thinking, resource and processing efficiencies. It introduced us to the theories of linear regression, which I am still trying to figure out. We studied test cases concerning real problems previously experienced in big business. A mock Foreign Exchange Dealing room exercise was held, requiring steady nerves and quick thinking. Each syndicate had to plan an extension to the existing Betchworth College, giving layout and explanations of design and the reasoning behind it. Explanations as to how we would cope with local residents' objections, costing and planning permission were required. We then had to construct our proposed building to scale, with polystyrene and to video our efforts inside and out of doors. Our team made a video in which I was the narrator and much of it was filmed outside, where shots of the existing premises and environs were shown, whilst I explained our plans, positioning and the reasons behind them. I was in full flow at one point, standing in the main driveway, when a delivery van passed recklessly by, almost knocking me and the cameraman over. I didn't miss a breath and continued my oration with undiminished enthusiasm. When shown to the audience and tutors later, it caused much laughter and interest. Unknown to me, this video was used at future courses, over a period of about two years.

After eight weeks of this intensive programme, we set about applying our new ideas. I was appointed as Operations representative on the Committee, organising the move to the new building in Park Street, Southwark, to co-ordinate the timing and needs of all other departments scheduled to move. Before that move I had some major decisions to take regarding Sterling Clearing. The PCA team had suggested a programme of re-alignment to amalgamate Leicester Cheque Centre, Currency Cheques UK and Sterling Clearing..

I was promoted to Senior Manager to carry out this project and set about establishing a team to proceed. I was fortunate to obtain the services of Bob Croft, who had worked with me before, in the Currency Accounts Department, who afforded good experience in systems application and general reorganisation, as did Bob Hurle, who had a good analytical mind. Kevin Gardner, the Manager of Currency Cheques, also joined the team and he introduced me to a young lady, a clerk in his department, suggesting she would make an ideal secretary.

I interviewed her and found her to be intelligent, enthusiastic, of good appearance and personality. I had already known of her willingness to be helpful to others at all times. Her mother was Irish and her father Norwegian. Her name was Tonia Rasmussen and she proved invaluable to me throughout the remainder of my time with the bank. She adapted immediately to using the personal computer, essential for word processing, spread-sheets, budget preparation and general records.

I held regular meetings with the implementation team and we considered PCA's proposals. I took a major decision not to re-equip the department with new, in-house, cheque computer processing systems. I decided to proceed in the direction of centralised processing in the District Service Centre and to link our business through that channel. Maintaining our own stand-alone systems would have produced data to tape, for overnight running through the bank's mainframe computer at the South Yorkshire Data Centre. I assigned a representative from Sterling Clearing to liaise with the bank's general clearing at Mariner House, to explore that possibility, whilst the managers and supervisors of the other departments, tackled their responsibilities with enthusiasm. At the time, we were working on three floors in one building and we planned for the future move to the new building at Park Street, where a single floor of 33,000 square feet, would accommodate us, along with Currency Disposals, Inland Payments and Outward Payments Departments.

The decision not to re-equip showed immediate financial benefits. The project went well and we established the new amalgamated department under the title of Wholesale Cheques Processing. We gradually de-commissioned our own out-moded in-house systems. Business was increasing rapidly as Correspondent Banking and Marketing Departments promoted our services. The project was successful and I was further promoted to amalgamate and assimilate the three previously mentioned payments departments. Electronic Communications was also brought under my jurisdiction to form Transaction Processing, within Wholesale Operations. We subsequently assimililated Head Office Sterling Clearing and commenced the run-down of Town Clearing. I was now Head of Transaction Processing.

This was all going on as the bank was undergoing major

cost-cutting initiatives and many managers were becoming redundant. The bank had been negotiating a merger with the Hong Kong and Shanghai Banking Corporation, which had taken a 15% interest in Midland, an initiative instigated by our own Chairman, Sir Kit McMahon. He visited me, along with Andy Hanges, to be shown around the amalgamated Wholesale Cheques operation at Martin Lane. Sir Kit proved to be pleasant and showed great interest in what I had to say and show him. We covered the entire operation, visiting the various floors and discussing the work flow and how our planning had been implemented. He was also interested in how we avoided fraud and how low our sustained losses were, considering the volumes with which the department had to contend. He thanked me, shook me warmly by the hand and left.

Andy Hanges came to see me later to say how impressed Sir Kit had been, having asked why could he not get more, such enthusiastic managers as me! In fact, he told Andy that he was going to the opera the next night but would be in the Royal Box at Covent Garden, so he passed on his four tickets in the stalls, for use by myself and the Wholesale Operations Chief. We attended a performance of Turandot with our wives that night and I was fortunate thereafter, for a period, to receive tickets from time to time, affording stall seats for some memorable performances at Covent Garden.

The merger with HSBC did not go ahead at that time and Sir Kit McMahon retired. In 1992 we were taken over completely, when HSBC bought the bank, though we continued to trade as Midland Bank for a number of years.

CHAPTER 29

Being Head of Transaction Processing I was now responsible for six major departments as well as sitting on various committees. These included the systems development for the Clearing House Automated Payments System (CHAPS), the London Currency Clearing Committee and the Committee for the Park Street relocation project. The LCC consisted of representatives of the major banks and I attended meetings at their plush offices at Moorgate. This was a pleasantly relaxed atmosphere compared with the daily grind and meetings were conducted in a very gentlemanly way, discussing such topics as to which currencies and which banks should participate in this specialised clearing.

I had an annual budget of £45m to cover the entire running costs of the six departments and initiatives were introduced to reduce costs further. Product costs had to be set, so as to remain profitable but at the same time, to keep us competitive and we were under constant pressure to seek efficiencies in our processing. Computer systems played an increasing part in our work, able to embrace the complexity of our operations in sterling and foreign currencies. There were many deadlines to be met, such as, foreign banks cut-off times, clearing schedules and Bank of England settlement times. Because of the multiplicity of our products and the inter-relation of other departments, such as, Correspondent Banking, Marketing and the computer systems, product costing was a complex problem.

We eventually reduced the operational budget to £28m and by 1992, my departments were responsible for a daily turnover of £70 billion in the payments departments and the processing of millions of currency, sterling and travellers' cheques with major reliance on the payments systems. The Electronic Communications Systems department, maintained the bank's links worldwide and in the UK, with CHAPS and on on-line computer services to the UK domestic branches.

We were under constant pressure of different deadlines to be met, so as to avoid costly interest claims, brought about by delay in payments delivery. An example of this failure to meet the CHAPS cut-off time will illustrate the point. An inter-bank payment for £80m was missed on one Christmas Eve. This resulted in five days' delay in effecting the payment after the Christmas break, incurring an interest claim for £247,000, which had to be paid on our return to work. Likewise, different cut-off times for foreign currency settlements, were much in mind. For instance, a payment to the USA in dollars, could be made by SWIFT, for the same day, up to 5 p.m. London time, due to the time zone differences, whereas payments in most European currencies could only be effected today, for value date settlement abroad on the next day. Some Far Eastern currencies required two days or more forward value.

About this time in the bank, I had a visit from a young lady. Her name was Dr Isabel Gouveia Lima, whose name had appeared in the bank's internal telephone directory and had caused some interest. She had been directed to me by Jacques de Mandat Grancey, another French aristocratic colleague of Herve de Carmoy, to discuss product costing. She appeared, a beautiful Brazilian lady in a red suit, smartly setting off her luxuriant black hair, accompanied by her charming smile and lustrous dark eyes. Her manner was as charming as her smile and overall appearance. We discussed product costing and I outlined my own theories on the subject, which were very basic compared with the multitude of incomprehensible theories and calculations that the boffins had thrust upon us. My dictum had always been 'simple solutions for complex problems'. I outlined my philosophy in this respect and my own methodology for assessing the individual costs of different products and off she went. Whether she made any sense of this or not, I never found out, but we did meet later and became friends.

This came about by a strange coincidence. Peter Middleton, who had been Head of Operations, and who went on to transform Thos Cooks, and then to Chief Executive of Lloyds of

London, before being Knighted and becoming Chairman of Barclays Bank, had issued an edict that anyone in International Division who wanted to learn a foreign language could do so at the bank's expense. I decided to try to enhance my limited Italian, picked up during my time in Milan, but without any basic structure or grounding in grammar. Isabel also joined the Italian class. She was already proficient in several languages and thought to improve her already adequate knowledge of Italian. Another young lady, who had studied Italian to A level, joined, wishing to improve her conversational skills. We were all considered quite able to a fair degree and consequently our lessons were pitched at quite an advanced level. Lessons were conducted weekly in the Scuola Linguarama, at their premises near St Paul's Cathedral. All lessons were conducted in Italian. No English was spoken, except when we were asked to translate extracts from newspapers or other periodicals. Each week we had to write an essay or story in Italian and read it out to the class at the next lesson. Somehow, my stories were considered interesting, not because of my mastery of the language, but for their content. Isabel encouraged me to write more of them in English. So it is due to her in no small measure that I finally took up the pen to complete this saga of my life, in response to her constant encouragement. I invited Isabel and her husband, Phil, to lunch. He is a Professsor of Computer Studies at London University. They came to our house and Isabel and Elsie struck an immediate rapport, both being interested in fashion and jewellery. Phil was endlessly interested in discussing computer solutions to some of my banking problems. This meeting led to a continuing friendship and Isabel finally went on to work for Citibank.

Mr Middleton also introduced another initiative for management improvements. Several of us were encouraged to seek short attachments to major customers of the bank, to explore and exchange management ideas. I elected to go to the headquarters of Grand Metropolitan at Northampton where I was well received and learnt much of interest and benefit in widening my outlook. I was also able to meet many of their Senior Executives and to suggest ideas to them where Midland Bank might improve their own operations.

I suffered much pain during my working life but only missed a day of work through illness on three major occasions. Firstly, the kidney stone episode which saw me absent for a week. Secondly, the tonsils operation accounted for another week. I succumbed on one other occasion, when I suffered thrombo phlebitis. There had been much talk in the papers at the time, when a Bulgarian diplomat had been mysteriously murdered. It was discovered that he had been killed by a tiny pellet embedded in his leg, shot from an adapted umbrella - an unusual form of execution, only revealed by the Coroner's enquiry and minute forensic investigation. I had been out at lunchtime and was rushing up the escalator to catch the Central Line at Oxford Circus to get back to the City. I was suddenly halted in my tracks by a fierce pain in the calf of my left leg. The thought instantly sprang to my mind that I had been stabbed. I turned quickly round to see a gentleman behind with a rolled umbrella. I yelled out, 'You've got me you bastard!', thinking that he had attacked me. I was unable to move; the man gave me a quizzical look and passed on by.

I hobbled back to work and next morning my entire lower leg and foot were black and hideously painful.

I staggered down to the doctor's surgery for an emergency appointment. An elderly retired locum doctor was in attendance. He was more than half deaf and very aged. I had difficulty in explaining my problem. However, as soon as he took a look at my leg, he pronounced that I had suffered a clot and a burst blood vessel. He asked how I had got to the surgery. I told him I had walked, he said that I couldn't possibly have done so, considering the state of my leg. When I told him that I had suffered the attack the previous lunchtime and had completed my day's work and journey home, he was astounded. Emphasising the gravity of my condition and ordering me to rest up for a couple of weeks, he prescribed medication to reduce the pain and the risk of further blood clotting. I was off work for three weeks and they were so concerned about me at the bank that a couple of colleagues visited me at home, bringing me a present.

Elsie's father had suffered ill-health and had been in hospital for a number of years. We visited him as often as possible. We went to Belfast at Christmas 1984. His condition deteriorated during our visit. We prepared to return to London and on our way to the airport, the day after Boxing Day, we learnt of his death. We returned immediately, so that Elsie could be with her mother and she and her sisters started to make the funeral arrangements.

The funeral took place at Lambeg Parish Church, where Elsie's father was well known from frequent visits over the years in his capacity as a Lay Reader. There was a good attendance and the minister, who was a close friend, conducted a service and a fitting tribute to his good work. We then returned to London with sadness.

I had developed severe arthritis in my right knee, about 1980. I suffered agonies for months, dragging my leg and shuffling along. The knee creaked. In those days, train and tube strikes occurred frequently. This meant that the road traffic was snarled up and I often had to walk from Elephant & Castle, to the office in Upper Thames Street. I went to my doctor who dismissed me, saying I was getting on a bit (I was only 44) and there was no worthwhile treatment, except to take an aspirin a day. Aspirin kills me, being very severe on my stomach and, in fact, I suffered a duodenal ulcer some years later. I therefore didn't follow his advice for long.

On a visit to Bangkok, we were on Silom Road, near our antique dealer's shop. Passing by a small alley, we noticed a queue of people. They were awaiting treatment in the clinic of a small Japanese man, a chiropractor, who was doing good business by the look of it. I decided to give him a try and awaited my turn in the queue. His premises were tiny and he spoke no English. He had a few charts on the wall, showing the human form with red dots outlining the points of neck, shoulder, back and joints, where pain is experienced. I indicated my knee. He seized my leg and began to bend it up and down. I screamed. All he could say was 'Tension, tension'. He made me lie face down on the couch, without my trousers. He leapt upon me, grabbing my foot and jamming his heel into the back of my knee joint. He pumped the leg up and down, gradually rotating it at the same time. I continued to grunt in protest, he re-doubled his efforts. Leaping off me, he then tried to force my foot up my back, to touch my head with my heel. He didn't succeed at first. He desisted from his attack, indicating that I should return the next day. I was not so sure, but the fact that he was doing such a roaring trade in an area usually given over to more pleasurable forms of massage, at lower prices, persuaded me that he must be good. I went back next day and he recommenced his torture, repeating over and over 'Tension, tension'. The treatment worked and he was able to force my leg behind me. I walked free and, touch wood, have never had a twinge in that knee in the last 20 years or so.

My nephew, Andrew, married a girl from Yorkshire. They had been living in Wandsworth not far from us. We attended the wedding in a church, somewhere near Bradford. I sang 'Panis Angelicus' in a freezing church, to very poor accompaniment and with little enthusiasm. It was a nice wedding with the men in morning suits and the ladies suitably attired. The bride arrived in a vintage Rolls Royce. Apart from Fred, Nina and Deborah, Elsie and I were the only other members of our family to attend. They had three beautiful children but his wife got restless and they eventually separated. Andrew came to London and is now Head of the Accident and Emergency Unit at the Chelsea and Westminster Hospital. He now lives with his partner in Kent.

My sister Valerie and her husband divorced. He married a Mormon and Valerie later married a surgeon, an ex-Naval man, called Louis Prendergast. They came to Ireland for a marriage blessing in Ballylinney Church. Louis asked me to sing Panis Angelicus and the Bach/Gounod Ave Maria. I said that if I sang these in Latin in a Presbyterian Church, I'd probably get shot. To balance things up, I included the song 'Thanks be to God'. George Gibson played the organ. The church was freezing but we survived.

Valerie's son Robbie was the youngest student at Harvard, where he went at age 16, and achieved an Honours Degree, summa cum laude, followed by a First at Queen's, Cambridge. We had a large family party at our house, where Elsie once again provided and prepared all the food. We hired a mini coach and driver and all went to Cambridge to attend the graduation ceremony. In the evening, Robbie treated us all to a lively tap-dance show in the West End, called Hot Shoe Shuffle. It was tremendously fast moving and was enjoyed by all, from Mother in her 80s down to my young nephew, Ben, who was about ten years old. Our celebrations continued the next day at home, before the family had to disperse. Robbie subsequently took up banking in the City with Swiss Bank Corp., directly opposite my office on the banks of the Thames and near to St Paul's

I was invited to sing at the wedding of Elizabeth, the daughter of Suzanne and Trevor Fulton, our friends at Canford Cliffs. The wedding was a lavish affair and took place in the Presbyterian Church in Bournemouth. The organist was terrific, a man from Yorkshire and full of enthusiasm. We rehearsed and I sang three items at the service - 'Where'e'r You Walk', 'Thanks be to God' and 'The Holy City'. I was in ringing voice, inspired by the good accompanist and was much congratulated afterwards, particularly by a number of attractive young ladies who joined us at the reception in a local hotel, beautifully situated overlooking the bay. Later in the evening, we met at the splendid apartment at Canford Cliffs for further refreshments.

Some years later, Stephanie, Valerie's daughter, came to London and met a young man from Hampshire. They announced their marriage and once again, the family assembled to attend the wedding in a small country church near Ringwood. I was asked to sing and was pleased that there was an excellent organist but the Vicar only allowed one song, 'I'll Walk Beside You', which I'm told I sang beautifully and was congratulated by Stephanie's father, who was there with his new wife. Stephanie was beautifully attired in a velvet and silk dress, designed and made in Dublin, and her husband wore a kilt. They eventually went to live near Valerie in California, where they now have two daughters.

We were invited to attend the World Airlines Entertainment Association's 12th Annual Conference at the Grosvenor House Hotel in Park Lane in October 1991. This was being hosted by

British Airways, which was to receive several awards for in-flight entertainment and advertising initiatives. I was loath to go, for I'd had so many formal events to attend to do with the bank that I was beginning to tire of such social occasions. Elsie and her friends persuaded me to go and a limousine was sent to take us there. The driver asked what time we would like to be collected afterwards and I suggested that midnight would be late enough. Elsie wore a black velvet outfit and a cream silk blouse, I was in the usual black tie format.

On arrival at the hotel we were ushered into a lobby, where a formal photograph was taken, and a nicely mounted copy was presented to us during the evening. I was impressed and mighty pleased. Pre-dinner drinks were served and we mingled with the guests, meeting several of Elsie's colleagues. The ladies present were in formal evening gowns. We were then seated at tables for ten, mostly with people connected with the entertainments industry whom we didn't know. Amongst them was one of Elsie's colleagues, a pretty young Indian girl called Tara, and her husband, who worked for a branch of the Midland Bank. I sat next to her and found her to be very chatty.

The Guest of Honour was HRH Prince Edward and the after-dinner speaker was Ned Sherrin, who later announced the awards, as well as entertaining us with his witticisms. During the excellent meal, Mr Sherrin made himself known amongst the tables and he was very genial and in sparkling form. After the meal, the formalities commenced with the announcement that there would be a ball at the end of the proceedings. I hate dancing. Ned Sherrin continued with his witty entertainment throughout the awards-giving ceremony. The prizes were presented by HRH Prince Edward, who spoke well, and seemed a nice young man. Tara received an award on behalf of British Airways and was loudly applauded. The atmosphere was good and I relaxed, contentedly. Then it was time for the dance.

Although I hate dancing I was always pretty vigorous on the floor and was usually the first up at the office parties, whilst the younger men were still fortifying themselves with alcohol. I danced the first number with Elsie, who was more restrained than myself, my unconventional approach being too vigorous for her. Next up was Tara and we got on well for she didn't inhibit my style and moved easily. I finshed up by inviting each of the ladies to a dance and got on well with them, except for one serious-looking Chinese girl, who plodded around unsmiling, as if wondering what it was all about. I returned to Tara to revitalise my efforts. Elsie was having a fine old time with her various admirers and the whole floor was filled with enthusiastic couples. I was introduced to a stunning lady and I invited her to dance. She was a great mover, matching my every move with a feather-like grace, floating along and letting herself be guided by my vigorous dashes across the floor in the jive numbers and making me feel like a good dancer in the slower ballroom numbers. We laughed and talked as we waited for each next dance. She was a teacher of English at Eton College. We had one great thing in common: she hated her job and I liked her all the more for it.

Elsie and Tara sat laughing at our antics, for they were becoming exhausted and were sitting out a few numbers. Elsie knew this lady's husband and I think she had met her before, when she visited BA. Our driver had arrived to take us home. We asked if he could return at 2 a.m. instead, which he was glad to do, so off we went again. I decided to give Tara and Elsie another fling, leaving my new friend time to re-acquaint herself with her husband and friends. She joined us afterwards at our table, where we all had a good laugh, confirming our enjoyment of the entire evening.

Mark Horton, one of Elsie's friends, was that year's President of the WAEA and had arranged this most excellent evening , which we all enjoyed thoroughly. Tara's comment was, 'So much for Ronnie having to be persuaded to attend!' Our patient driver finally conveyed us safely home.

I continued in the bank after the takeover by HSBC and was visited by many of their senior executives, including Sir John Bond, at the time Group Chief Executive, but now Chairman, having taken over after Sir William Purves retired. I was assigned three more departments to control, including Foreign Currency Accounts (my old department), Nostro Reconciliations, now based in Sheffield and Loans Administration. This was new to me, the department being responsible for control and realignment of all Latin American and Third World debts. I was now head of nine departments with a total staff of 640.

In 1991 our major relocation of the Payments and Clearing Depatments to Park Street, took place, where 420 staff were relocated on one floor. We moved the entire lot over one weekend and were up and running on the Monday morning. All staff had new desks and office furniture and their belongings all awaiting them with their computer terminals ready, when we commenced business at 9 a.m.

Many of my managerial colleagues had left by this time, either through voluntary or compulsory redundancy, including some of my previous tormentors, particularly my former outspoken Assistant Manager, who had so rudely reminded me that I was only the manager's assistant, thus confirming the old adage, 'Be nice to those you meet on the way up, for you may meet them on the way down'. Many of the Senior Executives of Midland had been replaced by the new HSBC hierarchy. Generally when one was promoted it meant that with the improved status would come a bigger desk or larger car, the best in ergonomically designed chair and so on. Many laid great store by these trappings of office. I never bothered but I did have a very nice private office at Park Street, overlooking the river, beside the Globe Theatre, with a view across to St Paul's. We were situated beside the house in which Sir Christopher Wren had lived, when he was building that great edifice.

I always refused all offers of a new chair. I had suffered a bad back, aching shoulders and neck, for years. I had acquired an old grey, tattered, straight backed office chair, no wheels or reclining or swivelling devices on it. Eventually, that chair was used by workmen one weekend to mix cement on it and I came in to find it with the arm broken and the seat covered in dried cement, so it had to go. I inherited an old wooden chair which had been used by one of the typists. She had been a competition dancer and had developed severe arthritis and could only use that chair, so I was delighted to acquire it after she left. She had joined our Currency Department from Head Office years earlier. Her first job was answering the telephones which rang constantly. After a couple of weeks, she came to me, asking to speak to me in confidence. I was a supervisor at the time. She was rather embarrassed but asked if I could possibly get her moved off that job and was reluctant to tell me why. She then revealed that she was nearly deaf and she couldn't hear what the customers were shouting about! We both howled with laughter and I got her assigned to typing duties, which she liked.

When I moved to Park Street where all the furniture was completely new, I insisted on bringing my old chair with me. It was taken away and the seat re-upholstered in a deep blue fabric, to match the new decor and furniture elsewhere. I retained it to the day I retired. I still use a similar chair at home which I bought for £2 in a junk shop and I re-upholstered it myself.

The only accolade I really welcomed was the fact that my status as Head of Transaction Processing required that my facsimile signature had to appear on all pre-printed and computer-produced cheques and payments, which meant that my name was known throughout the world. Of course, there were huge lists of signatories throughout the bank, but with the large volumes produced in our Payments Departments, my signature, along with the counter signature of my boss, was ubiquitous. The largest individual payment I ever had to sign manually, was for £200m, in respect of an inter-bank transfer.

The takeover by HSBC presented two major fundamental problems. The first was the integration with their staff and work practices and the second was to replace many of our own major processing, dealing and accounting systems, with the HSBC systems. Theirs had a broader worldwide application, being in use throughout all their foreign offices and subsidiary companies. This meant that I was on more committees relating to systems integration and development and contingency planning. This latter, was extremely important, for the HSBC Headquarters at Bishopsgate, had been bombed by the IRA and completely destroyed. They very quickly had to re-locate to a completely new building, at the corner of Southwark Bridge and Upper Thames Street, where they developed the largest Foreign Exchange Dealing Room in Europe, with 400 positions on one floor, to accommodate the combined HSBC and Midland dealing operations. The Chairman, Sir Wm Purves at the time, re-located to a new blue-glass building, beside Billingsgate, on the north side of the river, with fine views of Tower Bridge.

We developed a 'warm' standby site at Canary Wharf, to ensure that main systems could be used, should any of our major buildings in the City be attacked. The new District Service Centres throughout the country, played a major role in centralising processing functions, resulting in the closure of many small localised branches, but giving the benefits of lower processing costs.

I was fortunate to have a very efficient secretary and a good management team, who were adaptable to change. John Chappenden, one of my senior managers who had survived the merger, was our Systems Co-ordinator, who was indispensable both to my department and the bank in general. He was one of the few senior systems managers to survive the swathe of redundancies.

CHAPTER 30

In 1995 when I was in my 58th year of life and my 28th year of banking, I felt that I'd had enough. Technology was playing too great a part in our lives and we were running to keep up with it. I preferred things the other way around. Technology should have been reducing the individual's workload, instead of which it was reducing the individuals whilst increasing the workload. We had been cornered by a total reliance on systems which were expected to be perfect at all times, able to work wonders when they were up and running. Any glitch or down-time could thrust an unbearable burden on the 'down-sized' workforce. I decided to request retirement.

I was not ungrateful, for Midland Bank and HSBC had treated me very well. I had been given excellent training, both in-house and on external courses, allowing me to reveal whatever potential I had, and the banks had rewarded me accordingly when I was given responsibility commensurate with my ability. My slow reluctant start in banking had been entirely due to my own intransigence and failure to realise that sooner or later I would have to settle down.

The time of my retirement in October 1995 was agreed by my new 'boss', Rod Duke, a gentleman with whom I had worked years earlier and who had always been supportive. He has since gone on to even greater success. I was more than pleased to make way for those younger, more eager and more energetic from the up and coming generation.

I had decided that in retirement I would go back to Ireland, where I could be of some assistance to Mother in her few, but not feeble, remaining years. My desire to go back to Ireland accorded with Elsie's own sentiments. In early 1995 we set about searching for a house near Belfast. Elsie's mother had died in 1987 and it was to my wife's regret that she had been unable to spend more time with her. She had been in hospital and we had been to see her. She had been released and for about a year she appeared to be quite well. She suffered from heart trouble and blood pressure, but with medication she led a normal life and enjoyed getting out and about and had travelled to London on different occasions. Her death was sudden and was a great shock that left us both feeling very sad. The funeral service was conducted by the same minister at Lambeg Church, who gave a deeply moving eulogy, emphasising her kindness and patience throughout her life and I thought it was a perfect tribute to a lady who had always treated me with the greatest consideration. She was laid to rest beside her husband in the charmingly situated churchyard nearby. So our ideas to go back to Ireland were in accord, for Elsie was keen to be able to visit her two sisters more often, for they all were deeply saddened by their mother's passing.

Elsie had resigned earlier from British Airways, for her offices had been relocated from Buckingham Palace Road in London which was easily accessible from home. The office moved to a new centre at Heathrow and the travelling to get there and back became too arduous. We were both anxious to make our home elsewhere rather than remain permanently in London. Elsie's new found leisure gave her the opportunity to travel to Belfast to research the housing market.

We had had excellent neighbours in Streatham. The Doshi family had bought the house next to us some years before. Kirit Doshi was an accountant with offices in Wardour Street and he handled the affairs of several well-known film and TV personalities, including Chris Evans. He appeared on his TV show, where he had been introduced as the William Hague Indian lookalike. He was a keen golfer, liked a gamble at the casinos and was an avid gourmet. We often ate out together. His wife had worked for a time for Sainsbury's and his sister-in-law, who lived with them, worked for Lloyd's Bank. Kirit had great acumen and ambitions and became involved with Bollywood, the burgeoning Indian film industry.

There was a Greek family across the road, who spent most of the year at their house in Cyprus. Two doors up from them were the Patel family. The husband ran several retail establishments in the West End of London and they had a seven-year-old daughter, Roshni, who was at Thomas's School in Clapham. His wife, Pritti, worked for the Silver Seas Cruiseship Company. She had asked if Roshni could come over to play the piano and we made her welcome. She was a very bright child, endlessly inventive in making up games, which she used to exhaust me playing. She particularly liked dancing and singing and we had to stage 'concerts' for her, she herself hiding behind the sitting room curtains, then emerging to perform her own turns.

Priscilla had come from Florence to stay with us. Pritti invited us all to luncheon on the Silver Seas new luxury cruise ship, which was docked in the Pool of London, alongside the HMS Belfast battleship. It was Sunday and Raj with his wife and daughter, arrived in his large Mercedes, to drive us up to Tower Bridge where the ship was docked. We first boarded the Belfast, to cross her decks onto the adjoining cruise ship, resplendent in the sunlight, immediately beside Tower Bridge, which was raised while we were on the ship. We were greeted on board and plied lavishly with champagne, before being conducted to our table for a splendid lunch, accompanied by the finest vintage wines, which Priscilla particularly appreciated, she being a connoiseur. After lunch we were conducted throughout the luxury liner to view how the rich spend their leisure time, cruising the world's exotic locations. It was a truly enjoyable day out for us all.

We had also become friendly with a gentleman who lived across the road from us. He was an actor called Gordon Clyde and was well-known, having appeared on TV for many years as the straight man with the noted comedian, Dick Emery. We had known of him for years, but only met him one evening, when we were invited to a party by his American neighbours, who were leaving the district. The family next to them were in the music business, for the wife's father was the famous Johnny Douglas, who had written the theme music for the film 'The Railway Children', which increased his renown and wealth. He was leader of his own orchestra, The Johnny Douglas Strings.

They moved to Tadworth in Surrey and we were sorry to see them go for we had much in common.

We were pleased to meet Gordon Clyde, who was very friendly. He mentioned that he had often heard me singing in the bathroom and expressed an interest in coming over to visit us to play the piano. He had also starred in West End musicals in Drury Lane and proved to be a useful accompanist. We, in turn, visited him and after dinner he played his own piano for me, till I exhausted him as we performed operatic arias and he also joined me in singing the duet from the Pearl Fishers.

At the time I was to retire, we put the house up for sale and Gordon was also trying to sell his own, to move to Twickenham. The market conditions were not propitious. However, we pressed ahead and advertised with a couple of agents. We had already been going regularly to Northern Ireland looking for a suitable house to buy. There were many large properties available at that time, but too large for our requirements and Elsie had had enough of looking after a large house. Others were too remote outside Belfast. We even considered the prospect of living in the Republic, for we had previously taken a trip with Mother across to Enniskillen, going on to Sligo and Galway, and continued down the west coast of Ireland through Tralee and Killarney and as far as Cork and we had found many of the places to be enchanting. That was in 1994.

Prior to our departure, I had a bad fall off a chair, which slipped under me as I leapt upon it to retrieve an item from a shelf in the back pantry. The chair slipped on the tiled surface, shattered as I fell on it and I crashed backwards, knocking myself out as my head hit the back wall. I came to, my legs entangled with the remains of the chair, unable to move, for I was partially doubled up in the narrow confines and dazed. I couldn't figure out what was preventing me from extracting my legs from the debris. My head was in agony.

I eventually realised my predicament as my thoughts rearranged themselves. Elsie was upstairs and couldn't hear my feeble cries, so I lay for a while, till I could decide how to get up. I managed to crawl out to the bottom of the stairs, calling for assistance. A bump the size of an orange had appeared at the back of my head and I seemed to have torn my shoulder and leg muscles. I later learnt that I had cracked two ribs. Elsie was horrified and set about assisting me to a seat, where she applied a cold compress to my head. She then administered a cup of hot sweet tea. She insisted on ringing our doctor, a charming Welsh girl who had taken over the practice from our previous Maltese doctor, who had retired to live as a country gentleman.

Dr Britton, for so she was called, suggested the remedies which Elsie had already so efficiently prescribed, but insisted that I should go at once to the local hospital Casualty Department for x-ray and to ensure no internal damage had been caused. By this time, I was feeling somewhat better, though my head ached fearfully, so I did not follow that advice, much to Elsie's disgust. In the end she left me to my own devices. I seemed to recover, but where the large bump went to I've no idea, for it subsided within an hour or two and I suspect I've had water on the brain ever since!

We proceeded with our holiday and had a great trip. Our first night was spent in a B & B in Galway city. We chose a likely looking establishment from our guide book and called at the door in the early evening. The lady of the house greeted us warmly, but she was on her way out to a funtion with her husband. She said we could certainly have rooms for the night, so she gave us the keys to the house and left, saying she would see us later. We were struck by her ready trustfulness. We went out for a meal and returned later, glad of a nice house to stay in for the weather was inclement. There was a piano, so I encouraged Mother to play while I sang a number of songs. Unbeknown to us, the owners had returned and when we had finished our recital, the husband rushed in to congratulate me on my singing, saying I'd be great at a party and he was really sorry that we could only stay for one night.

We had a comfortable night and parted friends after a lavish breakfast next day. He had several pictures of himself with the former President of the US, Jimmy Carter, taken when he was in America on a business trip and he pressed us to come again. We started off for Tralee, where we decided to stay a further two nights in a new bungalow, run by a nurse, who was most friendly. We used this as a base as we explored the surrounding area, taking in Killarney - a most beautiful spot, Kenmare - a lovely old-fashioned country town and where I could have easily settled. We saw The Burren, startling in its remote and lunar-like landscape.

We went on to Blarney, for I wanted to see the Castle there and to kiss the Blarney Stone. We arrived there in the late afternoon. We hadn't booked anywhere to stay and had, so far, been lucky in finding accommodation. At Blarney our luck changed for everywhere was full due to some Festival and it was also a Bank Holiday weekend. After we'd tried several places, a lady offered us one room with a double bed, adding that a folding bed could be installed as well, should we find that acceptable. Mother readily agreed to take anything, for she was by now prepared to sleep on the floor and we were all tired. We made ready for bed and Mother prepared first in the bathroom. We saw her safely tucked up, just the top of her head above the blankets, chuckling at the absurdity of our situation. Elsie went to the bathroom whilst I partially disrobed in the bedroom. Elsie reappeared in her nightdress and I went forward to hear Mother scoffing. "What a sight" as I passed by in my underbags! This was followed by other ribald mutterings.

We slept well, before arising to a cold morning, the windows streaming with condensation. We impatiently awaited our various turns in the bathroom before going to breakfast. This was another hearty meal of eggs, bacon, sausages and wheaten bread, so enjoyable when properly made and served with a thick spreading of Kerrygold butter.

We explored the small town of Blarney, the castle, its grounds and the woollen mills, where the finest of tartans are woven. I fulfilled my ambition to kiss the Blarney Stone. This entailed lying on my back, arching backwards over a gap in the Castle walls, my feet being held by a guide. Craning my neck enabled me to kiss the stone in the upside down, reverse position, resulting in a severe crick in the neck and dislocation of the vertebrae. The town was lovely and the people were friendly. I decided to have a lunch of Irish stew, which is, when well made with mutton, potatoes, turnips, onions and carrots, delicious. Accompanied by additional vegetables and a pint of Guinness, it is a splendid simple meal. I asked to be served without any additional mashed turnip, but would take the rest. The meal was on the menu at an inclusive price and I was amused and touched when paying, as the young lady cashier said that she had made a deduction in respect of the discarded vegetables. Memories are full of such little niceties, as much as of the more grandiose things in life.

We pressed on to Bantry and Cork, where Mother indulged her shopping for shoes , declaring Cork to be a fine town. We stayed the night and decided to go on to Waterford to see the famous glassworks there. When we arrived it was closed. We made our way back home through central Ireland, passing Kilkenny and Mulingar and into Monaghan, across the border into Armagh and on to Belfast. I can declare it to have been one of the best holidays I have had.

We had been searching for a house near Belfast and were deciding it might be best to buy a convenient plot and to build a new house on it. We found a plot for sale in the village of Templepatrick, but thought it too expensive. On our next visit we found the site had already been sold, cleared and with two detached houses being erected thereon. They were in the neo-Georgian style and were very appealing, so we decided to buy one of them. Templepatrick is convenient to Aldergrove Airport. It is served by the modern M2 motorway, giving an easy 12-mile access journey to the centre of Belfast. My sister Winifred lives on the Ballyrobin Road, the main route to the airport. Mother was living in her flat on the Somerton Road, a short distance from the Fortwilliam motorway Junction. So the situation was eminently suitable, being convenient to family and some old friends. The Village is a pleasant spot and lies opposite the entrance to Castle Upton, the estate of the late Sir Robin Kinaghan, now occupied by his son. Peacocks roam freely about the estate and are often found in local gardens. Much expansion has taken place in the surrounding area, which lies in the town land of Ballyclare and near the town of Antrim.

We were finally committed and bought the house in June

1995. Elsie was able to visit Belfast regularly whilst I worked the required period of notice till my agreed retirement date of 30th October. Meantime, we had had considerable interest in our London house and settled for two most likely purchasers. One was an Austrian lady, who had lived for many years in London. She had sold a considerable property in Vienna, so she had money, although it was safely tucked away in Vienna. She sought my advice on how to get it out. I soon put her in touch with one of our main agent banks in Vienna and encouraged to get on with it, for she had made us a substantial offer.

The other prospective buyer was a Chinese lady from Calfornia. She had two sons at University in London and was seeking a property for them and herself. She was a widow, whose husband had died tragically of food poisoning. His death had incurred substantial compensation. She was a businesswoman of considerable acumen, who bought run-down companies and built them up into profitability, or realised the asset value of others and liquidated them for gain.

She was a rare character but struck a hard bargain. I was keen to take the higher offer from the Austrian lady, but as she seemed somewhat of a ditherer, Elsie thought that Mrs Thelma Chan was the better prospect. She had a keen business attitude to things and wanted an early settlement. I agreed and we accepted her offer, which was quickly realised. We arranged a settlement date for handover, to coincide with my retirement from the bank. We became friendly with Thelma, who took endless photographs of the house with her sons, our friends, the Patels and the Doshis and ourselves. The boys were very keen on the house and immediately laid claim to their various rooms. Thelma agreed to buy some furniture, including the snooker table in the attic.

These few months between buying our new house and before our move out of London, were busily spent divesting ourselves of many items which we had collected throughout the years, for we couldn't hope to accommodate them all in our smaller house. Tony Fowle, an antique dealer friend, came and took away a truck load of 50 assorted items. We spent several weekends driving to Arundel to deliver six car loads of assorted antiques and small items of furniture to a Welsh lady, who had an antique shop in the town. Lady Langham, who was from Tempo in Fermanagh, but lived in Belgravia, had previously arranged the purchase of a rare Belleek vase for us, by the Museum in Enniskillen, where it is now on display. She came with a picture dealer friend to assess some of our paintings. She purchased small items of silver, china and glass of interest to her. In spite of this we had to hire the largest lorry that the firm of removers, Morgans of Belfast, could provide, to transport our effects to Ireland.

My retirement party at the bank attracted a large gathering of friends and previous colleagues and I gratefully accepted their generous parting gift. There was much eating and drinking and humorous reminiscing.

We had sold the house which we left reluctantly. It had provided us with comfortable, commodious accommodation for 14 good years. There, we had entertained many guests and celebrated many occasions, such as Robbie's graduation, birthdays, visits by Valerie and her family from California, friends from Italy, America, China, the Phillipines, Ireland and Scotland. Both our mothers had enjoyed holidays through the years with us and members of both our families had visited us frequently. We had held many musical parties and entertained many interesting people as well as many of our banking and airline colleagues. The house had afforded us the opportunity of reciprocating the many visits we had spent with Fred and Nina in their various abodes and our frequent sojourns with Winifred and her family in Ireland. Several of our nephews and nieces had stayed with us while employed in London for summer work. Equally important was having the facility to make as much operatic noise as I liked without disturbing the neighbours.

I had put a deal of work and effort in decorating the house and had spent many busy and fulfilling weekends in the back garden and garage, restoring the many antiques that I had bought from George Nichol and elsewhere, many of which we still use in Ireland.

So I left the job, moved house and country, all simultaneously. Thelma allowed us to stay in the empty house on the last night, after the removers had loaded up, using the fold-up bed that she had purchased from us. We left the next day to drive to Stranraer, with a car load of the last remaining items we were taking, to board the Larne Ferry to our new life of retirement in Ireland.

The drive to Stranraer was rather different from that on which we had embarked before we were married. This time we planned the route with maps to hand and we were travelling in a new Audi Estate car, which ate up the miles. The weather was good and I determined to have a look at Shap Fell, scene of our previous mishap. How different it looked in the sunshine. Although remote, the drama of the previous situation was lost, for the scenery was inviting, the roads were good and no blizzards barred our way. We arrived at Larne in the late dark evening and drove the 15 miles or so to Templepatrick and then to Winifred's, to stay the night there as we still had no furniture installed.

CHAPTER 31

Though I had looked forward to retirement almost since the day I started in the bank, the reality hit me hard. Suddenly released from 28 years of constant tension and pressure, with no regime to order my life, was quite a shock. Elsie had already experienced similar feelings in London after she left BA. We also had to come to terms with being thrust together day and night and with the changes that had occurred in Northern Ireland since we left 30 years previously. However, we did have much to do in getting our new house in order. This gave Elsie plenty of scope to indulge her interest in interior design. Carpets and curtains, kitchen and bathroom equipment had to be installed and internal decoration carried out. Installation of our furniture was left to me, as well as the heavy work needed to make the garden attractive. There were 54 large cardboard packing cases of smaller effects sitting in the garage, to be unpacked and stowed away.

The house had four bedrooms, two bathrooms, a large hallway with cloakroom off, a dining room and sitting room and a large bright kitchen overlooking the back garden. I drew up plans of the rooms and set out positions for the larger items of furniture. I was able to comfortably accommodate most of them which I wished to keep. In the hallway I placed a loo-table and chairs, card table, bureau desk and another writing desk. The piano sat nicely in the sitting room by the front window and the large bureau bookcase fitted snugly into the corner at the other end. I enjoyed this part of the work, measuring and positioning the various furniture. Elsie had already arranged for the carpets to be laid. She sought out a lady to make the curtains to her design and had them installed throughout as well as blinds. Her brother-in-law completed the internal painting and in no time the house was looking good. The curtain maker was so impressed with Elsie's ideas and the results, that she suggested that the house should be featured in the Magazine Northern Woman, a quality production which featured "House of the Month" in each edition. We agreed and a photographer and reporter arrived and took some beautiful pictures and the reporter interviewed us to make up her description of the house and its contents. The results, when published over four pages of the magazine, were most pleasing.

The garden was bare except for five apple trees and a plum and a pear tree at the back. In the front there were a number of trees and one other small apple tree outside the front door. The property shared a communal entrance and driveway, it and the surrounding areas laid with pebbles and grass lawns back and front. The site was well positioned, with the two houses set back from the roadway at the top of the sloping driveway and gardens, presenting a very attractive prospect. It took us several weeks thereafter to unpack all the items stored in the garage and determined us not to acquire any more possessions.

With the relaxation from the tension of banking and the sudden unaccustomed vigorous work that I was doing, all my aches and pains emerged. I joined the Dunadry Health Club at the local hotel to get me into some better physical shape. This only increased my discomfort. I then decided to get involved in opera again and joined the chorus of Opera Northern Ireland in February 1996.

Elsie had her two sisters, one at Glengormley and one in Lisburn, whom she met quite frequently, as well as many of her old friends to meet in town. Elsie does not drive but a regular half-hourly bus service passing on the main road at the end of the village, ensured her independence and the means to get to and from the centre of Belfast. She always found something to do and to keep herself active, whereas I tended to need to be organised, except when I found something of particular interest to inspire me, when I would then become quite vigorous.

I auditioned for the opera, sang Lungi dal Caro Bene and was warmly praised by the Chorus Master, who had accompanied me. He asked was I a professional singer and would I join the chorus there and then and stay for that night's rehearsal. The

President of the Board and a fellow chorister, his Honour, Judge Curran, shook me warmly by the hand, welcoming me to their ranks.

Rehearsals were already well under way for Mozart's Marriage of Figaro, to be given four performances, commencing in March at Belfast Grand Opera House, with the Ulster Orchestra. I wasn't involved with that, but was asked to join the Gala Concert to be performed in the same period. Later in the year, preparations and rehearsals would take place for four performances of 'La Traviata' and 'Fidelio', in which I was asked to participate, commencing 14 September.

I attended a performance of 'The Marriage of Figaro', which was sung in English. The Countess was sung by an Icelandic soprano, Sola Braga, a beautiful and friendly girl, who received acclaim from the local critics. Suzanna was sung by Linda Kitchen, from the famous Leeds-based Opera North. I had seen her at Covent Garden in the role of Jemmy, son of William Tell, in that opera and thought she and the whole opera were great. In fact, Elsie and I were so impressed at the time that we went twice.

Chris Merritt, the American tenor, was singing the taxing role of Arnold. I had bought an LP disc in Milan in 1988 of him, recorded 'dal vivo in concerto', in Vercelli the previous year which included arias by Rossini, Donizetti, Meyerbeer and Verdi. It was a fantastic performance, so I was determined to see and hear him in the flesh. I paid £55 each for tickets to go to Covent Garden. At the first night's performance, fighting broke out in the street between opposing factions regarding their opinions of his interpretation of the role. Later in the run it was announced that Merritt had had to cancel, because of a viral infection. His place on that occasion was taken at short notice by Justin Lavender. He had been singing the small role of the fisherman and was suddenly launched before an international audience, for the performance was broadcast European wide. I heard it on the radio and he did a great job. Next it was announced that the entire performance was cancelled for other members of the cast had succumbed to the infection and a performance of La Boheme was substituted. By this time I despaired of ever hearing Merritt, but he did appear for the performances I had booked and he managed quite well in spite of obvious vocal discomfort. He is a huge fellow, taller and fatter than Pavarotti, but I have not seen him since, except on TV in 'Il Viaggio a Reims'.

Linda Kitchen was perfect for the role of Suzanna in Figaro, for she is diminutive and pretty and the opera was a sell-out, as was our Gala Concert, performed in the Opera House. I met the cast after the opening night at a reception in the Europa Hotel and had a long chat with Sola Braga, before meeting the others. I had a pleasant time chatting with Linda Kitchen, who was pleased with my appraisal of her performance in William Tell. After circulating a while, Sola came to bid me good night, shaking hands and hoping to see me again. I still await that pleasure.

We began rehearsals for four performances of 'La Traviata' and three of 'Fidelio'. A new Artistic Director of ONI had been appointed, in the person of Maestro Stephen Barlow, a conductor and pianist. He was married to the beautiful Joanna Lumley, who we were to meet later. Maestro Barlow arrived on the scene to conduct a rehearsal of Fidelio. Normally a pleasant and genial gentleman, he upbraided us roundly for our ineptitude, inferring that we were more or less useless. Fidelio is a tough assignment, quite demanding, particularly on the male chorus and we were made to feel very humble. In the meantime, rehearsals for 'La Traviata' were going well, for the company had performed it before, so most were acquainted with it, to be sung in Italian. Fidelio was a first for us all and even though to be sung in English, instead of the original German, we found it heavy going. The maestro was more conciliatory at our next rehearsal, realising we were all he was going to get and he persevered with us. We were to perform with the Ulster Orchestra which he would conduct and one performance was to be broadcast on BBC radio, so much was at stake.

We rehearsed at the Arts Council premises and at the BBC Blackstaff Studios and eventually came to terms with the score and staging, before production rehearsals at the Opera House. Things had been going better with 'La Traviata', except that it was discovered that the elaborate stage set which had been designed for the production, would not fit into the rehearsal rooms and so we had to seek other quarters. The Conductor was Martin Andre, very patient with the singers and I always enjoyed singing under his direction in this and other productions.

'Fidelio' was authentically staged and although not a sell-out, it was acclaimed and the maestro was able to relax. 'Traviata', much better known, *was* a sell-out and Elsie and here friend, Jo Valentine, from Australia, along with Mother attended one performance and enjoyed it very much. We had met members of both casts on a day out in the grounds of the mansion of William Montgomery, Chairman of the opera, at Greyabbey near the shores of Strangford Lough. We had been driven in Barry's Rolls Royce and our pictures subsequently appeared in Ulster Tatler.

The tenor, Florestan, in 'Fidelio', was an American called John Haughton Murray, resident singer in Germany, who had once taken over from Domingo at short notice, at the arena di Verona. He was a pleasant and confident young chap who tackled the difficult role with distinction. The baritone, Keith Latham, from Opera North, sang the role of Don Pizzaro, and I was sorry to read of his death recently, for he had been a pleasant companion and a fine singer.

I had seen Fidelio in Edinburgh, courtesy of the Royal Bank of Scotland, when they invited us there and I was pleased to meet our tenor for 'Traviata', who, it turned out, had sung the role of Jocquaino in 'Fidelio' in Edinburgh, where I had met a young lady at the supper provided after the performance. I mentioned to her that I had enjoyed the tenor who had sung that part, to be told that she was his fiancee. It was lucky that I hadn't said anything derogatory instead! I related the incident to him in Belfast and he told me that the young lady was now his wife. The soprano in 'Traviata' was an attractive young Canadian, who had sung the role of Cosette in 'Les Miserables' and the lead role in Phantom of the Opera' in the West End of London.

We decided to attend the Opera Ball to be held at the Culloden Hotel near Holywood in County Down, which has a splendid location overlooking Belfast Lough. Winifred and Peter and their friends, Alister and Esther McCourt, joined us and we hired a stretch limo to drive us there and back. Maestro Barlow did the honours and we had a nice table at the window with the beautiful view and we all enjoyed a thoroughly good evening of dining and dancing. The opera was advancing nicely under the new Artistic Director. There has been much publicity in the press and on TV. It was reported that Barlow and his wife, Joanna Lumley, had been seeking a permanent residence in N.I.

At the end of November 1995, we had flown to Pisa to get to Florence. We had missed the Vendemmia that year, due to my involvement at the Bank and our various necessary trips to Belfast as we prepared to move. We had previously met Ronald Kaftanski at a Vendemmia and he visited us twice in London. In the same year we had attended a lecture at the Harvard Club with Robbie, my nephew, who was a member. The guest speaker was Sir Georg Solti, the great conductor, whom we met afterwards. Robbie had already been invited to lunch at this home in Hampstead for Sir Georg and his wife maintained close links with Harvard and often entertained past members of the university.

Ronald Kaftanski encouraged us to visit and stay with him in Chicago, which we did at Halloween in 1996. He had come and stayed with us in Templepatrick earlier that year. We liked Chicago very much and met many of Ron's friends and members of his family, including his beautiful sister, Kathleen, a most gracious lady. She entertained us at her home, a fine Frank Lloyd Wright house at Barrington Hills. Ronald lived in the old family house in Chicago, occupying the ground floor, the uppper story having been let out as a self-contained unit. It was a huge house. They are a Polish family and Ronald continued to run the family delicatessen, till he retired and sold the business to a lady who was employed by him. He later sold the house and moved to his summer house at Beverley Shores, on Lake Michigan, in Indianna, not far from Michigan City.

We enjoyed the elegant Chicago house, where Ron held parties for us on two occasions. We met several interesting people, amongst them Alan Stone, founder of the Chicago Opera Theatre, where operas are performed in English. It is well known. The main theatre in Chicago is the Lyric Opera House, where works are performed in the original languages and we were to attend both of them during our second trip to the city, before Ronald moved permanently to Beverley Shores. I went with Ron's friend, Sara Leonard, to a performance of Don Carlos at the Lyric. The opera house has a capacity of 3,600. The auditorium is built on straight lines instead of the horseshoe shape more common in older opera houses and therefore affords good viewing and acoustics from every part. Don Carlos was well performed, which I enjoyed, although it presented a rather ludicrous ending. Most notable amongst the cast was the bass, Samuel Ramey.

Elsie and I then went to see 'Il Trittico', three operas composed by Puccini, which can be performed in the same evening, but which are rarely heard together. They each last about one hour and are of contrasting styles, from the severely Verismo (Il Tabarro), to the Romantic tragedy, (Suor Angelica), notable for having an all-female cast and the comic (Gianni Schicchi) entertaining and brilliant, which includes the famous aria 'O Mio Babbino Caro', always a hit and much performed by sopranos in recital. The evening was also memorable in that the soprano, Catherine Malfitano, sang all three contrasting roles. We also attended a performance of 'The Barber of Seville's at the Chicago Opera Theatre, which was most enjoyable and boasted a particularly fine tenor, Gregory Schmidt, as Almaviva, sung with panache and considerably more power than the usual *tenore di grazia.*

We were to visit Ronald on another occasion to stay with him in Indiana, where he had added a 40 ft square sitting room to his house, a main feature of which was a large open fireplace serving both the main sitting room and the dining room next door. The central attraction in the room was a water feature with gurgling jet, flowing into a square pool. Around this on the spacious floor he had a Steinway grand piano, a large refectory table, a circular dining table, two sofas and various chairs. Everything was done in fine style with subdued lighting and a glass dome in the ceiling affording plenty of sunlight. He had spent a great deal of time designing it himself and it had caused the builders considerable difficulty in constructing the walls to enclose such a space and to support the roof without pillars. The floor was laid in herringbone design of small terracotta bricks imported from Italy. This had also caused the tiler much minute planning to ensure an even pattern. To do this he had inserted pegs all over the floor from which strings were stretched at various angles for guidance. Notices were posted prominently, saying, please avoid the strings on the floor. We were there while some of this was going on ,when a friend walked in. Greeting me loudly, she plundered across the floor, the strings snapping round her ankles as she ploughed across. The poor tiler had to begin again.

Another incident occurred once the floor was completed. I had been sitting reading one afternoon and enjoying a glass or two of very good Californian wine. Rising without thinking, I walked across the room into the pool and out the other side, only realising when I was halfway through and up to my ankles in water, what I was doing. I ploughed on, fortunate not to fall on my face at the other edge. I was unobserved and made hurriedly to the bedroom to change my shoes and socks. To save my embarrassment, I said nothing, only to be discovered when Ronald came back, as I had left a trail of watery footprints right through the house.

We met a couple of Ronald's elderly lady friends in Chicago. Among these, was Mrs Sheila Putzel, an English lady who had lived for years in America and who was a Professor of Physics. Now widowed, she lived in a magnificent apartment at Lake Shore and was most gracious and interesting. We met another lady, the widow of a very famous architect, who invited us to supper at a restaurant specialising in spare ribs. This was the favourite haunt of Frank Sinatra when he visited Chicago. Throughout the meal (which wasn't very good, for we had stupidly selected tuna steaks instead of the delicious spare ribs), we were regaled by records of Sinatra singing 'Chicago My Home Town', amongst others.

Ronald spends two or three days in Chicago each week and he left us off at the Opera House one evening to attend a splendid performance of Verdi's Falstaff, sung by the great Bryn Terfel, a much better production than that staged at Covent Garden and broadcast on TV about a year later. I was also able to go with Ronald to see a very fine play, 'The Odyssey', by Mary Zimmerman. She had achieved renown through her dramatisation of the diaries of Leonardo da Vinci and this latest play only added to that fame, for it was quite brilliant.

On our return home I began rehearsals for 'Madama Butterfly' and 'Aida', to be sung in Italian, at the Belfast Grand Opera House. In that same season, the company performed 'Hansel and Gretel' by the composer Engelbert Humperdinck, whose name was subsequently adopted by the famous crooner. Several performances of 'Idomeneo' by Mozart, were given, both operas well performed but not attracting full audiences. I was not involved in either of these productions but attended performances of each of them. 'Hansel and Gretel' is a beautiful opera which should be seen more often. 'Idomeneo', on the other hand, though well sung, was interminably boring. The opera is too long and like much of Mozart, suffers from too much recitative and is rather static and classical in performance, lacking dramatic movement. Nevertheless, Mozart's music requires technical expertise and is subtly difficult to sing well and his operas contain delightful arias. I would class 'Don Giovanni' as his greatest dramatic work.

Aida was the greatest farce of a production I ever witnessed. The stage director had the bright idea of setting the opera in the period of the Franco/Prussian war instead of ancient Egypt. He also had tried to draw parallels with the situation in Northern Ireland, which was a mistake. That was bad enough, but the scenery was minimalist and the stage was severely raked (sloped) with two gaps in the floor, stretching in a V-shape from a point at the front, right across to the back corners. These were to allow for two moveable sliding screens to be operated in the slots and the stage was almost bare, except for these and a few isolated props, such as a chaise longue and a table. We were dressed in magnificent Prussian Army uniforms. During rehearsals, several incidents occurred, one resulting in a chorus member being taken to the hospital casualty, having slipped down one of the slots in the stage and badly damaging her leg. Several other minor incidents added to the drama and a dancer's left leg also disappeared into a hole during a performance, from which he had to be, rather unceremoniously, extracted by members of the cast. He did not suffer injury, except to his pride.

Apart from that, the opera was well-performed musically. The tenor originally contracted to perform the role of Radames had withdrawn after rehearsals had commenced. A replacement was only found after the Asst Artistic Director had spent two days on the telephone, searching and negotiating worldwide.

The replacement arrived during one of our later rehearsals and created some speculation. Was he Italian? He might have been, judging by his stout frame, dark Mediterranean looks and black hair. He looked ominous and one of my colleagues said that he didn't know what he was but that he would not like to see him let out of his cage. It turned out that he was from the Republic of Georgia in the USSR, a soloist with the Tbilisi State Opera and with the Bolshoi Opera in Moscow. His name was Badri Maissouradze. He had just flown in and was very tired, so we didn't hear him that night. When he did begin to sing at rehearsals, we knew immediately that here was a force to be reckoned with, a voice of considerable power and beauty, with a fine dramatic ring. In subsequent reviews, one local critic declared him to have been the best dramatic tenor ever heard in Belfast. Another said of him "Here is the stuff of greatness." The soprano was American and the mezzo, singing Amneris, was from the West Indies. Both were acclaimed and the baritone, Jonathan Veira, as the king, was excellent.

The tenor took a great interest in me. During the grand march I had to approach him, greet him and shake his hand, all the while singing lustily. He didn't speak English, I no Russian, but we found that we could communicate in Italian. He asked me where had I sung before and declared that I 'sang like a singer' and he was impressed with my voice.

He would not believe that I had been a reluctant banker for 28 years. I was much pleased with his appraisal. His wife and daughter had come with him and were staying at his hotel. His wife attended several rehearsals and he told me that she was a Professor at the Moscow Music Academy and that she was an excellent pianist and coach, who gave him great help and support. We discussed this and other aspects of learning a role and the advantages of having a good accompanist.

The critics were scathing of the production, saying "Pantomime comes to the opera", but were adulatory in respect of the singing, the orchestra and the chorus. Martin Andre was the excellent conductor.

'Madama Butterfly' had the benefit of an experienced, demanding and well renowned American producer and a good designer. The sets and costumes paid great attention to authentic Japanese detail. We were all given specially tailored wigs, costing up to £2,000 each and special make-up. The soprano was from Hong Kong, so had an authentic Oriental look and a fine voice. Although the role of Cio Cio San (Butterfly) depicts a 15-year-old girl, the music demands the voice and power of a lirico-dramatic soprano and can be very taxing. In all respects we were lucky and the performances went well. There is not a lot of chorus work in the opera, with the famous 'Humming Chorus', being sung off-stage. However, we appear throughout the opera, if only fleetingly on occasion, so there was no getting off early.

Makeup took a considerable time each evening, for the wigs first of all required a tightly fitting rubber skull to be applied and stuck down around the edges. Then the tight wigs were applied and the side burns similarly fixed in position. General makeup was then applied, with much emphasis on the shaping of the eyes and in my case, because I had a moustache at the time, extensions had to be stuck on, giving me the appearance of an ancient sage. The tight wig caused me severe headaches each evening throughout the run but the various shawls, cloaks, trousers and sashes added to the extremely good visual effect. It was all worth it in the end.

There is a great thrill in performing with a full orchestra and company on a large stage, particularly in the rousing numbers of Aida, which make good use of the chorus. Another mishap of that production occurred in my case. I had been assigned, with another colleague, at one point during the Grand March, to 'strike' the chaise longue from the stage as the action continued. Using one hand only, for the other was occupied in holding a large helmet and in controlling a long sword by my side, I had to lift the couch across and off the stage. That, with the steep slope, caused me severe back strain, which later took its toll, resulting in my having a serious back operation later.

During that particular run of the two operas in March 1997, Barlow organised a Gala Concert, an evening of entertainment at the opera house, to raise funds for the company. Appearing with him, were his wife, Joanna Lumley, the singer Jonathan Veira, and an actor friend. Barlow played all the accompaniments, from Verdi songs, to Noel Coward numbers and played a solo piece, 'Rustle of Spring', by Sinding, joining in several sketches as well. His wife did not sing, but lit up the stage with her elegant presence, moving stunningly and gracefully. She only alluded briefly to the show in which she was very famous at the time, 'Absolutely Fabulous', performing instead, light romantic comedy routines ,to great effect. The show was a sell-out and Barlow showed his considerable prowess as musician, pianist and all-round entertainer.

CHAPTER 32

Now that we were living in Ireland we needed somewhere to stay on our visits to London. We became members of the New Cavendish Club in Upper Berkeley Street, close to Marble Arch. We had already been members of the Ulster Reform Club in Belfast and had enjoyed visits at the New Cavendish on a reciprocal arrangement. Its convenience was the main attraction and so we joined, for it afforded a good stopping off point on our trips abroad, when flight connections were sometimes difficult on the same day.

A splendid event occurred in Belfast, in May 1997. A magnificent new concert hall had been built at a cost of £32m, beside the River Lagan, to seat 2,300. It was named the Waterfront Hall. The official opening ceremony was arranged to take place on 6th May, to be performed by HRH Prince Charles. There was to be a Gala Concert, with the Ulster Orchestra, international soloists and a large chorus, providing the entertainment, in support of the Prince's Trust. The whole event was to be broadcast live on BBC 2 nationwide TV. Opera Northern Ireland was asked to provide the chorus and 127 singers were assembled, with a relatively short period of rehearsals, to be made ready. Our chorus master, John Dallas, rose to the occasion and intensive rehearsals began at once. We would be required to perform six excerpts from operas in French, German and Italian.

The fine array of soloists engaged for the event, were Dame Kiri Te Kanawa, Gregory Yurisich and Dennis O'Neill from Covent Garden and our own Belfast mezzo, Kate McCarney. The Ulster Orchestra, with trumpeters from the Royal Irish Regiment, would accompany us, conducted by the resident conductor of the BBC, Robin Stapleton. We had only two rehearsals with the orchestra, one on the eve of the concert and the other on the afternoon before the evening's performance. This gave us our first glimpse of the soloists with brief samples of what they were to sing and the treats in store for the audience. Dame Kiri was a beauty, slight of figure in casual wear, her dark hair beautifully styled with blonde highlighting. She confirmed her greatness immediately she opened her mouth to sing. Gregory Yurisich was large and corpulent, as befits a famous baritone and Dennis O'Neill was a short, plump and jolly, in the tradition of the operatic tenor.

We received our programmes. The chorus, orchestra and trumpeters were to open the concert with the greeting of the guests (*Freudig, Begrussen, Wir di Edle Halle*), from Tannhauser and we would also perform the Anvil Chorus, join Kate McCarney in the Habanera from 'Carmen', the Grand March from 'Aida' and the concert version of 'Nessun Dorma' with Dennis O'Neill. Other exciting individual solos and orchestral excerpts, would be included. After this rehearsal, we had a couple of hours' break and were able to go home for a rest and to change into evening attire.

We were assembled early on the evening of the concert. Security was tight, so much so, that our chorus master couldn't gain admittance, as the organisers had forgotten to issue a pass in his name, for he wasn't performing. This was amusing, but upsetting for John, though the situation was eventually resolved and he got in to stand at the back. The audience, admitted strictly by previously issued tickets, were assembled and the chorus took their places on the platform, seated high behind the orchestra. HRH arrived to a fanfare by the trumpeters, specially written for the event. There had been a bomb scare in the street outside, but the authorities decided to let the concert go ahead and no alarm was raised in the hall. The whole house then rose, joining in a fine rendition of the National Anthem and so commenced the evening's entertainment.

The Lord Mayor introduced the concert, emphasising that it was in aid of the Prince's Trust and inviting HRH to perform the opening ceremony. This he did with a short and pleasant speech, unveiling the plaque to commemorate the event, which later would be mounted in the appropriate prominent spot.

Princes Charles looked well and spoke of his pleasure at being there and thanked all involved for their efforts on behalf of the Trust.

The orchestra opened with the introduction to our first piece from Tannhauser, which was very rousing. This was neatly followed by Yurisich, in the great aria, 'O du Mien Holder Abendstern', from the same opera. Kate McCarney then appeared, an attractive blonde in a beautiful red, off-the-shoulder gown, with billowing ruffles and a magnificent sparkling necklace and earrings, to sing 'Una Voce Poco Fa'. We followed with the Anvil Chorus from 'Il Trovatore', with two great clanging anvils adding to the effect on stage. O'Neill followed with the tenor aria from Luisa Miller, all well received by the audience. Dame Kiri then appeared to rapturous applause in a long dark blue gown, her shoulders draped in a fine, filmy blue, full length gown, looking radiant. She sang Marietta's Lied, from 'Die Tote Stadt' by Korngold. Until the rehearsal, none of us had heard this beautiful and touching aria from an otherwise gloomy, depressing opera, in which the heroine's lover strangles her with her own hair, following her infidelity. Dame Kiri sang it exquisitely and was soundly applauded. This was a hard act to follow for Kate, who then sang the 'Habanera', accompanied by the chorus and orchestra, which was warmly received.

Yurisich and O'Neill appeared to sing 'Era la Notte' and the great duet, 'Si Pel Ciel', from Verdi's 'Otello'. This was magnificent, with the orchestra at full blast at the dramatic end of the duet. This brought us to the interval.

The orchestra recommenced with the overture to Mozart's opera,' Die Entfuhrung Aus Dem Serail'. Dame Kiri reappeared to sing 'Depuis le Jour' from 'Louise', quite exquisitely. Yurisich followed with Prince Igor's Monologue from that opera by Borodin, a lengthy and sombre piece, sung with great technical expertise and expressiveness. Things then livened up with the orchestra in 'The Polonaise' from 'Eugene Onegin'. Kate reappeared, this time in a light blue toga-like gown clasped at her left shoulder, draped in long folds down her side, to sing the beautiful and sentimental aria, 'I Dreamt I Dwelt in Marble Halls', from 'The Bohemian Girl', by Michael Balfe. He was an Irish composer who, after a short singing career as a baritone, had turned to composing. His works contained many tuneful melodies, and were much performed in London and contributed to the development of British opera at the beginning of the 19th century. He produced over 20 operas and they were great favourites amongst Victorian audiences. 'The Bohemian Girl' was his most successful, last seen at Covent Garden in 1951 and the rest are now forgotten, except for the odd excerpt heard in concert. Kate brought the house down to thunderous applause, following her rendition of the aria.

The chorus then returned for its tour de force, 'The Grand March' from 'Aida', with the orchestra and the trumpeters of the Royal Irish Regiment, which attracted sustained applause. Dame Kiri then came on to further applause, in a long black, shoulderless dress with glittering highlights and three sparkling clasps on her left side, with star-shaped earrings to match. She sang 'Vissi D'arte' from 'Tosca' and 'O Mio Babbino Caro' from 'Gianni Schicchi', both of which received enthusiastic applause.

O'Neill finished with Nessun Dorma, with the chorus joining him at the end, reaching a tremendous fortissimo climax to huge applause and a standing ovation. That was the end of the programme, but all the soloists returned to the stage as the applause continued. So commenced the unannounced encore, 'The Brindisi' from 'Traviata', with Dame Kiri and O'Neill, joined by the chorus and other principals, to produce a rousing finale to a well-publicised and successful concert.

Elsie and I decided to go to Florence in late September for the Vendemmia. Our wedding anniversary on 29th September usually found us there or in Milan, for Andrew Sullivan's birthday was on the 30th and we had been in the habit of having a joint celebration. It was a good year, the grapes were luscious and the vintage turned out well. Varo, approaching 80 years of age, seemed fit and well in spite of having had an operation several years earlier. He was very strong and worked until the late evening to finish the wine making. We had the usual lively party afterwards, with large dishes of beef stew and polenta, and chargers of spare ribs with barbecue sauce. Endless wine was drunk, of course, and I was called upon to sing as usual, by which time I was helpless with tiredness, wine and too much food. Also, I hate having to sing unaccompanied. But it didn't matter for the audience by that time was never discriminating.

All seemed to be going well at Opera Northern Ireland, under the new Artistic Director and Management. In March1998, the great Russian soprano, Galina Gorchakova, was engaged for a concert of Russian music, accompanied by the chorus and orchestra, in numbers by Tchaikovsky, Borodin, Rimsky Korsakov and Moussorgsky. She was splendid, large and beautiful, with a glorious voice to match. However, due to her relative obscurity in the West, and a distinct lack of publicity, the concert was very poorly attended. Similarly, a concert given by the great and famous Nicolai Gedda, aged 70, on his fare-well tour, had attracted an abysmally small audience and the critic slated the population of Northern Ireland for their igno-rance and crass disregard of singing. The previous week, Gedda had packed Covent Garden in a similar concert.

We were scheduled to give four performances of 'The Magic Flute' and a Gala Concert in November 1998. This was a popu-lar choice and was given much publicity by our new fund rais-ing manager. Each of us had a photograph taken, to be dis-played in our different local newspapers. My photo appeared in four papers, The Antrim Guardian, The Antrim Times, The Belfast Telegraph and The Belfast Newsletter. The conductor was Martin Andre, who was always excellent, paying great heed to the singers and the chorus and making our job that much easier.

A fine array of principal soloists was assembled and the Director was a young man called Stephen Langridge, who knew what he was about. I commented to him during rehearsals that he knew the opera well, for he had not only been paying atten-tion to the action but was acquainted with the words and music as well. I enquired had he done any singing. He accepted the compliment and told me that he came from a musical back-ground but was not a singer himself. It was only later that the penny dropped and I realised he was the son of the noted British tenor, Philip Langridge, and the well known mezzo, Anne Murray.

One evening during a lull in the rehearsal, I was chatting to Martin about the programme for the Gala and he mentioned that it would include the Rigoletto quartet, which he started to play. I sang the opening passage with him and he then started to play La Donna e Mobile and I sang the first verse. Martin was a great accompanist, all from memory and I was enthused. I asked him to play 'Questa O Quella', which he did and I sang the complete aria. Stephen had come in as we commenced and at the end he came to tell me that he was very impressed indeed. I was pleased.

Having commenced rehearsals with the enthusiastic promotion of the production, we were buoyed up, when a bombshell dropped. The Arts Council decided to withdraw our future annual funding of about £400K and so this would be our last production. The reason they gave was that they wished to encourage the merging of ONI with the smaller company, Castleward Opera, with a view to ultimately forming an all-Ireland Grand Opera Company. Castleward is a privately run smaller company, which operates along the lines of Glyndebourne, performing work in their small theatre at Castleward Mansion, near Strangford.

We were shattered but I hoped that something would come of it anyway. The merger did not take place, Castleward preferring to remain independent. We went ahead with our production of 'The Magic Flute', which was a sell out and one performance was broadcast on BBC radio. The Gala Concert was also a great success. The tenor was Jeffrey Stewart as Tamino and I was to meet him some time later. The rest of the cast were very fine and the Irish soprano, Franzita Whelan, went on to great things. We went out on a high note but there was great regret that we were to be disbanded thereafter.

At the last night party in the Belfast Arts Club, we said goodbye to Martin Andre and I gave him a tape of Jose Cura's recordings of Puccini arias. I had previously heard him in Stiffelio at Covent Garden in 1994 and was very impressed and tipped him as a future star. He is now world famous and was acclaimed in Milan a couple of years ago as 'Il Nuovo Otello'. I bade Martin a sad goodbye, but he said that he expected to be back in Belfast the next year, which did not transpire. So, ONI was disbanded and I said goodbye to my colleagues.

I was now at a bit of a loose end, for the regular productions and concerts and the frequent rehearsals over the previous two or three years with ONI had taken up a good deal of my time. This had curtailed my travelling somewhat, of course, so Elsie and I decided to go to Florence just before Christmas 1998. We had missed the Vendemmia for two or three years and I was never involved in that again. Janine had had a severe car crash in July and was seriously injured. She was recuperating at her beautiful new apartment at Piazza Donatello, after a long spell in Intensive Care. So she pressed us to go over and stay for a few days, which we were glad to do.

Her injuries were severe and for a time she had lost the power in her right side. With treatment and physiotherapy she was now responding and she was fortunate to have found a very reliable daily help, a young lady from Latin America called Sylvia. She also had a very helpful neighbour downstairs and regular visits of the physiotherapist to keep her going. One of her big worries was the beautiful property which she had inherited at Lerici, situated on the cliff with magnificent of the Gulf, with an orchard of olive and walnut trees. Although she had let it for rental, she decided that she would sell it, for the burden of maintaining it and having the garden attended to, became too much. There was no shortage of eager prospective buyers.

We stayed with her and we enjoyed our time with her. Janine loves opera so we enjoyed the various CDs I had brought for her, whilst Elsie was out as usual, buying her favourite leather goods. Priscilla and Varo were able to join us for supper and Janine had managed to prepare a Swiss fondue for us. Varo, who is a property owner, was very much against Janine's decision to sell her house at Lerici but she went ahead to divest herself of that burden.

We returned to Ireland for Christmas and the family gathering at Winifred's house, overeating as usual. We always have a Christmas Eve Party at one of or other of our friends' houses, followed by Christmas morning church service, followed by pre-lunch champagne and caviar, at Winifred's. Peter, her hus-

317

band, who works in Moscow always manages to produce the best. Then we await the roasting of the turkey and all the usual over-rich, stomach distending extras. I am always glad when its over, but we then have to go on Boxing Day to Elsie's sister, or her niece at Annahilt, for another family gathering and generous dinner, returning home sated and several pounds heavier.

I eventually received a postcard from Martin Andre from Cologne, where he was conducting performances of Verdi's Macbeth. He was playing my tape in his hotel room he said and was minded to write to me to say how good it was, wishing me well and thanking me again. I hope I shall see him in the future.

I decided to approach Castleward Opera, following the demise of Opera Northern Ireland, and was invited for an audition. I sang Lungi dal Caro Bene and the Serenade from the Fair Maid of Perth, accompanied by the Musical Director, Michael McGuffin, who immediately invited me to join the company and to start rehearsals for La Sonnambula, which was to be given eight performances at Castleward in June 1999 and for 'La Traviata', which was to be given four performances at the Belfast Grand Opera House at the end of March that year.

We were in the last week's rehearsals for 'Traviata' when my back gave up altogether. I had been enjoying the rehearsals very much and was looking forward to appearing with the new company. I suffered a prolapsed disc at lumbar three and four, which trapped a sciatic nerve, causing screaming agony. I persevered up to the production rehearsals but had to retire. I was in constant agony and spent two nights half standing, hanging over the piano at home, unable to sit or lie down and sleep was impossible. I was seen by an eminent surgeon who set about arranging an MRI scan, to determine the extent of the trouble. He was not a back specialist, dealing mainly with hip problems, but there was a long waiting list for back surgeons, even going privately. The scan showed severe damage. I had been going for emergency treatment in the physiotherapy department of the Antrim Hospital and all their efforts to relieve the pain were in vain. I eventually got an appointment with a brilliant young surgeon and had to visit his surgery in Moira. By that time the pain had been so severe, that I had begun to feel numb from it

318

and my left leg was dragging as I walked.

I managed to drive over to Moira in March 1999 and immediately he saw me and had examined the x-rays and MRI scan, he diagnosed the trouble. He urgently suggested that I come in for immediate surgery. I explained about the opera, opening next week, saying that I would have liked to have taken part in it. He said it was up to me, but if I didn't get in immediately I would be left with a permanent limp in my left leg. With his and Elsie's urging, I accepted his offer to operate that weekend and was admitted to the Ulster Clinic.

The operation was quite long and after it I was heavily sedated. The surgeon had performed key-hole surgery, which meant that I didn't have a large scar, but he said that the sciatic nerve had been so severely damaged that it would not recover. He advised that I would have permanent discomfort in my left foot but that other nerves would compensate for the ruined one which was now defunct. Thus I had to miss both 'Traviata' and 'La Sonnambula'. I made a quick recovery and was soon mobile, but now, four years later the surgeon's predictions still hold true. I have a permanent feeling of my foot being swollen and I suffer severe cramps in bed, when the foot and ankle sieze up, curling downwards like a talon. I take a strong form of codeine as prescribed, but suffer from head and neck aches.

I was to re-join Castleward some while later and we gave three performances of 'Die Fledermaus' in the Autumn of 1999. Meantime, Elsie and I were in London in May 1999 staying at the New Cavendish Club. My nephew, Robbie, had acquired tickets for a concert version of 'Otello' at the Barbican, with Jose Cura in the title role. Robbie had also invited Edna Royston, our elderly friend with whom we occasionally stayed, at her house in Amersham. We had first met her when she had come over to Ireland to stay with our friend Barry Quin. He had previously met her on a trans-Atlantic voyage on the QE2.

Edna is a lively character, whose mother was of the Rothchild family. She had led a very exciting life in America, where her mother had been a patron and regular visitor to the New York Metropolitan Opera. It was there that Edna had heard all the great operas and singers, throughout the 1930s and up to the

70s. Edna had been a rally driver, had married the same man twice, divorced him twice and was ready to re-marry him yet again, but he died. She is very knowledgeable about opera and classical music generally and had heard all the great conductors, piano and cello soloists and many of the great singers of the world. She had driven carriage and horses with the Duke of Edinburgh and was familiar with many of the Royals. She had been an ardent admirer and friend of Noel Coward and had seen all his shows, of which she has autographed programmes. She continued to drive up until she was 80 years old, travelled frequently first class on the QE2 to New York, took the Orient Express to Venice and often visited Italy and France. The only aircraft she would fly on is Concorde, as she feels it's the safest.

Robbie generously treated us to tea at the Ritz before going on to the Barbican. Edna's chauffeur drove us there. She often comes up to London by car to her hairdresser in Bond Street and usually tries to take in a show as well. We have been several times to Covent Garden with her. The concert at the Barbican was excellent and as well as Cura, the Spanish baritone, Carlos Alvarez, as Iago, was outstanding. The Slovak soprano, Andrea Dankova, as Desdemona, was equally thrilling, with the LSO in great form, conducted by Sir Colin Davis.

I was now back with Castleward and we were beginning rehearsals for eight performances of Martha, at Castleward House in June 2000, with a further two performances at the Belfast Opera House, scheduled for 8th and 10th February 2001. The company was also presenting ten performances of Madama Butterfly, plus two at the Opera House to run concurrently.

In February, Barry invited us to join him at a lecture, at the Royal Geographical Society in London. This was to be given by the American explorer, Norman Vaughan, who had travelled to the South Pole with Admiral Byrd on his 1928-30 expedition. So here was Norman Vaughan, now 91 years of age, travelling the world and lecturing on his experiences, talking without notes. He was still active in husky trekking in Canada. He was quite a character and after the lecture, I bought his book. The ticket price also included supper, which turned out to be a pretty miserable offering of cold chicken and couscous.

On our return to Belfast, we found Mother, now in her 91st year, to be somewhat unwell. She had spent a week in the Belfast City Hospital with pneumonia, the previous winter, but had made an excellent recovery. She was now losing weight and complained of always feeling cold. She kept the heat on so high in her flat that I could only stay for short periods. In March she was quite weak, but still active. By mid-month, it was evident that she was really sick. She was staying with Winifred for the weekend as usual, when she began to complain of severe stomach pains and weakness. I went up to see her and she was sitting miserably on the edge of the bed, refusing and unable to move. We called for the ambulance and she was taken to the Antrim Area Hospital for tests. Winifred went with her in the ambulance and mother was fortunate to get a bed after a few hours wait. She was examined by a specialist, an elderly Indian gentleman, who was very nice to her. He advised us that she was seriously ill but that further tests would be carried out. Valerie decided to come over from California with her daughter Stephanie and my brother, Fred, was preparing to come over from Berkhamsted.

The tests which were carried out were very severe and caused mother a good deal of discomfort, but she seemed to rally quite well and was glad to see some friends who visited her. Valerie and Winifred remained in attendance, for we had accepted an invitation to go to London to attend a 50th birthday party of David Newbery, one of Elsie's BA colleagues. So we decided to go and join the party there on a boat on the Thames, on which there were over 100 guests.

The boat cruised down the Thames from the Festival Hall Pier, past Canary Wharf through Greenwich and around the Dome and on through the Thames Barrier and beyond. It was a splendid occasion and the Thames, the City, Tower Bridge and the Tower of London all looked magnificent, lit up at night as we cruised by. The same applied all the way down-river. Canary Wharf and the new 'City' built there looked splendid, as did the Dome and other sights. During the evening as we cruised, we were feted with champagne and dinner on board, all done in magnificent style. It was a great evening but we were ever mindful of mother and 'phoned to check on her condition, which was stable.

We had also been asked to go to stay a few days with Edna at Amersham, so we went there the next day. On 20th March we received an urgent call from Fred on my mobile phone to say that mother appeared to be in a coma. Edna arranged for her driver to take us immediately to Heathrow for our return to Belfast, where Valerie met us at Aldergrove Airport to convey us straight to the hospital.

Mother was unconscious but breathing with the aid of oxygen. Valerie had discussed the situation with the surgeon, who had tentatively suggested an operation but warned that it was deemed unwise in the circumstances. I remained at Mother's side, so that Val and Win could take a break. It was painful to see her so shrunken and breathless.

She was lying at a very awkward angle, propped up sideways on three pillows, and I tried to straighten her up to make her more comfortable. The nurse kept coming in and out. She eventually came in to change the breathing tube and as she removed it, Mother seemed to give a slight sigh, whereupon the nurse said, 'Oh she's gone.'

And so Mother died, less than two months short of her 91st birthday, which we had all planned to celebrate with her. I touched her forehead, said 'Goodbye, Mum' and with tears in my eyes sought out Val and Win to break the bad news. They came running in distress and rushed to Mother's side as the curtains were drawn around her bed. I went to telephone Fred who was equally distressed at the news and he prepared to come over at once.

The funeral was arranged to take place at Loanends Presbyterian Church, where Mother had worshipped for a number of years. Winifred decided to have the coffin delivered to her house, where Mother lay in the large sitting room. This was not in accordance with Mother's previously expressed wishes, for though she had done the same with Father, she had wanted to be kept private. However, Win wanted Fred and others to have a last sight of our mother before she was cremated, as was her express desire.

It was something of a shock to see how old she looked, for up to the time of her death, she had always looked fresh and sprightly. She was dressed in her favourite green two-piece costume, one which I had always liked. And so we made our farewells.

At the church next day, a good crowd assembled, which was pleasing, as so many of her friends and contemporaries had already died. Mother had always liked flowers and had often complained that Father wouldn't let her cut them in the garden to spoil his display, so we ensured that the coffin was bedecked with a fine arrangement. I gave the tribute which, unknown to me, was recorded along with the rest of the service. The Rev Noel Williamson played the organ and his wife, who was one of the doctors with whom Mother had worked at the surgery, also attended, along with friends, neighbours and family.

Robbie, Fred and my nephew, Christopher, who is a Presbyterian Minister, read passages from the Scriptures. The Rev Weir, minister of the church, preached a short sermon and enlarged on my tribute. He was inspired and those from the congregation who heard him said he surpassed himself in eloquence on that occasion. I was required afterwards to produce 14 copies of the tape which the sexton had given me after the service, for friends who requested them.

The funeral then proceeded to Roselawn Crematorium, on the outskirts of Belfast. After a further brief service at which Stephanie read a portion of Scripture, Mother's remains were committed to the Almighty. We then repaired to a local restaurant for refreshments, reminiscences and regrets. We returned home, sad but thankful that Mother had enjoyed a long and fruitful life and had not lingered in death, which at the end came swiftly. Hers was the 21st funeral I had had to attend since my retirement and return to Ireland in November 1995. It was not to be the last but it was certainly the saddest.

At the end of March, I decided to go with Barry to Poznan in Poland, for a tram-driving course. These courses were started by an Englishman, twice divorced, who had gone to Poland to escape his misery. He had bought a house at Wolsztyn, where there is a large steam engine yard. He acquired an engine and started advertising steam-driving courses. He finished up with 15 working steam engines, which he leased to the national railway, and offered steam enthusiasts the opportunity to learn, and to drive them, on scheduled rail services. The courses became very popular, attracting English, German, American and Japanese clients. He called his business 'The Wolsztyn Experience', and had later decided to do the same with trams.

Barry and I had been to a luncheon at the Harlequins Rugby Club and the match afterwards. Barry doesn't drink but I had enjoyed the wine served at lunch. When we got back to his house, amongst his post was a brochure advertising these courses. Passing it over to me, he asked, 'What do you think of that?', whereupon I said that we should sign up immediately. He got on the phone there and then to the English agent and booked us up to go.

We flew to Birmingham, took a flight to Berlin and then a train to Poznan, via Frankfurt Oder, a journey of over four hours. East Germany is quite desolate, as was the trek across the Silesian Plain, for the country was flat and uninteresting, much covered in sombre pine forests. But the train was quite pleasant and we had a good meal in the dining car. We arrived in the late evening at Poznan and were met by our guide, who conveyed us to the Park Hotel near the outskirts of the city. It was a pleasant hotel, set beside a man-made rowing lake of about 2000 metres, with a dry ski slope at the top end and in lovely surroundings. The food was excellent and cheap, with good pork and beef, cheeses, pickles and excellent fresh vegetables. The city was sprawling, somewhat dowdy, but showed remnants of previous grandeur.

We started the tram driving in the early mornings. We were assigned an old ex-German, double-carriage, single-deck tram. Unlike the trains, we did not carry passengers but otherwise plied the city's corporation tram routes in the normal traffic, thundering across the length and breadth of the entire city, often in excess of 70 kph . There wasn't a lot to it but it was a novel experience. In some cases, points were changed automatically as we approached the junctions, on other occasions we had to descend to manually alter them with a lever. We also had to be alert to the various electronic signals. We were concerned that we might hit a car or two, for there was not a lot you could do to avoid obstacles, as the tracks circumvented your movements. Our guide assured us that there would be no problem but that if we did hit something, we should try and ensure that it was Russian, for which we would score 20 points. Other cars of different nationalities would attract lower scores.

After our first day's driving the guide invited us for a drink of beer and we landed up in an Irish pub, where he ordered Guinness. It was at least three times the cost of the local beer, which I would have preferred anyway, as it was very good. We had dinner and breakfast at the hotel. Breakfast was a feast of salami and other sliced meats, yoghurts, cereals, pickles, breads of infinite variety, salads and cheeses. Fried eggs and bacon could be had if required, and it was all excellent.

As a bonus we were invited to take a steam train to Wolsztyn one afternoon, riding on the footplate, which was something new. The drivers were two Englishmen and made us welcome on board. They drove the engine with great panache and enthusiasm and we thundered along. The journey took about two hours till we arrived at the station yard, which we were given the opportunity to explore at our leisure. A large shed housed ten engines, standing alongside each other in a semi-circular formation. They were being prepared for action next day. Fires were lit and stoked to build up steam and oilers and greasers were at work in amongst the wheels and pistons. On the tracks outside, other engines, already fired up, were taking on coal and water and we were free to clamber aboard and inspect the mechanics and the work in progress. In the evening we were invited to a dinner at a local restaurant where we met a number of steam enthusiasts and had a very pleasant meal together. The train drivers on the course were housed in a large hostel within the engine yard complex, where they enjoyed mutual interests and had catering facilities at their disposal.

One evening I decided to go to the opera. I was assured at the hotel desk that tickets would be available at the opera house, where Verdi's Nabucco was to be performed. I took a taxi over and approached the ticket desk. A seat in the grand circle was available for twenty-six Zloty, about £5 at the prevailing rate, which I eagerly accepted. The opera house seated just over 1,000 and the performance was in Italian but with Polish surtitles! The performance was great, with a chorus of 80 (which I counted) and they and all principals were excellent. The rendering of the great 'Va Pensiero' was sublime, the huge chorus expertly controlled and the tone well modulated, from the pianissimo to the forte, and sung with great expression. Altogether, our experience in Poland was most pleasant, as was the weather for the time of year. I would like to go again some time, but it is a long journey from Belfast.

My next venture was for Elsie and I to go with Barry on a boat trip on the Gloucester and Worcester Canals. That was in July 2000. We hired a barge, received basic instruction and off we went. Elsie and I shared one double bedroom and Barry took the other at the front of the boat. It had a good kitchen and a serviceable bathroom and Elsie was able to prepare most of our meals on board. In the week, we traversed 53 locks and visited places of scenic interest, enjoying the occasional meal at canalside pubs along the way. We had been staying with Edna Royston at Amersham, where Barry had picked us up in his recently acquired Bentley Continental, and afterwards he delivered us back to Heathrow for our return to Belfast. Barry drove on to Somerset to stay with a friend. It was a very enjoyable, more or less incident-free holiday, much to be recommended.

The eight performances of Martha (otherwise known as 'Der Markt Von Richmond'), by Friedrich von Flotow, took place. It is not much heard outside Germany these days and was last seen in Ireland in 1941. It was often performed in Italian translation by the great Caruso, Gigli and others, and is famous for the aria 'M'Appari Tutt'amor'. It also incorporates 'The Last Rose of Summer'. It is a very tuneful and amusing opera. We performed it in English and received excellent notices in the English national papers, the critic in the Independent going so far as to urge readers who were anywhere near Liverpool to take a boat over to hear our performances. The tenor on this occasion was Jeffrey Stewart, whom I mentioned earlier, who had sung with me in the last performances with ONI in the

Magic Flute. He was subsequently going to Germany, where he had negotiated a three-year contract to sing on a regular basis, and to live.

We gave the final two performances of Martha at the Grand Opera House in Belfast and that was the last time I appeared there. It was interesting that an elderly couple, who had been on their honeymoon in 1941, had attended the previous performance of the opera in Cork and they came up to celebrate their wedding anniversary with us, to hear the opera again.

That and 'Die Fledermaus' were the only two operas I performed with Castleward. I had also joined them in a number of concerts, most notably at Castle Leslie in County Monaghan (where Sir Paul McCartney of Beatles fame, was recently married). Castle Leslie is a popular venue and boasts gourmet cuisine which attracts diners, who are also entertained by visiting groups. County Monaghan lies on the border with Armagh and is a notorious hotbed of revolution.

We had travelled down by coach and were late in arriving and the concert was also delayed as the diners indulged themselves. We commenced our programme, which was well received, but the coach driver had returned and advised that he would be departing at 11.30 pm, whether we were on the coach or not. We were determined to complete our scheduled offerings but had to run out during our last rendering still singing the chorus, 'Va Pensiero', as we scrambled out through the door.

The next concert was in the Grand Hall at Stormont Parliament Buildings. That was a splendid occasion and only the second time I'd ever been in that building. We followed that a month or two later with a concert at Harry Ramsden's fish and chip emporium, at Yorkgate in Belfast. For £14 the audience received a first-class fish supper and renderings of operatic choruses, solos and ensembles. The concert proved very popular, was a sell-out - and we got a fish supper for our efforts! These concerts supplemented the opera company's income and they have been back twice since that time.

Barry and I attended a lecture at the Scott Polar Institute in Cambridge. This followed on nicely from the previous lecture by Norman Vaughan, for it concerned tourism in the Antarctic and how popular it had become for cruise holidays. The average age of passengers on cruise ships was about 74, so the authorities were not too troubled; for although passengers were allowed to land, it was mainly for a quick look and no damage was being done. Of more concern was the advent of tours by younger back-packers, who were more vigorous and wanted to trek across the land. So rigid rules were applied about where to go, how to avoid spoiling areas of delicate habitat and disturbing the local wildlife, and preventing the rape of the area by souvenir hunters. It was a very interesting talk.

We had decided to take a tour on our way to Cambridge. We caught the overnight boat from Belfast to Liverpool. After embarking and stowing Barry's Rolls Royce, we had a substantial dinner on board as the ship set sail and then we retired to our berths. Aroused at 5.30.a.m., we had breakfast and prepared to disembark as the ship docked on a pleasant morning in Liverpool. We then drove to Coalbrookdale and Ironbridge, where Abraham Darby had founded the great iron industry, taking advantage of the locally available iron ore, limestone and coal. He was the first to use coke to smelt iron ore in 1790 and built the first famous iron bridge there, over the Severn Gorge. It is a very picturesque spot. We viewed the bridge, visited the local museums and toured the old smelting works. We saw the remains of the great blast furnaces and watched local artisans still at work fashioning intricate iron-work items, for sale to tourists. We saw an original pit engine at work, used to raise and lower the miners' cages in the old days and to pump air through the mines to prevent dangerous build-up of gas and toxic fumes. The size and sense of power of the massive blast furnaces was overwhelming.

We next went to Ludlow, a beautiful town, where we met an antiques restorer to collect a couple of items, and then stayed the night. Next morning we met Barry's antique-dealing friend before proceeding on our lengthy journey to Cambridge via Crewe. We visited the Rolls Royce factory there. Barry had recently acquired a new Bentley Continental and wanted to discuss the various modifications to it. We were warmly received at the Rolls Royce works and shown all over the 'Total Build', the repair workshop and the display of vintage cars maintained there. What struck us about the total build, where the cars are made from scratch, was the quietness of the place. We saw cars at each stage of development, from the chassis up. We saw the raw leather used in upholstery, through the various processes of pattern making, design, cutting, stretching, sewing and tailoring, as well as the various fine woods used in the provision of interior elegance.

In the workshop we saw cars of many potentates, in for modification, repair or complete refurbishment. Of particular interest was a Phantom V belonging to the King of Thailand, who had a fleet of 13 of them. They are all painted in a creamy fawn colour and the king was having all their engines modified to suit the particular climatic excesses in Thailand (ie humidity) and the quality of petroleum there. We also saw a Rolls Royce that had been painted a garish red, with all mountings and trimmings changed to gold. This had been done by the son of a Middle Eastern Royal, who had now decided to have his car restored to its original, more sedate colours. In the display area we saw the oldest Rolls in existence, originally owned by a Scottish doctor and now used for pageants and shows, still in pristine condition.

Going on to Cambridge, we met Bob Headland, Curator of the Scott Polar Institute. Barry had been to the Antarctic twice and met him on a cruise there, for Bob spends a lot of his time lecturing on such cruises and carrying out his own researches when there. He is a very likeable chap and we had lunch with him; he had reserved two seats for us at the evening lecture. We met him again when he invited us to another lecture in October 2000. This was to be given by Caroline Hamilton, the young lady who had led a team of women walking to the South Pole. She has recently been in the news in June 2002, having just completed and returned from a similar walk to the North Pole.

Barry decided to make another expedition on his way to Cambridge for this lecture and invited me to join him. He had recently bought a Rolls Phantom VI, a massive brute, and wanted to carry out 109 modifications to it to suit his idiosyncrasies. Elsie and I had taken a ride in it when he had first brought it

329

back to Belfast from Clapham, where he had bought it. We drove with him to Ballynahinch and were able to accommodate Elsie in the back along with two winged armchairs, while we sat in the front in the chauffeur's department, in rigid discomfort. The car was now at Crewe.

His new Bentley Continental was at a place near Stanstead for its final yearly overhaul under guarantee. Elsie and I would fly to London, where I would wait for Barry coming from London on a later flight, while Elsie went her own way to Leatherhead to stay with friends.

So off we went. I saw Elsie on her way and waited for Barry to arrive. He had arranged to meet an engineer from Weybridge, who was installing air conditioning in his vintage Bentley Continental and he wanted to discuss the final modifications. We met him over coffee at the Marriott Hotel and they discussed their plans for about an hour. Our next destination was a place near Stanstead, where we had to collect the other car. The gentleman foolishly offered to drive us there, which we accepted, for we had intended going by coach and taxi to our destination.

Traffic was bad as usual on the M25 but he made good time. However, as is usual with Barry's negotiations, they were protracted and our kind driver was glad to get away. Barry was then attracted by the large number of Rolls Royces and Bentleys on display at the Dealers and spent quite a while viewing and discussing them. There was a Phantom IV that had once belonged to the late Princess Margaret, up for sale at a huge price. This gave Barry ideas and he decided he would like to trace another such car with Royal provenance. This meant a deviation from our already exhausting planned route to Cambridge. He had booked us to stay at the Cobham Hilton, even though we had to come back next day to Stanstead to meet an elderly couple, friends of Barry, who were also related to Caroline Hamilton, who was to give the lecture.

We drove to Cobham, round the M25 at the worst time of the rush-hour and arrived about four hours later. The hotel had well appointed rooms and we went for dinner. Barry had negotiated a deal with the Hilton and he saved £10 on the cost of his room and was entitled to a free starter with dinner. There is no such thing as a free lunch! We had already spent ten times the amount saved on our rambling journey.

Next morning a change of plan entailed a visit to Isleworth, to go to a bookshop, specialising in books on rare vintage and classic cars. Some of the books were also rare and cost hundreds of pounds. Barry wanted to research ex-Royal limousines which might be acquired and said he would only be about 20 minutes, which turned into an hour and a half. As we were in the vicinity, I asked Barry to call at Twickenham to visit a mutual friend and colleague of Elsie's who lived there. Her door was answered by a friend who said that she had gone to Rome for the weekend. We proceeded to Stanstead and met Barry's friends, who then joined us for dinner at an Italian restaurant and so to the lecture.

Caroline is an attractive girl and we enjoyed her talk. I bought her book detailing her adventure. She had already extended an invitation to us to join her and her mother and several of her erudite friends for dinner afterwards. We went, but ate sparingly. She was very friendly and embraced us as we parted.

Next day we met Bob Headland, for Barry had long lists of books on Polar exploration. He wanted Bob to review them and advise him which would be worth buying. Many of them were very highly priced and once again, Barry said it would take about 20 minutes. He had 20 pages of lists and it took hours, so I invited them to share a pub lunch as they continued their discussions, to which Bob eagerly agreed.

Finally, getting on our way, we next headed for Hebden Bridge. Barry had purchased a couple of stick barometers at Olympia the previous year. They had cost thousands of pounds and he could not fly them home because of their sensitive nature. The lady who sold them had agreed to keep them till he could collect them, which meant a visit to her home and workshop, at Hebden Bridge. We decided to go via York, for we wanted to look over the Tram Museum. It rained heavily so we abandoned that and looked instead for a car sales lot, where direct imports from the Continent of Europe were being sold at greatly reduced prices. We found it by accident and had a look around the good bargains in the top range quality cars. A TV programme was being made about the project and we were interviewed and filmed. I don't know if we ever appeared on the final programme!

We drove on to Hebden Bridge in a constant downpour and in the deepening gloom, found the lady's house perched perilously on the side of the steep slopes, high above the town. The house looked like it might slide away at any time. We had a chat and a cup of tea and eventually got under way for Liverpool, bypassing Manchester, in pouring rain and arrived in good time for our sailing. We had a good hearty dinner on board before going to our separate berths. It was a wild crossing, but without incident, although I slept badly. We finally disembarked at Belfast - home at last. I retained fond memories of Caroline Hamilton and was pleased to see her interviewed recently, following her last trek across the snowy wastes to the North Pole.

Early in February 2001, Elsie and I decided to take a week's holiday in Dubai. I had recently been talking to my brother, Fred, on the phone, about my operatic appearances and he had expressed interest. Shortly afterwards I received an Express Delivery package from him, which contained a note and a pair of my father's gold cuff-links, engraved with his initials, RAF, the same as my own. The note explained that father had always worn them with his tie and tails when appearing with the Belfast Philharmonic over the years. Fred said that I might like them. I was delighted and called him to say so, saying he needn't have gone to the extra expense of special delivery. He replied that he was anxious I should have them quickly, so I thanked him. On reflection, I thought it a little odd, for he must have had them since father's death and could have given them to me on any occasion.

Elsie and I stayed at the Club in London before flying off to Dubai. We had been there two or three times before, but now found the city and surrounding beaches almost unrecognisable, as so much rapid development had taken place. We felt that the whole character of the city had changed for the worse and we were disappointed. On the second day I booked to go on a desert safari, which Elsie refused. It included a trip in a four-wheel drive vehicle, miles across the desert into the dunes, where we were scared witless by the switchback drive that was to come - not good in view of my recent back operation! The trip had also promised a view of a desert sunset, which didn't happen, for the weather was dull. A visit to a camel farm was equally disappointing. Several travellers were offered a ride, on a couple of mangy camels, which I refused.

A display of belly dancing at the sprawling and unimpressive desert camp was not much better. The dancer was pathetic, a white girl who looked like she was on a trip from Southend and was supplementing her finances. She gracelessly gyrated her elongated pale body with its long legs and big feet, more or less to the rhythm of the accompanying recorded music. One young girl in the party got up and gave her own version of the dance, which attracted others to follow, outdoing the 'professional', who was ignored. The evening was redeemed by a late night barbecue of plentiful and tasty food.

We were exhausted at the end of the evening and glad to be returning to our hotels. I had shared a car with an Indian in the front beside the driver, myself between two Pakistanis in the middle seats and an elderly American couple in the rear. On the way back we had to call at a filling station to re-inflate the tyres, which had been deflated considerably, so as to afford better traction on the steep and shifting sand slopes. The generator for the air pump was locked and we spent a long time waiting for it to be made ready. The Americans fretted, for they had to catch a midnight flight out of Dubai.

I arrived back at our hotel at 11.30 pm, to be greeted by Elsie with the words 'I've got some awful news for you - Fred has suffered a massive stroke and is unlikely to survive'. I was deeply upset but Elsie had already packed and booked us on the 1.10 a.m. flight back to London. We made haste by taxi to the airport and embarked for the long journey, exhausted and downcast.

When we arrived at London Heathrow at about 5 am, I immediately phoned Winifred, to be told that Fred had died 15 minutes before our arrival. This was a terrible shock and I surmised that he must have had a premonition, which was why he had so urgently despatched the cuff-links to me.

We continued on our journey to Belfast, where Winifred met us at the airport and began preparations to attend the funeral. Meantime, Valerie and her daughter, Stephanie, were on their way from California and we were to meet them in London. Fred had died on 16th February 2001 at the age of 65.

There was some discussion with his wife and daughter as to where and how he should be buried, and a humanist funeral was suggested, which news we received with some misgiving. That idea was finally abandoned. My niece, Deborah, lives in Newnham, Kent, so she was able to arrange with the vicar to have Fred interred in the local churchyard. The vicar was most kind and understanding. Fred's family didn't want a crowd at the funeral, hoping to keep it strictly family, but a few of Fred's close colleagues insisted on attending. Elsie and I, along with Peter Nicholas and Winifred, went to London and stayed at the Club. Next day we were joined by Christopher, our clergyman nephew, who had been in Glasgow. Valerie and Stephanie were staying in an hotel near Newnham and on the morning of the funeral we travelled there by train , where Robbie had also arrived and we all met at Deborah's house. She had arranged for us to eat something there and to meet the other friends.

Deborah owned the adjoining house, which was let to a friend who was trying to make a living writing and performing her own songs. She was invited to sing a few soulful numbers at the house, which Nina said Fred would have enjoyed. Deborah had laid on a lavish spread and we tucked in. It was arranged that another friend would play some jazz on the saxophone at the church, for Fred had played the trumpet and was fond of traditional jazz. Later we would repair to a local hostelry where soup, sandwiches and drinks had been ordered in a private room.

The vicar was understanding and allowed the jazz, as well as letting Fred's little dog sit beside Nina in the church. Nina asked if I would sing but I declined, as I was too emotional. I agreed to deliver a tribute to Fred instead. The church was freezing but there was a good organist and we sang a couple of hymns.

Christopher read a passage and offered a prayer. Fred's son, Andrew, also paid tribute to his father and I, of necessity, reiterated much of what he had said, but interlaced it with anecdotes of our times at school, in the business and on the farm. Other events were related which brought some humour to the proceedings and the vicar preached a short and moving sermon. The saxophonist took some time to warm up his instrument before he got underway with his musical offerings. Finally the coffin was taken out to the graveyard and we bade Fred goodbye as it was lowered into the ground. It was intensely cold.

We were glad to reach the warm pub and soon things took on a more jolly aspect. Colleagues of the singer were there and accompanied her in a few numbers. Everybody had a good time and we were pleased that Fred had had a good send-off, which he would have enjoyed himself. Back at Deborah's house, a young lady played unaccompanied Bach on her fine and venerable cello, before we departed for London.

Elsie and I stayed on in London, the others returning home. I had already booked a concert at the Barbican on the 21st February 2001. That year was the centenary of Verdi's death, which had occurred on 27th January 1901 and much of his music was being performed there and at the Royal Opera House. I invited Robbie and his girlfriend, Valika, a young lady from Crete whom we had recently met, when Edna Royston had treated us all to a night at Covent Garden to see Bellini's 'I Capuletti e I Montecchi'.

The concert was given by Jose Cura and Daniela Dessi, a soprano from Rome, who treated us to a feast of Verdi operatic solos and duets, accompanied by the LSO. The conductor was Pier Giorgio Morandi, but Cura conducted a number of items himself. It was a great evening.

Elsie and I had decided to take a holiday in Switzerland with the Railway Touring Company in June 2001. I had been suffering excruciating headaches and blocked sinuses for months and a specialist I had consulted suggested various medications, all of them useless; some I was allergic to, causing further annoyance. In the end he decided that cauterisation of the nasal turbanates was necessary. This meant a visit in May to the Ulster Clinic for a daytime operation under general anaesthetic. The result was horrifying and although the operation made breathing easier, I suffered the most appalling problems with my nose for months afterwards.

We had decided to buy a studio flat in Nell Gwynn House in Sloane Avenue. This would give us a convenient and comfortable pied a terre, for we intended to visit London a lot more in the future to meet friends and to enjoy the opera and theatre. Negotiations were protracted, so we still had to stay at the Club and we only took possession of the flat at the end of June 2001.

Our journey to Switzerland began with an early taxi ride to Waterloo Station, to join the Eurostar for the first leg of our journey to Paris. We were travelling first-class throughout and a good breakfast was efficiently served on a crowded but comfortable train. We had to change stations at Paris, to the Gare du Nord, whence we were transported to Lausanne, where a coach finally conveyed us to our first hotel in Montreux. The hotel was modern, on the lakeside, well appointed and comfortable, and the food was good. Daily tours by train had been arranged and we were only five minutes from the station.

We stayed for two days and enjoyed trips up the mountains in steam 'pusher' trains, with small sturdy engines, specially designed to push us up the steep slopes to the glaciers. On the way we enjoyed spectacular scenery and the weather was perfect.

We went on by train to Lucerne, where we stayed for three nights. The city was very fine and we enjoyed daily trips by boat on the lake and by train to more distant parts. My nose had been troubling me greatly and I was having permanent headaches. A chemist in Montreaux had prescribed some cream which helped to some degree. I did not let my indisposition upset my enjoyment of the tour. We went on to stay a further two nights at Chur, always travelling by first-class train and enjoying lunch or dinner on board as the occasion arose. Switzerland was delightful. The food was good, the scenery spectacular and the trains ran on time.

One thing did amuse us. For dinner, we were frequently

given chicken with noodles in a creamy sauce. We supposed this to be a favourite national dish and it was very tasty. However, on arriving at Chur and finding the same dish on the menu for the first night, a family trio left a message for the guide to say that they would not be dining at the hotel, but were going to a nearby MacDonald's for a decent meal!

We saw the length, breadth and heights of the country and returned via Paris to Calais and the Eurostar back to London. We enjoyed a good dinner on board the train to complete a memorable trip. The train was delayed into Waterloo and, exhausted, we all queued for taxis to get to our individual destinations. We stayed at the club for the night before returning to Belfast. Others, not so lucky, had missed their onward connections and had to seek out hotels.

We were unable to take possession of the flat in Sloane Avenue until 1st July, due to the protracted negotiations over the leasehold. The flat was in good order but we decided to have the bathroom floor re-tiled and new taps and a power shower installed. I painted the place throughout, put up a couple of blinds and we have used it regularly ever since. It has given us the opportunity to entertain some long-standing friends and is very convenient to all amenities. Elsie likes the shops, I like the opera and we both enjoy the shows in the West End.

Our previous travels had included a couple of trips to Lake Garda, staying near Malcesine. All around the lake was very beautiful with small towns, Bordolino and Limone being particularly attractive. On another occasion we took a trip to Bellagio on Lake Como, which was very enjoyable. However, the journey to get to these places from Belfast was arduous, requiring many changes of transport, so we decided one year instead of take a Mediterranean cruise sailing out of Genova.

The journey to join the ship was nearly as bad as that to Lake Garda but we felt that the cruise would afford us access to other ports more conveniently. We were late getting to Genova and the ship had delayed sailing, awaiting the arrival of our party from Northern Ireland. This was a good thing for the other 1200 people sailing on the ship had already embarked and so we were rushed on board without the necessity of queuing, and quickly ushered into dinner, as the ship put to.

Our itinerary was to take us to Livorno, Salerno, Crete, Alexandria, Port Said, Haifa and Beirut, returning via Capri and Naples to Genova. At our departure it was announced that terrorists had bombed Luxor, so our calls at Egypt were off and instead, we would be going to Kusadasi in Turkey. Livorno was a short stop but Salerno gave us the opportunity to go ashore in rainy weather and there wasn't a lot going on.

Crete proved to be a much nicer place and we tied up at Iraklion. The harbour was pleasant, in an historically run-down way and the town was busy, with good weather to cheer us. We made some purchases, finding that the rate of exchange was favourable and the people were pleasant. Going on, Haifa was nothing to write home about but we got excellent value at the Duty Free port and spent the day walking around the outskirts of the city. Beirut was in a worse state than parts of Belfast, which had suffered 30 years of terrorism, and we felt some rapport with the locals as we wandered amongst the craters and ruins.

Kusadasi was beautiful. By now it was off-season, being December, and our ship had not been expected. When we hove to and were docked, the entire town became alive. Shops opened up, the rain stopped and we spent the best part of the day exploring and buying items we didn't need. Elsie did buy a very nice Lapis Lazuli 22-carat gold necklace, which I approved. The locals were friendly and good bargains were to be had, but who needed them? It was enough to enjoy the local scene and the pleasant harbour, where the ship seemed to be docked right on the beach, for it was a small place.

The cruise afforded several opportunities to go on shore excursions. I was discouraged from this, particularly when I wanted to go to the Dead Sea, by the uninvited attentions of a middle-aged lady, who became persistent when she heard that Elsie didn't want to go. Several people who took the trip to Jerusalem were mugged in the Garden of Gethsemane. One of the visitors was a detective, and the muggers, finding his official ID card in his wallet, dropped it and fled the scene. Others were not so fortunate and lost their possessions.

Sailing back to Capri and Naples, we were subjected to a force-nine gale for two days and a night. Many on board were ill, including Elsie. When I went to the reception area to ask for some medication to ease her misery, most of the staff had been laid low and the remaining young lady on duty had only time to pass me a few pills, before she rushed off to be sick. The ship's doctor was also sick. We were unable to approach the harbour at Capri because of the storm and had to go straight to Naples, where the ship was delayed in berthing and we were unable to disembark. We felt somewhat cheated for I would have liked to have seen the city of Naples, birthplace of the great Caruso and home of the San Carlo Opera House.

The onboard evening cabaret entertainment was very good.. There were some excellent acts, good dancing and some fine singers, particularly a girl who joined the troupe at Naples for the last leg of the journey. Generally the food was good but rich; eating seemed to go on day and night, till I cried out for a simple boiled egg and a slice of toast.

Arriving back at Genova we were subjected to a lengthy disembarkation process and then the long drive back to Milan for our flight home. As far as Elsie was concerned, the best thing about the cruise was getting off it and she has refused to join me on another ever since.

To tell the truth, most holidays bore me and I'm usually glad to get back home. I'm no sooner there than I want to be off again but modern day flying is a complete curse, with endless air traffic delays, overcrowded airports and longer and longer check-in procedures, with extra security precautions delaying things further. That is one of the reasons I bought the flat in London; I can reach it easily and stay for ten days or so each month, visiting the things I missed during my 30 years living and working in London.

So here I am in 2002, having just completed the celebration of my 65th birthday, with a tour of the Isle of Skye and other parts of Scotland, with the Railway Touring Company on their Cock O' the North tour, in July. We boarded the Highland Chieftan train at Kings Cross Station and travelled for eight hours via Peterborough, Newcastle, Berwick, Edinburgh and

Perth, before arriving at Inverness Station, where we were taken to the Marriot Hotel to stay the night. We had enjoyed excellent meals and service in the first-class carriage, and were served a full Scottish breakfast next morning at the hotel, departing by coach to travel the scenic route to Kyle of Lochalsh Station, for a good lunch. We drove on to visit Eilean Donan Castle and admired the views before crossing the new bridge to Skye and onwards to the Skeaboat House Hotel. This is a fine Victorian mansion, situated on a lake and affording comfortable accommodation and excellent cuisine. The proprietors have maintained the essence and ambience of a Victorian mansion household, with a billiards room and a fine drawing room with large open fireplace with a welcoming turf fire and elegant furnishings. The dining room was similarly well appointed and we enjoyed good dinners, where we were joined each evening by another couple, who were pleasant dining companions. The lady had been an opera singer and so I was able to have lively discussions with her. Our bedroom overlooking the lake was well appointed and the bed very comfortable.

We had a beautiful trip by coach next day, exploring the Isle of Skye and visiting the Flora MacDonald memorial in the north. The views were magnificent, with a 20-mile vista all around. In spite of inclement weather and heavy skies, the visibility was startlingly clear. We had lunch at Portree, another beautiful spot, before visiting Dunvegan Castle and our return to Skeaboat Hotel for dinner. On the second day we went by coach to Armadale to take the ferry to Malaig. Not far away at Moran, steam enthusiasts were given the opportunity to photograph a steam train coming up a gradient, on its way to Malaig from Fortwilliam. I enjoyed seeing it pass. It recalled memories of the steam trains I had watched as a boy, on the Derry line as they passed through our land at Ballyrobert, one of my fonder memories of that place. We then took the 'Jacobite' steam train from Malaig to Fortwilliam, before the coach took us on to the Boat Hotel at Boat of Garten, where we stayed the night. Next day we departed by special steam train, for Aviemore, where we boarded the Highland Chieftan, for our long return journey to London. We had enjoyed Skye very much and found it remote, wet and beautiful - well worth another visit.

We returned to Belfast after a couple of days in London to prepare to go to my nephew Andrew's second wedding, which was to take place at Plane Castle, some 20 minutes away from Stirling.

We had attended a good number of weddings in our time, including one in Hong Kong, several in Italy, England, Ireland and Scotland and at least five Indian weddings of staff members during my time at the bank. We only attended one Jewish wedding, that of Rosalind, the daughter of a friend, Mr Joe Frankel, who had lived near us in Culverhouse Gardens. He was an accountant and I first met him on the way to work in the City, when I started travelling by bus. We travelled up regularly together, joined by another Irish fellow, who lived near us and who worked for Nat West, about which he moaned constantly. Joe and I became good friends and he had an amusing turn of phrase and stories to tell. His wife was an attractive lady. Their one daughter was a pretty girl, also an accountant.

Elsie and I were invited to her wedding in 1984, which was in a Synagogue at Golders Green. Joe advised me that I should wear a bow tie and he provided me with a little skull cap, which had to be worn throughout the day. I bought a new dress suit for the occasion but he later told me that the bow tie with a lounge suit or jacket would have done as well. The ladies were to be in evening wear. In the service at the synagogue, where the men wore hats and were segregated from the ladies on the other side of the church, I enjoyed hearing the cantors. Several famous singers had been cantors, or the sons of cantors. The great American tenors, Richard Tucker and his brother-in-law, Jan Peerce, and Al Jolson, the great entertainer, come to mind. Incidentally, Jan Peerce had also been a jazz violinist and was one of Toscanini's favourite tenors, for he was very musical, as well as vocally secure.

We attended the lavish reception at banqueting halls in North London. The event lasted all afternoon, starting with light snacks and drinks, a meal in themselves, before the main banquet, which was followed later by a supper and dance. Eating took place at different intervals and times, set aside during the proceedings, to comply with Jewish orthodoxy, when no food is consumed. There were many guests and the singer, Vince Hill, had been engaged to perform later with the band. To start with, we sang the Jewish national anthem. I didn't know the words but knew the tune and sang along enthusiastically. The British national anthem was also sung. We were seated beside a chap who looked and sounded like Walter Matthau, very amusing and droll. He commended my singing and we enjoyed his company throughout the evening. Many Jews are very musical, amongst them are famous instrumentalists and conductors, as well as singers. We ate and drank heartily and it was a rare experience and privilege to have attended the affair. Rosalind married a young man who was involved in the fur trade, a member of a family eminent in that business. Afterwards she went to live with her husband in North London. Joe and I remained friendly for many years, till he moved, after his wife died and I lost touch. He was a good deal older than myself but a great companion. Elsie met him several times in the Kosher area of Selfridges' Food Hall. He revealed that he was living in a flat in North London, near his daughter.

We attended another wedding in 1987. Craig Sullivan's daughter, Nadia, was to be married in Milan and we had been invited along. We went and stayed with Cecilia and Ashley at their apartment, where a big party was arranged on the eve of the wedding. Craig and his second wife were there along with his first wife, Lydia, and her sister and other relatives and old friends, including Peter Glossop, Eric and Mike Zacconi. Eric had rather too much to drink and grew somewhat argumentative. He became engaged in a heated exchange with Lydia's sister. As she turned away, he took a run at her, like a rugby player taking a place kick and landed his boot, fair in the middle of her arse. She turned, startled, indignant and no doubt hurt - he, losing his balance, hurtled backwards, collapsing onto an antique dining chair, which also collapsed under him, in a heap of splintered wood and dust, for it was riddled with woodworm. The guests were startled and Cecilia and Ashley were outraged. Ashley ordered him out of the house. I suggested to Ashley that Eric was in no fit state to make his way home, but he was adamant and would not hear of driving him there. I decided to go with him, which was just as well.

Outside the door, on the landing, Eric stumbled against the low banister and I emerged just in time to catch him by the collar, before he plunged over. With the jolt, his glasses became dislodged and plummeted down the five-storey drop, to shatter on the ground floor. We staggered down the stairs, for there was no lift, Eric by now literally 'blind drunk', for he had worn powerful lenses and was useless without them. We found them below, shattered to smithereens. We gained the outside quadrangle, where Eric felt the need to have a pee in the flowerbed. He was staggering and, as I could not dissuade him, I had to assist him, by holding his top coat open from behind, keeping him upright as he carried on.

At that moment, the great doors of the Portico, always locked at night, swung open to reveal the building's owner about to drive through with his wife, the headlamps of the car catching us in full glare. I quickly wrapped the folds of Eric's coat about him, not caring whether he had finished or not and heaved him out past the astonished pair, greeting them 'good-night', making a great show of helping a sick man.

Upstairs, the confrontation had not gone unnoticed and Ashley reneged and decided to come down and drive Eric home, to avoid further indignities, if nothing else. I went with them, but Ashley determined to leave Eric at the front door of his apartment block, refusing to be seen with him by any of the other residents or the caretaker. He propped him against the door and we drove off, leaving Eric fumbling for his keys.

Next day the wedding took place, but there was no sign of Eric, nor any word of him. It was concluded that he was sleeping it off, or too embarrassed to appear. It was only a couple of days later that the real cause of his absence was revealed. He had been unable to find the lock with his key - not surprising, considering his lack of spectacles and the state he was in - so he had pushed all of the entrance buzzers of the other flats and gained admittance to the stone stairway, stumbling and fumbling up, trying to locate his own door. He had fallen and tumbled down into the basement. The commotion roused the caretaker, who found him unconscious in the stairwell of the basement, a large gash on his forehead. She summoned the ambulance and he was whisked off to the casualty ward, where he was laid up for a couple of days with concussion. When he got the bill for their services, he soon recovered his senses.

In retrospect, we were all able to laugh at the whole episode, which could have been tragic. It had its good side too, for Eric never touched a drop of alcohol thereafter. He became a vegetarian and pursued an obscure form of Eastern religion for years, seeking the inner truth, or possibly the 'Third Eye', an advanced stage of Tibetan enlightenment.

I met Eric in Milan in May 2002. He was then 80 years of age, fit as a fiddle and in right good humour. He came to see me at Ashley's flat, greeting me warmly and calling out to Ashley 'When are you going to repay me all that money I promised to lend you?'. Ashley's immediate rejoinder was 'When are you going to have that antique chair you shattered, repaired and restored?' The remains still lie in Ashley's loft. Eric continues to dine with Ashley and Cecilia, each Saturday evening as usual.

A few years after Nadia's wedding, Andrew Sullivan got married in Milan, to a young Japanese girl, whom he had met when studying in Sydney, Australia. We had a quieter party on that occasion and the wedding took place in a huge church, where the reception was held afterwards, in the hall downstairs. In the evening we had a smaller dinner party at a restaurant. Andrew and his wife now live and work in London and we see them there from time to time.

A year or so after we left London, Thelma Chan, who had bought our house, announced that she was to be married to a well-to-do gentlemen from Ashtead, Surrey. We were invited to the wedding, held in the Royal Enclosure at Epsom Race Course. This was a grand affair and the guests arrived in their hundreds, from various parts of the world. These included many of our previous neighbours and the friends that Thelma had acquired in England. Within months of arriving in London, she had started a theatrical costume business, providing dresses for West End shows. She made friends wherever she went. Dr Ung, our last GP in London, and his wife, with whom we have remained friends, were also there. The celebrations lasted throughout the afternoon and evening, with much eating, drinking and dancing to a band, till midnight. Throughout the event, Thelma appeared in three different outfits, each more colourful and startling than the last. Her brother sang Ave Maria, to a recorded accompaniment, which broke down, and he had to continue unaccompanied to the end. I felt for him! Cine cameras recorded us all as we arrived and throughout the proceedings. Everything was spectacular. We left exhausted, wishing the happy couple well in their new life in Ashtead. We subsequently received loads of photographs from Thelma and we continue to receive a Christmas card each year.

Preparations to attend my nephew's wedding had been completed. Valerie and Winifred joined us on the Easyjet flight to Edinburgh, delayed for two hours. Val hired a car to drive us to Stirling. Where she gets the energy from, I don't know, for she had just recently arrived from California. Being used to driving on the 'wrong' side of the roads in the USA, she had to contend with that and the unfamiliar roads in Scotland. Elsie had booked for us to stay at a fine, large house in Stirling, a superior bed and breakfast establishment, decorated and furnished grandly in the Mackintosh style and very comfortable. The proprietor was an exceedingly stout gentleman, pleasant of manner, keenly interested in music. He had a large Beckstein grand piano in the drawing room, which he said he could play, but never did when we were there.

He and his wife ran the house together. He did the cooking and we were treated to huge breakfasts each morning, consisting of a half-grapefruit, and porridge served with maple syrup, fresh cream and a generous tot of malt whisky. There followed a choice of fried foods – two types of sausages, black pudding, bacon, mushrooms, poached eggs, tomatoes, fried bread and toast. To follow, or alternatively, varieties of fish (salmon, trout, pickled herrings, haddock and oysters) were pressed upon us. Coffee, tea and fresh juices were also served. When we had finished eating, he sat down and polished off quantities of everything.

Our bedrooms at the front of the house were large, with

most comfortable beds and en-suite bathrooms. The windows looked out across the green, to the elevated Stirling Castle in the near distance, which presented a fine prospect, lit up at night. Tea,coffee, chocolate, home made shortbread, fresh fruit and a bottle of single malt whisky were at our disposal. His wife brought round cups of good strong tea in the early morning, to liven us up before the marathon breakfasts. There were shelves of a good variety of books in the bedrooms and throughout the house. A Rolls Royce and several other cars, stood at the side of the house.

Stirling is a fine city and I would have enjoyed more time there. Plane Castle was undergoing restoration and stands in a desolate area, only accessible through a maze of winding, narrow, country roads, although the main motorway is visible nearby, but inaccessible across the fields. The castle was bought as a ruin by a clergyman, who has made a full-time job of restoring it and letting it out to groups for functions. It can accommodate 14 residents. It does boast a fine baronial hall, where receptions are held and a small private chapel, where marriages are carried out with due ceremony and solemnity. The brochure states that the castle is booked up two years in advance, for Christmas and New Year. There is a small lake in the grounds, with geese, ducks and peacocks wandering around. We decided to seek it out on our first evening, so as to be sure of our way to the wedding next day.

It was raining heavily when we got to the gate, which displayed a 'closed' notice. We were admitted by the owner, who had a resigned look, as if to say 'what next?' as we trudged in. His wife had a desolate look. Inside was apparent chaos, with Nina, Deborah, Liz (the bride) and her sister and others, in the midst of preparing the feast for the following day's celebrations. Andrew's party had driven up in his recently acquired four-wheel drive people carrier, together with three dogs and they had got marooned in the devastating floods which had hit the area. They were rescued by the Fire Brigade and their car had to be towed up to the yard where it stood, refusing to start. They faced the prospect of having to hire a car to return to Kent, where they were also in the middle of moving house. We didn't stay long, for we had only come out that evening to acquaint ourselves with the area.

Back in Stirling, we spent a fruitless hour searching for a place to eat, for it was after 9.p.m. We finished up in an Italian restaurant and were served massive, but tasty pizzas, which caused me a sleepless night. Next day, a good breakfast restored me somewhat and the day turned fine and sunny, as we prepared to attend the wedding. Back at the castle, things had taken on a rosier hue in the sunshine and we met the 20 or so guests, relatives and friends who had come. Andrew and his Best Man were attired in the full-dress and tartan of the Frazer Clan and looked magnificent. The bride, Elizabeth, wore a purple taffeta, Elizabethan gown, her hair flowing down her shoulders, presenting an image of a beautiful medieval painting, or a figure in a drawing by Aubrey Beardsley. Her two young daughters from a previous marriage, dressed in long mauve gowns and carrying bouquets, acted as bridesmaids. The wedding ceremony was tastefully performed in the chapel , with a lady playing some early Spanish guitar music in the background

Huge amounts of food had been prepared and most of us over-indulged in the two punch bowls of aperitifs provided, being a concoction of strong liquor, innocuously flavoured and coloured with strawberry and lemon extracts. Beer and wine were served with the meal. Endless reels of cine film and photographs were taken before, during and after the ceremony, when we tucked into delicious roast lamb, stuffed chicken and varieties of boiled, roasted and garlic potatoes and copious quantities of salads of every type.

After the repast, everyone was tiring, but a Scottish singer/musician had been hired to provide the evening's entertainment. He appeared in full tartan, with flowing hair and beard and a wild look resembling a 'hairy coo', one of those Highland cattle seen wandering in the hills. He was of pleasant demeanour as I helped him set us his equipment. He disappeared for a while, before returning to regale us with interminable ballads of a dozen verses or more, telling the sorry tales of the historical battles of the clans, gallow trees, hangings and the perfidy, perpetrated in ancient times. Val and Win tried to get the highland dancing going and gave us a vigorous display but no one volunteered to join them and some guests had already drifted off to bed, exhausted. We four decided to go, leaving the poor fellow with a much reduced audience and at least half of his repertoire still to be performed.

Next day, we travelled to Edinburgh, where Val and Win went off to museums and exhibitions. Elsie and I went on a bus tour of the city as the rain came down heavily, after which we enjoyed a lunch of fish and chips and mushy peas, at Harry Ramsdens. This restored me somewhat. We explored Princes Street in the continuing rain, till we met up with the others about 4 pm to make our way by car to the airport, in traffic as dense and slow-moving as that in London. Valerie had to return the car, so we had a long sojourn at the airport, till the scheduled time of 8.50 pm for our flight to Belfast. We were annoyed to be told that the flight would be delayed till 9.30.p.m. All Easyjet staff then disappeared, after which a sign came on the monitor, to advise that it would not leave until 10.30.p.m. In the end we waited till 11.50.p.m. before departing Edinburgh in a downpour and in a bad mood, for our half-hour flight to Belfast.

Meantime, Val and Win had departed for London, where Robbie had reserved a suite for them at the Savoy for a week. We arrived at Aldergrove and were fortunate to be offered a lift to our house in Templepatrick by another irate couple who were on their way to Limavady. At the beginning of the next week we went to London to meet Ashley and Cecilia, who had been staying in our flat for six days, on their way to Australia to visit Ashley's ageing mother. We then met up with Val and Nina, who had come up for lunch at the Savoy. Winifred had returned to Belfast. What a splendid suite they had, overlooking the river, with excellent views of the London Eye and all around. We went together, with Robbie and Valika as well, to a performance of My Fair Lady at Drury Lane. Valerie went home to California on the next day, which was Friday. Robbbie and Valika joined us for lunch on Saturday at Choy's on Kings Road, before we went on to a matinee performance of the Mikado at the Savoy Theatre, which was enjoying rave reviews. It was Robbie and Valika's third visit to the show.

I stayed in London for another couple of days, then returned to Belfast, leaving Elsie to meet her old friend and BA colleague, Jo Valentine, who was coming from Sydney. She had lived and worked in London for nearly 30 years and had a very nice flat in Lennox Gardens. Back home alone, I survived on a nice dish of stew which Elsie had left in the freezer, thereafter reduced to boiled eggs, cheese sandwiches and a slice or two of cold meat, coleslaw and beetroot. The reduced intake of food for four days was beneficial and my digestion improved. I was able to motivate myself to do a few jobs around the house, and to read and edit this volume. But I was missing Elsie and was glad to meet her at Belfast City Airport when she came home.

So here I am at the end of this saga and in my seventh year of retirement, living in Templepatrick, not far from Ballyrobert, where 18 years of my early life were spent. I am now a senior citizen and have received my first monthly State pension and free bus pass. Belfast, where I was born and bred, is not far away, still a troubled city, but with a cessation of the major troubles of the years since 1969, when the riots and bombing really began. The city thrives and some good redevelopment has taken place - it is now served by two major airports, Aldergrove where I used to work and the newer City Airport in the Docklands area - but much of the fabric of the old buildings has been destroyed. The Grand Central Hotel had become an Army base during the Troubles, before being demolished and giving way to a shopping complex. The city cinemas have disappeared, replaced by out of town Cineplexes, and Mackies has closed. Harland & Wolff is a greatly reduced shipbuilding industry, Gallagher's factory has given way to Yorkgate Cinema and shopping complex in York Street, though the company still thrives elsewhere.

The Short Bros aircraft factory, under the new name Bombardier, its present owners, still exists, but struggles to be competitive in the difficult Airlines' market. The Floral Hall at Bellevue has long been defunct. Once a thriving place of entertainment and a fine example of Art Deco architecture, it lies derelict, awaiting a developer with enough imagination to restore it to its former glory, attracting the public as it did in its

349

heyday. The Belfast Castle and the Zoo survive as places worth visiting, as does the impressive City Hall in the town centre. Much of the Docklands area and the Lagan River frontage has been transformed into fashionable dwellings and leisure areas, around and opposite the great new Waterfront Concert Hall, now the venue for large classical concerts, visiting opera companies and popular entertainers such as Daniel O'Donnell.

The Ulster Hall in the centre of town is still used for a variety of entertainment, and remains home to the Belfast Philharmonic. The Grand Opera House, fully refurbished (for it was blown up twice during the Troubles), is still a popular venue for plays, Broadway and West End musicals and Grand Opera. It stands near the Europa Hotel, which replaced the Grand Central as a popular meeting place, but it was the target of many attacks during the civil strife and was known as the most bombed hotel in the world. The King's Hall at Balmoral continues to host large events, such as the Royal Agricultural Show, the Motor Show and the Ideal Homes Exhibition. A new, large arena, The Odyssey, opened a couple of years ago in the Docklands area, where ice hockey has become very popular, played before large crowds supporting the Belfast Giants, as well as accommodating large events, such as rock concerts and other popular forms of entertainment.

The Stormont Buildings still gleam in the sunlight where, hopefully, the new ecumenical and multi-party government, currently suspended, will eventually begin working together for the good of the community and the country at large. A new air of prosperity and hope prevails and the countryside and coastal regions remain serenely beautiful. The weather hasn't changed much but on a good day, there is no more beautiful spot than the Antrim coast and the beaches at Portrush, the White Rocks and Whitepark Bay, with the picturesque Ballintoy Harbour nearby. The views from Carrickfergus Castle up Belfast Lough to the shipyards, are an inspiring sight.

So what next? I have given up singing, for since my back and nose operations, I can hardly sing a song without incurring severe headaches. So I will continue to enjoy and encourage others in their endeavours and my wife and I visit London regularly, to enjoy the best that Covent Garden has to offer. Banking, which claimed twenty-eight years of my life, is a receding nightmare. I am blessed with a good home, a wonderful and supportive wife and some good friends.

Is there a God? Probably, but not the one I envisioned in my early childhood: a stern, bearded, all-seeing figure, filling me with dread. Whatever His form, I hope to meet Him and to get answers to some of life's imponderables. Is there a hereafter? I think so, and I look forward to finding that out at least, whatever it may be, for I can't believe that this life is the end of it all.

But not too soon I hope, for I still want to explore some of the mysteries of this present existence, and experience the joys of living - made more pleasant when miseries have been dispelled, as long as good health affords me the strength to get around to the next adventure.

Caricature by Geoff Kidman,
Colleague at Babcock and
Wilcox, London 1966.

Enniskillen 1954, rowing at school

Milan 1959/60 Bohemian life of singing students. Eric (centre),
Ashley (left), Craig (right) and Ron (front)

1973 now a respectable! banker on a visit to New York

Singing party - London Aug 1980

Z (Polish Tenor) David Sutton (Pianist) and Ron

Ron, Karen, Z, David (Pianist), Sean Rea (Bass Singer) Rosemary Barnes (Pianist) and others

Thelma's wedding 7.11.98. (She bought our house in London)

Retirement in Templepatrick in 2001/2